CLINICAL TOXICOLOGY

ESSENTIAL TEXTBOOK FOR PHARM.D

DR. SANTHI SREE VEMULAPALLI, DR. ANVESH RAJ MOTURI, DR. J. DINESH BABU

Contents

Preface

The field of clinical toxicology plays a critical role in modern healthcare, addressing the diagnosis and management of poisoning and the adverse effects of chemicals on human health. As pharmaceutical professionals, the ability to understand and respond to toxicological emergencies is essential. This book, "Clinical Toxicology: Essential Guide for Pharm D Students," has been meticulously crafted to provide a comprehensive and accessible resource for students pursuing their Doctor of Pharmacy (Pharm D) degrees.

Purpose and Scope

Our primary aim in writing this book is to bridge the gap between theoretical knowledge and practical application in the field of clinical toxicology. This guide offers a detailed exploration of various toxicological scenarios, ranging from common poisonings to complex envenomations and substance abuse cases. By integrating foundational concepts with clinical insights, we strive to equip Pharm D students with the tools necessary to excel in their future careers.

Key Features

1. **Comprehensive Coverage:** Each chapter delves into specific toxicological topics, including the mechanisms of toxicity, clinical manifestations, and evidence-based management strategies. Our goal is to provide a thorough understanding of both the theoretical and practical aspects of clinical toxicology.
2. **Case Studies and Real-World Examples:** To enhance learning and retention, we have included numerous case studies and real-world examples. These scenarios illustrate the application of toxicological principles in clinical practice, helping students to develop critical thinking and problem-solving skills.
3. **Clear and Accessible Language:** Recognizing the diverse backgrounds of Pharm D students, we have emphasized clarity and simplicity in our writing. Technical concepts are explained in straightforward language, ensuring that readers of all levels can grasp the material effectively.
4. **Current and Relevant Information:** The field of toxicology is continually evolving, with new research and clinical practices emerging regularly. We have incorporated the most up-to-date information and

guidelines to ensure that students are well-informed about current standards of care.

Acknowledgments

We extend our deepest gratitude to our colleagues at Vijaya College of Pharmacy for their unwavering support and encouragement throughout the creation of this book. Their valuable feedback and insights have been instrumental in shaping the content and structure of this guide.

We also wish to acknowledge the contributions of our students, whose curiosity and dedication have inspired us to strive for excellence in our teaching and writing. It is our hope that this book will serve as a valuable resource in their academic journey and future professional endeavors.

"Clinical Toxicology: Essential Guide for Pharm D Students" is more than just a textbook; it is a comprehensive resource designed to empower students with the knowledge and skills needed to navigate the complexities of toxicological emergencies. We are confident that this book will be an indispensable tool for Pharm D students, fostering a deeper understanding of clinical toxicology and enhancing their ability to deliver high-quality patient care.

We invite you to embark on this educational journey with us, exploring the fascinating and vital field of clinical toxicology. Together, let us advance the frontiers of pharmaceutical education and contribute to the well-being of our communities.

Dr. Santhi Sree Vemulapalli
Dr. M. Anvesh Raj
Dr. J. Dinesh Babu

Clinical Toxicology: Essential Guide For Pharm D Students

Dr. Santhi Sree Vemulapalli
Professor
Vijaya College of Pharmacy
Hayatnagar, Munagnoor
India

Dr. M. Anvesh Raj
Associate Professor
Vijaya College of Pharmacy
Hayatnagar, Munagnoor
India

Dr. J. Dinesh Babu
Associate Professor
Vijaya College of Pharmacy
Hayatnagar, Munagnoor
India

Published by Notion Press
Notion Press, Inc.
800, West El Camino Real #180,
California USA 94040

Notion Press Media Pvt Ltd
#7, Red Cross Road,
Egmore, Chennai, Tamil Nadu 600008

Email ID: publish@notionpress.com
Phone Number: +91 44 46315631

July 2024

CHAPTER I

General Principles Involved in the Management of Poisoning

Introduction

The management of poisoning is a critical and often urgent aspect of medical care that requires a systematic and multidisciplinary approach. Poisoning can result from a wide array of substances, including pharmaceuticals, household chemicals, industrial agents, and natural toxins. The diverse nature of poisons and their varied effects on the human body necessitate a comprehensive understanding of the principles and strategies involved in their management.

In this chapter, we will explore the general principles involved in the management of poisoning, emphasizing the importance of a structured approach from initial assessment to treatment implementation. The primary goals in the management of poisoning are to stabilize the patient, prevent further absorption of the toxin, enhance its elimination, and provide supportive care to mitigate the effects of the poison.

Importance of Initial Assessment and Triage

The initial assessment and triage are crucial steps in managing poisoning cases. Rapid evaluation of the patient's airway, breathing, and circulation (ABCs) is essential to identify and address any life-threatening conditions. Obtaining a detailed history of the poisoning incident, including the type of substance involved, the amount, and the time of exposure, is vital for guiding further management. Assessing the level of consciousness and prioritizing care based on the severity of the poisoning are fundamental in ensuring that patients receive timely and appropriate interventions.

Stabilization of the Poisoned Patient

Stabilizing the patient involves managing the airway, supporting breathing, and ensuring adequate circulation. Techniques such as airway clearance, supplemental oxygen administration, and fluid resuscitation are critical in this phase. Neurological assessment and continuous monitoring are necessary to evaluate the patient's response to initial interventions and to guide further treatment.

Diagnosis and Risk Assessment

Accurate diagnosis and risk assessment are essential for effective management of poisoning. This involves detailed history taking, thorough physical examination, and appropriate use of laboratory tests and imaging studies. Identifying the specific poison, understanding its pharmacokinetics, and assessing the risk of complications help in formulating a targeted treatment plan.

Treatment Planning and Implementation

Treatment planning and implementation focus on setting clear goals, both immediate and long-term, for the management of poisoning. Immediate interventions may include administering antidotes and performing decontamination procedures to prevent further absorption of the toxin. Enhancing elimination of the poison through methods such as urinary alkalinization, hemodialysis, and hemoperfusion is also considered. Symptomatic and supportive care, including pain management and maintaining fluid and electrolyte balance, is crucial in the overall treatment strategy.

Ongoing Monitoring and Patient Education

Continuous monitoring and reassessment are vital to ensure the effectiveness of the treatment and to make necessary adjustments based on the patient's condition. Proper documentation and communication among healthcare providers are essential for coordinated care. Educating the patient and their family about preventive measures and ensuring appropriate follow-up care are important steps in preventing future poisoning incidents and promoting recovery.

1.1 Initial Assessment and Triage

1.1.1 Rapid Evaluation of Airway, Breathing, and Circulation

The **rapid evaluation of airway, breathing, and circulation (ABCs)** is a fundamental and urgent step in the initial management of a poisoned patient. This process involves a systematic and thorough assessment to ensure that the patient's vital functions are stable and to identify any immediate life-threatening conditions that require prompt intervention.

Airway Assessment: The first priority in the rapid evaluation is to ensure that the airway is patent and not obstructed. An obstructed airway can lead to hypoxia, which can rapidly result in brain damage or death. Healthcare providers should check for signs of airway obstruction such as stridor, gurgling sounds, or the absence of breath sounds. If the patient is unconscious or has a compromised airway, immediate actions such as repositioning the head, using airway adjuncts like oropharyngeal or nasopharyngeal airways, or performing endotracheal intubation may be necessary. Ensuring a clear airway is critical because even brief periods of oxygen deprivation can have severe consequences.

Breathing Assessment: After securing the airway, the next step is to assess the patient's breathing. This involves evaluating the respiratory rate, depth, and effort, as well as checking for symmetry of chest movements. Healthcare providers should look for signs of inadequate ventilation such as cyanosis, use of accessory muscles, or abnormal breathing patterns like tachypnea or bradypnea. The use of a pulse oximeter to measure oxygen saturation can provide valuable information about the patient's oxygenation status. In cases of respiratory compromise, interventions such as providing supplemental oxygen, using a bag-valve-mask, or initiating mechanical ventilation may be required. Ensuring adequate oxygenation and ventilation is crucial to prevent hypoxia and its associated complications.

Circulation Assessment: The third component of the ABC evaluation is assessing circulation. This involves checking the patient's pulse, blood pressure, and perfusion status. Signs of poor perfusion, such as pallor, diaphoresis, or delayed capillary refill (greater than 2 seconds), indicate potential circulatory compromise. Establishing intravenous access is often necessary for the administration of fluids and medications. In cases of hypotension, fluid resuscitation with isotonic saline or lactated Ringer's solution is typically initiated. If the patient does not respond to fluid therapy, vasopressors such as norepinephrine may be administered to maintain adequate blood pressure and perfusion. Monitoring heart rate and rhythm through electrocardiography (ECG) can also provide insights into the patient's circulatory status and help identify any cardiac dysrhythmias that need to be addressed.

The rapid evaluation of airway, breathing, and circulation is not a one-time event but an ongoing process. Continuous monitoring and reassessment are vital to detect any changes in the patient's condition and to ensure that interventions remain effective. This systematic approach to evaluating and managing the ABCs forms the cornerstone of emergency care in poisoning cases and is essential for stabilizing the patient and preventing further deterioration.

1.1 Initial Assessment and Triage

1.1.2 Obtaining a History of the Poisoning Incident

Obtaining a history of the poisoning incident is a critical step in the initial assessment of a poisoned patient. This process involves gathering detailed and accurate information about the circumstances surrounding the poisoning event. The primary goal is to identify the type of substance involved, the amount ingested, the time of exposure, and the route of administration. This information is vital for diagnosing the poisoning and formulating an effective treatment plan.

Substance Identification: The first aspect of history taking is to identify the specific substance that caused the poisoning. This can be challenging, especially if the patient is un

conscious or unable to communicate. In such cases, family members, bystanders, or first responders may provide valuable information. Healthcare providers should look for any containers, labels, or remnants of the substance at the scene. Additionally, in cases of multiple potential toxins, obtaining samples of the substance for laboratory analysis can be helpful.

Dose and Timing: Understanding the dose and timing of the exposure is crucial for assessing the severity of the poisoning and predicting its clinical course. The amount of substance ingested can determine the potential toxicity and the need for specific interventions. The timing of exposure helps in estimating the duration of action and the likely time frame for symptoms to manifest. For example, knowing that a patient ingested a large dose of acetaminophen several hours ago would prompt immediate consideration of antidotal therapy with N-acetylcysteine to prevent liver damage.

Route of Administration: The route by which the toxin entered the body—whether oral, inhalational, dermal, or intravenous—affects the absorption, distribution, and overall impact of the poison. For instance, inhalation of toxic gases may lead to rapid onset of respiratory symptoms, while dermal exposure to certain chemicals might require decontamination procedures.

Patient's Medical History and Concurrent Medications: It is also important to obtain information about the patient's medical history and any concurrent medications they are taking. Pre-existing conditions such as liver or kidney disease can affect the metabolism and excretion of toxins, while interactions with other medications can complicate the clinical picture.

Circumstances of the Incident: Understanding the context of the poisoning incident can provide additional insights. Accidental poisonings may involve different substances and doses compared to intentional overdoses. In cases of suspected intentional poisoning, psychiatric evaluation and support may also be necessary.

Effective communication and empathy are essential when obtaining a history of the poisoning incident. Patients and their families may be distressed, and clear, compassionate questioning can help elicit accurate information. Utilizing a structured approach, such as the SAMPLE (Symptoms, Allergies, Medications, Past medical history, Last meal, Events leading to the incident) mnemonic, can ensure that all relevant aspects are covered.

1.1.3 Assessing Level of Consciousness

Assessing the level of consciousness is a fundamental part of the initial evaluation of a poisoned patient. The patient's level of consciousness provides critical information about the severity of the poisoning and guides immediate management decisions. Various scales and tools are used to assess consciousness, with the Glasgow Coma Scale (GCS) being one of the most widely utilized.

Glasgow Coma Scale (GCS): The GCS is a standardized tool that evaluates three key components: eye opening, verbal response, and motor response. Each component is scored separately, and the total score ranges from 3 to 15. A lower GCS score indicates a more severe level of impaired consciousness. For example, a score of 8 or below is indicative of a coma, requiring immediate intervention to secure the airway and support breathing.

Alertness and Responsiveness: Initial assessment should determine if the patient is alert and responsive to verbal or physical stimuli. This can be done by calling the patient's name or gently shaking them. If the patient does not respond, painful stimuli, such as a sternal rub, may be used to assess responsiveness.

Pupillary Response: Examination of the pupils can provide additional information about the level of consciousness and potential causes of altered mental status. For instance, pinpoint pupils may suggest opioid toxicity, while dilated pupils can indicate anticholinergic poisoning or sympathomimetic toxicity.

Neurological Examination: A comprehensive neurological examination is essential to identify any focal deficits or signs of increased intracranial pressure. This includes assessing cranial nerve function, motor strength, and deep tendon reflexes. Any abnormalities may require further investigation, such as neuroimaging.

Vital Signs and Respiratory Pattern: Monitoring vital signs, including heart rate, blood pressure, and respiratory rate, is crucial. Abnormalities in these parameters can indicate systemic effects of poisoning, such as hypotension in cases of severe sedative overdose or tachycardia in stimulant poisoning. The respiratory pattern should also be observed, as irregular or depressed breathing may necessitate immediate intervention.

Continuous reassessment of the level of consciousness is necessary, as changes can occur rapidly in poisoning cases. Prompt identification of deteriorating mental status allows for timely interventions, such as securing the airway, providing ventilatory support, or administering antidotes.

1.1.4 Prioritizing Care Based on Severity

Prioritizing care based on severity is a critical aspect of the initial assessment and triage of poisoned patients. This process involves determining the urgency of medical interventions and ensuring that those with life-threatening conditions receive immediate attention. Triage systems are designed to categorize patients according to the severity of their symptoms and the potential for rapid deterioration.

Categorization of Patients: Triage categorizes patients into different levels based on the severity of their condition. For example, the Emergency Severity Index (ESI) is a commonly used system that ranges from level 1 (most urgent) to level 5 (least urgent). Patients with compromised airways, breathing difficulties, or severe circulatory collapse are given the highest priority (ESI level 1), requiring immediate life-saving interventions.

Life-Threatening Conditions: Identifying and addressing life-threatening conditions is the foremost priority. This includes managing airway obstruction, severe respiratory distress, profound hypotension, and altered mental status. Rapid interventions, such as securing the airway, administering oxygen, initiating fluid resuscitation, and providing antidotes, are critical in stabilizing these patients.

Symptom Severity and Potential for Deterioration: Patients presenting with moderate symptoms or those at risk of rapid deterioration are prioritized next. This group may include individuals with moderate respiratory distress, significant but not life-threatening hypotension, or persistent altered mental status. Continuous monitoring and timely interventions are essential to prevent their condition from worsening.

Less Severe Cases: Patients with mild symptoms and a lower risk of deterioration are triaged to lower priority levels. While their conditions are not immediately life-threatening, they still require thorough assessment and appropriate management. Examples include mild ingestions of non-toxic substances or stable patients with minimal symptoms.

Resource Allocation: Effective triage ensures the optimal use of available resources, such as medical personnel, equipment, and treatment facilities. By prioritizing care based on severity, healthcare providers can allocate these resources efficiently, ensuring that critically ill patients receive the necessary attention and interventions.

Reevaluation and Dynamic Triage: Triage is a dynamic process that requires continuous reevaluation of the patient's condition. As the clinical status of patients can change rapidly, regular reassessment ensures that any deterioration is promptly identified and addressed. Adjustments to the priority level may be necessary based on the patient's response to initial treatments and any new symptoms that arise.

1.2 Stabilization of the Poisoned Patient

1.2.1 Airway Management

Airway management is the first and most critical step in stabilizing a poisoned patient. Ensuring a patent airway is essential to prevent hypoxia, which can lead to brain damage or death within minutes. Effective airway management involves a series of techniques and interventions aimed at maintaining or restoring airway patency.

1.2.1.1 Techniques for Airway Clearance

Techniques for airway clearance are fundamental in the initial management of a poisoned patient. These techniques include basic maneuvers such as the head-tilt-chin-lift and jaw-thrust methods, which help open the airway by repositioning the head and neck. The head-tilt-chin-lift maneuver involves tilting the patient's head back and lifting the chin to open the airway, while the jaw-thrust maneuver is particularly useful in trauma patients as it avoids movement of the cervical spine.

In cases where the airway is obstructed by foreign materials, suctioning is necessary to remove secretions, vomit, or other debris. Suctioning should be performed carefully to avoid injury to the airway tissues and should be done using a sterile, flexible catheter.

Another technique for airway clearance is the use of airway adjuncts such as oropharyngeal and nasopharyngeal airways. An oropharyngeal airway is inserted into the mouth to keep the airway open, particularly in unconscious patients without a gag reflex. A nasopharyngeal airway, which is inserted through the nose, can be used in conscious or semiconscious patients and is helpful in maintaining airway patency when the oral route is not suitable.

1.2.1.2 Endotracheal Intubation

Endotracheal intubation is an advanced airway management technique used when basic methods are insufficient to maintain a patent airway. This procedure involves inserting a tube into the trachea through the mouth or nose to secure the airway and provide a direct route for ventilation.

The intubation process begins with pre-oxygenation, providing the patient with 100% oxygen to maximize oxygen reserves and minimize hypoxia during the procedure. The patient is then sedated and given a muscle relaxant to facilitate intubation.

Using a laryngoscope, the healthcare provider visualizes the vocal cords and guides the endotracheal tube into the trachea. Once the tube is in place, it is secured, and its position is confirmed by auscultation of breath sounds, observing chest rise, and verifying with end-tidal carbon dioxide (ETCO2) monitoring or a chest X-ray.

Endotracheal intubation is critical in cases of severe poisoning that result in respiratory failure, decreased level of consciousness, or the need for prolonged ventilatory support. It provides a secure airway, allows for precise control of ventilation, and facilitates the administration of medications directly into the lungs if necessary.

1.2.2 Breathing Support

Breathing support is essential in managing poisoned patients who exhibit signs of respiratory distress or failure. Ensuring adequate oxygenation and ventilation is crucial to prevent hypoxia and its associated complications.

1.2.2.1 Supplemental Oxygen

Supplemental oxygen is often the first intervention in providing breathing support. It involves administering oxygen to patients to improve their oxygen saturation levels and enhance tissue oxygenation. Oxygen can be delivered through various devices, depending on the severity of the patient's condition.

For patients with mild to moderate respiratory distress, nasal cannulas or simple face masks are commonly used. Nasal cannulas deliver oxygen at flow rates of 1-6 liters per minute, providing an oxygen concentration of 24-40%. Simple face masks can deliver higher concentrations of oxygen, typically 40-60%, at flow rates of 6-10 liters per minute.

In cases of severe respiratory distress or hypoxia, non-rebreather masks or high-flow oxygen systems are utilized. Non-rebreather masks can deliver oxygen concentrations up to 90-100% at flow rates of 10-15 liters per minute, providing a high concentration of oxygen to patients in critical condition.

1.2.2.2 Mechanical Ventilation

Mechanical ventilation is necessary for patients who cannot maintain adequate ventilation on their own. This intervention involves using a machine to assist or fully control the patient's breathing. Mechanical ventilation is indicated in cases of respiratory failure, severe hypoxia, or when the patient's respiratory muscles are fatigued.

There are two primary modes of mechanical ventilation: invasive and non-invasive. Invasive mechanical ventilation requires endotracheal intubation, while non-invasive mechanical ventilation uses masks or other devices to deliver positive pressure ventilation without the need for intubation.

In invasive mechanical ventilation, parameters such as tidal volume, respiratory rate, and positive end-expiratory pressure (PEEP) are set based on the patient's condition. Tidal volume typically ranges from 6-8 mL/kg of ideal body weight, and PEEP is adjusted to maintain adequate oxygenation without causing barotrauma. Continuous monitoring of blood gases and ventilator settings is essential to ensure optimal ventilation and oxygenation.

Non-invasive ventilation, such as continuous positive airway pressure (CPAP) or bilevel positive airway pressure (BiPAP), can be used in patients with mild to moderate respiratory distress who can protect their airway and have adequate respiratory drive. These modes provide positive pressure to keep the airways open and support breathing without the need for invasive procedures.

Effective breathing support, whether through supplemental oxygen or mechanical ventilation, is crucial in stabilizing poisoned patients, preventing respiratory failure, and improving overall outcomes.

1.2 Stabilization of the Poisoned Patient

1.2.3 Circulation Management

Circulation management is a critical component in the stabilization of a poisoned patient, ensuring that blood flow and oxygen delivery to vital organs are maintained. Effective management of circulation involves securing intravenous access, administering fluids for resuscitation, and using vasopressors when necessary.

1.2.3.1 Intravenous Access

Intravenous access is the initial step in managing circulation in poisoned patients. Establishing IV access allows for the rapid administration of fluids, medications, and antidotes. In emergency situations, the peripheral veins are typically used first due to their accessibility. Common sites include the antecubital fossa, the dorsal hand veins, and the cephalic or basilic veins.

When peripheral access is difficult or impossible, central venous access may be required. Central lines are placed in larger veins such as the internal jugular, subclavian, or femoral veins. Central venous access provides a more reliable route for administering large volumes of fluids and medications and is also used for central venous pressure monitoring.

1.2.3.2 Fluid Resuscitation

Fluid resuscitation is essential in treating patients with hypotension or shock due to poisoning. The primary goal is to restore adequate intravascular volume and improve tissue perfusion. Isotonic crystalloids, such as normal saline (0.9% sodium chloride) or lactated Ringer's solution, are commonly used for initial resuscitation.

The amount and rate of fluid administration depend on the patient's clinical condition and response to therapy. In cases of hypovolemic shock, rapid infusion of 1-2 liters of isotonic crystalloids is often required to restore blood pressure and perfusion. Monitoring urine output, blood pressure, heart rate, and central venous pressure can help guide the effectiveness of fluid resuscitation.

Patients who do not respond adequately to initial fluid resuscitation may require additional fluids or alternative therapies. Colloids or blood products might be considered in specific cases, such as severe hemorrhage or significant plasma losses.

1.2.3.3 Use of Vasopressors

Vasopressors are indicated when fluid resuscitation alone is insufficient to maintain adequate blood pressure and tissue perfusion. These medications constrict blood vessels, increasing systemic vascular resistance and blood pressure. Commonly used vasopressors include norepinephrine, dopamine, and epinephrine.

Norepinephrine is often the first-line vasopressor for treating septic shock and other forms of distributive shock. It is administered via continuous IV infusion, with doses titrated based on the patient's blood pressure and clinical response. Dopamine and epinephrine can also be used, depending on the specific clinical scenario and the patient's response to norepinephrine.

The use of vasopressors requires careful monitoring in an intensive care setting, as these medications can have significant side effects, including arrhythmias, tissue ischemia, and increased myocardial oxygen demand. Continuous hemodynamic monitoring is essential to adjust the dosages appropriately and to ensure the patient's safety.

1.2.4 Neurological Assessment

Neurological assessment is a crucial aspect of stabilizing a poisoned patient, providing insights into the severity of poisoning and guiding further management. It involves evaluating the patient's level of consciousness, motor function, and potential complications such as seizures.

1.2.4.1 Glasgow Coma Scale

The **Glasgow Coma Scale (GCS)** is a standardized tool used to assess a patient's level of consciousness. It evaluates three components: eye opening, verbal response, and motor response, each scored individually and summed to give a total score ranging from 3 to 15.

- **Eye Opening:** Scored from 1 to 4, with 4 indicating spontaneous eye opening, 3 to voice, 2 to pain, and 1 indicating no response.
- **Verbal Response:** Scored from 1 to 5, with 5 indicating oriented conversation, 4 confused conversation, 3 inappropriate words, 2 incomprehensible sounds, and 1 no response.
- **Motor Response:** Scored from 1 to 6, with 6 indicating obeying commands, 5 localizing pain, 4 withdrawing from pain, 3 flexing to pain (decorticate posture), 2 extending to pain (decerebrate posture), and 1 no response.

A total GCS score of 15 indicates a fully alert and oriented patient, while a score of 8 or below indicates a severe decrease in consciousness, often requiring airway protection and intensive monitoring.

1.2.4.2 Management of Seizures

Management of seizures is critical in patients with poisoning, as seizures can exacerbate the toxicity and lead to further complications such as hypoxia, metabolic acidosis, and rhabdomyolysis. Seizures can result from various toxic agents, including organophosphates, tricyclic antidepressants, and amphetamines.

Initial management involves ensuring patient safety by protecting the airway, preventing injury, and monitoring vital signs. Benzodiazepines, such as diazepam or lorazepam, are the first-line treatment for seizure control. Diazepam can be administered intravenously at doses of 5-10 mg, repeated as necessary, while lorazepam is given at 2-4 mg IV, also repeatable.

If seizures persist despite benzodiazepine administration, additional anticonvulsants such as phenobarbital or phenytoin may be required. Phenobarbital is administered at a dose of 15-20 mg/kg IV, while phenytoin is given at 15-20 mg/kg IV. Continuous EEG monitoring may be necessary in refractory cases to guide further treatment.

In severe or prolonged seizures, rapid sequence intubation and general anesthesia may be necessary to control the seizures and protect the airway. Patients with persistent seizures or status epilepticus require intensive care and continuous monitoring.

Effective neurological assessment and management of seizures are vital for stabilizing poisoned patients and preventing long-term complications. Continuous monitoring and timely interventions are essential to improve outcomes and ensure patient safety.

1.2 Stabilization of the Poisoned Patient

1.2.5 Decontamination Procedures

Decontamination procedures are essential steps in the management of poisoned patients to prevent further absorption of the toxic substance. These procedures are aimed at removing the toxin from the skin, eyes, or gastrointestinal tract, depending on the route of exposure.

1.2.5.1 Skin and Ocular Decontamination

Skin and ocular decontamination are critical in cases where the poison has come into contact with the skin or eyes. Prompt and effective decontamination can significantly reduce the absorption of the toxin and prevent further injury.

Skin Decontamination: The initial step in skin decontamination is to remove any contaminated clothing and to thoroughly wash the affected skin with copious amounts of water. If the substance is a dry chemical, it should be brushed off the skin before washing. It is important to use mild soap and water for washing, as harsh detergents can further irritate the skin. The duration of washing should be at least 15-20 minutes to ensure thorough removal of the toxin. Special care should be taken to avoid cross-contamination to other areas of the body or to healthcare providers.

Ocular Decontamination: For ocular exposure, immediate and copious irrigation of the eyes is essential. Normal saline or sterile water is preferred for irrigation, and the process should continue for at least 15-30 minutes. The eyelids should be held open to ensure thorough irrigation of the entire surface of the eye and the conjunctival sacs. After irrigation, an ophthalmologic examination is necessary to assess for any residual damage or need for further treatment. In cases of exposure to caustic substances, prolonged irrigation may be required, and pH testing of the eye may guide the duration of irrigation.

1.2.5.2 Gastrointestinal Decontamination

Gastrointestinal decontamination is performed to limit the absorption of ingested toxins. The choice of method depends on the type and amount of poison ingested, the time since ingestion, and the patient's clinical condition.

Activated Charcoal: Activated charcoal is the most commonly used method for gastrointestinal decontamination. It adsorbs the toxin in the gastrointestinal tract, preventing its absorption into the bloodstream. The recommended dose of activated charcoal is 1 gram per kilogram of body weight, administered orally or via nasogastric tube. It is most effective when given within one hour of ingestion. However, activated charcoal is not effective for all toxins, such as alcohols, heavy metals, and hydrocarbons.

Gastric Lavage: Gastric lavage, or stomach pumping, involves the insertion of a large-bore orogastric tube to aspirate gastric contents and rinse the stomach with saline or water. This procedure is typically reserved for life-threatening ingestions where the toxin is known to be present in the stomach, and it is performed within one hour of ingestion. Gastric lavage carries risks such as aspiration, esophageal perforation, and electrolyte imbalances, so it should be done with caution and under specific indications.

Cathartics and Whole Bowel Irrigation: Cathartics, such as sorbitol or magnesium citrate, are sometimes used in conjunction with activated charcoal to hasten the elimination of the toxin from the gastrointestinal tract. Whole bowel irrigation with polyethylene glycol-electrolyte solution is used for certain types of poisonings, such as sustained-release or enteric-coated drugs and toxins not adsorbed by activated charcoal. The solution is administered orally or via nasogastric tube until the rectal effluent is clear, indicating that the gastrointestinal tract has been thoroughly cleansed.

1.2.6 Continuous Monitoring and Support

Continuous monitoring and support are vital components in the stabilization of poisoned patients. These processes involve the ongoing assessment of the patient's vital signs, neurological status, and metabolic parameters to detect any changes in condition and to guide further treatment.

Vital Signs Monitoring: Continuous monitoring of vital signs, including heart rate, blood pressure, respiratory rate, and oxygen saturation, is crucial. Automated monitoring devices are often used in emergency and intensive care settings to provide real-time data. Any abnormalities in these parameters can indicate a deterioration in the patient's condition, necessitating prompt intervention.

Neurological Monitoring: Regular assessment of the patient's level of consciousness, using tools such as the Glasgow Coma Scale, helps in detecting any changes in neurological status. Continuous EEG monitoring may be necessary in patients with seizures or altered mental status to detect subclinical seizure activity and guide treatment.

Metabolic Monitoring: Blood tests, including arterial blood gases, electrolytes, renal function tests, and glucose levels, should be monitored regularly. These tests provide important information about the patient's metabolic status and help in identifying complications such as acidosis, electrolyte imbalances, or renal failure. Continuous capnography can be used to monitor ventilation and detect respiratory failure early.

Cardiac Monitoring: Continuous ECG monitoring is essential for detecting cardiac arrhythmias, which are common in many types of poisoning. Poison-induced arrhythmias can be life-threatening and require immediate treatment. Monitoring for signs of myocardial ischemia or infarction is also important in patients with cardiotoxic poisonings.

Supportive Care: Supportive care involves maintaining adequate oxygenation, ventilation, and perfusion. This may include the use of supplemental oxygen, mechanical ventilation, intravenous fluids, and vasopressors. Pain management, sedation, and temperature control are also important aspects of supportive care.

Frequent Reassessment: The patient's condition can change rapidly in cases of poisoning, so frequent reassessment is necessary. This includes regular physical examinations, repeated vital signs measurements, and continuous monitoring of clinical and laboratory parameters. Adjustments to the treatment plan should be made based on the patient's response and any new clinical findings.

Documentation and Communication: Accurate documentation of all interventions, monitoring parameters, and patient responses is essential for effective management and continuity of care. Clear communication among healthcare providers, including handovers during shift changes, ensures that all team members are aware of the patient's status and treatment plan.

1.3 Diagnosis and Risk Assessment

1.3.1 History Taking

History taking is a crucial initial step in diagnosing and assessing the risk in poisoning cases. It involves gathering comprehensive information about the exposure to understand the nature and extent of the poisoning.

1.3.1.1 Substance Identification

Substance identification is paramount in history taking. Identifying the specific toxin or toxins involved guides the subsequent management and treatment decisions. Healthcare providers should ask detailed questions to ascertain the exact substance, including the product name, chemical composition, and concentration if known. In situations where the patient is unable to provide this information, family members, bystanders, or first responders can be valuable sources. Additionally, examining the scene for containers, labels, or remnants of the substance can provide critical clues. Understanding the properties of the substance, such as whether it is a caustic agent, a neurotoxin, or a cardiotoxin, helps in predicting the clinical course and potential complications.

1.3.1.2 Dose and Timing

Dose and timing are equally important aspects of history taking. The dose of the toxin ingested, inhaled, or absorbed correlates directly with the severity of poisoning. Healthcare providers should aim to determine the amount of substance the patient was exposed to. Questions should include the quantity taken, the form (e.g., liquid, solid), and the duration of exposure. Timing of exposure is critical, as it affects the absorption, distribution, and metabolism of the toxin. Knowing the time elapsed since exposure helps in predicting the onset of symptoms and the window for certain interventions, such as the administration of activated charcoal or antidotes. For instance, the effectiveness of many decontamination procedures decreases significantly as more time passes after ingestion.

1.3.2 Physical Examination

Physical examination is an essential component in the diagnosis and risk assessment of poisoned patients. It involves a thorough assessment of vital signs and specific physical findings that provide clues to the type and severity of poisoning.

1.3.2.1 Vital Signs and Symptoms

Vital signs and symptoms offer immediate information about the patient's physiological state and the impact of the poisoning. Vital signs include temperature, pulse, blood pressure, respiratory rate, and oxygen saturation. Each of these parameters can indicate specific effects of toxins:

- **Temperature:** Hypothermia or hyperthermia can be seen in various poisonings. For example, salicylate poisoning can cause hyperthermia, while opioid overdose may lead to hypothermia.
- **Pulse:** Tachycardia can result from stimulant poisonings such as amphetamines, while bradycardia may be seen in cases of beta-blocker or calcium channel blocker overdoses.
- **Blood Pressure:** Hypertension can be a sign of stimulant poisoning, whereas hypotension is often seen with sedative or cardiovascular toxin overdoses.
- **Respiratory Rate:** Tachypnea might indicate metabolic acidosis, as seen in salicylate poisoning, whereas bradypnea suggests central nervous system depression, commonly due to opioid toxicity.
- **Oxygen Saturation:** Low oxygen saturation indicates respiratory compromise, necessitating immediate intervention.

1.3.2.2 Specific Physical Findings

Specific physical findings provide further insight into the nature and extent of poisoning. A detailed head-to-toe examination can reveal critical signs associated with specific toxins:

- **Pupils:** Miosis (pinpoint pupils) is characteristic of opioid poisoning, while mydriasis (dilated pupils) can be seen with anticholinergic or sympathomimetic toxicity.
- **Skin:** Skin findings can be very telling. Cyanosis indicates hypoxia, while flushing might be seen in anticholinergic poisoning. Pallor or diaphoresis can be signs of shock or severe stress responses.
- **Mucous Membranes:** Dry mucous membranes are often seen in anticholinergic poisoning, whereas salivation might be excessive in organophosphate poisoning.
- **Neurological Findings:** Assessing motor function, reflexes, and coordination is important. Tremors, hyperreflexia, or seizures can occur with stimulant poisonings, whereas flaccidity and diminished reflexes might be seen in sedative overdoses.
- **Cardiovascular Examination:** An irregular heartbeat or murmurs may suggest cardiotoxic effects, requiring immediate attention.

1.3 Diagnosis and Risk Assessment

1.3.3 Laboratory Tests

Laboratory tests are essential in the diagnosis and management of poisoning, providing crucial information about the patient's physiological status and the presence of specific toxins.

1.3.3.1 Basic Metabolic Panel

The **basic metabolic panel (BMP)** includes a group of tests that measure different chemicals in the blood. These tests provide valuable information about the patient's overall metabolic state and can indicate specific complications related to poisoning.

- **Electrolytes:** Sodium, potassium, chloride, and bicarbonate levels help assess electrolyte imbalances that can result from or contribute to poisoning. For instance, hypokalemia can be seen in diuretic abuse, while hyperkalemia may occur in potassium-sparing diuretic overdose or rhabdomyolysis.
- **Glucose:** Blood glucose levels can indicate hyperglycemia or hypoglycemia, both of which can occur with various poisonings. For

example, hypoglycemia is common in insulin or oral hypoglycemic agent overdose.

- **Renal Function:** Blood urea nitrogen (BUN) and creatinine levels assess kidney function. Elevated levels may indicate renal impairment, which can affect the elimination of toxins and require adjustment in treatment strategies.
- **Calcium:** Abnormal calcium levels can occur in poisonings involving fluoride, ethylene glycol, or phosphate-containing substances.

1.3.3.2 Specific Toxicology Screens

Specific toxicology screens are targeted tests that detect the presence of specific toxins in the blood, urine, or other body fluids. These screens help confirm the diagnosis and guide appropriate treatment.

- **Blood Toxicology:** Blood tests can measure levels of specific toxins, such as acetaminophen, salicylates, ethanol, methanol, and ethylene glycol. Blood carboxyhemoglobin levels are measured in suspected carbon monoxide poisoning.
- **Urine Toxicology:** Urine screens can detect a wide range of substances, including drugs of abuse like amphetamines, cocaine, opioids, benzodiazepines, and barbiturates. Urine tests are useful for detecting recent exposure to these substances.
- **Gas Chromatography-Mass Spectrometry (GC-MS):** GC-MS is a highly sensitive and specific method for identifying and quantifying various toxins. It is often used in complex cases where the toxin is unknown or when confirmatory testing is required.

1.3.4 Electrocardiography (ECG)

Electrocardiography (ECG) is a critical diagnostic tool in poisoning cases, as many toxins can affect the heart's electrical activity and lead to life-threatening arrhythmias.

1.3.4.1 Common ECG Findings in Poisoning

Common ECG findings in poisoning can provide important clues about the nature and severity of the exposure:

- **QT Prolongation:** Prolonged QT interval is common in poisonings with drugs like tricyclic antidepressants, antipsychotics, and certain antihistamines. QT prolongation increases the risk of torsades de pointes, a potentially fatal arrhythmia.
- **QRS Widening:** Widened QRS complexes can indicate sodium channel blockade, seen in tricyclic antidepressant overdoses. This finding suggests a higher risk of ventricular arrhythmias and requires immediate intervention.
- **ST Segment Changes:** ST segment elevations or depressions may occur with toxic effects on the heart, such as in carbon monoxide poisoning or with certain drugs like cocaine and amphetamines.
- **Bradycardia:** Slow heart rate can be seen in beta-blocker or calcium channel blocker overdoses and may require treatment with atropine, glucagon, or intravenous calcium.
- **Tachycardia:** Fast heart rate is common in stimulant poisonings (e.g., amphetamines, cocaine) and can lead to complications like myocardial ischemia.

1.3.5 Imaging Studies

Imaging studies provide visual information about the internal structures of the body and can help identify complications related to poisoning.

1.3.5.1 Chest X-ray

Chest X-rays are useful in identifying respiratory complications and other abnormalities associated with poisoning:

- **Aspiration Pneumonia:** Common in patients with decreased consciousness who have aspirated gastric contents.
- **Pulmonary Edema:** Can occur in poisonings with opioids, organophosphates, and other toxins.
- **Pneumonitis:** Inflammation of lung tissue seen with inhalation of toxic gases or chemical pneumonitis from hydrocarbon ingestion.
- **Foreign Bodies:** Radiopaque substances ingested or aspirated can be visualized on chest X-ray.

1.3.5.2 Abdominal Radiographs

Abdominal radiographs help in detecting ingested foreign bodies or toxins that are radiopaque:

- **Tablets or Capsules:** Certain medications like iron or enteric-coated tablets can be seen on abdominal X-rays.
- **Body Packers:** Individuals who smuggle drugs by ingesting packets can be identified with abdominal radiographs, showing the presence of multiple foreign bodies.
- **Intestinal Obstruction:** Radiographs can identify obstructions caused by bezoars or concretions of ingested material.

1.3.6 Risk Assessment Tools

Risk assessment tools help clinicians evaluate the severity of poisoning and guide management decisions.

1.3.6.1 Poison Severity Score (PSS)

The **Poison Severity Score (PSS)** is a standardized tool used to assess the severity of poisoning based on clinical symptoms and signs:

- **Grades:** PSS categorizes poisoning into four grades: Minor (Grade 0), Moderate (Grade 1), Severe (Grade 2), and Fatal (Grade 3).
- **Application:** This scoring system helps in triaging patients, predicting outcomes, and standardizing communication among healthcare providers. For instance, a PSS of Grade 2 indicates severe poisoning with life-threatening symptoms requiring intensive care.

1.3.6.2 Toxicological Consultation

Toxicological consultation involves seeking expert advice from poison control centers or toxicologists:

- **Poison Control Centers:** These centers provide 24/7 expert guidance on managing poisoning cases. They can offer specific treatment recommendations, antidote information, and support in identifying unknown toxins.
- **Toxicologists:** Consulting a medical toxicologist can be invaluable in complex cases. They can assist with advanced diagnostic techniques, interpret toxicology results, and provide specialized care

recommendations.

Effective diagnosis and risk assessment through comprehensive history taking, physical examination, laboratory tests, ECG, imaging studies, and the use of risk assessment tools are vital in the management of poisoned patients. These steps ensure accurate identification of the toxin, evaluation of the severity of poisoning, and formulation of an appropriate treatment plan.

1.4 Treatment Planning and Implementation

1.4.1 Setting Treatment Goals

Setting treatment goals is a critical step in managing poisoning cases. This involves defining both immediate and long-term objectives to ensure comprehensive care and optimal outcomes for the patient.

1.4.1.1 Immediate and Long-Term Goals

Immediate goals focus on stabilizing the patient and preventing further harm. These goals typically include:

- **Stabilizing Vital Signs:** Ensuring airway patency, adequate breathing, and circulatory support to maintain oxygenation and perfusion.
- **Administering Antidotes:** Providing specific antidotes to neutralize the toxin if available and indicated.
- **Preventing Further Absorption:** Implementing decontamination procedures to prevent additional toxin absorption.
- **Symptomatic Management:** Addressing acute symptoms such as seizures, pain, or severe agitation.

Long-term goals aim at preventing complications, ensuring complete recovery, and educating the patient and family to avoid future poisoning incidents. These goals include:

- **Monitoring and Reassessment:** Regularly monitoring the patient's condition and reassessing the effectiveness of interventions.
- **Rehabilitation:** Providing physical and psychological rehabilitation to address any residual effects of the poisoning.

- **Patient Education:** Educating the patient and their family about the prevention of future poisoning incidents and the proper use and storage of toxic substances.
- **Follow-Up Care:** Arranging follow-up visits to monitor recovery and manage any long-term health issues related to the poisoning.

1.4.2 Immediate Interventions

Immediate interventions are crucial for counteracting the effects of the poison and stabilizing the patient.

1.4.2.1 Administering Antidotes

Administering antidotes is one of the most effective immediate interventions when a specific antidote is available for the toxin involved. Antidotes work by neutralizing the toxin, blocking its effects, or enhancing its elimination from the body.

- **N-acetylcysteine (NAC):** Used for acetaminophen overdose. NAC replenishes glutathione stores, detoxifies the reactive metabolite, and prevents liver damage. It is most effective when administered within 8 hours of ingestion.
- **Atropine:** Used in organophosphate or carbamate poisoning. Atropine blocks the effects of excessive acetylcholine at muscarinic receptors, alleviating symptoms such as bradycardia, bronchospasm, and excessive salivation.
- **Naloxone:** An opioid antagonist used to reverse the effects of opioid overdose. Naloxone rapidly restores normal respiration in patients with opioid-induced respiratory depression.
- **Flumazenil:** A benzodiazepine antagonist used in benzodiazepine overdose. Flumazenil competitively inhibits the action of benzodiazepines at the GABA receptor, reversing sedation and respiratory depression.

Administering antidotes should be done promptly and according to established protocols to maximize their effectiveness and minimize the risk of complications.

1.4.3 Preventing Further Absorption

Preventing further absorption of the toxin is essential to limit its systemic effects and reduce the severity of poisoning. This involves various decontamination procedures depending on the route of exposure.

1.4.3.1 Gastrointestinal Decontamination

Gastrointestinal decontamination aims to remove ingested toxins from the gastrointestinal tract before they are absorbed into the bloodstream.

- **Activated Charcoal:** The most common method of gastrointestinal decontamination. Activated charcoal adsorbs a wide range of toxins, reducing their absorption. It is typically administered in a dose of 1 gram per kilogram of body weight. For maximum effectiveness, it should be given within one hour of ingestion.
- **Gastric Lavage:** This procedure involves inserting a large-bore orogastric tube into the stomach and washing it out with saline or water to remove the ingested toxin. Gastric lavage is usually reserved for life-threatening ingestions where the toxin is still in the stomach and performed within one hour of ingestion.
- **Whole Bowel Irrigation:** This method involves administering large volumes of polyethylene glycol-electrolyte solution to flush out the entire gastrointestinal tract. It is useful for substances that are not adsorbed by activated charcoal, such as sustained-release or enteric-coated drugs and certain metals.

1.4.3.2 Dermal and Ocular Decontamination

Dermal and ocular decontamination are crucial for cases where toxins have come into contact with the skin or eyes.

- **Skin Decontamination:** Promptly removing contaminated clothing and washing the skin with copious amounts of water and mild soap can significantly reduce toxin absorption. It is important to avoid vigorous scrubbing, which can cause further irritation or damage. Washing should continue for at least 15-20 minutes.
- **Ocular Decontamination:** Immediate and thorough irrigation of the eyes with sterile water or normal saline is essential to remove toxins and prevent further damage. The eyelids should be held open during irrigation to ensure thorough cleansing of the entire ocular surface.

Irrigation should continue for at least 15-30 minutes. Following irrigation, an ophthalmologic evaluation is necessary to assess for any residual damage.

1.4 Treatment Planning and Implementation

1.4.4 Enhancing Elimination

Enhancing elimination of the toxin from the body is a critical aspect of managing poisoning. Various techniques are used to accelerate the removal of the toxin, thereby reducing its systemic effects and facilitating recovery.

1.4.4.1 Urinary Alkalinization

Urinary alkalinization involves increasing the pH of the urine to enhance the excretion of certain toxins. This technique is particularly effective for weak acids, such as salicylates and phenobarbital.

- **Mechanism:** Alkalinizing the urine increases the ionization of weak acids, reducing their reabsorption in the renal tubules and promoting their excretion.
- **Procedure:** Sodium bicarbonate is commonly used to alkalinize the urine. It is administered intravenously, typically as a bolus followed by a continuous infusion. The goal is to maintain a urinary pH of 7.5 to 8.5.
- **Monitoring:** Frequent monitoring of blood pH, serum electrolytes, and urine pH is essential to avoid complications such as metabolic alkalosis and hypokalemia.

1.4.4.2 Hemodialysis

Hemodialysis is a medical procedure that involves the removal of toxins directly from the bloodstream using a dialysis machine. It is highly effective for certain poisons, particularly those that are water-soluble and have a low molecular weight.

- **Indications:** Hemodialysis is indicated for poisoning with substances such as methanol, ethylene glycol, lithium, and severe cases of salicylate overdose.

- **Procedure:** Blood is passed through a dialysis machine, which filters out the toxins and returns the cleaned blood to the patient. The process is repeated over several hours until the toxin levels are significantly reduced.
- **Monitoring:** Continuous monitoring of the patient's vital signs, electrolyte levels, and acid-base balance is crucial during hemodialysis to ensure safety and effectiveness.

1.4.4.3 Hemoperfusion

Hemoperfusion is another extracorporeal technique used to enhance the elimination of toxins. It involves passing blood through a cartridge filled with adsorbent material, such as activated charcoal or resin, which binds the toxins.

- **Indications:** Hemoperfusion is particularly effective for toxins that are poorly dialyzable but highly protein-bound or lipid-soluble, such as theophylline, carbamazepine, and certain pesticides.
- **Procedure:** Blood is circulated through the hemoperfusion cartridge, allowing the adsorbent material to bind and remove the toxins from the bloodstream. The cleaned blood is then returned to the patient.
- **Monitoring:** Similar to hemodialysis, close monitoring of the patient's hemodynamic status, electrolyte levels, and overall clinical condition is essential during the procedure.

1.4.5 Symptomatic and Supportive Care

Symptomatic and supportive care is a cornerstone of managing poisoned patients, addressing the clinical symptoms and maintaining physiological stability while specific treatments are administered.

1.4.5.1 Pain Management

Pain management is crucial in providing comfort and improving the overall well-being of the patient. Pain can result from the toxic effects of the poison or from complications such as tissue injury or inflammation.

- **Assessment:** Pain should be assessed using appropriate pain scales, taking into account the patient's verbal and non-verbal cues.

- **Medications:** Analgesics, such as acetaminophen or nonsteroidal anti-inflammatory drugs (NSAIDs), are commonly used for mild to moderate pain. For severe pain, opioids such as morphine or fentanyl may be required, administered with caution to avoid respiratory depression, especially in patients with compromised respiratory function.
- **Non-Pharmacological Measures:** Complementary techniques such as ice packs, heat therapy, or relaxation exercises can also be beneficial in managing pain.

1.4.5.2 Anticonvulsants

Anticonvulsants are used to manage seizures, which can be a complication of various poisonings. Prompt control of seizures is essential to prevent further neurological damage and systemic complications.

- **First-Line Agents:** Benzodiazepines, such as diazepam and lorazepam, are the first-line agents for controlling seizures. They are effective in rapidly terminating seizures by enhancing the inhibitory effects of gamma-aminobutyric acid (GABA).
- **Second-Line Agents:** If seizures persist, additional anticonvulsants such as phenobarbital or phenytoin may be administered. Phenobarbital works by increasing the duration of chloride channel opening, while phenytoin stabilizes neuronal membranes and reduces excitability.
- **Monitoring:** Continuous EEG monitoring may be necessary in cases of refractory seizures to guide treatment adjustments and assess the effectiveness of therapy.

1.4.5.3 Fluid and Electrolyte Balance

Maintaining fluid and electrolyte balance is critical in managing poisoning cases, as many toxins can disrupt homeostasis and lead to significant imbalances.

- **Fluid Therapy:** Intravenous fluids are administered to maintain hydration, support circulatory function, and facilitate toxin elimination. Isotonic crystalloids, such as normal saline or lactated Ringer's solution, are commonly used.
- **Electrolyte Monitoring:** Regular monitoring of serum electrolytes, including sodium, potassium, calcium, and magnesium, is essential. Electrolyte imbalances are corrected based on the specific deficits

identified.

- **Acid-Base Balance:** Monitoring and correcting acid-base imbalances is crucial. Metabolic acidosis, for example, may occur in poisoning with substances such as methanol or ethylene glycol, and may require administration of sodium bicarbonate or other alkalinizing agents.

1.4 Treatment Planning and Implementation

1.4.6 Monitoring and Reassessment

Monitoring and reassessment are continuous processes crucial to the effective management of poisoning cases. These steps ensure that the patient's condition is stable, interventions are effective, and any changes in status are promptly addressed.

1.4.6.1 Vital Signs and Laboratory Parameters

Monitoring vital signs and laboratory parameters provides ongoing information about the patient's physiological status and the effectiveness of treatment:

- **Vital Signs:** Regular monitoring of heart rate, blood pressure, respiratory rate, and oxygen saturation is essential. Automated monitoring systems are often used in emergency and intensive care settings to provide continuous data. Any deviations from normal ranges can indicate deterioration and necessitate immediate intervention.
- **Laboratory Parameters:** Frequent blood tests are necessary to monitor electrolytes, renal function, liver function, and blood glucose levels. Serial measurements of toxicology screens can assess the effectiveness of decontamination and elimination efforts. Blood gas analysis helps monitor acid-base balance, crucial in cases of metabolic acidosis or alkalosis due to poisoning.
- **Reassessment Frequency:** The frequency of monitoring depends on the severity of the poisoning and the patient's clinical status. In critically ill patients, continuous monitoring may be required, while stable patients may need periodic reassessment.

1.4.7 Documentation and Communication

Documentation and communication are vital for ensuring effective management and continuity of care. Accurate records and clear communication among healthcare providers facilitate coordinated and efficient treatment.

1.4.7.1 Recording Interventions and Outcomes

Recording interventions and outcomes involves maintaining detailed and accurate records of all medical actions taken and the patient's response to those actions:

- **Interventions:** Document all interventions, including medications administered, doses, times, and routes of administration. Note any procedures performed, such as gastric lavage or hemodialysis, and the rationale for these interventions.
- **Patient Response:** Record the patient's response to treatments, including changes in vital signs, laboratory parameters, and clinical symptoms. This information is critical for assessing the effectiveness of interventions and making necessary adjustments.
- **Communication:** Clear and timely communication among healthcare providers is essential, especially during shift changes. Use standardized handover protocols to ensure that all team members are aware of the patient's status, treatment plan, and any changes that have occurred.

1.4.8 Patient Education and Follow-Up

Patient education and follow-up are key components of comprehensive poisoning management. Educating the patient and their family helps prevent future incidents and ensures ongoing care.

1.4.8.1 Preventive Measures

Preventive measures focus on educating patients and families about the risks of poisoning and strategies to avoid future exposures:

- **Safe Storage:** Emphasize the importance of storing medications, chemicals, and other toxic substances out of reach of children and in secure locations.

- **Proper Usage:** Educate patients on the correct usage of medications and household chemicals, including reading labels and following dosage instructions carefully.
- **Disposal:** Provide guidance on the safe disposal of unused or expired medications and chemicals to prevent accidental ingestion or exposure.
- **Emergency Plan:** Advise on the development of an emergency plan, including keeping the contact information for poison control centers readily available and knowing the steps to take in case of accidental poisoning.

Method	Description	Advantages	Limitations
Activated Charcoal	Adsorbs toxins in the GI tract, preventing absorption	Effective for many toxins; easy to administer	Ineffective for alcohols, metals, and hydrocarbons
Gastric Lavage	Washing out stomach contents via a tube	Useful for life-threatening ingestions within 1 hour	Risk of aspiration, esophageal perforation
Whole Bowel Irrigation	Cleansing the entire GI tract with polyethylene glycol solution	Effective for sustained-release or enteric-coated drugs	Requires patient cooperation; time-consuming
Skin Decontamination	Washing skin with water and mild soap	Prevents further absorption; simple procedure	Risk of cross-contamination; needs thorough washing
Ocular Decontamination	Irrigating eyes with saline or water	Essential for eye exposure; prevents further damage	Requires prolonged irrigation; may need ophthalmologic follow-up

Table 1: Comparison of Decontamination Methods

Antidote	Indication	Mechanism of Action	Dosage and Administration
N-acetylcysteine (NAC)	Acetaminophen overdose	Replenishes glutathione, detoxifies reactive metabolite	IV or oral; loading dose followed by maintenance
Atropine	Organophosphate or carbamate poisoning	Blocks effects of excess acetylcholine	IV; titrate to effect, frequent dosing required
Naloxone	Opioid overdose	Opioid receptor antagonist	IV, IM, or nasal; initial dose followed by repeat doses as needed
Flumazenil	Benzodiazepine overdose	Competitive inhibition at GABA receptor	IV; single dose, may repeat based on response
Sodium Bicarbonate	Tricyclic antidepressant overdose	Alkalinizes blood, reduces cardiotoxic effects	IV; bolus followed by continuous infusion

Table 2: Common Antidotes and Their Uses

Tool	Purpose	Key Findings
Glasgow Coma Scale (GCS)	Assess level of consciousness	Eye, verbal, and motor response scores
Electrocardiography (ECG)	Detect cardiac effects of toxins	QT prolongation, QRS widening, arrhythmias
Basic Metabolic Panel (BMP)	Evaluate metabolic state and organ function	Electrolytes, glucose, BUN, creatinine levels
Specific Toxicology Screens	Identify and quantify specific toxins	Presence and concentration of drugs/toxins
Imaging Studies (X-ray, CT)	Visualize complications and ingested materials	Pulmonary edema, aspiration pneumonia, radiopaque substances

Table 3: Diagnostic Tools in Poisoning Cases

Aspect	Details
Rapid ABC Evaluation	Ensure Airway, Breathing, and Circulation are stable
History Taking	Identify substance, dose, timing, and route of exposure
Physical Examination	Assess vital signs and specific physical findings (e.g., pupils, skin)
Neurological Assessment	Use GCS to determine level of consciousness
Triage	Prioritize care based on severity of symptoms

Table 4: Key Considerations in Initial Assessment of Poisoned Patients

Fig 1 : Initial Assessment and Triage

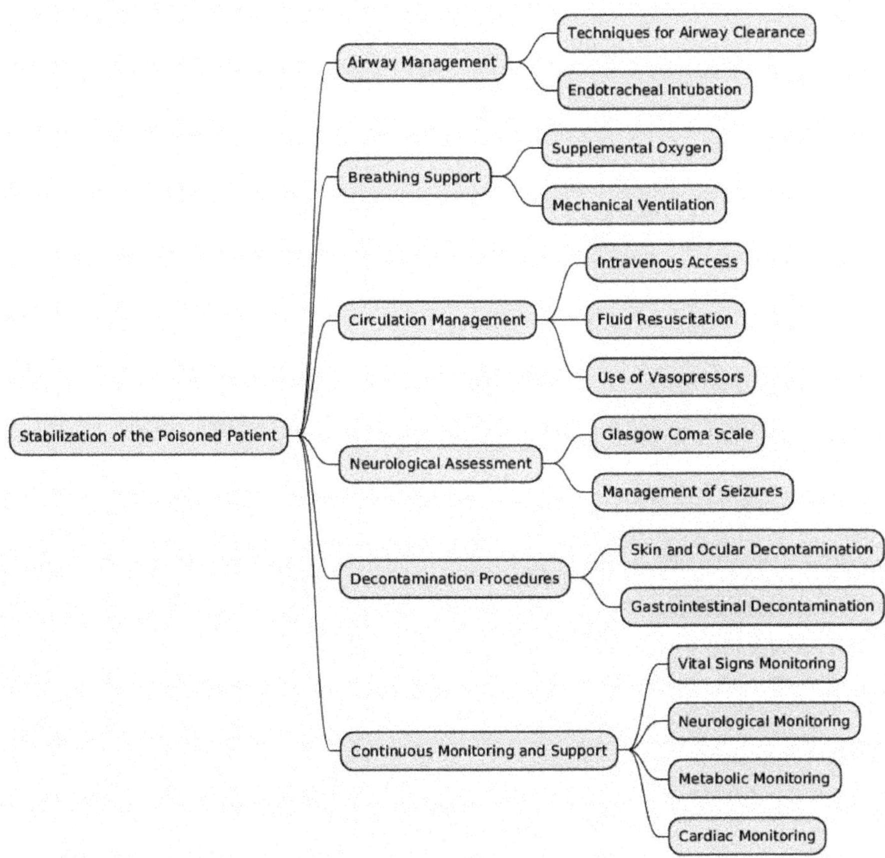

Fig 2. Stabilization of the Poisoned Patient

CHAPTER II

Antidotes and Clinical Applications Introduction

Antidotes play a pivotal role in the management of poisoning cases, providing specific therapeutic agents that counteract the toxic effects of various substances. The development and application of antidotes have significantly improved outcomes for patients exposed to potentially life-threatening toxins. This chapter delves into the diverse range of antidotes available, their mechanisms of action, clinical indications, and practical applications in the treatment of poisoning.

Understanding the appropriate use of antidotes requires comprehensive knowledge of toxicology, pharmacokinetics, and the pathophysiology of poisoning. Each antidote is tailored to neutralize a specific toxin, mitigate its effects, or enhance its elimination from the body. The timely and accurate administration of antidotes can be lifesaving, underscoring the importance of prompt diagnosis and intervention.

Scope of the Chapter

This chapter covers the following key areas:

1. **Mechanisms of Action**: Explaining how various antidotes work at a molecular and physiological level to counteract the effects of toxins.
2. **Clinical Indications**: Detailing the specific poisoning scenarios in which each antidote is indicated, including the types of toxins they target and the clinical signs that warrant their use.
3. **Dosage and Administration**: Providing guidelines on the appropriate dosages, routes of administration, and timing for antidote administration to ensure maximum efficacy and safety.
4. **Case Studies and Clinical Applications**: Presenting real-world examples and case studies that illustrate the practical application of antidotes in clinical settings, highlighting best practices and common challenges.
5. **Adverse Effects and Contraindications**: Discussing potential side effects, contraindications, and precautions associated with antidote use, ensuring that healthcare providers can make informed decisions and manage complications effectively.
6. **Advances in Antidote Development**: Exploring recent advances in antidote research and development, including novel therapeutic agents

and emerging trends in toxicology.

Importance of Antidotes in Poisoning Management

The use of antidotes is integral to the comprehensive management of poisoning. While supportive care and symptomatic treatment are crucial, antidotes provide a targeted approach to neutralize toxins and reduce their harmful effects. For example, N-acetylcysteine (NAC) is essential in treating acetaminophen overdose by replenishing glutathione stores and preventing liver damage. Similarly, naloxone is a critical antidote for opioid overdoses, rapidly reversing respiratory depression and saving lives.

Antidotes not only improve survival rates but also enhance the quality of recovery, reducing long-term complications and improving patient outcomes. The ability to promptly administer the correct antidote can mean the difference between life and death, making it a cornerstone of emergency medical care in toxicology.

Educational Objectives

By the end of this chapter, readers should be able to:

- Understand the fundamental principles underlying the action of various antidotes.
- Identify clinical situations where antidotes are indicated and apply the appropriate treatment protocols.
- Administer antidotes effectively, considering factors such as dosage, timing, and potential side effects.
- Utilize case studies to enhance practical understanding and application of antidotes in real-world scenarios.
- Stay informed about new developments and emerging trends in antidote therapy.

2.1 Definition and Types of Antidotes

Introduction

Antidotes are therapeutic agents specifically designed to counteract the toxic effects of poisons. They play a critical role in poisoning management by neutralizing toxins, preventing their absorption, or promoting their elimination from the body. Antidotes can be classified into different types based on their mechanism of action and the nature of their interaction with the toxin. Understanding the various types of antidotes is essential for selecting the appropriate treatment in cases of poisoning.

2.1.1 Chemical Antidotes

Chemical antidotes directly interact with the toxin to neutralize it or render it harmless. These antidotes typically work through chemical reactions that alter the structure or properties of the toxin, preventing it from exerting its harmful effects.

- **Chelating Agents:** These are used to treat heavy metal poisoning. Examples include **dimercaprol** (used for arsenic, gold, and mercury poisoning), **EDTA** (used for lead poisoning), and **penicillamine** (used for copper poisoning in Wilson's disease). Chelating agents bind to heavy metals, forming complexes that are more easily excreted by the body.
- **Neutralizing Agents:** These antidotes chemically neutralize the toxin. For instance, **sodium thiosulfate** is used in cyanide poisoning, where it converts cyanide to thiocyanate, a less toxic compound that is excreted in the urine.
- **Oxidizing Agents:Methylene blue** is used in cases of methemoglobinemia, where it reduces methemoglobin back to hemoglobin, restoring its oxygen-carrying capacity.

2.1.2 Pharmacological Antidotes

Pharmacological antidotes work by counteracting the effects of the toxin on the body's physiological systems. These antidotes often act on specific receptors or biochemical pathways affected by the toxin.

- **Receptor Antagonists:** These drugs block the action of the toxin at its receptor site. For example, **naloxone** is an opioid antagonist that competes with opioids for binding to the mu-opioid receptor, reversing the effects of opioid overdose such as respiratory depression.
- **Receptor Agonists:** In some cases, antidotes may act as receptor agonists to counteract the effects of toxins. **Atropine**, an anticholinergic agent, is used to treat organophosphate poisoning by blocking the effects of excessive acetylcholine at muscarinic receptors.
- **Enzyme Reactivators:Pralidoxime** (2-PAM) reactivates acetylcholinesterase inhibited by organophosphates, restoring its function and alleviating the toxic effects of acetylcholine accumulation.

2.1.3 Mechanical Antidotes

Mechanical antidotes involve physical methods or devices used to remove or prevent the absorption of toxins. These methods do not chemically or pharmacologically interact with the toxin but rather employ mechanical means to mitigate its effects.

- **Activated Charcoal:** This is a widely used mechanical antidote that adsorbs toxins in the gastrointestinal tract, preventing their absorption into the bloodstream. Activated charcoal is effective for many ingested toxins if administered promptly after ingestion.
- **Gastric Lavage:** Also known as stomach pumping, this procedure involves inserting a tube into the stomach and washing it out with saline or water to remove ingested toxins. Gastric lavage is typically used in severe poisoning cases within an hour of toxin ingestion.
- **Whole Bowel Irrigation:** This method involves the administration of large volumes of polyethylene glycol solution to flush out the entire gastrointestinal tract. It is particularly useful for eliminating sustained-release or enteric-coated drugs and certain metals not effectively adsorbed by activated charcoal.
- **Hemodialysis and Hemoperfusion:** These extracorporeal techniques mechanically remove toxins from the bloodstream. Hemodialysis is effective for water-soluble toxins with low molecular weight, while hemoperfusion uses adsorbent materials like activated charcoal to remove protein-bound or lipid-soluble toxins.

2.2 Mechanism of Action

Introduction

Understanding the **mechanism of action** of antidotes is crucial for their effective application in clinical toxicology. Antidotes function through various mechanisms to counteract the harmful effects of toxins. This section delves into the fundamental mechanisms by which antidotes neutralize toxins and mitigate their effects on the body.

2.2.1 Neutralization of Toxins

Neutralization of toxins is one of the primary mechanisms by which antidotes exert their therapeutic effects. This process involves chemically altering the toxin to render it harmless or less toxic. The neutralization can occur through various biochemical reactions, such as oxidation, reduction, or chelation. Here, we explore different methods of toxin neutralization:

Chemical Neutralization

Chemical neutralization involves a direct reaction between the antidote and the toxin, resulting in the formation of a less toxic compound. This is often seen with antidotes that chemically transform the toxin into a safer substance that can be easily eliminated from the body.

- **Sodium Thiosulfate in Cyanide Poisoning:** Sodium thiosulfate serves as a sulfur donor in the detoxification of cyanide. It reacts with cyanide to form thiocyanate, a much less toxic compound that is excreted in the urine. This reaction significantly reduces the toxicity of cyanide, thereby protecting the patient from its lethal effects.

Chelation

Chelation therapy involves the binding of metal ions with chelating agents, forming stable, non-toxic complexes that can be excreted from the body. This method is particularly effective in cases of heavy metal poisoning.

- **Dimercaprol for Arsenic Poisoning:** Dimercaprol, also known as British Anti-Lewisite (BAL), forms stable complexes with arsenic, mercury, and other heavy metals. These complexes are more water-soluble and can be excreted via the kidneys, reducing the body's toxic burden of heavy metals.
- **EDTA for Lead Poisoning:** Ethylenediaminetetraacetic acid (EDTA) is another chelating agent that binds to lead ions, forming a stable complex that is excreted in the urine. This process reduces the concentration of free lead in the bloodstream, mitigating its toxic effects on the nervous system and other organs.

Oxidation and Reduction

Oxidation and reduction reactions are employed by certain antidotes to neutralize toxins by altering their oxidation state, making them less harmful or more easily excretable.

- **Methylene Blue for Methemoglobinemia:** Methemoglobinemia occurs when hemoglobin is oxidized to methemoglobin, which cannot effectively carry oxygen. Methylene blue acts as a reducing agent, converting methemoglobin back to hemoglobin, thereby restoring its oxygen-carrying capacity. This is a classic example of how altering the oxidation state of a toxin can neutralize its harmful effects.

- **Ascorbic Acid (Vitamin C) for Methemoglobinemia:** Ascorbic acid is another reducing agent that can convert methemoglobin to hemoglobin. It is particularly useful in cases where methylene blue is contraindicated or unavailable.

Formation of Inactive Complexes

Some antidotes work by forming inactive complexes with the toxin, preventing it from interacting with biological targets and exerting its toxic effects.

- **Protamine Sulfate for Heparin Overdose:** Protamine sulfate neutralizes heparin by forming a stable complex with it. This complex is inactive, thereby reversing the anticoagulant effects of heparin and reducing the risk of bleeding.
- **Vitamin K for Warfarin Overdose:** While not a direct neutralizer, Vitamin K promotes the synthesis of clotting factors inhibited by warfarin, counteracting its anticoagulant effects and restoring normal blood clotting.

Enzyme Inhibition

Certain antidotes neutralize toxins by inhibiting enzymes involved in their activation or metabolism.

- **Fomepizole in Methanol or Ethylene Glycol Poisoning:** Fomepizole inhibits alcohol dehydrogenase, the enzyme responsible for converting methanol and ethylene glycol into their toxic metabolites. By blocking this conversion, fomepizole prevents the formation of toxic compounds that cause metabolic acidosis and organ damage.

2.2 Mechanism of Action

2.2.2 Receptor Antagonism

Receptor antagonism is a mechanism by which antidotes block the interaction between a toxin and its biological target, usually a receptor. By preventing the toxin from binding to its receptor, receptor antagonists mitigate the toxic effects and restore normal physiological functions.

Mechanism of Action

- **Competitive Inhibition:** Receptor antagonists typically work through competitive inhibition, where the antidote competes with the toxin for binding to the receptor. By occupying the receptor sites, the antagonist prevents the toxin from exerting its effects.
- **Reversal of Receptor Activation:** In cases where the toxin has already activated the receptor, the antagonist can reverse this activation, thereby neutralizing the toxic effects.

Examples of Receptor Antagonism

- **Naloxone for Opioid Overdose:** Naloxone is a competitive antagonist at the mu-opioid receptors. It rapidly displaces opioids from these receptors, reversing the effects of opioid toxicity, including respiratory depression, sedation, and hypotension. Naloxone's rapid onset of action makes it an essential antidote in emergency settings.
- **Flumazenil for Benzodiazepine Overdose:** Flumazenil is a competitive antagonist at the benzodiazepine receptor, a part of the GABA-A receptor complex. By blocking benzodiazepines from binding, flumazenil reverses their sedative and respiratory depressant effects. It is used cautiously due to the risk of precipitating seizures, particularly in patients with mixed-drug overdoses or chronic benzodiazepine use.
- **Atropine for Organophosphate Poisoning:** Organophosphates inhibit acetylcholinesterase, leading to an accumulation of acetylcholine and overstimulation of muscarinic receptors. Atropine, a muscarinic receptor antagonist, blocks the effects of excessive acetylcholine, alleviating symptoms such as bradycardia, bronchorrhea, and salivation.

2.2.3 Chelation Therapy

Chelation therapy is a treatment modality used to remove heavy metals from the body by administering chelating agents. These agents form stable, water-soluble complexes with metal ions, facilitating their excretion and reducing their toxicity.

Mechanism of Action

- **Binding to Metal Ions:** Chelating agents contain functional groups that can bind tightly to metal ions, forming stable complexes. These complexes are typically non-toxic and are excreted via the kidneys or the gastrointestinal tract.

- **Enhancing Excretion:** By forming these complexes, chelation therapy enhances the renal or fecal excretion of heavy metals, reducing their burden in the body and preventing further damage.

Examples of Chelation Therapy

- **Dimercaprol (BAL):** Used for arsenic, mercury, and lead poisoning. Dimercaprol contains sulfhydryl groups that bind to heavy metals, forming stable, non-toxic complexes that are excreted in the urine.
- **Ethylenediaminetetraacetic Acid (EDTA):** Primarily used for lead poisoning. EDTA forms strong complexes with lead, which are then excreted in the urine. EDTA is often administered as calcium disodium EDTA to prevent hypocalcemia.
- **Penicillamine:** Used for copper poisoning, particularly in Wilson's disease. Penicillamine forms soluble complexes with copper, facilitating its excretion. It is also used in the treatment of lead and mercury poisoning.
- **Deferoxamine:** An iron chelator used for acute iron toxicity and chronic iron overload conditions such as thalassemia. Deferoxamine binds free iron, forming a complex that is excreted in the urine, reducing the risk of iron-induced organ damage.

Conclusion

Receptor antagonism and chelation therapy are critical mechanisms by which antidotes counteract the effects of toxins. Receptor antagonists work by blocking or reversing the interaction between toxins and their biological targets, effectively neutralizing their effects. Chelation therapy, on the other hand, involves binding heavy metals with chelating agents to form stable complexes that can be excreted from the body, reducing toxicity. Understanding these mechanisms allows healthcare providers to effectively utilize antidotes in the management of poisoning, ensuring better patient outcomes.

2.3 Indications and Contraindications

2.3.1 Specific Indications for Common Antidotes

Naloxone

Indications:

- **Opioid Overdose:** Naloxone is the first-line antidote for opioid overdoses, indicated for reversing life-threatening respiratory depression, sedation, and hypotension caused by opioids such as heroin, morphine, and fentanyl.
- **Suspected Opioid Toxicity:** It can be administered when opioid toxicity is suspected, even if the diagnosis is not confirmed, due to its rapid action and low risk of adverse effects.

Contraindications:

- **Known Hypersensitivity:** Naloxone should not be used in patients with a known hypersensitivity to the drug.
- **Precaution:** Caution is required in patients with opioid dependence, as naloxone can precipitate acute withdrawal symptoms.

N-acetylcysteine (NAC)
Indications:

- **Acetaminophen (Paracetamol) Overdose:** NAC is indicated for the treatment of acute and chronic acetaminophen poisoning. It replenishes glutathione stores, detoxifies the reactive metabolite, and prevents liver damage. It is most effective when administered within 8 hours of ingestion.

Contraindications:

- **Known Hypersensitivity:** NAC should be avoided in patients with a known hypersensitivity to it.
- **Precaution:** Anaphylactoid reactions can occur, especially with intravenous administration, requiring careful monitoring.

Atropine
Indications:

- **Organophosphate and Carbamate Poisoning:** Atropine is used to counteract the muscarinic effects of excessive acetylcholine, such as bradycardia, bronchorrhea, and salivation.

- **Bradycardia:** It is also indicated for the treatment of bradycardia that does not respond to other measures.

Contraindications:

- **Glaucoma:** Atropine is contraindicated in patients with narrow-angle glaucoma due to the risk of increasing intraocular pressure.
- **Tachycardia:** It should be used cautiously in patients with tachycardia, as it can exacerbate this condition.

Flumazenil
Indications:

- **Benzodiazepine Overdose:** Flumazenil is indicated for reversing the sedative effects of benzodiazepine overdose. It is particularly useful in cases of iatrogenic overdose during medical procedures.

Contraindications:

- **Mixed-Drug Overdoses:** Flumazenil is contraindicated in patients with mixed-drug overdoses, especially those involving tricyclic antidepressants, due to the risk of seizures.
- **Chronic Benzodiazepine Users:** It should be avoided in patients with long-term benzodiazepine use because of the risk of precipitating withdrawal seizures.

Dimercaprol (BAL)
Indications:

- **Arsenic, Mercury, and Lead Poisoning:** Dimercaprol is used for chelation therapy in cases of arsenic, mercury, and severe lead poisoning. It forms stable complexes with these metals, facilitating their excretion.

Contraindications:

- **Hepatic Insufficiency:** Dimercaprol is contraindicated in patients with hepatic insufficiency, except in cases of metal poisoning, as it can exacerbate liver dysfunction.

- **Renal Impairment:** Caution is required in patients with renal impairment due to the risk of nephrotoxicity.

Ethylenediaminetetraacetic Acid (EDTA)
Indications:

- **Lead Poisoning:** EDTA is primarily indicated for the treatment of lead poisoning. It binds to lead ions, forming a stable complex that is excreted in the urine.

Contraindications:

- **Anuria:** EDTA is contraindicated in patients with anuria (absence of urine production) due to the risk of accumulating the chelated metal complex, which can exacerbate toxicity.
- **Precaution:** It should be used cautiously in patients with renal insufficiency and monitored closely for potential nephrotoxicity.

Deferoxamine
Indications:

- **Iron Poisoning:** Deferoxamine is indicated for acute iron poisoning and chronic iron overload conditions such as thalassemia. It binds free iron, forming a complex that is excreted in the urine.

Contraindications:

- **Severe Renal Disease:** Deferoxamine is contraindicated in patients with severe renal disease where iron-chelate complexes cannot be adequately excreted.
- **Precaution:** Long-term use can lead to ocular and auditory disturbances, requiring regular monitoring.

2.3 Indications and Contraindications

2.3.2 Contraindications and Precautions

Understanding the **contraindications and precautions** for antidote administration is essential for ensuring patient safety and optimizing treatment outcomes. Each antidote has specific situations where its use may be harmful or require special consideration.

Naloxone

Contraindications:

- **Known Hypersensitivity:** Naloxone is contraindicated in patients with a known hypersensitivity to the drug, although this is rare.

Precautions:

- **Opioid Dependence:** Use with caution in opioid-dependent patients as naloxone can precipitate acute withdrawal symptoms, which may include agitation, hypertension, tachycardia, and nausea.
- **Cardiovascular Disease:** Monitor patients with pre-existing cardiovascular conditions closely, as the stress of acute withdrawal can exacerbate cardiac conditions.

N-acetylcysteine (NAC)

Contraindications:

- **Known Hypersensitivity:** NAC should not be administered to patients with a known hypersensitivity to the medication.

Precautions:

- **Anaphylactoid Reactions:** Be aware of the potential for anaphylactoid reactions, particularly with intravenous administration. Symptoms can include rash, wheezing, and hypotension. Slow infusion rates and pre-treatment with antihistamines can help mitigate these reactions.
- **Asthma:** Use cautiously in asthmatic patients, as NAC can cause bronchospasm.

Atropine

Contraindications:

- **Narrow-Angle Glaucoma:** Atropine is contraindicated in patients with narrow-angle glaucoma due to the risk of increased intraocular pressure.

- **Obstructive Uropathy:** Should not be used in patients with obstructive uropathy (e.g., benign prostatic hyperplasia) as it can exacerbate urinary retention.
- **Myasthenia Gravis:** Contraindicated in patients with myasthenia gravis unless used to manage side effects of anticholinesterase medications.

Precautions:

- **Cardiovascular Disease:** Use with caution in patients with cardiovascular disease, as atropine can cause tachycardia and increase myocardial oxygen demand.
- **Elderly Patients:** Be cautious in elderly patients due to the increased risk of side effects such as confusion and constipation.

Flumazenil
Contraindications:

- **Mixed-Drug Overdoses:** Flumazenil is contraindicated in cases of mixed-drug overdoses, especially if tricyclic antidepressants are involved, due to the risk of seizures.
- **Long-Term Benzodiazepine Use:** Avoid in patients with chronic benzodiazepine use to prevent withdrawal seizures.

Precautions:

- **Seizure Disorders:** Use cautiously in patients with a history of seizures or head injury, as flumazenil can lower the seizure threshold.
- **Liver Disease:** Reduced doses may be required in patients with liver impairment due to slower metabolism.

Dimercaprol (BAL)
Contraindications:

- **Hepatic Insufficiency:** Contraindicated in patients with hepatic insufficiency, except in cases of acute metal poisoning where the benefit outweighs the risk.
- **Renal Impairment:** Use cautiously in patients with renal impairment, as dimercaprol and its metal complexes can be nephrotoxic.

Precautions:

- **Hypertension:** Monitor blood pressure closely as dimercaprol can cause hypertension.
- **Allergy:** Be aware of potential allergic reactions, including urticaria and fever.

Ethylenediaminetetraacetic Acid (EDTA)
Contraindications:

- **Anuria:** Contraindicated in patients with anuria due to the risk of accumulating chelated metal complexes.
- **Hypocalcemia:** EDTA can bind calcium, potentially causing hypocalcemia, so it should not be used in patients with pre-existing hypocalcemia.

Precautions:

- **Renal Insufficiency:** Monitor renal function closely, as EDTA and its complexes can be nephrotoxic. Dose adjustments may be necessary.
- **Electrolyte Imbalances:** Regularly monitor electrolytes to detect and manage potential imbalances.

Deferoxamine
Contraindications:

- **Severe Renal Disease:** Contraindicated in patients with severe renal disease due to the risk of toxic accumulation of iron-deferoxamine complexes.

Precautions:

- **Ocular and Auditory Disturbances:** Long-term use can lead to ocular and auditory disturbances, requiring regular monitoring for visual and hearing impairments.
- **Allergic Reactions:** Be vigilant for signs of allergic reactions, including urticaria and anaphylaxis.

2.4 Common Antidotes and Their Clinical Use

2.4.1 Activated Charcoal

Activated charcoal is a commonly used antidote in the management of various poisonings due to its ability to adsorb toxins in the gastrointestinal tract, preventing their absorption into the bloodstream.

2.4.1.1 Mechanism of Action

Activated charcoal works by **adsorption**, a process where toxins bind to the surface of the charcoal particles. This binding reduces the bioavailability of the toxin, limiting its absorption from the gastrointestinal tract into the systemic circulation. The large surface area of activated charcoal allows it to adsorb a wide range of substances effectively. It is important to note that activated charcoal adsorbs toxins rather than absorbing them, meaning it holds the toxins on its surface without incorporating them into its structure.

2.4.1.2 Clinical Indications

Activated charcoal is indicated for the treatment of acute poisoning from a variety of substances. It is most effective when administered within one hour of toxin ingestion. Specific indications include:

- **Drug Overdoses:** Effective in adsorbing drugs such as acetaminophen, aspirin, barbiturates, benzodiazepines, tricyclic antidepressants, and theophylline.
- **Chemical Poisonings:** Useful for certain chemicals like pesticides and herbicides.
- **Food Poisonings:** Can be used in cases of food poisoning to adsorb bacterial toxins.
- **Toxins with Enterohepatic Circulation:** Beneficial in cases where toxins undergo enterohepatic recirculation, such as carbamazepine and phenobarbital, as it interrupts the reabsorption process.

Activated charcoal is not effective for all substances. It does not adsorb well with alcohols, heavy metals, corrosives, and certain inorganic substances like lithium and iron.

2.4.1.3 Dosage and Administration

Dosage:

- The typical dose of activated charcoal for adults and adolescents is **50-100 grams.**
- For children, the dose is usually **25-50 grams.**

- The dose may be repeated every 4-6 hours in cases of sustained-release or large ingestions if the toxin is known to undergo enterohepatic recirculation.

Administration:

- Activated charcoal is administered orally or via a nasogastric tube.
- It is usually mixed with water to form a slurry, which can be more easily ingested.
- It should be given as soon as possible after the ingestion of the toxin, ideally within one hour. The effectiveness decreases significantly with time due to the absorption of the toxin into the bloodstream.
- Activated charcoal can be administered alongside a cathartic, such as sorbitol, to speed up the elimination of the charcoal-toxin complex from the gastrointestinal tract. However, the use of cathartics is controversial due to potential side effects like dehydration and electrolyte imbalances.
- In cases where a large amount of a toxin has been ingested, or if the toxin undergoes enterohepatic recirculation, multiple doses of activated charcoal may be given. This is known as **multiple-dose activated charcoal (MDAC)** therapy, and it involves administering additional doses every 4-6 hours.

Precautions:

- **Aspiration Risk:** Avoid use in patients with a decreased level of consciousness unless the airway is protected by intubation, as there is a risk of aspiration.
- **Gastrointestinal Obstruction:** Caution in patients with gastrointestinal obstruction or those who have ingested caustic substances, as charcoal can obscure endoscopic visualization and complicate management.
- **Dehydration and Electrolyte Imbalances:** Repeated doses or administration with cathartics can lead to dehydration and electrolyte imbalances, so monitoring and supportive care are essential.

2.4 Common Antidotes and Their Clinical Use

2.4.2 N-acetylcysteine (NAC)

N-acetylcysteine (NAC) is a critical antidote used primarily for the treatment of acetaminophen (paracetamol) overdose. Its effectiveness in preventing severe liver damage has made it a cornerstone in toxicology.

2.4.2.1 Mechanism of Action

The **mechanism of action** of NAC in acetaminophen overdose involves several pathways:

- **Glutathione Precursor:** NAC serves as a precursor to glutathione, a vital intracellular antioxidant. In acetaminophen overdose, the liver's glutathione stores are depleted, leading to the accumulation of a toxic metabolite, N-acetyl-p-benzoquinone imine (NAPQI). NAC replenishes glutathione stores, allowing for the detoxification of NAPQI.
- **Direct Binding:** NAC can also directly conjugate with NAPQI, neutralizing its toxic effects and preventing it from binding to cellular proteins and causing liver damage.
- **Anti-inflammatory and Antioxidant Effects:** NAC has additional benefits due to its anti-inflammatory and antioxidant properties, which help reduce oxidative stress and inflammation in the liver.

2.4.2.2 Clinical Indications

Clinical indications for NAC include:

- **Acetaminophen Overdose:** The primary indication for NAC is the treatment of acute and chronic acetaminophen toxicity. Early administration, ideally within 8 hours of ingestion, significantly reduces the risk of severe hepatotoxicity and liver failure.
- **Chronic Acetaminophen Toxicity:** NAC is also effective in chronic acetaminophen toxicity cases, where patients have ingested supratherapeutic doses over a prolonged period.
- **Other Indications:** While less common, NAC is sometimes used in the treatment of other conditions, such as:

  - **Contrast-Induced Nephropathy:** As a preventive measure for renal toxicity in patients undergoing radiographic contrast studies.
  - **Acute Liver Failure:** In cases of acute liver failure from non-acetaminophen causes, although this is an off-label use.

2.4.2.3 Dosage and Administration

Dosage and administration of NAC vary depending on the route of administration (oral or intravenous) and the clinical scenario.

Oral Administration:

- **Loading Dose:** 140 mg/kg initially.
- **Maintenance Dose:** 70 mg/kg every 4 hours for 17 doses, completing a 72-hour regimen.
- **Preparation:** NAC has an unpleasant odor and taste. It is often diluted in a soft drink or juice to improve palatability.

Intravenous Administration:

- **Loading Dose:** 150 mg/kg over 60 minutes.
- **Second Dose:** 50 mg/kg over 4 hours.
- **Third Dose:** 100 mg/kg over 16 hours.
- **Total Duration:** The IV regimen typically lasts 20-21 hours. This protocol can be adjusted based on the patient's clinical condition and acetaminophen levels.

Considerations for Dosage and Administration:

- **Early Administration:** The efficacy of NAC is highest when administered within 8 hours of acetaminophen ingestion. However, it can still provide benefits even if given later.
- **Anaphylactoid Reactions:** IV administration can cause anaphylactoid reactions, characterized by rash, wheezing, or hypotension. Slowing the infusion rate and pre-treating with antihistamines can help manage these reactions.
- **Monitoring:** Regular monitoring of liver function tests (LFTs), acetaminophen levels, and coagulation profiles is crucial to assess the response to NAC and the progression of liver injury.

2.4 Common Antidotes and Their Clinical Use

2.4.3 Atropine

Atropine is a widely used antidote with significant applications in treating various types of poisonings, particularly those involving cholinergic agents. Its effectiveness stems from its ability to antagonize the effects of excessive acetylcholine.

2.4.3.1 Mechanism of Action

The **mechanism of action** of atropine involves competitive antagonism at muscarinic acetylcholine receptors:

- **Muscarinic Receptor Blockade:** Atropine binds to muscarinic receptors, blocking the action of acetylcholine. This prevents the overstimulation of these receptors, which is common in organophosphate and carbamate poisoning.
- **Reduction of Cholinergic Symptoms:** By blocking muscarinic receptors, atropine alleviates symptoms such as bradycardia, bronchoconstriction, excessive salivation, lacrimation, urination, diarrhea, gastrointestinal cramping, and emesis (SLUDGE syndrome).

2.4.3.2 Clinical Indications
Clinical indications for atropine include:

- **Organophosphate and Carbamate Poisoning:** Atropine is the antidote of choice for treating poisoning by organophosphates and carbamates, commonly found in pesticides. These substances inhibit acetylcholinesterase, leading to an accumulation of acetylcholine.
- **Bradycardia:** Atropine is indicated for the treatment of symptomatic bradycardia not responding to other measures. It increases heart rate by blocking the vagal effects on the heart.
- **Pre-anesthetic Medication:** To reduce secretions and prevent bradycardia during surgery, although this use has become less common with modern anesthesia practices.

2.4.3.3 Dosage and Administration
Dosage and administration of atropine vary depending on the clinical scenario.

Organophosphate and Carbamate Poisoning:

- **Initial Dose:** 1-3 mg IV or IM, depending on the severity of symptoms.
- **Repeat Doses:** Administer 2-4 mg every 5-10 minutes until cholinergic symptoms (e.g., bronchorrhea, bradycardia) are significantly reduced. Large doses may be required, and continuous infusion may be necessary in severe cases.
- **End Point:** Adequate atropinization is indicated by the drying of bronchial secretions and a heart rate of more than 80 beats per minute.

Symptomatic Bradycardia:

- **Initial Dose:** 0.5 mg IV.
- **Repeat Doses:** Can be repeated every 3-5 minutes if needed, up to a total dose of 3 mg.
- **Precautions:** Use with caution in patients with acute coronary ischemia or myocardial infarction due to the risk of increasing myocardial oxygen demand.

Pre-anesthetic Medication:

- **Dose:** 0.4-0.6 mg IV or IM, administered 30-60 minutes before anesthesia induction to reduce secretions and prevent bradycardia.

Considerations for Dosage and Administration:

- **Route of Administration:** Atropine can be administered intravenously, intramuscularly, or subcutaneously. The IV route is preferred for rapid action in emergency situations.
- **Monitoring:** Continuous monitoring of vital signs, particularly heart rate and respiratory status, is essential during atropine administration. ECG monitoring is recommended for patients receiving atropine for bradycardia.
- **Side Effects:** Common side effects of atropine include dry mouth, blurred vision, tachycardia, urinary retention, and confusion, particularly in elderly patients.

2.4 Common Antidotes and Their Clinical Use

2.4.4 Flumazenil

Flumazenil is an antidote specifically used to reverse the effects of benzodiazepines. It acts quickly to counteract sedation, respiratory depression, and other central nervous system effects caused by benzodiazepine overdose.

2.4.4.1 Mechanism of Action

The **mechanism of action** of flumazenil involves competitive antagonism at the benzodiazepine binding site on the GABA-A receptor:

- **Competitive Inhibition:** Flumazenil binds to the benzodiazepine site on the GABA-A receptor, displacing benzodiazepines and preventing their action. By blocking the effects of benzodiazepines, flumazenil reverses sedation, respiratory depression, and other central nervous system effects.
- **Rapid Onset:** Flumazenil has a rapid onset of action, typically within 1-2 minutes, with peak effects occurring at about 6-10 minutes after administration.

2.4.4.2 Clinical Indications

Clinical indications for flumazenil include:

- **Benzodiazepine Overdose:** Flumazenil is primarily indicated for the reversal of benzodiazepine overdose, especially in cases where there is significant central nervous system depression or respiratory compromise.
- **Iatrogenic Benzodiazepine Sedation:** It is also used to reverse benzodiazepine sedation in medical settings, such as during diagnostic procedures or after anesthesia, when rapid recovery of consciousness is desired.

Contraindications and Precautions:

- **Mixed-Drug Overdoses:** Flumazenil is contraindicated in patients with mixed-drug overdoses, particularly involving tricyclic antidepressants, due to the risk of seizures.
- **Chronic Benzodiazepine Use:** Avoid use in patients with long-term benzodiazepine use or dependency, as it can precipitate withdrawal seizures.

2.4.4.3 Dosage and Administration

Dosage and administration of flumazenil must be carefully managed to minimize the risk of adverse effects.

Initial Dosing:

- **Initial Dose:** 0.2 mg IV, administered over 15 seconds.
- **Repeat Doses:** If the desired level of consciousness is not achieved, additional doses of 0.2 mg can be administered at 1-minute intervals, up

to a maximum total dose of 1 mg.

- **Titration:** Doses should be titrated carefully based on the patient's response. In some cases, doses up to 3 mg may be required, but exceeding this is rarely necessary.

Maintenance Dosing:

- **Continuous Infusion:** In cases where prolonged reversal of benzodiazepine effects is necessary, a continuous infusion of flumazenil can be used. The infusion rate typically ranges from 0.1 to 0.5 mg per hour, adjusted based on the patient's response and the duration of action of the benzodiazepine involved.

Considerations for Dosage and Administration:

- **Monitoring:** Continuous monitoring of the patient's respiratory and cardiovascular status is essential during and after flumazenil administration. ECG monitoring is recommended, particularly in patients with pre-existing cardiac conditions or mixed-drug overdoses.
- **Re-sedation:** Due to the shorter half-life of flumazenil compared to most benzodiazepines, re-sedation can occur. Patients should be observed for at least 2 hours after the last dose of flumazenil to ensure that re-sedation does not occur. In cases of long-acting benzodiazepines, extended monitoring may be necessary.
- **Adverse Effects:** Common side effects include dizziness, nausea, vomiting, and agitation. Serious side effects such as seizures are more likely in patients with a history of epilepsy or chronic benzodiazepine use.

2.4 Common Antidotes and Their Clinical Use

2.4.5 Naloxone

Naloxone is a crucial antidote used to reverse the effects of opioid overdose. It acts rapidly to counteract life-threatening respiratory depression and sedation caused by opioid toxicity.

2.4.5.1 Mechanism of Action

The **mechanism of action** of naloxone involves competitive antagonism at opioid receptors:

- **Competitive Inhibition:** Naloxone is a competitive antagonist at mu-opioid receptors, with some affinity for kappa and delta opioid receptors as well. By binding to these receptors, naloxone displaces opioids and blocks their effects, reversing the symptoms of opioid overdose.
- **Rapid Onset:** Naloxone has a rapid onset of action, typically within 2-3 minutes when administered intravenously, making it highly effective in emergency situations.

2.4.5.2 Clinical Indications

Clinical indications for naloxone include:

- **Opioid Overdose:** Naloxone is primarily indicated for the treatment of acute opioid overdose, particularly when there is significant respiratory depression, altered mental status, or other signs of opioid toxicity.
- **Suspected Opioid Toxicity:** It can be administered when opioid toxicity is suspected but not yet confirmed, due to its low risk of adverse effects and significant potential benefit.
- **Postoperative Opioid Depression:** Naloxone is used to reverse opioid-induced respiratory depression following surgery, although this is less common with modern opioid-sparing anesthesia techniques.
- **Neonatal Resuscitation:** Used in newborns with respiratory depression resulting from maternal opioid use.

2.4.5.3 Dosage and Administration

Dosage and administration of naloxone vary depending on the route of administration and the clinical scenario.

Intravenous (IV) Administration:

- **Initial Dose:** 0.4 to 2 mg IV. If there is no response, doses can be repeated every 2-3 minutes.
- **Maximum Dose:** If there is no response after a total of 10 mg, the diagnosis of opioid overdose should be reconsidered.
- **Continuous Infusion:** For patients with long-acting opioid overdose, an initial bolus dose may be followed by an infusion. The infusion rate is usually calculated based on the effective bolus dose administered per hour (e.g., if 2 mg effectively reverses symptoms, an infusion rate of 2 mg/hour can be started).

Intramuscular (IM) or Subcutaneous (SC) Administration:

- **Initial Dose:** 0.4 to 2 mg IM or SC. The onset of action is slower compared to IV administration, but it is useful when IV access is not available.
- **Repeat Doses:** Additional doses can be administered every 2-3 minutes if needed.

Intranasal Administration:

- **Initial Dose:** 2 to 4 mg intranasally, using a prefilled device. This route is particularly useful for out-of-hospital settings and first responders.
- **Repeat Doses:** If there is no response, additional doses can be given every 2-3 minutes in alternate nostrils.

Considerations for Dosage and Administration:

- **Titration:** The goal is to administer the smallest effective dose to restore adequate ventilation without precipitating acute withdrawal symptoms, especially in opioid-dependent patients.
- **Monitoring:** Continuous monitoring of respiratory rate, heart rate, blood pressure, and level of consciousness is essential. ECG monitoring is recommended for patients with a history of cardiovascular disease.
- **Duration of Action:** Naloxone's duration of action (30-90 minutes) is shorter than that of most opioids. Therefore, patients should be observed for recurrent symptoms of opioid toxicity, and additional doses or a continuous infusion may be necessary for long-acting opioids.
- **Adverse Effects:** Naloxone can precipitate acute withdrawal symptoms in opioid-dependent individuals, which may include agitation, nausea, vomiting, tachycardia, and hypertension. While these symptoms are uncomfortable, they are usually not life-threatening.

CHAPTER III

Supportive Care in Clinical Toxicology

Introduction

Supportive care is a cornerstone of clinical toxicology, providing essential measures to stabilize patients and manage symptoms while specific treatments or antidotes are administered. In cases of poisoning and overdose, supportive care focuses on maintaining vital physiological functions, alleviating symptoms, and preventing complications. This holistic approach is critical for ensuring patient safety and improving outcomes, regardless of the specific toxin involved.

Supportive care encompasses a wide range of interventions, including airway management, respiratory support, cardiovascular stabilization, fluid and electrolyte balance, and monitoring of neurological status. It also involves addressing secondary issues such as pain, agitation, and potential complications that may arise during the course of treatment.

Scope of the Chapter

This chapter will cover the following key aspects of supportive care in clinical toxicology:

1. **Airway Management:** Techniques and strategies for ensuring a patent airway and adequate ventilation in poisoned patients.
2. **Respiratory Support:** Methods for providing supplemental oxygen, mechanical ventilation, and other interventions to support respiratory function.
3. **Cardiovascular Stabilization:** Approaches to managing hypotension, hypertension, arrhythmias, and other cardiovascular issues that may arise in poisoning cases.
4. **Fluid and Electrolyte Balance:** Strategies for maintaining and restoring fluid and electrolyte homeostasis, which is often disrupted in poisoning scenarios.

5. **Neurological Monitoring:** Continuous assessment of the patient's neurological status, including level of consciousness and seizure management.
6. **Symptom Management:** Addressing pain, agitation, nausea, and other symptoms to improve patient comfort and facilitate recovery.
7. **Complication Prevention:** Identifying and preventing potential complications such as aspiration pneumonia, rhabdomyolysis, and secondary infections.

Importance of Supportive Care

Supportive care is crucial in the management of poisoning for several reasons:

- **Immediate Stabilization:** It provides immediate measures to stabilize the patient's condition, ensuring that vital functions are maintained while specific treatments are initiated.
- **Symptom Relief:** By managing symptoms such as pain, agitation, and respiratory distress, supportive care improves patient comfort and quality of life during the acute phase of poisoning.
- **Prevention of Complications:** Proactive supportive care can prevent the development of serious complications that could worsen the patient's prognosis and complicate recovery.
- **Foundation for Specific Treatments:** Effective supportive care creates a stable platform from which specific antidotes or treatments can be administered more safely and effectively.

3.1 Airway Management

Effective **airway management** is a critical component of supportive care in clinical toxicology. Ensuring that the airway remains open and functional is essential for maintaining adequate oxygenation and ventilation in poisoned patients. Airway management involves various techniques to maintain airway patency and, when necessary, advanced procedures such as endotracheal intubation.

3.1.1 Techniques for Maintaining Airway Patency

Maintaining airway patency is the first step in managing a patient with poisoning, especially if they are unconscious or have compromised airway reflexes. Several techniques are used to ensure the airway remains open:

- **Positioning:** Proper positioning of the patient can help keep the airway open. The head-tilt-chin-lift maneuver is used to lift the tongue away from the back of the throat. This is particularly useful in patients without spinal injuries. In patients with potential spinal injuries, the jaw-thrust maneuver is preferred, as it minimizes neck movement.
- **Airway Adjuncts:** Various airway adjuncts can be used to maintain patency:

  - **Oropharyngeal Airway (OPA):** An OPA is inserted into the mouth to keep the tongue from obstructing the airway. It is suitable for unconscious patients with no gag reflex.
  - **Nasopharyngeal Airway (NPA):** An NPA is inserted through the nose and is useful for both conscious and unconscious patients, especially if there is a risk of oral obstruction or if the patient has a gag reflex.

- **Suctioning:** Suction devices are used to remove secretions, vomit, or blood from the airway. This is crucial in preventing aspiration and ensuring a clear path for air to reach the lungs.
- **Manual Ventilation:** If the patient is not breathing adequately, manual ventilation using a bag-valve-mask (BVM) device can provide positive pressure ventilation. Proper technique and mask fit are essential to ensure effective ventilation and oxygenation.

3.1.2 Endotracheal Intubation

Endotracheal intubation is an advanced airway management technique used when basic measures are insufficient to maintain airway patency or when the patient requires prolonged ventilatory support.

- **Indications for Intubation:**

- **Airway Protection:** Patients who are at risk of aspiration due to decreased consciousness or inability to protect their airway.
- **Respiratory Failure:** Patients with severe respiratory distress or failure, who require mechanical ventilation.
- **Anticipated Clinical Course:** Patients who are expected to deteriorate, such as those with significant toxin ingestion, may benefit from early intubation.

- **Procedure for Endotracheal Intubation:**

  - **Preparation:** Gather necessary equipment, including an endotracheal tube, laryngoscope, suction device, and BVM. Pre-oxygenate the patient with 100% oxygen to maximize oxygen reserves.
  - **Medications:** Administer sedatives and paralytics to facilitate intubation. Commonly used agents include etomidate, propofol, or midazolam for sedation, and succinylcholine or rocuronium for paralysis.
  - **Intubation:** Using a laryngoscope, visualize the vocal cords and insert the endotracheal tube through the mouth into the trachea. Confirm placement by auscultating breath sounds bilaterally, observing chest rise, and using capnography to verify exhaled CO_2.
  - **Securing the Tube:** Secure the endotracheal tube with tape or a commercial tube holder to prevent displacement. Connect the tube to a mechanical ventilator or BVM for ventilation.

- **Post-Intubation Care:**

  - **Monitoring:** Continuously monitor the patient's vital signs, oxygen saturation, and end-tidal CO_2. Obtain a chest X-ray to confirm tube placement.
  - **Sedation and Analgesia:** Administer ongoing sedation and analgesia to keep the patient comfortable and to prevent agitation that could compromise the airway.
  - **Ventilator Management:** Adjust ventilator settings based on the patient's respiratory status and underlying condition. Monitor for complications such as barotrauma, volutrauma, and ventilator-associated pneumonia.

3.2 Breathing and Oxygenation

Maintaining adequate breathing and oxygenation is crucial in the management of poisoned patients. Ensuring that the patient receives sufficient oxygen and can adequately ventilate is a key component of supportive care. This section discusses the use of supplemental oxygen and mechanical ventilation in the context of clinical toxicology.

3.2.1 Supplemental Oxygen

Supplemental oxygen is often the first intervention in managing patients with respiratory compromise due to poisoning. It helps improve oxygenation and reduce the risk of hypoxia, which can lead to severe organ damage and worsening of the patient's condition.
Indications:

- **Hypoxia:** Any patient showing signs of hypoxia (low oxygen saturation, cyanosis) should receive supplemental oxygen.
- **Respiratory Distress:** Patients experiencing respiratory distress, even if oxygen saturation levels are normal initially, may benefit from supplemental oxygen.
- **Specific Poisonings:** Certain toxins, such as carbon monoxide or cyanide, impair the body's ability to utilize oxygen, making supplemental oxygen particularly important.

Methods of Administration:

- **Nasal Cannula:** Delivers low to moderate concentrations of oxygen (24-44%) at flow rates of 1-6 liters per minute. It is comfortable and allows the patient to speak and eat.
- **Simple Face Mask:** Provides higher concentrations of oxygen (40-60%) at flow rates of 6-10 liters per minute. It is used when higher oxygen delivery is required.
- **Non-Rebreather Mask:** Delivers very high concentrations of oxygen (up to 90-100%) at flow rates of 10-15 liters per minute. It is used in severe cases of hypoxia where maximum oxygen delivery is needed.

- **Venturi Mask:** Allows precise control of oxygen concentration, making it useful for patients who require specific oxygen levels, particularly those with chronic respiratory conditions.

Monitoring:

- **Pulse Oximetry:** Continuous monitoring of oxygen saturation (SpO2) is essential to ensure adequate oxygenation. The target SpO2 is generally >94%.
- **Arterial Blood Gases (ABGs):** In more severe cases or when accurate assessment of oxygenation, ventilation, and acid-base status is needed, ABGs should be monitored.

3.2.2 Mechanical Ventilation

Mechanical ventilation is required when a poisoned patient cannot maintain adequate ventilation on their own. This can be due to respiratory failure, decreased consciousness, or severe respiratory distress.

Indications:

- **Respiratory Failure:** Patients with inadequate respiratory effort or failure, evidenced by low oxygen levels (PaO2) and high carbon dioxide levels (PaCO2) on ABGs.
- **Severe Respiratory Distress:** When non-invasive methods are insufficient to maintain adequate oxygenation and ventilation.
- **Coma or Decreased Consciousness:** Patients who are unable to protect their airway due to decreased level of consciousness.
- **Specific Poisonings:** Toxins that cause significant central nervous system depression or neuromuscular paralysis, such as organophosphates, opioids, and certain sedatives.

Modes of Mechanical Ventilation:

- **Volume-Controlled Ventilation (VCV):** Delivers a preset tidal volume with each breath. It is useful for ensuring consistent ventilation in patients with varying lung compliance.

- **Pressure-Controlled Ventilation (PCV):** Delivers breaths at a preset pressure, allowing for more control over peak airway pressures, reducing the risk of barotrauma.
- **Continuous Positive Airway Pressure (CPAP) and Bi-level Positive Airway Pressure (BiPAP):** Non-invasive ventilation methods that provide positive pressure to keep airways open and improve oxygenation. They are used in less severe cases where intubation might be avoidable.

Settings and Adjustments:

- **Tidal Volume:** Typically set at 6-8 mL/kg of ideal body weight to minimize the risk of ventilator-induced lung injury.
- **Respiratory Rate:** Adjusted to maintain adequate minute ventilation, usually between 12-20 breaths per minute.
- **Positive End-Expiratory Pressure (PEEP):** Used to keep alveoli open and improve oxygenation, typically set at 5-10 cm H2O.
- **FiO2 (Fraction of Inspired Oxygen):** Adjusted to maintain adequate oxygenation with the goal of minimizing oxygen toxicity. The lowest FiO2 that maintains SpO2 >94% is preferred.

Monitoring:

- **Continuous Monitoring:** Vital signs, including heart rate, blood pressure, and SpO2, should be continuously monitored.
- **ABGs:** Regular ABGs are necessary to assess ventilation and oxygenation status, allowing for adjustments in ventilator settings.
- **Peak and Plateau Pressures:** Monitoring these pressures helps in identifying issues like barotrauma or changes in lung compliance.

3.3 Circulation and Fluids

Maintaining proper circulation and fluid balance is crucial in the supportive care of poisoned patients. Effective management involves securing intravenous access, administering appropriate fluids, and ensuring cardiovascular stability. This section focuses on the importance and methods of establishing intravenous access.

3.3.1 Intravenous Access

Intravenous (IV) access is a critical step in managing poisoned patients, as it allows for the rapid administration of fluids, medications, and antidotes. Establishing IV access promptly and efficiently is essential, especially in emergency situations.

Importance of Intravenous Access

- **Rapid Fluid Administration:** IV access enables the quick infusion of fluids to treat dehydration, shock, or hypotension, which are common complications in poisoning cases.
- **Medication Delivery:** Many antidotes and supportive medications need to be administered intravenously for rapid effect. This includes medications for symptomatic relief, antidotes, and drugs for managing complications such as seizures or arrhythmias.
- **Blood Sampling:** IV access allows for the collection of blood samples for laboratory testing, including toxicology screens, electrolyte levels, and blood gas analysis, which are critical for diagnosing and monitoring the patient's condition.

Types of Intravenous Access

- **Peripheral IV Lines:** These are the most commonly used and are inserted into peripheral veins, typically in the arms or hands. Peripheral lines are suitable for most situations requiring fluid and medication administration.

  - **Procedure:** Clean the insertion site, apply a tourniquet, insert the catheter into the vein, and secure it with adhesive tape or a securement device. Ensure patency by flushing with saline.

- **Central Venous Catheters (CVCs):** These are used when peripheral access is difficult or when long-term IV therapy is needed. CVCs are inserted into large central veins such as the internal jugular, subclavian, or femoral veins.

- ○ **Procedure:** Perform under sterile conditions, usually with ultrasound guidance. Secure the catheter and confirm placement with a chest X-ray. CVCs provide reliable access for administering large volumes of fluids, medications, and for central venous pressure monitoring.

- **Intraosseous (IO) Access:** This is used in emergency situations when IV access cannot be quickly established. IO access involves inserting a needle into the bone marrow cavity, typically in the proximal tibia or humerus, to provide a route for fluid and medication administration.

  - ○ **Procedure:** Clean the insertion site, insert the IO needle using a manual or powered driver, confirm placement by aspirating bone marrow or seeing a flash of blood, and secure the needle. IO access is a temporary solution until more permanent IV access can be established.

Considerations for Intravenous Access

- **Site Selection:** Choose an appropriate site based on the patient's condition, availability of veins, and the expected duration of therapy. Avoid sites with signs of infection, trauma, or previous unsuccessful attempts.
- **Aseptic Technique:** Use strict aseptic techniques to prevent infections, including hand hygiene, wearing gloves, and using sterile equipment.
- **Patency and Maintenance:** Regularly check for patency by flushing the line with saline. Monitor for signs of complications such as phlebitis, infiltration, or infection.
- **Patient Comfort:** Ensure patient comfort by using appropriate techniques for insertion and securing the IV line to minimize movement and discomfort.

Challenges and Troubleshooting

- **Difficult Access:** In patients with poor venous access, use techniques such as warm compresses, limb elevation, or ultrasound guidance to improve success rates.
- **Complications:** Be vigilant for signs of complications like infection, thrombosis, or catheter dislodgement. Address these issues promptly to

prevent further complications.

3.3 Circulation and Fluids

3.3.2 Fluid Resuscitation

Fluid resuscitation is a key component in the management of poisoned patients, particularly those presenting with shock, hypotension, or dehydration. Proper fluid resuscitation helps restore intravascular volume, improve tissue perfusion, and stabilize hemodynamics.

Indications:

- **Hypotension:** Due to vasodilation or fluid loss caused by toxins.
- **Shock:** Particularly distributive shock, often seen in sepsis or severe poisoning.
- **Dehydration:** Resulting from vomiting, diarrhea, or inadequate fluid intake in the context of poisoning.

Types of Fluids:

- **Crystalloids:** These are the most commonly used fluids for resuscitation. They include:

  - **Normal Saline (0.9% NaCl):** Suitable for most patients and readily available.
  - **Lactated Ringer's Solution:** Contains electrolytes and a buffer (lactate), which can be beneficial in metabolic acidosis.

- **Colloids:** These fluids contain larger molecules and stay in the intravascular space longer. They are less commonly used due to cost and potential for adverse effects.

  - **Examples:** Albumin, hydroxyethyl starch, and dextrans.

Administration:

- **Initial Bolus:** Administer an initial bolus of 20-30 mL/kg of crystalloid solution over 15-30 minutes, reassessing the patient's response frequently.
- **Ongoing Resuscitation:** Continue fluid administration based on the patient's hemodynamic response, clinical assessment, and ongoing losses. Monitor for signs of fluid overload, such as pulmonary edema and worsening oxygenation.

Monitoring:

- **Vital Signs:** Continuous monitoring of heart rate, blood pressure, respiratory rate, and oxygen saturation.
- **Urine Output:** An important indicator of renal perfusion and overall fluid balance; aim for a urine output of 0.5-1 mL/kg/hr.
- **Central Venous Pressure (CVP):** In critical care settings, CVP monitoring can guide fluid resuscitation, although its use is controversial and should be interpreted in conjunction with other clinical findings.
- **Lactate Levels:** Serial lactate measurements can help assess the effectiveness of resuscitation efforts and tissue perfusion.

3.3.3 Use of Vasopressors

When fluid resuscitation alone is insufficient to maintain adequate blood pressure and tissue perfusion, **vasopressors** are used to support circulation. These medications constrict blood vessels and increase cardiac output to improve blood pressure and organ perfusion.

Indications:

- **Persistent Hypotension:** After adequate fluid resuscitation in patients with distributive or septic shock.
- **Cardiogenic Shock:** When there is a need to improve cardiac output and perfusion.
- **Severe Poisoning:** With toxins that cause profound vasodilation or myocardial depression.

Common Vasopressors:

- **Norepinephrine:** Often the first-line vasopressor in septic and distributive shock. It primarily acts on alpha-1 adrenergic receptors to induce vasoconstriction and increase blood pressure, with some beta-1 adrenergic activity to support cardiac output.
- **Epinephrine:** Used in anaphylactic shock and as a second-line agent in septic shock. It has potent alpha-1, beta-1, and beta-2 adrenergic activity, providing both vasoconstriction and cardiac stimulation.
- **Dopamine:** Acts on dopaminergic, beta-1, and alpha-1 receptors depending on the dose. It can be used in certain scenarios but is less preferred due to variable effects and higher risk of arrhythmias.
- **Phenylephrine:** A pure alpha-1 agonist that causes vasoconstriction without significant cardiac stimulation. It is useful when tachyarrhythmias preclude the use of other vasopressors.

Administration:

- **Central Venous Access:** Vasopressors should be administered via a central venous catheter to avoid the risk of tissue necrosis from extravasation.
- **Titration:** Start at a low dose and titrate upwards based on the patient's response. Frequent monitoring and dose adjustments are necessary to achieve the desired hemodynamic goals.

Monitoring:

- **Blood Pressure:** Continuous arterial blood pressure monitoring is preferred for accuracy and real-time assessment.
- **Heart Rate and Rhythm:** Monitor for tachyarrhythmias and other cardiac complications.
- **Organ Perfusion:** Assess urine output, mental status, and lactate levels to ensure adequate perfusion and adjust therapy as needed.

3.4 Monitoring and Observation

Continuous **monitoring and observation** are essential components of supportive care in clinical toxicology. These practices help detect changes in the patient's condition, guide treatment decisions, and identify potential complications early.

3.4.1 Vital Signs Monitoring

Vital signs monitoring is crucial for assessing the overall stability of the patient and the effectiveness of interventions. The primary vital signs to monitor include:

Heart Rate:

- **Normal Range:** 60-100 beats per minute (bpm) in adults.
- **Tachycardia:** Can indicate pain, anxiety, hypovolemia, or a response to certain toxins like stimulants.
- **Bradycardia:** May be caused by toxins affecting the heart or central nervous system depressants such as opioids or sedatives.

Blood Pressure:

- **Hypotension:** May result from fluid loss, vasodilation, or cardiac depression caused by toxins. Requires prompt fluid resuscitation and possibly vasopressors.
- **Hypertension:** Can be seen with stimulant poisoning or as a stress response. Requires careful management to avoid end-organ damage.

Respiratory Rate:

- **Normal Range:** 12-20 breaths per minute in adults.
- **Tachypnea:** May indicate respiratory distress, metabolic acidosis, or central nervous system stimulation.
- **Bradypnea:** Often seen in opioid or sedative overdose, requiring immediate intervention to prevent respiratory failure.

Oxygen Saturation (SpO2):

- **Normal Range:** 94-100%.
- **Hypoxia:** Low oxygen saturation necessitates supplemental oxygen and possibly advanced airway management.

Temperature:

- **Hyperthermia:** Can be a sign of infection, toxin-induced hypermetabolism, or drug effects such as serotonin syndrome.
- **Hypothermia:** May result from environmental exposure, certain toxins, or prolonged resuscitation efforts.

3.4.2 Laboratory Monitoring

Laboratory monitoring provides valuable information about the patient's metabolic state, organ function, and the presence and concentration of toxins. Key laboratory tests include:

Blood Glucose:

- **Hypoglycemia:** Common in alcohol, salicylate, or insulin overdose. Requires immediate correction with glucose administration.
- **Hyperglycemia:** Can be seen in stress responses or with certain drugs like corticosteroids.

Electrolytes:

- **Sodium, Potassium, Chloride, Bicarbonate:** Monitoring these helps detect and manage electrolyte imbalances, which can be life-threatening.
- **Calcium and Magnesium:** Essential for cardiac and neuromuscular function, often disrupted in poisoning cases.

Renal Function Tests:

- **Blood Urea Nitrogen (BUN) and Creatinine:** Indicators of renal function. Acute kidney injury can result from toxins or dehydration and requires careful management.

Liver Function Tests:

- **AST, ALT, Alkaline Phosphatase, Bilirubin:** Elevated levels may indicate hepatic injury from toxins like acetaminophen, requiring specific antidotal therapy and supportive care.

Arterial Blood Gases (ABGs):

- **pH, PaCO2, PaO2, HCO3-:** Provide information on the patient's acid-base status and respiratory function. Metabolic acidosis, for example, may necessitate specific interventions such as sodium bicarbonate.

Complete Blood Count (CBC):

- **White Blood Cell Count (WBC):** Elevated WBC can indicate infection or inflammation.
- **Hemoglobin and Hematocrit:** Useful for assessing overall blood volume and detecting anemia.
- **Platelet Count:** Important for coagulation status, especially in cases of liver dysfunction or disseminated intravascular coagulation (DIC).

Toxicology Screens:

- **Drug Panels:** Detect specific drugs or their metabolites in blood or urine, guiding appropriate antidote administration and supportive care.
- **Specific Toxin Levels:** Measuring levels of specific toxins like acetaminophen, salicylates, or alcohols can be crucial for guiding treatment.

Coagulation Profile:

- **Prothrombin Time (PT), Activated Partial Thromboplastin Time (aPTT), International Normalized Ratio (INR):** Important for assessing coagulation status, particularly in cases of liver damage or toxin-induced coagulopathy.

Additional Tests:

- **Lactate Levels:** Elevated levels indicate tissue hypoperfusion and can guide resuscitation efforts.
- **Cardiac Enzymes:** Useful in assessing myocardial injury, particularly in cases of cardiotoxic drug overdose.

3.5 Pain and Symptom Management

Effective **pain and symptom management** is a critical aspect of supportive care in clinical toxicology. Addressing pain, nausea, vomiting, and seizures not only improves patient comfort but also prevents further complications and facilitates recovery.

3.5.1 Analgesics

Analgesics are essential for managing pain in poisoned patients. Pain can result from the toxic effects of substances, injuries sustained during the poisoning event, or medical interventions.

Types of Analgesics:

- **Non-Opioid Analgesics:**

  - **Acetaminophen:** Often used for mild to moderate pain. It is important to monitor dosing to avoid further liver injury, especially in cases of overdose.
  - **Nonsteroidal Anti-Inflammatory Drugs (NSAIDs):** Examples include ibuprofen and naproxen. These are effective for mild to moderate pain but should be used cautiously in patients with renal impairment or gastrointestinal issues.

- **Opioid Analgesics:**

  - **Morphine, Fentanyl, Hydromorphone:** Used for moderate to severe pain. These should be administered with caution due to the risk of respiratory depression and potential for exacerbating the effects of opioid toxicity.
  - **Tramadol:** A centrally acting analgesic with a lower risk of respiratory depression. It should be used with caution in patients with a history of seizures.

Administration and Monitoring:

- **Route of Administration:** Analgesics can be given orally, intravenously, intramuscularly, or subcutaneously, depending on the patient's condition and the severity of pain.

- **Monitoring:** Regularly assess pain levels using pain scales and monitor for side effects, especially respiratory depression with opioids. Adjust dosing based on patient response and side effects.

3.5.2 Antiemetics

Antiemetics are used to control nausea and vomiting, which are common symptoms in poisoning cases. These symptoms can be directly related to the toxin or a side effect of medical treatments.

Common Antiemetics:

- **Ondansetron:** A serotonin 5-HT3 receptor antagonist. It is highly effective and has a favorable side effect profile.
- **Metoclopramide:** A dopamine antagonist that also has prokinetic properties, helping to promote gastric emptying.
- **Promethazine:** An antihistamine with antiemetic and sedative properties. It should be used cautiously due to its potential for causing sedation and hypotension.

Administration and Monitoring:

- **Route of Administration:** Antiemetics can be administered orally, intravenously, or intramuscularly. The choice of route depends on the severity of symptoms and patient tolerance.
- **Monitoring:** Monitor for effectiveness in controlling symptoms and for potential side effects such as sedation, extrapyramidal symptoms (with metoclopramide), and prolonged QT interval (with ondansetron).

3.5.3 Anticonvulsants

Anticonvulsants are critical for managing seizures, which can be a life-threatening complication of poisoning. Seizures may result from direct neurotoxic effects of substances or as a secondary effect of metabolic disturbances.

Common Anticonvulsants:

- **Benzodiazepines:** First-line treatment for acute seizures.

  - **Diazepam and Lorazepam:** Administered intravenously for rapid control of seizures. Lorazepam is often preferred due to its longer duration of action.
  - **Midazolam:** Can be administered intramuscularly or intranasally if IV access is not available.

- **Barbiturates:**

  - **Phenobarbital:** Used for ongoing seizure control or when benzodiazepines are ineffective. It has a longer onset of action but provides sustained control.

- **Other Anticonvulsants:**

  - **Phenytoin or Fosphenytoin:** Used for longer-term management of seizures. These are not first-line for acute seizures due to their slower onset.
  - **Levetiracetam:** An alternative with a favorable side effect profile and fewer drug interactions.

Administration and Monitoring:

- **Initial Control:** Use benzodiazepines for rapid seizure control, followed by longer-acting anticonvulsants if needed.
- **Monitoring:** Continuous monitoring of vital signs and neurological status is crucial. Ensure airway protection and adequate oxygenation during seizures. Monitor for side effects such as respiratory depression with benzodiazepines and sedation or hypotension with barbiturates.

Chapter 4: Gut Decontamination

Introduction

Gut decontamination is a critical aspect of managing acute poisoning cases. The primary goal of gut decontamination is to remove or neutralize ingested toxins before they can be absorbed into the systemic circulation. This intervention can significantly reduce the severity of poisoning and improve patient outcomes.

Gut decontamination involves various techniques and agents, each with specific indications, mechanisms of action, and limitations. The choice of method depends on factors such as the type of toxin, the time since ingestion, the patient's clinical condition, and the risks and benefits of the procedure.

4.1 Indications for Gut Decontamination

Gut decontamination is not universally indicated for all poisoning cases. Specific criteria must be met to justify its use, ensuring that the benefits outweigh the potential risks. Understanding the indications and criteria for gut decontamination is essential for making informed clinical decisions.

4.1.1 Criteria for Use

Criteria for the use of gut decontamination involve assessing the type of toxin, the time elapsed since ingestion, and the patient's overall condition. The decision to proceed with gut decontamination should be based on the following considerations:

Type of Toxin:

- **Potentially Life-Threatening Toxins:** Gut decontamination is particularly indicated for ingestions involving toxins that are highly toxic or potentially fatal, such as cyanide, methanol, ethylene glycol, certain pesticides, and large doses of medications like tricyclic antidepressants or calcium channel blockers.
- **Substances with Delayed Absorption:** Toxins that have delayed gastrointestinal absorption, such as sustained-release or enteric-coated medications, may benefit from gut decontamination even if several hours have passed since ingestion.
- **Substances Not Effectively Removed by Other Means:** Some toxins are poorly removed by hemodialysis or other extracorporeal methods, making gut decontamination a preferred option.

Time Since Ingestion:

- **Within One Hour:** Gut decontamination is most effective when performed within one hour of toxin ingestion. This is when the toxin is still primarily located in the stomach and upper gastrointestinal tract.
- **Beyond One Hour:** In certain cases, gut decontamination may be considered beyond one hour if the toxin has a prolonged gastric retention time, the patient has ingested a large amount, or if the toxin is known to form bezoars or slow-release formulations.

Patient's Clinical Condition:

- **Stable Vital Signs:** The patient should have stable vital signs or be stabilized to ensure safe decontamination. Unstable patients may require initial stabilization before gut decontamination can be safely attempted.
- **Protected Airway:** Patients should have a protected airway, either naturally or through intubation, to prevent aspiration, especially during procedures like gastric lavage or when administering activated charcoal.
- **Cooperation and Consciousness:** Conscious and cooperative patients are more likely to tolerate procedures like activated charcoal administration. In unconscious or uncooperative patients, the risk of complications may outweigh the benefits.

Contraindications:

- **Caustic or Corrosive Ingestions:** Gut decontamination is contraindicated in cases of caustic or corrosive substance ingestion, as it can cause additional injury to the gastrointestinal tract and increase the risk of perforation.
- **Hydrocarbon Ingestions:** For hydrocarbons, such as gasoline or kerosene, gut decontamination is generally contraindicated due to the high risk of aspiration and chemical pneumonitis.
- **Risk of Aspiration:** Patients with an unprotected airway or those at high risk of aspiration should not undergo gut decontamination procedures that increase this risk.

Specific Considerations:

- **Activated Charcoal:** Indicated for a wide range of toxins, especially those that bind well to charcoal. Not effective for metals, alcohols, and certain other substances.
- **Gastric Lavage:** Considered for life-threatening ingestions if performed within one hour. Requires careful consideration of risks versus benefits.
- **Whole Bowel Irrigation:** Indicated for substances that do not bind well to activated charcoal or have a delayed release. Suitable for ingestions of sustained-release formulations or body packers.

4.1 Indications for Gut Decontamination

4.1.2 Timing and Effectiveness

The **timing** of gut decontamination is a crucial factor in its effectiveness. The sooner the intervention is performed after toxin ingestion, the more likely it is to prevent significant absorption of the toxin and reduce its systemic effects. Understanding the relationship between timing and effectiveness is essential for making informed clinical decisions about gut decontamination.

Timing Considerations:

- **Within One Hour:**

  - **Peak Effectiveness:** Gut decontamination is most effective when performed within the first hour after ingestion. During this time, the majority of the ingested toxin is likely to be present in the stomach, where it can be effectively removed or adsorbed.
  - **Activated Charcoal:** Administering activated charcoal within one hour can adsorb a significant amount of the toxin, preventing its absorption into the bloodstream. It is the preferred method for many toxins due to its broad efficacy and safety profile.
  - **Gastric Lavage:** This method is generally recommended only within the first hour for life-threatening ingestions, as the procedure itself carries risks and is less effective once the toxin has moved beyond the stomach.

- **Beyond One Hour:**

  - **Reduced Effectiveness:** The effectiveness of gut decontamination decreases significantly as more time elapses after ingestion. Toxins are progressively absorbed into the bloodstream or move further along the gastrointestinal tract, making removal more difficult.
  - **Special Cases:** Certain situations may still warrant gut decontamination beyond the one-hour mark:

    - **Delayed-Release Formulations:** Ingestions involving sustained-release or enteric-coated medications, which can remain in the gastrointestinal tract longer, may benefit from continued gut decontamination efforts.
    - **Bezoars and Body Packers:** In cases where large quantities of drugs form bezoars (solid masses) or body packers ingest packets of drugs, whole bowel irrigation or repeated doses of activated charcoal can be effective beyond the initial hour.

Effectiveness of Different Methods:

- **Activated Charcoal:**

  - **Mechanism:** Activated charcoal adsorbs toxins onto its surface, reducing their absorption in the gastrointestinal tract. It is effective for a wide range of substances, including many drugs and chemicals.
  - **Administration:** Typically given as a single dose (50-100 grams for adults, 25-50 grams for children), but multiple doses may be administered in specific cases like sustained-release drug ingestion or enterohepatic recirculation of the toxin.
  - **Timing:** Most effective when given within one hour of ingestion. Its effectiveness diminishes over time but can still provide some benefit if given later, especially in cases of delayed gastric emptying.

- **Gastric Lavage:**

  - **Mechanism:** Involves the insertion of a large-bore orogastric tube and the repeated instillation and aspiration of small volumes of saline or water to wash out the stomach contents.

- ◦ **Administration:** Performed within one hour of a life-threatening ingestion. Requires careful consideration of risks, such as aspiration and esophageal perforation.
- ◦ **Timing:** Effectiveness is greatest within the first hour, with rapidly diminishing returns thereafter. It is rarely indicated beyond this period due to the risks involved.

- **Whole Bowel Irrigation:**

  - ◦ **Mechanism:** Uses a polyethylene glycol-electrolyte solution to flush out the entire gastrointestinal tract, preventing further absorption of the toxin.
  - ◦ **Administration:** Indicated for substances not effectively adsorbed by activated charcoal, such as iron, lithium, and certain sustained-release medications.
  - ◦ **Timing:** Can be effective beyond the first hour, particularly in cases where the toxin remains in the gastrointestinal tract for an extended period.

Monitoring and Reassessment:

- **Clinical Monitoring:** Continuous monitoring of the patient's vital signs, mental status, and overall condition is essential during and after gut decontamination procedures.
- **Laboratory Tests:** Regular assessment of blood chemistry, toxicology screens, and other relevant laboratory tests helps guide ongoing management and determine the effectiveness of decontamination efforts.
- **Reevaluation:** Reevaluate the need for further decontamination or additional interventions based on the patient's response to initial treatments and evolving clinical status.

4.2 Methods of Gut Decontamination

4.2.1 Induced Emesis

Induced emesis involves the deliberate induction of vomiting to expel ingested toxins from the stomach. Historically, it has been used as a method of gut decontamination, but its use has become more limited due to the availability of more effective and safer alternatives.

4.2.1.1 Indications and Contraindications

Indications:

- **Specific Toxin Ingestions:** Induced emesis may be considered for certain ingestions where other methods are not feasible, and the toxin is not caustic or hydrocarbon-based.
- **Early Presentation:** It is most effective when the patient presents very soon after ingestion, ideally within one hour, when the toxin is still in the stomach.
- **Limited Resources:** In settings where activated charcoal or other decontamination methods are unavailable, induced emesis might be considered as an interim measure.

Contraindications:

- **Caustic Substances:** Ingestions involving caustic substances (e.g., acids, alkalis) can cause further injury to the esophagus and oral mucosa if vomited.
- **Hydrocarbons:** Vomiting hydrocarbons (e.g., gasoline, kerosene) increases the risk of aspiration and chemical pneumonitis.
- **Reduced Consciousness:** Patients with a decreased level of consciousness or those unable to protect their airway are at high risk of aspiration and should not be induced to vomit.
- **Seizure Disorders:** Patients with a history of seizures or currently seizing are at increased risk of aspiration.
- **Age Considerations:** Young children and elderly patients are at higher risk for complications and may not be suitable candidates for induced emesis.

4.2.1.2 Techniques and Complications

Techniques:

- **Syrup of Ipecac:**

- ◦ **Administration:** Ipecac syrup was traditionally used to induce vomiting. The recommended dose was 15-30 mL in adults and 10-15 mL in children, followed by 240 mL of water. Vomiting typically occurs within 15-30 minutes.
  - ◦ **Availability:** Its use has declined significantly, and it is no longer recommended in many guidelines due to the potential for adverse effects and the availability of better alternatives.

- **Mechanical Stimulation:**

  - ◦ **Technique:** Mechanical stimulation of the pharynx (e.g., using a finger or other object) to induce a gag reflex and vomiting.
  - ◦ **Risks:** This method is not recommended due to the risk of trauma to the oropharynx and the potential for aspiration.

Complications:

- **Aspiration:** One of the most serious complications, especially in patients with compromised airway protection or reduced consciousness.
- **Esophageal and Gastric Injury:** Induced vomiting can cause tears, perforations, or other injuries to the esophagus and stomach, particularly with caustic substances.
- **Electrolyte Imbalances:** Repeated vomiting can lead to significant electrolyte disturbances, including hypokalemia and metabolic alkalosis.
- **Persistent Vomiting:** Some patients may experience prolonged vomiting, leading to dehydration and further complications.
- **Ineffectiveness:** Induced emesis may not effectively remove all or even a significant portion of the ingested toxin, especially if delayed beyond the optimal time frame.

4.2 Methods of Gut Decontamination

4.2.2 Gastric Lavage

Gastric lavage is a procedure that involves the insertion of a tube into the stomach, followed by the repeated instillation and aspiration of fluid to remove ingested toxins. While its use has declined with the advent of more effective and safer methods, gastric lavage may still be considered in specific clinical scenarios.

4.2.2.1 Indications and Contraindications
Indications:

- **Life-Threatening Ingestions:** Considered when a potentially life-threatening amount of a toxin has been ingested, especially if the ingestion occurred within one hour.
- **Large Ingestions:** Particularly large ingestions of substances that do not bind well to activated charcoal, such as iron or lithium.
- **Toxins Not Amenable to Other Methods:** Situations where other methods, such as activated charcoal, are not suitable or available.
- **Delayed Gastric Emptying:** Certain cases where delayed gastric emptying is suspected, such as with bezoars or large pill masses.

Contraindications:

- **Caustic or Corrosive Substances:** Ingestions involving acids or alkalis, which can cause further damage to the esophagus and stomach if gastric lavage is performed.
- **Hydrocarbons:** Risk of aspiration and chemical pneumonitis outweighs the potential benefits.
- **Compromised Airway Protection:** Patients with a decreased level of consciousness who do not have a secured airway (e.g., intubation) are at high risk of aspiration.
- **High Risk of Perforation:** Situations where there is a high risk of gastrointestinal perforation, such as in cases of recent surgery or known pathology.

4.2.2.2 Techniques and Complications
Techniques:

1. **Preparation:**

   - **Patient Positioning:** Place the patient in the left lateral decubitus position with the head slightly lower than the body to reduce the risk of aspiration.

- **Equipment Preparation:** Use a large-bore orogastric tube (36-40 French for adults, 24-28 French for children), syringes or lavage set, and saline or water for lavage.

2. **Procedure:**

   - **Insertion of the Tube:** Insert the orogastric tube gently through the mouth or nose into the stomach, confirming placement by auscultation (listening for air insufflated through the tube) and aspiration of stomach contents.
   - **Initial Aspiration:** Aspirate as much gastric content as possible before beginning lavage.
   - **Lavage Process:** Instill 200-300 mL of warm saline or water into the stomach and then aspirate back the fluid. Repeat this process until the returned fluid is clear. For children, use smaller volumes (10 mL/kg).
   - **Monitoring:** Continuously monitor the patient's vital signs and oxygen saturation throughout the procedure.

Complications:

- **Aspiration:** One of the most serious complications, particularly if the patient's airway is not adequately protected. This can lead to aspiration pneumonia or chemical pneumonitis.
- **Esophageal or Gastric Perforation:** Risk of perforation, especially if excessive force is used during tube insertion or if the patient has underlying gastrointestinal pathology.
- **Electrolyte Imbalances:** Repeated lavage with large volumes of fluid can lead to electrolyte disturbances, particularly if electrolyte-free solutions are used.
- **Hypothermia:** Using large volumes of cold lavage fluid can lead to hypothermia, especially in small children or elderly patients.
- **Mechanical Injury:** Trauma to the oropharynx, esophagus, or stomach can occur, leading to bleeding or other complications.
- **Ineffectiveness:** If performed too late after ingestion, gastric lavage may not effectively remove the toxin, especially if it has already moved beyond the stomach or been absorbed.

4.2 Methods of Gut Decontamination

4.2.3 Activated Charcoal

Activated charcoal is a widely used method of gut decontamination in poisoning cases. It works by adsorbing toxins in the gastrointestinal tract, preventing their absorption into the bloodstream. Due to its effectiveness and relative safety, activated charcoal is often the preferred method for many types of poisoning.

4.2.3.1 Mechanism and Indications
Mechanism of Action:

- **Adsorption:** Activated charcoal has a large surface area due to its porous structure, which allows it to adsorb a wide range of toxins. The toxins adhere to the surface of the charcoal particles, reducing their absorption from the gastrointestinal tract into the bloodstream.
- **Prevention of Enterohepatic Recirculation:** In some cases, activated charcoal can interrupt the enterohepatic recirculation of certain toxins, further enhancing its effectiveness in reducing toxin levels in the body.

Indications:

- **Broad Range of Toxins:** Activated charcoal is effective for many drugs and chemicals, including acetaminophen, aspirin, barbiturates, tricyclic antidepressants, and many others.
- **Early Presentation:** Most effective when administered within one hour of toxin ingestion. It may still be beneficial beyond this period for certain substances with delayed absorption or prolonged gastric retention.
- **Multiple Doses:** In cases of substances that undergo enterohepatic recirculation (e.g., carbamazepine, phenobarbital) or sustained-release formulations, multiple doses of activated charcoal may be indicated.

Substances Not Effectively Adsorbed by Activated Charcoal:

- **Metals:** Iron, lithium, lead.
- **Alcohols:** Ethanol, methanol, ethylene glycol.
- **Corrosives:** Acids and alkalis.

- **Hydrocarbons:** Gasoline, kerosene.

4.2.3.2 Dosage and Administration
Dosage:

- **Single Dose:**

  - **Adults:** 50-100 grams of activated charcoal.
  - **Children:** 25-50 grams of activated charcoal.

- **Multiple Doses:** Used in specific cases where prolonged adsorption is beneficial. Subsequent doses are typically 12.5 grams per hour, 25 grams every 2 hours, or 50 grams every 4 hours, depending on the clinical scenario and toxin involved.

Administration:

1. **Preparation:**

   - **Formulation:** Activated charcoal is usually available as a powder that is mixed with water to form a slurry, or as a pre-prepared suspension. The slurry should be mixed thoroughly to ensure even distribution.
   - **Palatability:** Activated charcoal has an unpleasant taste and gritty texture. It can be mixed with a flavored beverage (e.g., juice) to improve palatability, though this should not significantly dilute the charcoal.

2. **Administration Technique:**

   - **Oral Route:** The charcoal slurry is given orally if the patient is conscious and able to swallow. Encourage the patient to drink the entire dose.
   - **Nasogastric Tube:** In cases where the patient is unconscious or unable to swallow, activated charcoal can be administered via a nasogastric tube. Confirm proper tube placement before administration to avoid complications.

3. **Post-Administration Care:**

- ○ **Hydration:** Ensure the patient stays adequately hydrated to facilitate gastrointestinal transit and reduce the risk of constipation.
- ○ **Monitoring:** Monitor for signs of gastrointestinal obstruction or aspiration, particularly in patients with decreased consciousness or compromised airway reflexes.

Complications:

- **Aspiration:** Risk of aspiration, particularly in patients with a decreased level of consciousness or those unable to protect their airway. This risk underscores the importance of securing the airway in at-risk patients.
- **Gastrointestinal Obstruction:** Rarely, activated charcoal can lead to intestinal obstruction, particularly with multiple doses. Ensure adequate hydration and monitor for signs of obstruction.
- **Emesis:** Vomiting is a common side effect and can complicate the administration, especially if large volumes are given quickly.

4.2 Methods of Gut Decontamination

4.2.4 Whole Bowel Irrigation

Whole bowel irrigation (WBI) is a method of gut decontamination that involves the administration of large volumes of an osmotically balanced polyethylene glycol-electrolyte solution to cleanse the entire gastrointestinal tract. This technique is used to prevent the absorption of ingested toxins by flushing them out of the gastrointestinal tract.

4.2.4.1 Indications and Contraindications
Indications:

- **Sustained-Release or Enteric-Coated Drugs:** WBI is particularly useful for ingestions involving sustained-release or enteric-coated medications that are not effectively removed by other methods.
- **Drugs Not Adsorbed by Activated Charcoal:** Substances such as iron, lithium, and certain heavy metals that do not bind well to activated charcoal.

- **Body Packers:** Individuals who have ingested packets of illicit drugs (e.g., cocaine, heroin) to smuggle them. WBI can help evacuate the packets before they rupture and cause severe toxicity.
- **Large Ingestions:** Situations where a significant amount of a toxin has been ingested, and rapid clearance from the gastrointestinal tract is desired.

Contraindications:

- **Bowel Obstruction or Perforation:** WBI is contraindicated in patients with known or suspected bowel obstruction or gastrointestinal perforation due to the risk of worsening the condition.
- **Gastrointestinal Bleeding:** Active gastrointestinal bleeding is a contraindication as WBI can exacerbate bleeding.
- **Unprotected Airway:** Patients with a compromised airway or those who cannot protect their airway are at risk of aspiration.
- **Hemodynamic Instability:** Patients who are hemodynamically unstable may not tolerate the large fluid volumes required for WBI.
- **Caustic Ingestions:** Ingestions involving caustic substances (e.g., acids, alkalis) should not undergo WBI as it can cause further injury to the gastrointestinal tract.

4.2.4.2 Techniques and Complications
Techniques:

1. **Preparation:**

   - **Solution:** Use a polyethylene glycol-electrolyte solution (e.g., GoLYTELY, Colyte). This solution is isotonic and osmotically balanced to prevent significant fluid and electrolyte shifts.
   - **Equipment:** A large-bore nasogastric tube may be necessary for administration, especially in unconscious or uncooperative patients.

2. **Administration:**

   - **Oral Route:** If the patient is conscious and cooperative, the solution can be ingested orally. Typically, the patient drinks 1.5-2 liters per hour until the effluent (stool) is clear.

- ◦ **Nasogastric Tube:** In unconscious or uncooperative patients, the solution is administered via a nasogastric tube. The rate is similar, 1.5-2 liters per hour, until the effluent is clear.
- ◦ **Duration:** The procedure usually lasts 4-6 hours but can vary depending on the amount of toxin ingested and the patient's gastrointestinal transit time.

3. **Monitoring:**

- ◦ **Vital Signs:** Continuous monitoring of vital signs to detect any signs of hemodynamic instability.
- ◦ **Electrolytes:** Regular monitoring of electrolyte levels, especially in patients with underlying medical conditions that could be exacerbated by large fluid volumes.
- ◦ **Output:** Monitor the output and clarity of the effluent to determine when the irrigation can be stopped.

Complications:

- **Nausea and Vomiting:** Common during the procedure and can complicate the administration of the solution.
- **Abdominal Distension:** The large volumes of fluid can cause discomfort and distension, particularly in patients with delayed gastric emptying.
- **Electrolyte Imbalances:** Although the solution is isotonic, there is still a risk of electrolyte disturbances, particularly if the procedure is prolonged or the patient has pre-existing electrolyte abnormalities.
- **Aspiration:** Risk of aspiration, especially in patients with compromised airway reflexes. This underscores the importance of airway protection in at-risk patients.
- **Mechanical Complications:** Insertion and use of a nasogastric tube can cause nasal or esophageal trauma, especially if not performed correctly.

Chapter 5: Elimination Enhancement

Introduction

Elimination enhancement refers to a range of medical interventions designed to accelerate the removal of toxins from the body. While the body's natural processes, primarily through the liver and kidneys, gradually eliminate most poisons, these processes can be too slow to prevent significant harm in cases of severe poisoning. Enhancing elimination can significantly reduce the duration of toxin exposure, mitigate its effects, and improve patient outcomes.

This chapter explores various techniques used to enhance the elimination of toxins, including urinary alkalinization, hemodialysis, hemoperfusion, and other extracorporeal methods. Each technique has specific indications, mechanisms of action, and potential complications. Understanding when and how to use these methods is critical for effectively managing cases of poisoning, particularly when dealing with substances that are highly toxic or have prolonged half-lives.

Scope of the Chapter

This chapter will cover the following key areas:

1. **Urinary Alkalinization:** Discussing its role in enhancing the renal excretion of certain toxins, particularly weak acids like salicylates and phenobarbital.
2. **Hemodialysis:** Exploring its effectiveness in removing toxins that are water-soluble, have low molecular weight, and are not highly protein-bound. This includes a discussion on indications, procedure, and potential complications.
3. **Hemoperfusion:** Detailing its use for removing toxins that are poorly removed by hemodialysis, such as those with high protein binding or large molecular size, including the setup, indications, and limitations.
4. **Other Extracorporeal Methods:** Briefly covering additional techniques like continuous renal replacement therapy (CRRT) and exchange transfusion, highlighting their specific applications and effectiveness in poisoning cases.

Importance of Elimination Enhancement

The primary goal of elimination enhancement is to reduce the toxin burden on the body more rapidly than would occur naturally. This is particularly important in the following scenarios:

- **Severe Poisoning:** When the ingested toxin is highly toxic and poses an immediate threat to life.
- **Prolonged Half-Life:** When the toxin has a long half-life, leading to sustained exposure and potential cumulative damage.
- **Impaired Natural Elimination:** In patients with compromised renal or hepatic function, where the natural elimination processes are insufficient to handle the toxin load.

5.1 Principles of Elimination Enhancement

5.1.1 Mechanisms of Enhanced Elimination

Enhanced elimination techniques are employed to accelerate the removal of toxins from the body. These mechanisms are particularly valuable when natural elimination processes are insufficient to mitigate the toxic effects rapidly enough. The primary mechanisms include urinary manipulation, extracorporeal removal, and chemical modification.

Urinary Manipulation:

- **Urinary Alkalinization:**

  - **Mechanism:** This process involves the administration of alkaline substances, such as sodium bicarbonate, to increase the pH of urine. Alkaline urine increases the ionization of weak acids, reducing their reabsorption in the renal tubules and enhancing their excretion.
  - **Applications:** Effective for toxins such as salicylates and phenobarbital. It enhances the renal clearance of these substances by trapping them in their ionized form within the urinary tract.

Extracorporeal Removal:

- **Hemodialysis:**

- **Mechanism:** Hemodialysis uses a semipermeable membrane to facilitate the diffusion of toxins from the blood into a dialysate solution, which is then removed from the body. It is effective for substances that are water-soluble, have low molecular weight, and are not highly protein-bound.
- **Applications:** Commonly used for toxins such as methanol, ethylene glycol, lithium, and certain barbiturates.

- **Hemoperfusion:**

  - **Mechanism:** In hemoperfusion, blood passes through a column containing adsorbent materials (e.g., activated charcoal or resin), which bind and remove toxins from the bloodstream. This technique is particularly useful for toxins that are highly protein-bound or have large molecular weights.
  - **Applications:** Effective for substances like theophylline, carbamazepine, and certain pesticides.

Chemical Modification:

- **Use of Antidotes:**

  - **Mechanism:** Some antidotes can chemically modify toxins, rendering them less harmful or more easily excretable. For example, N-acetylcysteine in acetaminophen poisoning helps replenish glutathione, facilitating detoxification.
  - **Applications:** Specific antidotes are used based on the type of poisoning and the mechanism of the toxin.

5.1.2 Indications and Contraindications

Indications for Enhanced Elimination:

- **Severe Poisoning:**

  - **Life-Threatening Toxins:** When the ingested toxin poses an immediate and severe risk to life, enhanced elimination is critical.

- **Examples:** Severe cases of methanol or ethylene glycol poisoning, significant salicylate toxicity, and life-threatening lithium overdose.

- **Prolonged Half-Life:**

  - **Toxins with Long Half-Lives:** Substances that remain in the body for extended periods, leading to prolonged toxic effects.
  - **Examples:** Barbiturates, theophylline, and certain sustained-release formulations.

- **Ineffective Natural Elimination:**

  - **Compromised Renal or Hepatic Function:** Patients with impaired kidney or liver function, where the natural elimination processes are inadequate.
  - **Examples:** Patients with pre-existing renal insufficiency who have ingested lithium or other renally excreted toxins.

Contraindications for Enhanced Elimination:

- **Hemodynamic Instability:**

  - **Unstable Patients:** Procedures like hemodialysis and hemoperfusion require stable hemodynamics. Severely unstable patients may not tolerate these procedures without first being stabilized.
  - **Management:** Initial stabilization of blood pressure and cardiovascular status is necessary before proceeding.

- **Coagulopathies:**

  - **Risk of Bleeding:** Patients with bleeding disorders or those at high risk of bleeding may not be suitable candidates for extracorporeal procedures.
  - **Considerations:** Careful assessment and correction of coagulopathies are essential before initiating procedures like hemodialysis or hemoperfusion.

- **Inadequate Access:**

- ◦ **Vascular Access Issues:** Difficulty in establishing reliable vascular access can preclude the use of certain extracorporeal techniques.
- ◦ **Alternatives:** Consider alternative methods of elimination or prioritize other supportive care measures.

- **Specific Toxin Properties:**

- ◦ **Ineffectiveness of Technique:** Not all toxins are amenable to enhanced elimination techniques. For instance, highly lipid-soluble or protein-bound toxins may not be effectively removed by hemodialysis.
- ◦ **Evaluation:** A thorough evaluation of the toxin's pharmacokinetics and properties is necessary to determine the appropriateness of the chosen method.

5.2 Methods of Elimination Enhancement

5.2.1 Urinary Alkalinization

5.2.1.1 Mechanism and Indications
Mechanism:

Urinary alkalinization involves the administration of substances that increase the pH of urine, typically sodium bicarbonate. This process enhances the renal excretion of certain toxins, particularly weak acids. When the urine becomes more alkaline, weak acids become ionized and less lipid-soluble. This ionized form is less likely to be reabsorbed by the renal tubules and more likely to be excreted in the urine. This mechanism is crucial for toxins like salicylates and phenobarbital, which are weak acids and can cause significant toxicity. By increasing the urinary pH to a target range of 7.5 to 8.0, these substances are trapped in the urine, facilitating their elimination from the body.

Indications:

Urinary alkalinization is primarily indicated for poisoning with weak acids that benefit from increased renal excretion. One of the most common indications is **salicylate poisoning**. Salicylates, found in medications like aspirin, can cause metabolic acidosis, respiratory alkalosis, and various systemic effects. Alkalinizing the urine enhances the elimination of salicylates, reducing their toxic effects. Another indication is **phenobarbital overdose**, a barbiturate that can cause central nervous system depression and respiratory failure. By promoting the excretion of phenobarbital, urinary alkalinization helps to decrease its sedative effects. Additionally, urinary alkalinization can be used for poisoning with other weak acids, although it is less commonly employed for these cases.

5.2.1.2 Techniques and Complications

Techniques:

To achieve urinary alkalinization, **sodium bicarbonate** is typically administered intravenously. The initial dose is usually **1-2 mEq/kg**, administered as an intravenous bolus. Following the bolus, a continuous infusion of sodium bicarbonate may be initiated. The infusion rate is adjusted based on the patient's urine pH and serum bicarbonate levels. The goal is to maintain the urine pH between 7.5 and 8.0. Frequent monitoring of urine pH is essential to ensure that the target range is achieved and maintained. In addition to urine pH, **serum electrolytes** and **blood gases** should be monitored regularly to avoid complications such as metabolic alkalosis and electrolyte imbalances. Potassium supplementation may be necessary because alkalinization can lead to hypokalemia.

Complications:

While urinary alkalinization can be highly effective, it is not without risks. One of the primary complications is **metabolic alkalosis**, which can occur if the bicarbonate dose is too high or if the patient has pre-existing conditions that predispose them to alkalosis. Metabolic alkalosis can cause symptoms such as confusion, muscle twitching, and cardiac arrhythmias. To prevent this, careful monitoring of blood gases and serum bicarbonate levels is necessary. Another potential complication is **hypokalemia**, which occurs because increasing the urinary pH enhances potassium excretion. Hypokalemia can lead to muscle weakness, cramps, and arrhythmias. Regular monitoring of serum potassium levels and appropriate supplementation are crucial. Additionally, rapid administration of sodium bicarbonate can lead to **volume overload** and **hypernatremia**, especially in patients with renal or cardiac dysfunction. It is important to adjust the rate of infusion and monitor fluid balance closely to avoid these issues.

5.2 Methods of Elimination Enhancement

5.2.2 Hemodialysis

5.2.2.1 Mechanism and Indications

Mechanism:

Hemodialysis is a procedure that utilizes a dialysis machine and a semipermeable membrane to remove toxins from the blood. The patient's blood is pumped through a dialyzer, where it flows on one side of the membrane while a dialysis solution (dialysate) flows on the opposite side. The semipermeable membrane allows small molecules, such as toxins and electrolytes, to diffuse from the blood into the dialysate based on concentration gradients. Large molecules and blood cells are retained, while toxins move into the dialysate, which is then discarded. This process effectively reduces the concentration of water-soluble, low molecular weight, and non-protein-bound toxins in the bloodstream, thus decreasing their toxic effects.

Indications:

Hemodialysis is indicated for the removal of specific toxins that meet certain criteria:

- **Water-Soluble Toxins:** Hemodialysis is effective for substances that are highly soluble in water.
- **Low Molecular Weight Toxins:** Toxins with low molecular weights can easily pass through the semipermeable membrane of the dialyzer.
- **Low Protein Binding:** Toxins that are not extensively bound to plasma proteins are more readily removed by hemodialysis.

Common indications for hemodialysis in poisoning include:

- **Methanol and Ethylene Glycol:** Both are toxic alcohols that can cause metabolic acidosis and severe organ damage. Hemodialysis rapidly removes these substances and their toxic metabolites.
- **Salicylates:** In cases of severe salicylate poisoning, where levels are dangerously high, hemodialysis can effectively reduce serum salicylate concentrations.
- **Lithium:** Hemodialysis is used in severe lithium toxicity, particularly when serum levels are high or in patients with impaired renal function.

- **Phenobarbital:** For barbiturate poisoning, especially when complicated by prolonged coma or significant respiratory depression, hemodialysis can enhance drug elimination.
- **Theophylline:** In cases of severe theophylline poisoning, hemodialysis can be used to rapidly reduce toxic levels, especially when standard therapies fail.

5.2.2.2 Techniques and Complications
Techniques:

1. **Vascular Access:**

   - **Central Venous Catheter:** A temporary large-bore catheter is placed in a central vein (e.g., femoral, jugular, or subclavian) to facilitate high blood flow rates required for hemodialysis.
   - **AV Fistula or Graft:** In patients requiring long-term dialysis, an arteriovenous (AV) fistula or graft is surgically created, but this is not typically used in acute poisoning scenarios.

2. **Dialysis Procedure:**

   - **Dialyzer Setup:** The dialyzer, containing the semipermeable membrane, is connected to the dialysis machine. The dialysate composition is selected based on the patient's needs, often mirroring normal plasma electrolyte concentrations.
   - **Blood Flow Rates:** Blood flow rates are typically maintained between 200-500 mL/min to ensure efficient toxin removal.
   - **Duration:** The duration of the dialysis session can vary but usually lasts 4-6 hours. In severe cases, continuous renal replacement therapy (CRRT) may be considered.

3. **Monitoring:**

   - **Vital Signs:** Continuous monitoring of blood pressure, heart rate, and respiratory rate is crucial to detect any hemodynamic instability.
   - **Electrolytes and Blood Gases:** Regular checks of serum electrolytes, blood gases, and toxin levels help guide the dialysis process and adjustments in treatment.

Complications:

1. **Hypotension:**

   - **Mechanism:** Rapid removal of fluids and toxins can lead to a drop in blood pressure, particularly in patients who are volume-depleted or have cardiovascular instability.
   - **Management:** Hypotension can be managed by adjusting the ultrafiltration rate, administering intravenous fluids, or using vasopressors if necessary.

2. **Electrolyte Imbalances:**

   - **Mechanism:** Rapid shifts in electrolytes can occur during hemodialysis, leading to imbalances such as hypokalemia or hypocalcemia.
   - **Management:** Regular monitoring and appropriate supplementation of electrolytes are essential to prevent complications.

3. **Dialysis Disequilibrium Syndrome:**

   - **Mechanism:** This condition can occur due to rapid removal of urea and other solutes, leading to cerebral edema. Symptoms include headache, nausea, vomiting, and in severe cases, seizures.
   - **Management:** Gradual reduction in solute removal and careful monitoring of neurological status can help mitigate this risk.

4. **Infections:**

   - **Mechanism:** The use of central venous catheters increases the risk of infections, including bacteremia and sepsis.
   - **Management:** Strict aseptic technique during catheter insertion and maintenance, along with prompt treatment of any signs of infection, is crucial.

5. **Bleeding:**

- ○ **Mechanism:** Heparin is often used during hemodialysis to prevent clotting in the dialysis circuit, which can increase the risk of bleeding.
- ○ **Management:** Monitoring coagulation parameters and adjusting heparin dosage as needed can help manage this risk.

5.2 Methods of Elimination Enhancement

5.2.3 Hemoperfusion

5.2.3.1 Mechanism and Indications

Mechanism:

Hemoperfusion involves passing the patient's blood through a cartridge filled with adsorbent materials, such as activated charcoal or resin, which can bind and remove toxins directly from the bloodstream. Unlike hemodialysis, which relies on diffusion across a semipermeable membrane, hemoperfusion uses adsorption to clear substances. The blood flows through the adsorbent material, which captures and holds onto the toxin molecules. This method is particularly effective for substances that are highly protein-bound or have large molecular weights, which are typically difficult to remove by hemodialysis.

Indications:

Hemoperfusion is indicated for certain types of poisonings where traditional methods, such as activated charcoal or hemodialysis, are less effective:

- **Highly Protein-Bound Toxins:** Toxins like theophylline, carbamazepine, and phenobarbital, which bind extensively to plasma proteins, making them poor candidates for hemodialysis.
- **Large Molecular Weight Toxins:** Substances with large molecular sizes, which are inefficiently cleared by hemodialysis membranes.
- **Lipid-Soluble Toxins:** Toxins that are highly lipid-soluble, such as certain pesticides and drugs that are difficult to remove by conventional methods.
- **Severe Poisoning:** Cases of life-threatening toxicity where rapid reduction of toxin levels is critical for patient survival.

5.2.3.2 Techniques and Complications

Techniques:

1. **Preparation:**

   - **Vascular Access:** Similar to hemodialysis, a central venous catheter is typically used to achieve the necessary blood flow rates. This catheter is placed in a large central vein, such as the femoral, jugular, or subclavian vein.
   - **Cartridge Selection:** The type of adsorbent material (activated charcoal or resin) is chosen based on the specific toxin to be removed. Each cartridge has specific properties suited to different types of toxins.

2. **Procedure:**

   - **Blood Flow:** Blood is drawn from the patient and pumped through the hemoperfusion cartridge. The flow rate is usually maintained between 200-300 mL/min to ensure efficient adsorption of toxins.
   - **Adsorption:** As blood passes through the cartridge, toxins bind to the adsorbent material, while the cleansed blood is returned to the patient. The duration of the procedure is typically 2-4 hours, depending on the severity of poisoning and the efficiency of toxin removal.
   - **Monitoring:** Continuous monitoring of vital signs, blood flow rates, and the condition of the hemoperfusion cartridge is essential to ensure the procedure's effectiveness and patient safety.

Complications:

1. **Hypotension:**

   - **Mechanism:** Rapid removal of large volumes of blood and the adsorption of certain substances can cause a drop in blood pressure.
   - **Management:** Hypotension can be managed by adjusting blood flow rates, administering intravenous fluids, or using vasopressors if necessary.

2. Thrombocytopenia:

- **Mechanism:** The adsorbent materials in the cartridge can adsorb platelets and clotting factors, leading to a reduction in platelet count and an increased risk of bleeding.
- **Management:** Regular monitoring of platelet counts and coagulation parameters is necessary. If thrombocytopenia is significant, the procedure may need to be discontinued, or additional supportive measures, such as platelet transfusions, may be required.

3. Electrolyte Imbalances:

- **Mechanism:** Similar to hemodialysis, hemoperfusion can cause shifts in electrolyte levels, particularly calcium, potassium, and magnesium.
- **Management:** Frequent monitoring of electrolytes and appropriate supplementation are essential to prevent complications.

4. Cartridge Saturation:

- **Mechanism:** Over time, the adsorbent material in the cartridge can become saturated with toxins, reducing its effectiveness.
- **Management:** The cartridge may need to be replaced during the procedure to maintain optimal toxin adsorption.

5. Infections:

- **Mechanism:** The use of central venous catheters increases the risk of bloodstream infections.
- **Management:** Strict aseptic techniques during catheter insertion and maintenance are essential, along with prompt treatment of any signs of infection.

6. Coagulopathy:

- **Mechanism:** Adsorption of clotting factors can lead to coagulopathy, increasing the risk of bleeding.
- **Management:** Monitoring coagulation parameters and adjusting treatment as necessary can help manage this risk.

5.2 Methods of Elimination Enhancement

5.2.4 Peritoneal Dialysis

5.2.4.1 Mechanism and Indications
Mechanism:

Peritoneal dialysis (PD) is a technique that uses the patient's peritoneal membrane as a semi-permeable dialysis membrane. A dialysis solution, or dialysate, is infused into the peritoneal cavity, where it remains for a period, allowing toxins and excess solutes from the blood to diffuse across the peritoneal membrane into the dialysate. After an appropriate dwell time, the dialysate, now containing the waste products and toxins, is drained out of the peritoneal cavity and replaced with fresh dialysate. This process can be repeated multiple times to enhance the removal of toxins from the bloodstream.

Indications:

Peritoneal dialysis is indicated in situations where other methods of enhanced elimination are not feasible or are contraindicated:

- **Limited Access to Hemodialysis:** In settings where hemodialysis facilities are not available, peritoneal dialysis can be an alternative for toxin removal.
- **Hemodynamic Instability:** Patients who are hemodynamically unstable and cannot tolerate the rapid fluid shifts associated with hemodialysis may benefit from the gentler nature of peritoneal dialysis.
- **Specific Toxins:** Although less commonly used for toxin removal compared to hemodialysis, peritoneal dialysis can be effective for certain toxins, particularly those that are water-soluble and have low molecular weights.
- **Pediatric Patients:** Peritoneal dialysis is often preferred in young children due to the relative ease of the procedure and the avoidance of large vascular access.

5.2.4.2 Techniques and Complications
Techniques:

1. **Catheter Insertion:**

   - **Peritoneal Catheter:** A peritoneal dialysis catheter is surgically or percutaneously inserted into the peritoneal cavity. This catheter provides access for infusing and draining the dialysate.
   - **Placement:** The catheter is placed under sterile conditions to reduce the risk of infection and is typically positioned in the lower abdomen.

2. **Dialysate Infusion:**

   - **Dialysate Composition:** The dialysate is an osmotic solution containing glucose or other osmotic agents, electrolytes, and sometimes buffers. The composition is selected based on the patient's needs and the specific toxins involved.
   - **Infusion Process:** The dialysate is infused into the peritoneal cavity through the catheter. The volume of dialysate used can vary, but typical volumes range from 1.5 to 2.5 liters per exchange.

3. **Dwell Time:**

   - **Duration:** The dialysate is allowed to dwell in the peritoneal cavity for a prescribed period, usually between 1 to 4 hours, depending on the specific protocol and the patient's condition.
   - **Diffusion and Osmosis:** During the dwell time, toxins and excess solutes diffuse from the blood vessels in the peritoneal membrane into the dialysate, driven by concentration gradients.

4. **Drain and Exchange:**

   - **Draining:** After the dwell time, the dialysate, now containing the removed toxins and waste products, is drained out of the peritoneal cavity.
   - **Exchange:** Fresh dialysate is then infused to start a new cycle. This process is repeated several times per day, depending on the severity of poisoning and the efficiency of toxin removal.

Complications:

1. **Peritonitis:**

   - **Mechanism:** Infection of the peritoneal cavity is a significant risk and can occur due to contamination during catheter insertion or dialysate exchanges.
   - **Symptoms:** Signs of peritonitis include abdominal pain, fever, cloudy dialysate, and elevated white blood cell count in the dialysate.
   - **Management:** Treatment involves prompt administration of intraperitoneal or systemic antibiotics, and in severe cases, removal and replacement of the catheter.

2. **Catheter-Related Issues:**

   - **Obstruction:** The peritoneal catheter can become obstructed by fibrin, blood clots, or kinks, preventing effective dialysate flow.
   - **Management:** Flushing the catheter, repositioning, or in some cases, surgical revision may be necessary to restore proper function.

3. **Fluid Overload:**

   - **Mechanism:** Inadequate removal of fluid during exchanges can lead to fluid retention and overload, causing symptoms such as edema, hypertension, and respiratory distress.
   - **Management:** Careful monitoring of fluid balance and adjusting the dialysate volume and dwell times can help prevent and manage fluid overload.

4. **Electrolyte Imbalances:**

   - **Mechanism:** Peritoneal dialysis can cause shifts in electrolytes, leading to imbalances such as hypokalemia or hyperglycemia (due to the glucose content in the dialysate).
   - **Management:** Regular monitoring of serum electrolyte levels and appropriate adjustments to the dialysate composition or supplementation are necessary to maintain electrolyte balance.

5. **Mechanical Complications:**

- ◦ **Leakage:** Leakage of dialysate around the catheter insertion site can occur, leading to suboptimal dialysis and risk of infection.
- ◦ **Hernias:** Increased intra-abdominal pressure from the dialysate can contribute to the development of hernias, particularly in patients with pre-existing risk factors.
- ◦ **Management:** Addressing leakage may require adjustments in the catheter placement or securement, and hernias may require surgical intervention.

Chapter 6: Toxicokinetics

Introduction

Toxicokinetics is the study of how toxins are absorbed, distributed, metabolized, and excreted by the body. Understanding these processes is essential for effectively managing poisoning cases and developing appropriate treatment strategies. The principles of toxicokinetics help predict the behavior of toxins within the body, influencing decisions about decontamination, antidote administration, and supportive care.

Toxicokinetics is closely related to pharmacokinetics, the study of how drugs move through the body, but focuses specifically on substances that cause harmful effects. By analyzing toxicokinetic data, healthcare providers can better understand the time course of toxin exposure and its impact on different organs and systems.

Scope of the Chapter

This chapter will cover the following key areas:

1. **Absorption:** How toxins enter the body through various routes, including oral, inhalation, dermal, and parenteral. Factors affecting the rate and extent of absorption will be discussed.
2. **Distribution:** The process by which toxins are transported throughout the body and distributed to various tissues and organs. This section will explore the concepts of volume of distribution, protein binding, and tissue affinity.

3. **Metabolism:** How the body biotransforms toxins into more or less harmful substances. The roles of the liver and other metabolic pathways, including phase I and phase II reactions, will be examined.
4. **Excretion:** The mechanisms by which toxins and their metabolites are eliminated from the body, primarily through the kidneys, liver, and lungs. Factors influencing renal and hepatic clearance will be discussed.
5. **Kinetic Models:** An overview of the different models used to describe the kinetic behavior of toxins, including zero-order and first-order kinetics, and how these models help predict toxin levels over time.

Importance of Toxicokinetics

Understanding toxicokinetics is crucial for several reasons:

- **Treatment Planning:** By knowing how a toxin is absorbed, distributed, metabolized, and excreted, healthcare providers can develop targeted treatment plans to enhance elimination and mitigate toxic effects.
- **Dose-Response Relationships:** Toxicokinetics helps elucidate the relationship between the dose of a toxin and its observed effects, aiding in the assessment of toxicity and risk.
- **Timing of Interventions:** Knowledge of toxicokinetic principles enables clinicians to time interventions, such as the administration of antidotes or enhanced elimination techniques, to maximize their effectiveness.
- **Predicting Outcomes:** By analyzing toxicokinetic data, it is possible to predict the likely course of poisoning and anticipate potential complications, leading to more proactive and effective management.

6.1 Absorption

6.1.1 Mechanisms of Absorption

Mechanisms of Absorption refer to the processes by which toxins enter the body and move from the site of exposure into the bloodstream. Understanding these mechanisms is crucial for predicting the onset and severity of toxic effects and for determining appropriate decontamination strategies.

Gastrointestinal Absorption:

- **Passive Diffusion:** Most toxins are absorbed through passive diffusion, where molecules move from an area of higher concentration (the gut) to an area of lower concentration (the blood) across the intestinal mucosa. This process does not require energy and depends on the concentration gradient.
- **Active Transport:** Some toxins, particularly those that resemble essential nutrients, are absorbed via active transport. This process involves carrier proteins and requires energy (ATP) to move substances against their concentration gradient. Examples include certain metals like lead, which mimic calcium.
- **Facilitated Diffusion:** This is similar to passive diffusion but involves specific carrier proteins that help transport molecules across the cell membrane without using energy.
- **Endocytosis:** Larger molecules or particles may be absorbed through endocytosis, where the cell membrane engulfs the toxin and forms a vesicle to transport it into the cell. This mechanism is less common but important for some biological toxins.

Dermal Absorption:

- **Transdermal Penetration:** Toxins can penetrate the skin through the outermost layer, the stratum corneum. Lipid-soluble substances penetrate more easily than water-soluble ones.
- **Intercellular Route:** Toxins can move between the cells of the stratum corneum, following the lipid matrix.
- **Transcellular Route:** This involves toxins moving through the cells of the epidermis.
- **Appendageal Route:** Some toxins enter through hair follicles and sweat glands, bypassing the stratum corneum.

Inhalational Absorption:

- **Alveolar Diffusion:** Gases and vapors are absorbed through the alveoli in the lungs by simple diffusion. The large surface area and rich blood supply of the alveoli facilitate rapid absorption.

- **Aerosol and Particulate Absorption:** Particles can be absorbed through the alveolar membrane or deposited in the respiratory tract and absorbed through the mucosa.

Parenteral Absorption:

- **Intravenous Injection:** Toxins introduced directly into the bloodstream provide immediate absorption and distribution.
- **Intramuscular and Subcutaneous Injection:** Toxins are absorbed from the injection site into the surrounding tissue and then into the bloodstream. This absorption depends on blood flow to the injection site.

6.1.2 Factors Influencing Absorption

Factors Influencing Absorption involve a variety of physiological and chemical characteristics that affect how quickly and efficiently toxins are absorbed into the body.

Physicochemical Properties of the Toxin:

- **Molecular Size and Weight:** Smaller molecules generally diffuse more easily across cell membranes compared to larger molecules.
- **Lipid Solubility:** Lipid-soluble toxins penetrate cell membranes more readily than water-soluble toxins, affecting absorption rates.
- **Ionization State:** The degree of ionization of a toxin affects its absorption. Non-ionized (neutral) molecules cross cell membranes more easily than ionized molecules. The ionization state is influenced by the pH of the environment and the pKa of the substance.

Concentration of the Toxin:

- **Concentration Gradient:** A higher concentration of the toxin at the site of exposure creates a stronger gradient, promoting faster absorption through passive diffusion.

Surface Area of the Absorptive Site:

- **Gastrointestinal Tract:** The extensive surface area of the intestines, with villi and microvilli, enhances absorption.
- **Lungs:** The alveoli provide a large surface area for gas and vapor absorption.
- **Skin:** The surface area available for dermal absorption can be increased with larger exposure areas.

Blood Flow to the Absorptive Site:

- **Enhanced Perfusion:** Increased blood flow to the site of absorption (e.g., intestines, lungs) enhances the removal of absorbed toxins, maintaining the concentration gradient and promoting further absorption.
- **Reduced Perfusion:** Conditions that decrease blood flow can reduce absorption rates.

Presence of Food or Other Substances:

- **Food in the Stomach:** The presence of food can slow gastric emptying, thereby slowing the absorption of some toxins but potentially increasing the absorption of lipid-soluble toxins due to bile secretion.
- **Interactions with Other Substances:** Some substances can bind to toxins, reducing their absorption. For example, activated charcoal binds many toxins in the gastrointestinal tract, preventing their absorption.

Physiological Conditions:

- **Age and Health Status:** Age-related changes, such as decreased gastric acidity and slowed gastrointestinal motility in the elderly, can influence absorption. Health conditions, such as gastrointestinal diseases, can also affect absorption.
- **Genetic Factors:** Genetic variations can influence enzyme activity and transporter proteins involved in toxin absorption and metabolism.

Exposure Route and Duration:

- **Route of Exposure:** Different routes (oral, inhalation, dermal, parenteral) have distinct absorption characteristics. For instance, inhalation provides rapid absorption due to the large surface area and rich blood supply of the alveoli.

- **Duration of Exposure:** Prolonged exposure can lead to increased absorption and accumulation of the toxin in the body.

6.2 Distribution

6.2.1 Mechanisms of Distribution

Mechanisms of Distribution describe how toxins move from the bloodstream to various tissues and organs after absorption. This process is influenced by the toxin's physicochemical properties and the body's physiological characteristics.

Blood Flow and Perfusion:

- **Initial Distribution:** Toxins are initially distributed to highly perfused organs such as the liver, kidneys, brain, and heart. These organs receive a large proportion of the cardiac output, leading to rapid distribution.
- **Subsequent Redistribution:** Over time, toxins redistribute to less perfused tissues like muscle and fat. This process depends on the toxin's solubility and affinity for different tissues.

Plasma Protein Binding:

- **Binding to Plasma Proteins:** Many toxins bind to plasma proteins, such as albumin and globulins. The extent of binding affects the free (unbound) fraction of the toxin available for distribution to tissues.
- **Equilibrium:** A dynamic equilibrium exists between the bound and unbound forms of the toxin. Only the unbound fraction can cross cell membranes and exert toxic effects or be metabolized and excreted.

Capillary Permeability:

- **Continuous Capillaries:** These capillaries, found in the brain and muscles, have tight junctions that restrict the movement of large molecules and hydrophilic substances. The blood-brain barrier (BBB) is an example of a continuous capillary system with selective permeability.

- **Fenestrated Capillaries:** Found in organs like the kidneys and endocrine glands, these capillaries have pores that allow larger molecules and hydrophilic substances to pass through more easily.
- **Discontinuous Capillaries:** Present in the liver and spleen, these capillaries have large gaps, permitting the passage of larger molecules and cells.

Transport Mechanisms:

- **Passive Diffusion:** Toxins move across cell membranes from areas of higher concentration to lower concentration. Lipid-soluble toxins diffuse more readily through the lipid bilayer of cell membranes.
- **Active Transport:** Some toxins are transported into cells via active transport mechanisms, involving specific carrier proteins and energy expenditure.
- **Facilitated Diffusion:** Carrier proteins facilitate the movement of toxins across cell membranes without using energy, driven by concentration gradients.
- **Endocytosis:** Cells engulf toxins through endocytosis, forming vesicles that transport the toxins into the cell. This mechanism is important for large molecules and particulate matter.

6.2.2 Factors Influencing Distribution

Factors Influencing Distribution involve various characteristics of the toxin and the physiological state of the body, affecting how toxins are distributed to different tissues and organs.

Physicochemical Properties of the Toxin:

- **Molecular Size:** Smaller molecules distribute more easily through capillary walls and cell membranes compared to larger molecules.
- **Lipid Solubility:** Lipid-soluble toxins readily cross cell membranes and are distributed to tissues with high lipid content, such as the brain and adipose tissue.
- **Ionization State:** The degree of ionization affects a toxin's ability to cross cell membranes. Non-ionized (neutral) molecules cross membranes more easily than ionized molecules.

Tissue Perfusion:

- **Highly Perfused Tissues:** Organs with high blood flow, such as the liver, kidneys, brain, and heart, receive a significant amount of the toxin quickly after absorption.
- **Less Perfused Tissues:** Tissues with lower blood flow, such as muscle and fat, receive the toxin more slowly. Redistribution to these tissues occurs over time.

Plasma Protein Binding:

- **Extent of Binding:** The proportion of the toxin bound to plasma proteins affects the free fraction available for distribution. Highly protein-bound toxins have a limited free fraction, reducing their immediate distribution to tissues.
- **Reversible Binding:** Binding to plasma proteins is usually reversible, allowing a dynamic equilibrium between bound and unbound toxin. Changes in binding dynamics can influence distribution.

Barriers to Distribution:

- **Blood-Brain Barrier (BBB):** The BBB restricts the passage of many toxins into the brain, protecting the central nervous system. Only lipid-soluble or actively transported toxins can cross the BBB easily.
- **Placental Barrier:** The placental barrier provides partial protection to the fetus from maternal toxins, although many substances can still cross and affect fetal development.

Tissue Affinity:

- **Tissue Binding:** Some toxins have a high affinity for specific tissues, leading to accumulation. For example, lead accumulates in bones, and certain pesticides accumulate in adipose tissue.
- **Receptor Interactions:** Toxins that interact with specific cellular receptors may have targeted distribution based on receptor availability in different tissues.

Pathophysiological Conditions:

- **Disease States:** Conditions such as liver or kidney disease can alter toxin distribution by affecting blood flow, plasma protein levels, and tissue permeability.
- **Age and Development:** Age-related changes, such as decreased plasma protein levels in neonates or altered blood-brain barrier function in the elderly, can influence toxin distribution.
- **Body Composition:** Variations in body fat and muscle mass affect the distribution of lipid-soluble and water-soluble toxins, respectively.

Drug Interactions:

- **Competitive Binding:** Co-administered drugs that bind to the same plasma proteins can displace toxins, increasing the free fraction available for distribution.
- **Metabolic Interactions:** Drugs that induce or inhibit metabolic enzymes can alter the distribution of toxins by affecting their metabolism and subsequent availability for distribution.

6.3 Metabolism

6.3.1 Mechanisms of Metabolism

Mechanisms of Metabolism refer to the biochemical processes by which the body transforms toxins into more water-soluble compounds that can be more easily excreted. These processes primarily occur in the liver but can also take place in other tissues such as the kidneys, lungs, and intestines. Metabolism of toxins generally occurs in two phases: Phase I and Phase II reactions.

Phase I Reactions:

- **Oxidation:** These reactions involve the addition of oxygen or the removal of hydrogen from the toxin, typically catalyzed by the cytochrome P450 enzyme system (CYP450). Common oxidative reactions include hydroxylation, dealkylation, and deamination.

- ○ **Example:** The oxidation of ethanol to acetaldehyde by alcohol dehydrogenase.

- **Reduction:** These reactions involve the gain of electrons or hydrogen by the toxin. Reduction reactions are less common than oxidation and often occur in anaerobic environments or low oxygen conditions.

  - ○ **Example:** The reduction of nitro compounds to amines.

- **Hydrolysis:** These reactions involve the cleavage of bonds by the addition of water, typically catalyzed by esterases, amidases, and other hydrolases.

  - ○ **Example:** The hydrolysis of aspirin (acetylsalicylic acid) to salicylic acid and acetic acid.

Phase II Reactions:

- **Conjugation:** Phase II reactions involve the addition of endogenous substrates to the toxin or its Phase I metabolites, making them more water-soluble and easier to excrete.

  - ○ **Glucuronidation:** Addition of glucuronic acid, catalyzed by UDP-glucuronosyltransferase (UGT).
  - ○ **Sulfation:** Addition of sulfate groups, catalyzed by sulfotransferases.
  - ○ **Acetylation:** Addition of acetyl groups, catalyzed by N-acetyltransferases.
  - ○ **Glutathione Conjugation:** Addition of glutathione, catalyzed by glutathione S-transferase.

These metabolic reactions transform lipophilic toxins into hydrophilic metabolites, which can be readily excreted by the kidneys or through bile.

6.3.2 Factors Influencing Metabolism

Factors Influencing Metabolism encompass a variety of physiological, genetic, and environmental factors that can affect the rate and efficiency of toxin metabolism.

Genetic Factors:

- **Genetic Polymorphisms:** Variations in genes encoding metabolic enzymes can lead to differences in metabolic activity. For instance, polymorphisms in the CYP450 enzymes can result in individuals being classified as poor, intermediate, extensive, or ultra-rapid metabolizers.

  - ◦ **Example:** CYP2D6 polymorphisms can affect the metabolism of drugs like codeine and its conversion to morphine.

Age:

- **Neonates and Infants:** Immature liver enzyme systems in neonates and infants can lead to slower metabolism and prolonged effects of toxins.

  - ◦ **Example:** The deficiency of UDP-glucuronosyltransferase in newborns can cause prolonged jaundice due to inefficient bilirubin conjugation.

- **Elderly:** Aging can reduce the metabolic capacity due to decreased liver size, blood flow, and enzyme activity.

  - ◦ **Example:** Decreased Phase I enzyme activity in elderly individuals can slow the metabolism of certain medications and toxins.

Sex:

- **Sex Differences:** Hormonal differences between males and females can influence the expression and activity of certain metabolic enzymes.

  - ◦ **Example:** Female sex hormones can modulate the activity of CYP3A4, affecting the metabolism of various drugs and toxins.

Diet and Nutrition:

- **Dietary Influences:** Certain foods and nutrients can induce or inhibit metabolic enzymes, affecting toxin metabolism.

- ◦ **Induction:** Cruciferous vegetables and charbroiled meats can induce CYP1A2, increasing the metabolism of some drugs.
- ◦ **Inhibition:** Grapefruit juice contains compounds that inhibit CYP3A4, leading to decreased metabolism of certain toxins and drugs.

Disease States:

- **Liver Disease:** Conditions such as hepatitis, cirrhosis, or liver cancer can impair hepatic metabolism, reducing the clearance of toxins.

  - ◦ **Example:** Cirrhosis can decrease the activity of CYP450 enzymes, leading to the accumulation of toxins and drugs.

- **Renal Disease:** Impaired renal function can affect the excretion of metabolites, leading to their accumulation and potential toxicity.

  - ◦ **Example:** Chronic kidney disease can reduce the elimination of conjugated metabolites, prolonging their effects.

Environmental Factors:

- **Exposure to Chemicals:** Environmental pollutants and chemicals, such as industrial solvents and pesticides, can induce or inhibit metabolic enzymes.

  - ◦ **Induction:** Exposure to polycyclic aromatic hydrocarbons (PAHs) can induce CYP1A1 and CYP1B1, affecting toxin metabolism.
  - ◦ **Inhibition:** Heavy metals like lead and mercury can inhibit various metabolic enzymes, reducing toxin clearance.

Drug Interactions:

- **Inducers and Inhibitors:** Concurrent use of drugs that induce or inhibit metabolic enzymes can significantly alter the metabolism of toxins.

  - ◦ **Induction:** Rifampin, an antibiotic, induces CYP3A4, increasing the metabolism of drugs and toxins.

- ○ **Inhibition:** Ketoconazole, an antifungal, inhibits CYP3A4, decreasing the metabolism of many substances.

Physiological Conditions:

- **Pregnancy:** Hormonal changes and increased blood volume during pregnancy can affect the metabolism of toxins.

  - ○ **Example:** Increased activity of CYP2D6 and CYP3A4 during pregnancy can enhance the metabolism of certain drugs.

6.4 Excretion

6.4.1 Mechanisms of Excretion

Mechanisms of Excretion involve the processes by which toxins and their metabolites are eliminated from the body. Excretion is a critical component of toxicokinetics, as it determines how long a toxin remains in the body and continues to exert its effects. The primary organs involved in excretion are the kidneys, liver, lungs, and to a lesser extent, the skin and gastrointestinal tract.

Renal Excretion:

- **Glomerular Filtration:** Blood is filtered through the glomeruli in the kidneys, allowing small, water-soluble molecules and unbound toxins to pass into the filtrate, forming urine. The rate of glomerular filtration depends on the blood flow to the kidneys and the integrity of the glomerular filtration barrier.

  - ○ **Example:** Small, hydrophilic toxins like methanol and ethylene glycol are efficiently excreted through glomerular filtration.

- **Tubular Secretion:** Toxins and metabolites that did not enter the filtrate through glomerular filtration can be actively secreted into the renal tubules from the peritubular capillaries. This process involves specific transporter proteins and energy expenditure.

- ◦ **Example:** Organic acids and bases, such as penicillin and morphine, are actively secreted into the renal tubules.

- **Tubular Reabsorption:** Some toxins and metabolites may be reabsorbed from the tubular fluid back into the bloodstream, depending on their lipid solubility and ionization state. Urinary pH can influence reabsorption; for example, alkaline urine enhances the excretion of weak acids by reducing their reabsorption.

  - ◦ **Example:** Weak acids like salicylates are reabsorbed less in alkaline urine, promoting their excretion.

Hepatic Excretion:

- **Biliary Excretion:** The liver plays a significant role in excreting toxins via bile. Hepatocytes secrete conjugated metabolites into the bile, which is then transported to the gallbladder and released into the intestines. Toxins can be eliminated in feces or undergo enterohepatic recirculation if reabsorbed from the intestines.

  - ◦ **Example:** Conjugated bilirubin and certain drug metabolites are excreted into the bile.

- **Enterohepatic Recirculation:** Some toxins and metabolites excreted in bile can be reabsorbed in the intestines and returned to the liver via the portal circulation. This recycling process can prolong the presence of the toxin in the body.

  - ◦ **Example:** Enterohepatic recirculation of estrogen metabolites can extend their biological activity.

Pulmonary Excretion:

- **Exhalation:** Volatile substances and gases can be excreted through the lungs by diffusion across the alveolar-capillary membrane. The rate of pulmonary excretion depends on the concentration gradient between the blood and alveolar air and the blood flow to the lungs.

- **Example:** Alcohol, anesthetic gases, and volatile solvents like benzene are excreted through exhalation.

Gastrointestinal Excretion:

- **Direct Excretion into the Gut:** Some toxins can be directly excreted into the gastrointestinal tract from the bloodstream. This mechanism is less common but can be significant for certain substances.

  - **Example:** Heavy metals like mercury can be excreted into the intestines and eliminated in feces.

Other Routes of Excretion:

- **Sweat and Saliva:** Minor routes of excretion include sweat and saliva. Toxins excreted in sweat can cause skin irritation, while those in saliva may lead to a metallic taste or other oral symptoms.

  - **Example:** Small amounts of drugs like amphetamines can be excreted in sweat and saliva.

- **Milk:** Lactating mothers can excrete toxins into breast milk, posing a risk to nursing infants. The excretion into milk depends on the toxin's lipid solubility and protein binding.

  - **Example:** Lipid-soluble drugs like diazepam can be excreted into breast milk.

6.4 Excretion

6.4.2 Factors Influencing Excretion

Factors Influencing Excretion include various physiological, biochemical, and external factors that affect how efficiently toxins and their metabolites are eliminated from the body. Understanding these factors is essential for predicting the duration of toxic effects and for designing effective treatment strategies.

Physiological Factors:

- **Renal Function:** The efficiency of renal excretion is directly related to kidney function. Conditions like chronic kidney disease (CKD) or acute kidney injury (AKI) can significantly reduce the elimination of toxins, leading to prolonged toxicity.

  - **Example:** Impaired renal function in patients with CKD can lead to the accumulation of drugs like digoxin, requiring dose adjustments.

- **Hepatic Function:** Liver health is crucial for the metabolism and subsequent excretion of many toxins. Liver diseases such as hepatitis or cirrhosis can impair hepatic metabolism and biliary excretion, leading to increased toxicity.

  - **Example:** Reduced hepatic function in cirrhosis can impair the excretion of bilirubin, leading to jaundice.

- **Age:** Both very young and elderly individuals often have reduced excretory capacity. Neonates have immature renal and hepatic functions, while elderly individuals may experience age-related declines in kidney and liver function.

  - **Example:** Newborns have immature glucuronidation pathways, affecting the excretion of drugs like chloramphenicol, which can lead to "gray baby syndrome."

- **Body Fluid pH:** The pH of body fluids, particularly urine, can influence the excretion of weak acids and bases. Alkaline urine enhances the excretion of weak acids by ionizing them, while acidic urine promotes the excretion of weak bases.

  - **Example:** Alkalinizing the urine with sodium bicarbonate is used to enhance the excretion of salicylates in cases of overdose.

Biochemical Factors:

- **Protein Binding:** Toxins that are highly bound to plasma proteins have a reduced free fraction available for filtration and excretion. Only the unbound fraction is freely filtered by the kidneys.

  - **Example:** Warfarin is highly protein-bound, limiting its renal excretion.

- **Molecular Size and Lipid Solubility:** Small, water-soluble molecules are more readily excreted by the kidneys, while larger, lipid-soluble molecules may require metabolism to more water-soluble forms before excretion.

  - **Example:** Lipid-soluble drugs like diazepam undergo hepatic metabolism to form more water-soluble metabolites for renal excretion.

- **Transporter Proteins:** Specific transport proteins in the kidneys and liver facilitate the secretion and reabsorption of various toxins and drugs. Genetic variations or drug interactions can affect the function of these transporters.

  - **Example:** P-glycoprotein is a transporter that pumps drugs out of cells and can influence the excretion of drugs like digoxin.

External Factors:

- **Drug Interactions:** Concurrent use of multiple drugs can affect the excretion of toxins through competition for the same transporters or enzymes, or through changes in urine pH.

  - **Example:** Probenecid inhibits the renal excretion of penicillin, prolonging its plasma levels and therapeutic effects.

- **Hydration Status:** Adequate hydration enhances renal excretion by increasing urine flow and dilution of toxins. Dehydration can reduce renal perfusion and urine output, slowing toxin elimination.

- ◦ **Example:** Adequate hydration is crucial for patients receiving methotrexate to prevent renal toxicity.

- **Diet and Nutrition:** Certain dietary components can influence the excretion of toxins. For example, a high-protein diet can acidify the urine, affecting the excretion of weak bases.

  - ◦ **Example:** A diet rich in green vegetables can alkalinize the urine, enhancing the excretion of weak acids.

- **Environmental Factors:** Exposure to environmental toxins, such as heavy metals, can saturate excretory pathways, reducing the body's ability to eliminate other toxins.

  - ◦ **Example:** Chronic exposure to lead can impair renal function, reducing the excretion of other nephrotoxic substances.

Pathophysiological Conditions:

- **Infections and Inflammation:** Conditions that affect the kidneys or liver, such as infections or inflammatory diseases, can impair the excretion of toxins.

  - ◦ **Example:** Acute pyelonephritis can impair renal function and reduce the excretion of drugs like aminoglycosides.

- **Genetic Disorders:** Genetic disorders affecting metabolic enzymes or transport proteins can significantly alter the excretion of toxins.

  - ◦ **Example:** Individuals with Gilbert's syndrome have a deficiency in glucuronosyltransferase, affecting the excretion of bilirubin and certain drugs.

6.5 Factors Affecting Toxicokinetics

6.5.1 Age and Gender

Age:

- **Neonates and Infants:**

  - **Absorption:** Gastrointestinal absorption is variable due to immature digestive enzymes and altered gastric pH. Dermal absorption is higher due to thinner skin.
  - **Distribution:** Higher body water content and lower fat content influence the distribution of hydrophilic and lipophilic toxins, respectively. Plasma protein binding is reduced due to lower albumin levels.
  - **Metabolism:** Liver enzyme activity is immature, leading to slower metabolism of many toxins.
  - **Excretion:** Renal function is immature, reducing glomerular filtration, tubular secretion, and reabsorption.

- **Elderly:**

  - **Absorption:** Gastrointestinal motility and blood flow decrease with age, potentially altering absorption rates.
  - **Distribution:** Increased body fat and decreased lean body mass affect the distribution of lipophilic and hydrophilic substances. Plasma protein binding may be reduced due to lower albumin levels.
  - **Metabolism:** Hepatic enzyme activity and liver blood flow decline, slowing the metabolism of many toxins.
  - **Excretion:** Renal function declines, reducing the clearance of toxins.

Gender:

- **Hormonal Differences:** Sex hormones influence the expression and activity of metabolic enzymes and transporters. For example, estrogen and progesterone can modulate CYP450 enzyme activity.
- **Body Composition:** Women generally have higher body fat percentages, affecting the distribution of lipophilic toxins. Men typically have higher lean body mass, influencing the distribution of hydrophilic toxins.

- **Renal Function:** Glomerular filtration rate (GFR) may differ slightly between genders, influencing renal excretion rates.

6.5.2 Genetic Factors

- **Genetic Polymorphisms:** Variations in genes encoding metabolic enzymes, transporters, and receptors can lead to differences in toxin metabolism and excretion among individuals.

  - **CYP450 Enzymes:** Polymorphisms in CYP2D6, CYP2C19, and CYP2C9 can lead to variations in the metabolism of many drugs and toxins, resulting in poor, intermediate, extensive, or ultra-rapid metabolizer phenotypes.
  - **Transport Proteins:** Variations in genes encoding transporters like P-glycoprotein (ABCB1) and organic anion transporters (OATs) can affect the uptake and efflux of toxins in tissues and organs.

- **Metabolic Enzymes:**

  - **UDP-Glucuronosyltransferases (UGTs):** Polymorphisms in UGT1A1 can affect the glucuronidation and excretion of bilirubin and drugs like irinotecan.
  - **N-Acetyltransferases (NATs):** Polymorphisms in NAT2 can lead to slow or fast acetylator phenotypes, affecting the metabolism of drugs like isoniazid.

- **Receptor Variants:** Genetic variations in receptors can alter sensitivity to toxins and influence their toxicokinetic profiles.

6.5.3 Disease States

Liver Disease:

- **Cirrhosis and Hepatitis:** These conditions impair hepatic metabolism and reduce the clearance of many toxins. Liver dysfunction can alter the synthesis of plasma proteins, affecting toxin binding and distribution.

- **Liver Enzyme Activity:** Enzyme activity may be reduced, leading to slower Phase I and Phase II reactions, which impairs the detoxification process.

Kidney Disease:

- **Chronic Kidney Disease (CKD):** Reduced glomerular filtration, tubular secretion, and reabsorption impair renal excretion of toxins. Accumulation of uremic toxins can interfere with the metabolism and excretion of other substances.
- **Acute Kidney Injury (AKI):** Sudden loss of renal function can lead to rapid accumulation of toxins and their metabolites, requiring immediate medical intervention.

Cardiovascular Disease:

- **Heart Failure:** Reduced cardiac output decreases blood flow to the liver and kidneys, impairing the metabolism and excretion of toxins.
- **Peripheral Edema:** Fluid accumulation can alter the distribution of hydrophilic toxins.

Endocrine Disorders:

- **Diabetes:** Diabetic nephropathy can impair renal function, while alterations in glucose metabolism can influence the metabolism of certain toxins.
- **Thyroid Disorders:** Hyperthyroidism and hypothyroidism can affect the metabolism and distribution of toxins due to changes in metabolic rate and protein binding.

Respiratory Disease:

- **Chronic Obstructive Pulmonary Disease (COPD):** Impaired pulmonary function can reduce the excretion of volatile toxins and affect the overall metabolic capacity.

Gastrointestinal Disorders:

- **Malabsorption Syndromes:** Conditions like celiac disease or Crohn's disease can alter the absorption of toxins and nutrients, influencing their toxicokinetic profiles.

Chapter 7: Clinical Symptoms and Management of Acute Poisoning

Introduction

Acute poisoning is a critical medical emergency that requires prompt recognition and management to prevent severe morbidity and mortality. The clinical presentation of acute poisoning can vary widely depending on the type of toxin, the route of exposure, the dose, and the patient's individual characteristics. Understanding the clinical symptoms and appropriate management strategies is crucial for healthcare providers to effectively address poisoning cases.

Acute poisoning can result from various substances, including pharmaceuticals, household chemicals, industrial agents, environmental toxins, and biological agents. The symptoms can range from mild, nonspecific complaints to severe, life-threatening conditions. Effective management involves a systematic approach to assessment, stabilization, diagnosis, and treatment.

Scope of the Chapter

This chapter will cover the following key areas:

1. **Clinical Symptoms:**

   - Identification of common and specific clinical signs and symptoms associated with various types of poisoning.
   - Understanding the pathophysiology behind the symptoms to aid in accurate diagnosis and management.

2. **Initial Assessment and Stabilization:**

- A systematic approach to the initial assessment of poisoned patients, focusing on airway, breathing, and circulation (ABCs).
- Rapid identification of life-threatening conditions and implementation of immediate stabilization measures.

3. Diagnosis:

- Strategies for obtaining a detailed patient history, including exposure history and previous medical conditions.
- Utilization of laboratory tests, imaging studies, and toxicology screens to identify the causative agent and assess the severity of poisoning.

4. Decontamination:

- Techniques for removing or neutralizing the toxin from the patient's body, including activated charcoal, gastric lavage, and whole bowel irrigation.
- Indications, contraindications, and potential complications of each decontamination method.

5. Supportive Care:

- Providing symptomatic and supportive care tailored to the specific needs of the poisoned patient.
- Monitoring vital signs, fluid and electrolyte balance, and organ function to prevent and manage complications.

6. Specific Antidotes:

- Overview of commonly used antidotes for specific toxins, including their mechanisms of action, indications, and administration protocols.
- Case studies highlighting the use of antidotes in real-world clinical scenarios.

7. Elimination Enhancement:

- ◦ Methods to enhance the elimination of toxins from the body, such as urinary alkalinization, hemodialysis, hemoperfusion, and peritoneal dialysis.
- ◦ Indications, techniques, and potential complications of each method.

8. **Prevention and Education:**

- ◦ Strategies for preventing poisoning incidents through public education, safe storage of hazardous substances, and regulatory measures.
- ◦ Importance of educating patients and caregivers about the risks and management of potential poisoning exposures.

Importance of Understanding Clinical Symptoms and Management

Effective management of acute poisoning requires a thorough understanding of the clinical symptoms and appropriate treatment protocols. Prompt recognition and intervention can significantly improve patient outcomes by preventing the progression of poisoning and minimizing complications. Healthcare providers must be equipped with the knowledge and skills to:

- **Identify Toxic Syndromes:** Recognize patterns of symptoms that suggest specific types of poisoning, enabling timely and accurate diagnosis.
- **Stabilize Patients:** Implement immediate stabilization measures to address life-threatening conditions and maintain vital functions.
- **Administer Appropriate Treatments:** Utilize the correct decontamination methods, supportive care, antidotes, and elimination enhancement techniques based on the specific toxin and patient condition.
- **Educate and Prevent:** Provide education to patients, families, and communities to prevent poisoning incidents and promote safe practices.

7.1 Pesticide Poisoning

7.1.1 Organophosphorous Compounds

Organophosphorous (OP) compounds are a group of pesticides that inhibit acetylcholinesterase, an enzyme responsible for breaking down acetylcholine in the nervous system. The accumulation of acetylcholine leads to overstimulation of cholinergic receptors, resulting in a wide range of clinical symptoms.

7.1.1.1 Clinical Symptoms

The clinical symptoms of organophosphorous poisoning can be divided into three categories: muscarinic, nicotinic, and central nervous system (CNS) effects. The onset of symptoms can be rapid, occurring within minutes to hours after exposure.

Muscarinic Effects:

- **Respiratory Symptoms:**

  - **Bronchorrhea:** Excessive secretion of mucus in the airways.
  - **Bronchospasm:** Constriction of the bronchi, leading to difficulty in breathing.
  - **Dyspnea:** Shortness of breath due to increased secretions and bronchospasm.

- **Gastrointestinal Symptoms:**

  - **Salivation:** Excessive salivation.
  - **Lacrimation:** Increased tearing.
  - **Diarrhea:** Watery stools due to increased gastrointestinal motility.
  - **Vomiting:** Stimulation of the emetic center in the brain.

- **Ophthalmic Symptoms:**

  - **Miosis:** Constriction of the pupils.
  - **Blurred Vision:** Due to the constriction of the pupils and increased tear production.

- **Cardiovascular Symptoms:**

- ◦ **Bradycardia:** Slowed heart rate.
- ◦ **Hypotension:** Low blood pressure due to vasodilation.

Nicotinic Effects:

- **Muscle Weakness:** Due to overstimulation of the nicotinic receptors at the neuromuscular junction.
- **Fasciculations:** Involuntary muscle twitching.
- **Paralysis:** Severe cases can lead to paralysis, including respiratory muscles, necessitating mechanical ventilation.

CNS Effects:

- **Anxiety:** Increased restlessness and nervousness.
- **Confusion:** Mental disorientation.
- **Seizures:** Due to overstimulation of the CNS.
- **Coma:** Severe poisoning can lead to loss of consciousness and coma.

7.1.1.2 Management Strategies

The management of organophosphorous poisoning involves a combination of supportive care, decontamination, and specific antidotal therapy. Prompt recognition and treatment are crucial to improve outcomes.

Supportive Care:

- **Airway Management:** Ensure a clear airway and provide oxygen. Mechanical ventilation may be necessary in cases of respiratory failure.
- **Cardiovascular Support:** Monitor heart rate and blood pressure. Administer intravenous fluids and vasopressors if needed to maintain blood pressure.

Decontamination:

- **Skin Decontamination:** Remove contaminated clothing and wash the skin thoroughly with soap and water to reduce dermal absorption of the toxin.
- **Gastric Lavage:** Consider gastric lavage if the patient presents within one hour of ingestion, especially if a large amount of pesticide has been

ingested. Ensure airway protection before performing gastric lavage.

- **Activated Charcoal:** Administer activated charcoal to reduce gastrointestinal absorption if the patient is alert and within one hour of ingestion.

Antidotal Therapy:

- **Atropine:** Atropine is a muscarinic antagonist that counteracts the muscarinic effects of acetylcholine. Administer an initial dose of 2-5 mg IV in adults (0.05 mg/kg in children), repeating every 5-10 minutes until secretions are dry, and bradycardia is resolved. Higher doses may be required in severe cases.
- **Pralidoxime (2-PAM):** Pralidoxime reactivates acetylcholinesterase by removing the organophosphorous compound from the enzyme. Administer an initial dose of 1-2 g IV in adults (20-50 mg/kg in children), followed by a continuous infusion if necessary. Repeat dosing may be required based on the clinical response.
- **Benzodiazepines:** Administer benzodiazepines, such as diazepam, to control seizures and reduce CNS agitation.

Monitoring and Follow-Up:

- **Vital Signs:** Continuously monitor vital signs, including heart rate, blood pressure, respiratory rate, and oxygen saturation.
- **Neurological Status:** Regularly assess the patient's neurological status, including mental status, muscle strength, and reflexes.
- **Laboratory Tests:** Perform serial blood tests to monitor acetylcholinesterase activity, electrolyte levels, and organ function.

Preventive Measures:

- **Education:** Educate patients and communities about the safe use and storage of pesticides to prevent accidental poisoning.
- **Personal Protective Equipment (PPE):** Encourage the use of PPE, such as gloves and masks, when handling pesticides.
- **Regulation:** Advocate for the regulation and control of organophosphorous pesticides to reduce the risk of poisoning.

7.1 Pesticide Poisoning

7.1.2 Carbamates

Carbamates are a class of pesticides similar to organophosphates in their mechanism of action but with some key differences in their clinical presentation and management. Like organophosphates, carbamates inhibit acetylcholinesterase, leading to an accumulation of acetylcholine and subsequent overstimulation of cholinergic receptors. However, carbamate poisoning tends to be less severe and of shorter duration compared to organophosphate poisoning because carbamates bind reversibly to acetylcholinesterase.

7.1.2.1 Clinical Symptoms

The clinical symptoms of carbamate poisoning are similar to those of organophosphate poisoning and can be categorized into muscarinic, nicotinic, and central nervous system (CNS) effects. Symptoms usually manifest within minutes to hours of exposure.

Muscarinic Effects:

- **Respiratory Symptoms:**

  - **Bronchorrhea:** Increased mucus production in the airways.
  - **Bronchospasm:** Constriction of the bronchial muscles, causing difficulty in breathing.
  - **Dyspnea:** Shortness of breath due to increased secretions and bronchospasm.

- **Gastrointestinal Symptoms:**

  - **Salivation:** Excessive production of saliva.
  - **Lacrimation:** Increased tear production.
  - **Diarrhea:** Frequent, watery bowel movements.
  - **Vomiting:** Expulsion of stomach contents through the mouth.

- **Ophthalmic Symptoms:**

- ◦ **Miosis:** Constriction of the pupils, leading to blurred vision.
- ◦ **Blurred Vision:** Due to pupil constriction and increased tear production.

- **Cardiovascular Symptoms:**

  - ◦ **Bradycardia:** Slow heart rate.
  - ◦ **Hypotension:** Low blood pressure due to vasodilation.

Nicotinic Effects:

- **Muscle Weakness:** Generalized muscle weakness due to overstimulation of nicotinic receptors at the neuromuscular junction.
- **Fasciculations:** Involuntary muscle twitching.
- **Paralysis:** Severe cases may lead to paralysis, including respiratory muscles, necessitating mechanical ventilation.

CNS Effects:

- **Anxiety:** Increased nervousness and restlessness.
- **Confusion:** Disorientation and difficulty in thinking clearly.
- **Seizures:** Convulsions due to excessive stimulation of the central nervous system.
- **Coma:** Loss of consciousness in severe poisoning cases.

7.1.2.2 Management Strategies

The management of carbamate poisoning involves supportive care, decontamination, and specific antidotal therapy. Given that carbamate poisoning tends to be less severe and shorter in duration than organophosphate poisoning, the management strategies are tailored accordingly.

Supportive Care:

- **Airway Management:** Ensure a clear airway and provide supplemental oxygen. Mechanical ventilation may be required in cases of severe respiratory compromise.
- **Cardiovascular Support:** Monitor heart rate and blood pressure. Administer intravenous fluids and vasopressors if necessary to maintain

adequate blood pressure.

Decontamination:

- **Skin Decontamination:** Remove contaminated clothing and wash the skin thoroughly with soap and water to reduce further absorption of the toxin.
- **Gastric Lavage:** Consider gastric lavage if the patient presents within one hour of ingestion, especially if a large amount of carbamate has been ingested. Ensure airway protection before performing gastric lavage.
- **Activated Charcoal:** Administer activated charcoal to reduce gastrointestinal absorption if the patient is alert and presents within one hour of ingestion.

Antidotal Therapy:

- **Atropine:** Atropine is a muscarinic antagonist that counteracts the muscarinic effects of acetylcholine. Administer an initial dose of 1-2 mg IV in adults (0.05 mg/kg in children), repeating every 5-10 minutes until secretions are dry and bradycardia is resolved. Higher doses may be required in severe cases.
- **Pralidoxime (2-PAM):** Unlike in organophosphate poisoning, pralidoxime is generally not indicated in carbamate poisoning because carbamates bind reversibly to acetylcholinesterase, and the enzyme reactivates spontaneously. However, in cases of severe poisoning where differentiation from organophosphate poisoning is unclear, pralidoxime may be administered.

Monitoring and Follow-Up:

- **Vital Signs:** Continuously monitor vital signs, including heart rate, blood pressure, respiratory rate, and oxygen saturation.
- **Neurological Status:** Regularly assess the patient's neurological status, including mental status, muscle strength, and reflexes.
- **Laboratory Tests:** Perform serial blood tests to monitor acetylcholinesterase activity, electrolyte levels, and organ function.

Preventive Measures:

- **Education:** Educate patients and communities about the safe use and storage of carbamate pesticides to prevent accidental poisoning.
- **Personal Protective Equipment (PPE):** Encourage the use of PPE, such as gloves and masks, when handling carbamate pesticides.
- **Regulation:** Advocate for the regulation and control of carbamate pesticides to reduce the risk of poisoning.

7.1 Pesticide Poisoning

7.1.3 Organochlorines

Organochlorines are a class of pesticides known for their environmental persistence and bioaccumulation in the food chain. These compounds include well-known pesticides such as DDT, chlordane, and lindane. They exert their toxic effects primarily by interfering with the normal function of the nervous system, particularly by prolonging the opening of sodium channels in nerve cells, leading to prolonged depolarization and subsequent neurotoxicity.

7.1.3.1 Clinical Symptoms

The clinical symptoms of organochlorine poisoning can vary depending on the level and duration of exposure. Symptoms may appear acutely or after chronic exposure due to the cumulative nature of these compounds.

Acute Exposure Symptoms:

- **Neurological Symptoms:**

  - **Seizures:** Prolonged depolarization of neurons can lead to seizures, which may be difficult to control.
  - **Tremors:** Muscle twitching and tremors due to overstimulation of nerves.
  - **Hyperexcitability:** Increased sensitivity to stimuli, resulting in exaggerated reflexes and restlessness.
  - **Dizziness and Headache:** General symptoms of central nervous system irritation.

- **Gastrointestinal Symptoms:**

- ○ **Nausea and Vomiting:** Common symptoms due to the irritative effects of organochlorines on the gastrointestinal tract.
- ○ **Abdominal Pain:** Discomfort and pain due to toxin exposure.

- **Dermatological Symptoms:**

- ○ **Rashes:** Skin irritation and rashes can occur upon dermal exposure.

Chronic Exposure Symptoms:

- **Neurological Symptoms:**

- ○ **Peripheral Neuropathy:** Long-term exposure can lead to sensory and motor deficits.
- ○ **Cognitive Impairment:** Memory loss, confusion, and other cognitive deficits due to chronic neurotoxicity.

- **Endocrine Disruption:**

- ○ **Hormonal Imbalances:** Organochlorines can interfere with endocrine function, leading to reproductive and metabolic disorders.

- **Carcinogenic Effects:**

- ○ **Increased Cancer Risk:** Chronic exposure to certain organochlorines is associated with an increased risk of cancers, particularly liver and breast cancer.

7.1.3.2 Management Strategies

Management of organochlorine poisoning involves supportive care, decontamination, and specific interventions to manage symptoms. Due to their persistence and bioaccumulation, long-term monitoring may also be necessary.

Supportive Care:

- **Neurological Support:**

- **Seizure Management:** Administer benzodiazepines such as diazepam or lorazepam to control seizures. Refractory seizures may require additional anticonvulsants like phenobarbital.
- **Monitoring:** Continuous monitoring of neurological status is essential to detect and manage ongoing neurotoxic effects.

- **Gastrointestinal Support:**

  - **Antiemetics:** Administer antiemetics such as ondansetron to control nausea and vomiting.
  - **Fluid and Electrolyte Balance:** Ensure adequate hydration and correct any electrolyte imbalances caused by vomiting or diarrhea.

Decontamination:

- **Skin Decontamination:**

  - **Immediate Washing:** Remove contaminated clothing and wash the skin thoroughly with soap and water to reduce further absorption.
  - **Activated Charcoal:** Administer activated charcoal if ingestion occurred within an hour and the patient is alert, to limit gastrointestinal absorption.

Specific Interventions:

- **Seizure Control:**

  - **Benzodiazepines:** Administer benzodiazepines for initial seizure control.
  - **Additional Anticonvulsants:** Use phenobarbital or phenytoin if seizures are refractory to benzodiazepines.

- **Monitoring and Follow-Up:**

  - **Vital Signs:** Continuous monitoring of vital signs, including heart rate, blood pressure, and respiratory rate, to manage acute symptoms.
  - **Neurological Assessments:** Regular neurological assessments to detect changes in mental status, seizure activity, and other neurotoxic

effects.

- ○ **Laboratory Tests:** Perform blood tests to monitor organ function and detect any metabolic abnormalities.

Preventive Measures:

- **Public Education:** Educate the public about the dangers of organochlorine exposure and the importance of proper handling and disposal.

  - ○ **Regulation:** Advocate for stricter regulations and monitoring of organochlorine use to minimize environmental contamination and human exposure.
  - ○ **Personal Protective Equipment (PPE):** Encourage the use of PPE, such as gloves and masks, when handling organochlorines to reduce the risk of exposure.

Long-Term Monitoring:

- **Neurological Monitoring:** Regular follow-up to monitor for long-term neurological effects, such as peripheral neuropathy and cognitive impairment.
- **Cancer Screening:** Periodic screening for cancers associated with chronic organochlorine exposure, particularly liver and breast cancer.

7.1 Pesticide Poisoning

7.1.4 Pyrethroids

Pyrethroids are a class of synthetic insecticides modeled after natural pyrethrins derived from chrysanthemum flowers. They are widely used due to their high insecticidal potency and relatively low toxicity to humans. However, in cases of significant exposure, pyrethroids can cause acute toxicity, particularly affecting the nervous system.

7.1.4.1 Clinical Symptoms

The clinical symptoms of pyrethroid poisoning primarily involve the nervous system but can also include other systemic effects. Symptoms vary depending on the type of pyrethroid (Type I or Type II) and the level of exposure.

Type I Pyrethroids (e.g., permethrin, tetramethrin):

- **Neurological Symptoms:**

  - **Tremors:** Fine, involuntary muscle twitching and shaking.
  - **Hyperexcitability:** Increased sensitivity to stimuli, leading to exaggerated reflexes.
  - **Ataxia:** Lack of muscle coordination, resulting in unsteady movements.

- **Systemic Symptoms:**

  - **Nausea and Vomiting:** Common gastrointestinal symptoms due to systemic absorption.
  - **Respiratory Distress:** Mild respiratory symptoms such as coughing and throat irritation.

Type II Pyrethroids (e.g., cypermethrin, deltamethrin):

- **Neurological Symptoms:**

  - **Seizures:** Convulsions due to overstimulation of the nervous system.
  - **Paresthesia:** Tingling or burning sensation on the skin, particularly at the site of contact.
  - **Choreoathetosis:** Involuntary, writhing movements of the limbs and trunk.

- **Systemic Symptoms:**

  - **Salivation:** Increased production of saliva.
  - **Lacrimation:** Excessive tearing.
  - **Bradycardia:** Slow heart rate.

General Symptoms:

- **Dermal Symptoms:**

  - **Skin Irritation:** Redness, itching, and burning sensation at the site of exposure.
  - **Allergic Reactions:** In rare cases, contact dermatitis or urticaria.

- **Respiratory Symptoms:**

  - **Respiratory Irritation:** Coughing, wheezing, and shortness of breath due to inhalation of pyrethroid particles.

7.1.4.2 Management Strategies

Management of pyrethroid poisoning involves supportive care, decontamination, and symptom-specific treatments. Prompt recognition and appropriate management are crucial to minimize toxicity and improve outcomes.

Supportive Care:

- **Neurological Support:**

  - **Seizure Management:** Administer benzodiazepines such as diazepam or lorazepam to control seizures. Severe cases may require additional anticonvulsants like phenobarbital.
  - **Monitoring:** Continuous monitoring of neurological status is essential to detect and manage ongoing neurotoxic effects.

- **Respiratory Support:**

  - **Oxygen Therapy:** Provide supplemental oxygen to patients experiencing respiratory distress.
  - **Ventilatory Support:** Mechanical ventilation may be necessary in cases of severe respiratory compromise.

Decontamination:

- **Skin Decontamination:**

- **Immediate Washing:** Remove contaminated clothing and wash the skin thoroughly with soap and water to reduce further absorption.
- **Activated Charcoal:** Administer activated charcoal if ingestion occurred within an hour and the patient is alert, to limit gastrointestinal absorption.

Symptom-Specific Treatments:

- **Tremors and Hyperexcitability:**

  - **Benzodiazepines:** Administer benzodiazepines to reduce tremors and hyperexcitability.
  - **Antihistamines:** Use antihistamines to alleviate skin irritation and paresthesia.

- **Gastrointestinal Symptoms:**

  - **Antiemetics:** Administer antiemetics such as ondansetron to control nausea and vomiting.
  - **Hydration:** Ensure adequate hydration to prevent dehydration from vomiting.

- **Respiratory Symptoms:**

  - **Bronchodilators:** Use bronchodilators to relieve bronchospasm and improve airflow.
  - **Corticosteroids:** Administer corticosteroids in severe cases of respiratory irritation and inflammation.

Monitoring and Follow-Up:

- **Vital Signs:** Continuous monitoring of vital signs, including heart rate, blood pressure, respiratory rate, and oxygen saturation.
- **Neurological Assessments:** Regular neurological assessments to detect changes in mental status, seizure activity, and other neurotoxic effects.
- **Laboratory Tests:** Perform blood tests to monitor organ function and detect any metabolic abnormalities.

Preventive Measures:

- **Public Education:** Educate the public about the safe use and storage of pyrethroid pesticides to prevent accidental poisoning.
- **Personal Protective Equipment (PPE):** Encourage the use of PPE, such as gloves and masks, when handling pyrethroids to reduce the risk of exposure.
- **Regulation:** Advocate for stricter regulations and monitoring of pyrethroid use to minimize environmental contamination and human exposure.

7.2 Opiates Overdose

7.2.1 Clinical Symptoms

Opiates are a class of drugs that include natural, synthetic, and semi-synthetic compounds derived from the opium poppy or designed to mimic its effects. Common opiates include morphine, heroin, codeine, oxycodone, and fentanyl. Overdose of opiates can lead to a range of symptoms, primarily due to their depressant effects on the central nervous system (CNS) and respiratory system.

Central Nervous System Symptoms:

- **Depressed Mental Status:** Opiate overdose typically results in marked sedation, drowsiness, and lethargy. Patients may become unresponsive or difficult to arouse.
- **Coma:** In severe cases, opiate overdose can lead to profound unconsciousness or coma.
- **Miosis:** Pinpoint pupils are a classic sign of opiate overdose, though this may not be present in cases involving mixed drug overdoses.

Respiratory Symptoms:

- **Respiratory Depression:** A hallmark of opiate overdose is slowed or absent breathing. This can lead to hypoxia, hypercapnia, and potentially fatal respiratory arrest.

- **Cyanosis:** Blue discoloration of the skin and mucous membranes due to inadequate oxygenation of the blood.

Cardiovascular Symptoms:

- **Hypotension:** Low blood pressure may occur due to the vasodilatory effects of opiates.
- **Bradycardia:** Slowed heart rate is common, although in severe cases, the heart rate may become erratic or lead to cardiac arrest.

Gastrointestinal Symptoms:

- **Nausea and Vomiting:** Common symptoms due to the activation of the chemoreceptor trigger zone.
- **Decreased Bowel Sounds:** Opiates can reduce gastrointestinal motility, leading to constipation or ileus.

7.2.2 Management Strategies

The management of opiate overdose focuses on supportive care, the administration of specific antidotes, and addressing any complications that arise. Timely intervention is critical to prevent severe outcomes and fatalities.

Supportive Care:

- **Airway Management:** Ensure the patient's airway is open. Use the jaw-thrust maneuver if necessary, and consider placing an oropharyngeal or nasopharyngeal airway to maintain patency.
- **Breathing Support:** Administer supplemental oxygen to all patients with suspected opiate overdose. For patients with significant respiratory depression, provide assisted ventilation using a bag-valve mask. Endotracheal intubation and mechanical ventilation may be required in severe cases.
- **Circulatory Support:** Monitor blood pressure and heart rate. Administer intravenous fluids to treat hypotension. Vasopressors may be necessary if hypotension persists despite fluid resuscitation.

Antidotal Therapy:

- **Naloxone:** Naloxone is a competitive opioid receptor antagonist that rapidly reverses the effects of opiates. It can be administered intravenously, intramuscularly, subcutaneously, or intranasally.

  - **Initial Dose:** Administer 0.4 to 2 mg of naloxone IV, IM, or SC. If there is no response, repeat every 2 to 3 minutes, up to a total dose of 10 mg. For intranasal administration, 2 to 4 mg can be given, and repeated as necessary.
  - **Observation:** After naloxone administration, monitor the patient closely for recurrent respiratory depression, as the duration of action of naloxone is shorter than that of many opiates. Additional doses may be required.
  - **Infusion:** In cases of long-acting opiate overdose, a continuous infusion of naloxone may be necessary to maintain adequate ventilation.

Monitoring and Follow-Up:

- **Vital Signs:** Continuous monitoring of respiratory rate, oxygen saturation, heart rate, and blood pressure.
- **Neurological Status:** Regular assessments of the patient's level of consciousness and neurological status.
- **Laboratory Tests:** Perform blood tests, including arterial blood gases (ABGs), to assess oxygenation, ventilation, and acid-base status. Check electrolytes, glucose, and renal function to detect any metabolic abnormalities.

Preventive Measures:

- **Education and Awareness:** Educate patients, families, and communities about the risks of opiate use and overdose. Promote the availability of naloxone kits for individuals at risk of overdose.
- **Safe Prescribing Practices:** Encourage healthcare providers to follow guidelines for the safe prescribing of opiates and to consider alternative pain management strategies.

- **Substance Abuse Treatment:** Refer patients with opiate dependence to addiction treatment programs and provide resources for long-term support.

Long-Term Management:

- **Observation:** Patients who have received naloxone should be observed for at least 2 to 4 hours after the last dose to ensure that respiratory depression does not recur.
- **Psychosocial Support:** Offer counseling and support services to address underlying issues related to opiate use and addiction.
- **Harm Reduction:** Promote harm reduction strategies, such as needle exchange programs and supervised injection sites, to reduce the risk of overdose and other complications.

7.3 Antidepressants Overdose

7.3.1 Clinical Symptoms

Antidepressants are a diverse group of medications used to treat depression and other psychiatric disorders. Overdoses can be life-threatening and present with a wide range of symptoms depending on the class of antidepressant involved. The main classes include tricyclic antidepressants (TCAs), selective serotonin reuptake inhibitors (SSRIs), serotonin-norepinephrine reuptake inhibitors (SNRIs), and monoamine oxidase inhibitors (MAOIs).

Tricyclic Antidepressants (TCAs):

- **Neurological Symptoms:**

  - **Sedation:** Patients may present with drowsiness, confusion, and coma in severe cases.
  - **Seizures:** TCAs lower the seizure threshold, leading to convulsions.

- **Cardiovascular Symptoms:**

- ◦ **Tachycardia:** Increased heart rate.
- ◦ **Hypotension:** Low blood pressure due to vasodilation and reduced cardiac output.
- ◦ **Arrhythmias:** Life-threatening arrhythmias, including ventricular tachycardia and fibrillation.
- ◦ **QRS Prolongation:** Widening of the QRS complex on ECG, indicative of sodium channel blockade.

- **Anticholinergic Effects:**

  - ◦ **Dry Mouth, Blurred Vision, Urinary Retention, Constipation:** Due to muscarinic receptor antagonism.

Selective Serotonin Reuptake Inhibitors (SSRIs):

- **Neurological Symptoms:**

  - ◦ **Agitation, Confusion:** Mild to moderate overdose can cause increased anxiety and confusion.
  - ◦ **Seizures:** Rare but can occur in severe overdoses.
  - ◦ **Serotonin Syndrome:** Characterized by agitation, hyperreflexia, tremor, clonus, and hyperthermia. It can be life-threatening.

- **Gastrointestinal Symptoms:**

  - ◦ **Nausea, Vomiting, Diarrhea:** Common due to increased serotonin in the gastrointestinal tract.

Serotonin-Norepinephrine Reuptake Inhibitors (SNRIs):

- **Neurological Symptoms:**

  - ◦ **Agitation, Confusion, Seizures:** Similar to SSRIs, with additional risk of increased blood pressure.

- **Cardiovascular Symptoms:**

- **Hypertension:** Increased blood pressure due to norepinephrine reuptake inhibition.
- **Tachycardia:** Increased heart rate.

Monoamine Oxidase Inhibitors (MAOIs):

- **Neurological Symptoms:**

  - **Agitation, Confusion, Seizures:** Due to excessive neurotransmitter accumulation.

- **Cardiovascular Symptoms:**

  - **Hypertension:** Severe, potentially leading to hypertensive crisis.
  - **Tachycardia:** Increased heart rate.

- **Serotonin Syndrome:** Especially when combined with other serotonergic agents.

7.3.2 Management Strategies

The management of antidepressant overdose involves supportive care, specific antidotal therapies where applicable, and careful monitoring to manage complications. Early recognition and treatment are crucial.

Supportive Care:

- **Airway Management:** Ensure a clear airway and provide supplemental oxygen as needed. Intubation and mechanical ventilation may be required in cases of severe respiratory depression or coma.
- **Circulatory Support:** Monitor blood pressure and heart rate. Administer intravenous fluids to maintain adequate blood pressure. Vasopressors may be necessary if hypotension persists despite fluid resuscitation.

Decontamination:

- **Activated Charcoal:** Administer activated charcoal if the patient presents within one hour of ingestion and is alert, to limit gastrointestinal absorption of the drug.

- **Gastric Lavage:** Consider gastric lavage if the patient presents within one hour of a large overdose and airway protection is assured.

Specific Treatments:

- **Tricyclic Antidepressants (TCAs):**

  - **Sodium Bicarbonate:** Administer sodium bicarbonate IV to treat QRS prolongation and arrhythmias. Typical dose is 1-2 mEq/kg, repeated as necessary based on ECG findings.
  - **Benzodiazepines:** Use benzodiazepines to control seizures and agitation.
  - **Lipid Emulsion Therapy:** Consider lipid emulsion therapy for severe, refractory cases, especially with significant cardiovascular instability.

- **Selective Serotonin Reuptake Inhibitors (SSRIs) and Serotonin-Norepinephrine Reuptake Inhibitors (SNRIs):**

  - **Benzodiazepines:** Administer benzodiazepines for seizures and severe agitation.
  - **Cyproheptadine:** An antihistamine with serotonin antagonistic properties, used to treat serotonin syndrome. The initial dose is 12 mg, followed by 2 mg every 2 hours as needed.
  - **Cooling Measures:** Use cooling blankets and antipyretics to manage hyperthermia associated with serotonin syndrome.

- **Monoamine Oxidase Inhibitors (MAOIs):**

  - **Phentolamine or Nitroprusside:** Administer phentolamine or nitroprusside IV to manage hypertensive crisis. Start with 1-5 mg of phentolamine IV or 0.3 mcg/kg/min of nitroprusside, titrated to effect.
  - **Benzodiazepines:** Use benzodiazepines for seizure control.

Monitoring and Follow-Up:

- **Vital Signs:** Continuous monitoring of respiratory rate, oxygen saturation, heart rate, and blood pressure.
- **ECG Monitoring:** Regular ECG monitoring to detect and manage arrhythmias, particularly in TCA overdose.
- **Neurological Status:** Frequent assessments of the patient's level of consciousness and neurological status.
- **Laboratory Tests:** Perform blood tests, including electrolytes, renal function, and toxicology screens, to assess the extent of the overdose and organ function.

Preventive Measures:

- **Patient Education:** Educate patients and caregivers about the risks of overdose and the importance of adhering to prescribed dosages.
- **Safe Prescribing Practices:** Encourage healthcare providers to follow guidelines for the safe prescribing of antidepressants and to consider alternative treatments for patients at risk of overdose.
- **Mental Health Support:** Provide resources and referrals for mental health support and counseling to address underlying issues related to depression and suicidal ideation.

7.4 Barbiturates and Benzodiazepines Overdose

7.4.1 Clinical Symptoms

Barbiturates and **benzodiazepines** are both central nervous system (CNS) depressants but differ in their mechanisms of action and toxicity profiles. Overdoses of these substances can lead to significant morbidity and mortality, particularly when taken in combination with other depressants such as alcohol.

Barbiturates:

- **Neurological Symptoms:**

  - **Sedation:** Profound drowsiness, lethargy, and, in severe cases, coma.

- **Respiratory Depression:** Slowed or absent breathing due to CNS depression.
- **Ataxia:** Lack of coordination and unsteady movements.
- **Nystagmus:** Rapid involuntary eye movements.

- **Cardiovascular Symptoms:**

  - **Hypotension:** Low blood pressure due to vasodilation and decreased cardiac output.
  - **Bradycardia:** Slowed heart rate.

- **Gastrointestinal Symptoms:**

  - **Nausea and Vomiting:** Common due to CNS effects on the vomiting center.

Benzodiazepines:

- **Neurological Symptoms:**

  - **Sedation:** Drowsiness, confusion, and difficulty in arousal.
  - **Ataxia:** Unsteady gait and impaired coordination.
  - **Dysarthria:** Slurred speech.
  - **Respiratory Depression:** Less common compared to barbiturates but can occur, especially with high doses or in combination with other CNS depressants.

- **Cardiovascular Symptoms:**

  - **Hypotension:** Less common but possible, especially in cases of severe overdose.

- **Paradoxical Reactions:**

  - **Agitation:** In rare cases, particularly in children and the elderly, paradoxical agitation and hyperactivity may occur.

7.4.2 Management Strategies

The management of barbiturate and benzodiazepine overdose involves supportive care, the use of specific antidotes, and addressing any complications that arise. Prompt recognition and appropriate intervention are crucial for improving patient outcomes.

Supportive Care:

- **Airway Management:** Ensure the patient's airway is open. Use the jaw-thrust maneuver if necessary, and consider placing an oropharyngeal or nasopharyngeal airway to maintain patency.
- **Breathing Support:** Administer supplemental oxygen to all patients with suspected overdose. For patients with significant respiratory depression, provide assisted ventilation using a bag-valve mask. Endotracheal intubation and mechanical ventilation may be required in severe cases.
- **Circulatory Support:** Monitor blood pressure and heart rate. Administer intravenous fluids to maintain adequate blood pressure. Vasopressors may be necessary if hypotension persists despite fluid resuscitation.

Decontamination:

- **Activated Charcoal:** Administer activated charcoal if the patient presents within one hour of ingestion and is alert, to limit gastrointestinal absorption of the drug. This is more effective for barbiturates than benzodiazepines.
- **Gastric Lavage:** Consider gastric lavage if the patient presents within one hour of a large overdose and airway protection is assured.

Specific Treatments:

- **Barbiturates:**

  - **Alkaline Diuresis:** For long-acting barbiturates like phenobarbital, consider using sodium bicarbonate to alkalinize the urine and enhance renal excretion. This involves administering 1-2 mEq/kg of sodium bicarbonate IV, followed by a continuous infusion to maintain urine pH above 7.5.

- ○ **Hemodialysis:** In severe cases of barbiturate overdose, particularly with long-acting agents, hemodialysis or hemoperfusion may be necessary to enhance drug clearance.

- **Benzodiazepines:**

  - ○ **Flumazenil:** Flumazenil is a competitive benzodiazepine receptor antagonist that can reverse the effects of benzodiazepines. However, it should be used with caution due to the risk of precipitating seizures, particularly in patients with a history of seizures, benzodiazepine dependence, or co-ingestion of proconvulsant substances.

    - ▪ **Initial Dose:** Administer 0.2 mg IV over 15 seconds. If there is no response, give an additional 0.3 mg IV over 30 seconds. Further doses of 0.5 mg can be administered at 1-minute intervals, up to a total dose of 3 mg.

Monitoring and Follow-Up:

- **Vital Signs:** Continuous monitoring of respiratory rate, oxygen saturation, heart rate, and blood pressure.
- **Neurological Status:** Frequent assessments of the patient's level of consciousness and neurological status.
- **Laboratory Tests:** Perform blood tests, including electrolytes, renal function, and toxicology screens, to assess the extent of the overdose and organ function.

Preventive Measures:

- **Patient Education:** Educate patients and caregivers about the risks of overdose and the importance of adhering to prescribed dosages.
- **Safe Prescribing Practices:** Encourage healthcare providers to follow guidelines for the safe prescribing of barbiturates and benzodiazepines and to consider alternative treatments for patients at risk of overdose.
- **Mental Health Support:** Provide resources and referrals for mental health support and counseling to address underlying issues related to substance use and dependency.

Long-Term Management:

- **Observation:** Patients who have received treatment for barbiturate or benzodiazepine overdose should be observed for several hours to ensure that symptoms do not recur.
- **Substance Abuse Treatment:** Refer patients with a history of substance abuse to addiction treatment programs and provide resources for long-term support.

7.5 Alcohol Poisoning

7.5.1 Ethanol

Ethanol is the type of alcohol found in alcoholic beverages. Ethanol poisoning, also known as alcohol intoxication, occurs when a person consumes a large amount of ethanol in a short period, leading to toxic effects on the central nervous system and other organs.

7.5.1.1 Clinical Symptoms

The clinical symptoms of ethanol poisoning vary depending on the blood alcohol concentration (BAC) and the individual's tolerance to alcohol. Symptoms can range from mild to severe.

Mild to Moderate Intoxication:

- **Euphoria:** Feeling of well-being and reduced inhibition.
- **Impaired Judgment:** Poor decision-making and risk-taking behavior.
- **Coordination Problems:** Unsteady gait, difficulty with fine motor skills.
- **Slurred Speech:** Difficulty articulating words clearly.
- **Nausea and Vomiting:** Gastrointestinal irritation and potential for aspiration.

Severe Intoxication:

- **Confusion:** Disorientation and impaired cognitive function.
- **Stupor:** Significant reduction in mental and physical activity, difficult to arouse.

- **Hypothermia:** Low body temperature due to vasodilation and impaired thermoregulation.
- **Hypoglycemia:** Low blood sugar levels, especially in individuals with poor nutritional status.
- **Respiratory Depression:** Slowed or irregular breathing, potentially leading to respiratory arrest.
- **Coma:** Unconsciousness, unresponsive to stimuli.
- **Death:** In severe cases, respiratory arrest, aspiration, or cardiac arrhythmias can lead to death.

7.5.1.2 Management Strategies

Management of ethanol poisoning focuses on supportive care, monitoring, and preventing complications.

Supportive Care:

- **Airway Management:** Ensure the airway is open and protected, especially if the patient is vomiting or has a reduced level of consciousness. Consider endotracheal intubation if there is a risk of aspiration.
- **Breathing Support:** Provide supplemental oxygen if needed. Assist ventilation if there is significant respiratory depression.
- **Circulatory Support:** Monitor blood pressure and heart rate. Administer intravenous fluids to maintain hydration and blood pressure. Correct electrolyte imbalances as needed.

Decontamination:

- **Activated Charcoal:** Not typically indicated for ethanol poisoning as it is not effective in adsorbing alcohol.

Symptomatic Treatment:

- **Hypoglycemia:** Administer intravenous glucose to treat or prevent hypoglycemia, particularly in children and individuals with poor nutritional status.
- **Thiamine:** Administer thiamine (100 mg IV or IM) to prevent Wernicke's encephalopathy, especially in chronic alcohol users.

- **Hypothermia:** Rewarm patients with hypothermia using external warming devices and warm IV fluids.

Monitoring and Follow-Up:

- **Vital Signs:** Continuous monitoring of respiratory rate, oxygen saturation, heart rate, and blood pressure.
- **Neurological Status:** Regular assessments of the patient's level of consciousness and neurological status.
- **Laboratory Tests:** Perform blood tests, including blood alcohol level, glucose, electrolytes, and liver function tests.

Preventive Measures:

- **Patient Education:** Educate patients about the dangers of excessive alcohol consumption and provide resources for alcohol use disorder treatment.
- **Safe Practices:** Encourage safe drinking practices and the use of designated drivers or alternative transportation.

7.5.2 Methanol

Methanol is a toxic alcohol found in industrial products, antifreeze, and some household products. Methanol poisoning occurs when methanol is ingested, inhaled, or absorbed through the skin. Methanol is metabolized to formaldehyde and formic acid, which are highly toxic.

7.5.2.1 Clinical Symptoms

The clinical symptoms of methanol poisoning can be delayed, typically appearing 12-24 hours after exposure, and are primarily due to the toxic metabolites.

Initial Symptoms:

- **Central Nervous System Symptoms:**

  - **Headache:** Common early symptom.
  - **Dizziness and Confusion:** Impaired cognitive function.
  - **Nausea and Vomiting:** Gastrointestinal distress.

- **Visual Symptoms:**

    - **Blurred Vision:** Difficulty focusing.
    - **Photophobia:** Sensitivity to light.
    - **"Snowfield" Vision:** Described as seeing a "snowstorm" effect in the visual field, which can progress to blindness.

Severe Symptoms:

- **Metabolic Acidosis:**

    - **Hyperventilation:** Rapid breathing to compensate for acidosis.
    - **Abdominal Pain:** Due to severe metabolic acidosis.
    - **Coma:** Depressed level of consciousness, potentially leading to coma.

- **Ocular Damage:**

    - **Optic Neuropathy:** Permanent damage to the optic nerve, leading to blindness.

- **Multi-Organ Failure:**

    - **Cardiovascular Collapse:** Severe hypotension and shock.
    - **Renal Failure:** Due to severe metabolic acidosis and toxicity.

7.5.2.2 Management Strategies

Management of methanol poisoning involves supportive care, specific antidotal therapy, and enhanced elimination techniques.

Supportive Care:

- **Airway Management:** Ensure the airway is open and protected. Consider intubation if the patient has a depressed level of consciousness.
- **Breathing Support:** Provide supplemental oxygen and assist ventilation if needed. Monitor for respiratory failure due to metabolic acidosis.
- **Circulatory Support:** Monitor blood pressure and heart rate. Administer intravenous fluids and vasopressors if necessary to maintain blood pressure.

Decontamination:

- **Activated Charcoal:** Not effective for methanol poisoning and not recommended.

Specific Treatments:

- **Antidotes:**

  - **Ethanol:** Competitive inhibition of alcohol dehydrogenase. Administer ethanol IV or orally to maintain a blood ethanol concentration of 100-150 mg/dL.
  - **Fomepizole:** Preferred antidote, inhibits alcohol dehydrogenase. Initial dose is 15 mg/kg IV, followed by 10 mg/kg every 12 hours.

- **Folic Acid:** Enhances the metabolism of formic acid to non-toxic metabolites. Administer folic acid (50 mg IV every 4-6 hours).
- **Correction of Metabolic Acidosis:**

  - **Sodium Bicarbonate:** Administer sodium bicarbonate IV to correct severe metabolic acidosis and maintain blood pH above 7.3.

Enhanced Elimination:

- **Hemodialysis:** Highly effective in removing methanol and its toxic metabolites. Indicated in cases of severe poisoning, significant metabolic acidosis, visual disturbances, or renal failure.

Monitoring and Follow-Up:

- **Vital Signs:** Continuous monitoring of respiratory rate, oxygen saturation, heart rate, and blood pressure.
- **Neurological Status:** Regular assessments of the patient's level of consciousness and neurological status.
- **Laboratory Tests:** Perform serial blood tests to monitor methanol levels, electrolytes, blood pH, and renal function.

Preventive Measures:

- **Public Education:** Educate the public about the dangers of methanol-containing products and the importance of safe storage and handling.
- **Regulation:** Advocate for stricter regulations on the availability and labeling of methanol-containing products to prevent accidental ingestion.

7.6 Paracetamol and Salicylates Overdose

7.6.1 Clinical Symptoms

Paracetamol (Acetaminophen)

Paracetamol overdose is one of the most common causes of poisoning worldwide. It can lead to severe liver damage and potentially fatal hepatic failure if not promptly treated. Symptoms of paracetamol overdose typically present in stages.

Stage 1 (0-24 hours):

- **Nausea and Vomiting:** Initial symptoms may include gastrointestinal upset.
- **Diaphoresis:** Excessive sweating.
- **Malaise:** General feeling of discomfort or unease.

Stage 2 (24-72 hours):

- **Right Upper Quadrant Pain:** Due to liver enlargement and damage.
- **Elevated Liver Enzymes:** AST and ALT levels begin to rise, indicating liver injury.
- **Jaundice:** Yellowing of the skin and eyes may start to appear.
- **Coagulopathy:** Impaired blood clotting due to liver dysfunction.

Stage 3 (72-96 hours):

- **Peak Hepatic Damage:** Liver enzymes peak, and hepatic failure may ensue.
- **Encephalopathy:** Confusion, altered mental status due to liver failure.
- **Hypoglycemia:** Low blood sugar levels.

- **Lactic Acidosis:** Metabolic acidosis due to liver failure.
- **Renal Failure:** Kidney injury may occur in severe cases.

Stage 4 (4 days to 2 weeks):

- **Recovery or Death:** Patients may either recover with supportive care and treatment or progress to multi-organ failure and death.

Salicylates (Aspirin)

Salicylate poisoning can result from acute overdose or chronic ingestion. Symptoms result from direct toxicity and metabolic disturbances.

Early Symptoms (0-12 hours):

- **Tinnitus:** Ringing in the ears.
- **Nausea and Vomiting:** Gastrointestinal upset is common.
- **Hyperventilation:** Due to stimulation of the respiratory center in the brain.
- **Respiratory Alkalosis:** Early acid-base disturbance from hyperventilation.

Progressive Symptoms (12-24 hours):

- **Metabolic Acidosis:** Accumulation of salicylic acid and lactic acid.
- **Dehydration:** Due to vomiting, hyperventilation, and fever.
- **Hyperthermia:** Elevated body temperature.
- **Confusion and Agitation:** Central nervous system effects from salicylate toxicity.

Severe Symptoms (24+ hours):

- **Seizures:** Due to severe metabolic disturbances.
- **Pulmonary Edema:** Fluid accumulation in the lungs.
- **Hypoglycemia:** Low blood sugar levels.
- **Renal Failure:** Due to direct toxicity and dehydration.
- **Coma:** Severe cases can lead to coma and death.

7.6.2 Management Strategies

Paracetamol (Acetaminophen)
    Supportive Care:

- **Airway Management:** Ensure airway patency and provide supplemental oxygen if needed.
- **Circulatory Support:** Administer intravenous fluids to maintain hydration and blood pressure.

Decontamination:

- **Activated Charcoal:** Administer activated charcoal if the patient presents within 1-2 hours of ingestion to limit gastrointestinal absorption of the drug.

Specific Treatments:

- **N-acetylcysteine (NAC):** NAC replenishes glutathione stores and enhances the detoxification of NAPQI, the toxic metabolite of paracetamol.

    - **Oral NAC:** Loading dose of 140 mg/kg followed by 70 mg/kg every 4 hours for 17 doses.
    - **Intravenous NAC:** Loading dose of 150 mg/kg over 1 hour, followed by 50 mg/kg over 4 hours, then 100 mg/kg over 16 hours.

Monitoring and Follow-Up:

- **Vital Signs:** Continuous monitoring of respiratory rate, oxygen saturation, heart rate, and blood pressure.
- **Liver Function Tests:** Regular assessment of AST, ALT, bilirubin, and coagulation parameters.
- **Renal Function Tests:** Monitor creatinine and urine output to detect renal involvement.

Preventive Measures:

- **Patient Education:** Educate patients about the risks of paracetamol overdose and the importance of adhering to recommended dosages.
- **Safe Storage:** Advise safe storage of paracetamol-containing products to prevent accidental ingestion, especially in children.

Salicylates (Aspirin)
Supportive Care:

- **Airway Management:** Ensure airway patency and provide supplemental oxygen if needed.
- **Circulatory Support:** Administer intravenous fluids to correct dehydration and maintain blood pressure.

Decontamination:

- **Activated Charcoal:** Administer activated charcoal if the patient presents within 1-2 hours of ingestion to limit gastrointestinal absorption of the drug.
- **Gastric Lavage:** Consider gastric lavage if the patient presents within 1 hour of a large overdose and airway protection is assured.

Specific Treatments:

- **Alkalinization:** Sodium bicarbonate IV to alkalinize the urine and promote renal excretion of salicylates.

  - **Initial Dose:** 1-2 mEq/kg IV bolus followed by continuous infusion to maintain urine pH above 7.5.

- **Hemodialysis:** Indicated in severe cases with renal failure, severe metabolic acidosis, or refractory symptoms. Hemodialysis effectively removes salicylates from the blood.

Monitoring and Follow-Up:

- **Vital Signs:** Continuous monitoring of respiratory rate, oxygen saturation, heart rate, and blood pressure.

- **Electrolytes and Acid-Base Status:** Regular assessment of electrolytes, blood gases, and bicarbonate levels.
- **Renal Function Tests:** Monitor creatinine and urine output to detect renal involvement.

Preventive Measures:

- **Patient Education:** Educate patients about the risks of salicylate overdose and the importance of adhering to recommended dosages.
- **Safe Storage:** Advise safe storage of salicylate-containing products to prevent accidental ingestion, especially in children.

7.7 Non-Steroidal Anti-Inflammatory Drugs (NSAIDs) Overdose

7.7.1 Clinical Symptoms

Non-Steroidal Anti-Inflammatory Drugs (NSAIDs) are commonly used medications for pain, inflammation, and fever. Overdose can lead to a variety of clinical symptoms, ranging from mild gastrointestinal discomfort to severe multi-organ toxicity.

Mild to Moderate Overdose:

- **Gastrointestinal Symptoms:**

  - **Nausea and Vomiting:** Common early symptoms due to direct irritation of the gastric mucosa.
  - **Abdominal Pain:** Often related to gastrointestinal irritation and potential for gastritis or peptic ulceration.
  - **Diarrhea:** Occasional symptom related to gastrointestinal upset.

- **Central Nervous System Symptoms:**

  - **Headache:** Common symptom, often mild.
  - **Dizziness:** Feeling of lightheadedness or unsteadiness.

- **Tinnitus:** Ringing in the ears, especially with salicylate-based NSAIDs.

Severe Overdose:

- **Renal Symptoms:**

  - **Acute Kidney Injury (AKI):** NSAIDs can cause reduced renal blood flow and direct renal toxicity, leading to AKI. Symptoms include decreased urine output, fluid retention, and elevated creatinine levels.
  - **Electrolyte Imbalances:** Hyperkalemia and hyponatremia can occur due to impaired renal function.

- **Cardiovascular Symptoms:**

  - **Hypertension:** Elevated blood pressure due to fluid retention and renal effects.
  - **Arrhythmias:** Rare but possible in severe overdose, particularly with medications like ibuprofen and naproxen.

- **Central Nervous System Symptoms:**

  - **Seizures:** Rare but possible, particularly with severe overdose or in individuals with underlying risk factors.
  - **Coma:** In very severe cases, CNS depression can lead to coma.

- **Gastrointestinal Symptoms:**

  - **Gastrointestinal Bleeding:** Significant risk in severe overdose, particularly with chronic use or pre-existing gastrointestinal conditions.
  - **Perforation:** Rare but serious complication due to severe gastrointestinal ulceration.

- **Metabolic Symptoms:**

- **Metabolic Acidosis:** Can occur in severe overdose, particularly with NSAIDs like ibuprofen.

7.7.2 Management Strategies

Management of NSAID overdose focuses on supportive care, decontamination, monitoring, and addressing any complications that arise.
Supportive Care:

- **Airway Management:** Ensure airway patency and provide supplemental oxygen if needed.
- **Circulatory Support:** Administer intravenous fluids to maintain hydration and blood pressure, particularly if there is evidence of renal impairment or significant gastrointestinal loss.

Decontamination:

- **Activated Charcoal:** Administer activated charcoal if the patient presents within 1-2 hours of ingestion and is alert, to limit gastrointestinal absorption of the drug.

Symptomatic Treatment:

- **Gastrointestinal Protection:**

  - **Proton Pump Inhibitors (PPIs):** Administer PPIs (e.g., omeprazole) to reduce gastric acid secretion and protect the gastric mucosa.
  - **H2 Receptor Antagonists:** As an alternative to PPIs, H2 receptor antagonists (e.g., ranitidine) can also be used to reduce gastric acid secretion.

- **Renal Support:**

  - **Hydration:** Ensure adequate hydration to support renal function and promote excretion of the drug.
  - **Monitoring:** Regularly monitor renal function through serum creatinine and urine output. Adjust treatment based on renal

function.

- **Electrolyte Management:**

  - **Hyperkalemia:** Treat hyperkalemia with measures such as sodium polystyrene sulfonate, insulin with glucose, or calcium gluconate, depending on severity.
  - **Hyponatremia:** Correct hyponatremia with appropriate intravenous fluids, avoiding rapid correction.

Monitoring and Follow-Up:

- **Vital Signs:** Continuous monitoring of respiratory rate, oxygen saturation, heart rate, and blood pressure.
- **Laboratory Tests:** Perform serial blood tests to monitor renal function, electrolytes, blood gases, and any evidence of metabolic acidosis.
- **Neurological Status:** Frequent assessments of the patient's level of consciousness and neurological status.

Preventive Measures:

- **Patient Education:** Educate patients about the risks of NSAID overdose and the importance of adhering to recommended dosages.
- **Safe Storage:** Advise safe storage of NSAID-containing products to prevent accidental ingestion, especially in children.
- **Regular Monitoring:** For patients on long-term NSAID therapy, ensure regular monitoring of renal function, gastrointestinal health, and cardiovascular status.

7.8 Hydrocarbons Poisoning

7.8.1 Petroleum Products

Petroleum products such as gasoline, kerosene, and motor oil are common hydrocarbons that can cause poisoning. Exposure can occur through ingestion, inhalation, or dermal contact, leading to a range of clinical symptoms.

7.8.1.1 Clinical Symptoms
Ingestion:

- **Gastrointestinal Symptoms:**

  - **Nausea and Vomiting:** Common initial symptoms.
  - **Abdominal Pain:** Due to irritation of the gastrointestinal tract.
  - **Diarrhea:** Occasionally seen following ingestion.

- **Central Nervous System Symptoms:**

  - **Headache and Dizziness:** Early neurological symptoms.
  - **Confusion and Drowsiness:** Progression to more severe CNS depression.
  - **Seizures and Coma:** Severe cases can lead to seizures and coma.

- **Respiratory Symptoms:**

  - **Coughing and Choking:** Due to aspiration risk.
  - **Respiratory Distress:** Difficulty breathing, wheezing, and cyanosis.
  - **Chemical Pneumonitis:** Inflammation of the lungs due to aspiration, leading to coughing, fever, and chest pain.

Inhalation:

- **Respiratory Symptoms:**

  - **Coughing and Wheezing:** Due to airway irritation.
  - **Shortness of Breath:** Difficulty breathing.
  - **Pulmonary Edema:** Severe cases can lead to fluid accumulation in the lungs.

- **Central Nervous System Symptoms:**

  - **Headache and Dizziness:** Common symptoms due to CNS effects.
  - **Confusion and Ataxia:** Impaired coordination and mental status.
  - **Unconsciousness:** In severe cases.

Dermal Contact:

- **Skin Irritation:** Redness, itching, and burning sensation.
- **Dermatitis:** Prolonged exposure can lead to skin inflammation and blistering.

7.8.1.2 Management Strategies
Supportive Care:

- **Airway Management:** Ensure airway patency and provide supplemental oxygen. Consider intubation if the patient has significant respiratory distress or risk of aspiration.
- **Breathing Support:** Administer supplemental oxygen and provide ventilatory support if needed. Monitor for signs of chemical pneumonitis.
- **Circulatory Support:** Administer intravenous fluids to maintain hydration and blood pressure.

Decontamination:

- **Ingestion:**

  - **Activated Charcoal:** Generally not recommended due to the risk of aspiration.
  - **Gastric Lavage:** Contraindicated due to the high risk of aspiration and chemical pneumonitis.
  - **Do Not Induce Vomiting:** Avoid inducing vomiting to prevent aspiration.

- **Inhalation:**

  - **Remove from Exposure:** Move the patient to fresh air immediately.
  - **Oxygen Therapy:** Provide high-flow oxygen to improve oxygenation.

- **Dermal Contact:**

  - **Skin Decontamination:** Remove contaminated clothing and wash the skin thoroughly with soap and water.

Symptomatic Treatment:

- **Respiratory Support:**

  - **Bronchodilators:** Administer bronchodilators such as albuterol to relieve bronchospasm.
  - **Corticosteroids:** Consider corticosteroids for severe inflammation and chemical pneumonitis.

- **Neurological Support:**

  - **Benzodiazepines:** Administer benzodiazepines for seizure control if necessary.

Monitoring and Follow-Up:

- **Vital Signs:** Continuous monitoring of respiratory rate, oxygen saturation, heart rate, and blood pressure.
- **Chest X-Ray:** Perform a chest x-ray to assess for chemical pneumonitis or pulmonary edema.
- **Laboratory Tests:** Monitor blood gases, electrolytes, and renal function.

Preventive Measures:

- **Public Education:** Educate the public about the dangers of hydrocarbon exposure and the importance of proper storage and handling.
- **Workplace Safety:** Implement safety protocols and provide personal protective equipment (PPE) in workplaces handling hydrocarbons.

7.8.2 Polyethylene Glycol (PEG)

Polyethylene glycol (PEG) is commonly used as a laxative and in various industrial applications. While generally considered safe, excessive ingestion can lead to toxicity.

7.8.2.1 Clinical Symptoms
Gastrointestinal Symptoms:

- **Nausea and Vomiting:** Common initial symptoms.
- **Abdominal Pain:** Cramping and discomfort.
- **Diarrhea:** Due to the osmotic effect of PEG in the gastrointestinal tract.
- **Dehydration:** Resulting from excessive diarrhea and fluid loss.

Central Nervous System Symptoms:

- **Dizziness and Headache:** Mild CNS effects.
- **Confusion:** In severe cases, particularly with significant fluid and electrolyte imbalances.

7.8.2.2 Management Strategies
Supportive Care:

- **Hydration:** Administer oral or intravenous fluids to maintain hydration and correct electrolyte imbalances.
- **Electrolyte Management:** Monitor and correct electrolyte imbalances, particularly sodium and potassium levels.

Decontamination:

- **Activated Charcoal:** Not typically indicated for PEG ingestion due to its poor adsorption of PEG.
- **Gastric Lavage:** Generally not recommended as PEG is rapidly absorbed and lavage is unlikely to be effective.

Symptomatic Treatment:

- **Anti-Nausea Medications:** Administer antiemetics such as ondansetron to control nausea and vomiting.
- **Anti-Diarrheal Medications:** Use cautiously to manage severe diarrhea, ensuring that underlying causes are addressed.

Monitoring and Follow-Up:

- **Vital Signs:** Continuous monitoring of heart rate, blood pressure, and respiratory rate.

- **Laboratory Tests:** Regular assessment of electrolyte levels, renal function, and hydration status.

Preventive Measures:

- **Patient Education:** Educate patients on the proper use of PEG-containing products and the risks of excessive ingestion.
- **Safe Storage:** Advise safe storage of PEG products to prevent accidental ingestion, especially in children.

7.9 Caustics Poisoning

Caustics, or corrosive substances, include inorganic acids and alkalis. These substances can cause severe tissue damage upon contact, leading to significant morbidity. Management of caustics poisoning requires prompt and effective intervention to prevent or minimize tissue injury.

7.9.1 Inorganic Acids

Inorganic acids, such as hydrochloric acid, sulfuric acid, and nitric acid, are commonly used in industrial processes and household cleaning products. Exposure can result from ingestion, inhalation, or dermal contact.

7.9.1.1 Clinical Symptoms
Ingestion:

- **Gastrointestinal Symptoms:**

  - **Severe Pain:** Intense pain in the mouth, throat, chest, and abdomen.
  - **Drooling:** Excessive salivation due to irritation.
  - **Dysphagia:** Difficulty swallowing.
  - **Hematemesis:** Vomiting blood due to gastrointestinal bleeding.
  - **Perforation:** Risk of esophageal or gastric perforation leading to severe pain, peritonitis, and shock.

Inhalation:

- **Respiratory Symptoms:**

- ○ **Coughing:** Due to irritation of the respiratory tract.
- ○ **Dyspnea:** Shortness of breath.
- ○ **Wheezing and Stridor:** Due to airway inflammation and potential obstruction.
- ○ **Pulmonary Edema:** Fluid accumulation in the lungs in severe cases.

Dermal Contact:

- **Skin Symptoms:**

  - ○ **Burns:** Redness, blistering, and severe pain at the site of contact.
  - ○ **Ulceration:** Deep tissue damage can lead to ulcer formation.

7.9.1.2 Management Strategies
Supportive Care:

- **Airway Management:** Ensure airway patency, provide supplemental oxygen, and consider intubation if there is significant respiratory distress.
- **Circulatory Support:** Administer intravenous fluids to maintain hydration and blood pressure, especially if there is significant blood loss or shock.

Decontamination:

- **Ingestion:**

  - ○ **Do Not Induce Vomiting:** Avoid inducing vomiting to prevent further esophageal damage.
  - ○ **Dilution:** Administer small amounts of water or milk to dilute the acid if the patient is conscious and can swallow safely.

- **Inhalation:**

  - ○ **Remove from Exposure:** Move the patient to fresh air immediately.
  - ○ **Oxygen Therapy:** Provide high-flow oxygen to improve oxygenation.

- **Dermal Contact:**

- ○ **Skin Decontamination:** Remove contaminated clothing and wash the skin thoroughly with copious amounts of water. Continue flushing for at least 15-20 minutes.

Symptomatic Treatment:

- **Pain Management:** Administer analgesics to control pain.
- **Gastrointestinal Protection:** Consider proton pump inhibitors (PPIs) or H2 receptor antagonists to reduce gastric acid secretion and protect the gastric mucosa.

Monitoring and Follow-Up:

- **Vital Signs:** Continuous monitoring of respiratory rate, oxygen saturation, heart rate, and blood pressure.
- **Endoscopy:** Perform early endoscopy (within 24 hours) to assess the extent of gastrointestinal injury and guide further management.
- **Laboratory Tests:** Monitor blood gases, electrolytes, renal function, and complete blood count.

Preventive Measures:

- **Public Education:** Educate the public about the dangers of inorganic acid exposure and the importance of proper storage and handling.
- **Workplace Safety:** Implement safety protocols and provide personal protective equipment (PPE) in workplaces handling inorganic acids.

7.9.2 Alkali

Alkalis, such as sodium hydroxide, potassium hydroxide, and ammonia, are commonly found in industrial cleaners, drain openers, and fertilizers. Alkali exposure can cause deep tissue damage due to liquefactive necrosis.

7.9.2.1 Clinical Symptoms
Ingestion:

- **Gastrointestinal Symptoms:**

- **Severe Pain:** Intense pain in the mouth, throat, chest, and abdomen.
- **Drooling:** Excessive salivation due to irritation.
- **Dysphagia:** Difficulty swallowing.
- **Hematemesis:** Vomiting blood due to gastrointestinal bleeding.
- **Perforation:** Risk of esophageal or gastric perforation leading to severe pain, peritonitis, and shock.

Inhalation:

- **Respiratory Symptoms:**

  - **Coughing:** Due to irritation of the respiratory tract.
  - **Dyspnea:** Shortness of breath.
  - **Wheezing and Stridor:** Due to airway inflammation and potential obstruction.
  - **Pulmonary Edema:** Fluid accumulation in the lungs in severe cases.

Dermal Contact:

- **Skin Symptoms:**

  - **Burns:** Redness, blistering, and severe pain at the site of contact.
  - **Ulceration:** Deep tissue damage can lead to ulcer formation.

7.9.2.2 Management Strategies
Supportive Care:

- **Airway Management:** Ensure airway patency, provide supplemental oxygen, and consider intubation if there is significant respiratory distress.
- **Circulatory Support:** Administer intravenous fluids to maintain hydration and blood pressure, especially if there is significant blood loss or shock.

Decontamination:

- **Ingestion:**

- ◦ **Do Not Induce Vomiting:** Avoid inducing vomiting to prevent further esophageal damage.
- ◦ **Dilution:** Administer small amounts of water or milk to dilute the alkali if the patient is conscious and can swallow safely.

- **Inhalation:**

  - ◦ **Remove from Exposure:** Move the patient to fresh air immediately.
  - ◦ **Oxygen Therapy:** Provide high-flow oxygen to improve oxygenation.

- **Dermal Contact:**

  - ◦ **Skin Decontamination:** Remove contaminated clothing and wash the skin thoroughly with copious amounts of water. Continue flushing for at least 15-20 minutes.

Symptomatic Treatment:

- **Pain Management:** Administer analgesics to control pain.
- **Gastrointestinal Protection:** Consider proton pump inhibitors (PPIs) or H2 receptor antagonists to reduce gastric acid secretion and protect the gastric mucosa.

Monitoring and Follow-Up:

- **Vital Signs:** Continuous monitoring of respiratory rate, oxygen saturation, heart rate, and blood pressure.
- **Endoscopy:** Perform early endoscopy (within 24 hours) to assess the extent of gastrointestinal injury and guide further management.
- **Laboratory Tests:** Monitor blood gases, electrolytes, renal function, and complete blood count.

Preventive Measures:

- **Public Education:** Educate the public about the dangers of alkali exposure and the importance of proper storage and handling.
- **Workplace Safety:** Implement safety protocols and provide personal protective equipment (PPE) in workplaces handling alkalis.

7.10 Radiation Poisoning

7.10.1 Clinical Symptoms

Radiation poisoning, also known as acute radiation syndrome (ARS), occurs after exposure to a high dose of ionizing radiation over a short period. The severity and onset of symptoms depend on the radiation dose and exposure duration. Clinical symptoms can be grouped into three phases: prodromal, latent, and manifest illness.

Prodromal Phase (Minutes to Days Post-Exposure):

- **Gastrointestinal Symptoms:**

  - **Nausea and Vomiting:** Often the earliest symptoms, occurring within hours of exposure.
  - **Diarrhea:** Can lead to dehydration and electrolyte imbalances.
  - **Anorexia:** Loss of appetite.

- **Neurological Symptoms:**

  - **Headache:** Common due to CNS involvement.
  - **Dizziness:** Feeling of lightheadedness or unsteadiness.
  - **Fatigue and Weakness:** General malaise and loss of energy.

Latent Phase (Hours to Weeks Post-Exposure):

- **Temporary Improvement:** Symptoms may diminish, leading to a deceptive period of well-being.
- **Duration:** Length of the latent phase depends on the radiation dose; higher doses result in shorter latent periods.

Manifest Illness Phase (Weeks to Months Post-Exposure):
Hematopoietic Syndrome (1-10 Gy):

- **Bone Marrow Suppression:**

- **Leukopenia:** Reduced white blood cell count, increasing infection risk.
- **Thrombocytopenia:** Reduced platelet count, leading to bleeding and bruising.
- **Anemia:** Reduced red blood cell count, causing fatigue and pallor.

Gastrointestinal Syndrome (10-50 Gy):

- **Severe Diarrhea and Vomiting:** Leading to dehydration and electrolyte imbalances.
- **Intestinal Damage:** Potential for severe mucosal damage, malabsorption, and bleeding.
- **Sepsis:** High risk due to mucosal barrier breakdown and immunosuppression.

Cardiovascular/Central Nervous System Syndrome (Above 50 Gy):

- **Neurological Symptoms:**

  - **Confusion and Disorientation:** Altered mental status due to CNS damage.
  - **Seizures:** Due to severe brain damage.
  - **Coma:** Loss of consciousness in severe cases.

- **Cardiovascular Collapse:**

  - **Hypotension:** Low blood pressure leading to shock.
  - **Multi-Organ Failure:** Due to extensive tissue damage.

7.10.2 Management Strategies

Management of radiation poisoning focuses on supportive care, symptom management, and specific treatments to mitigate the effects of radiation exposure.

Supportive Care:

- **Isolation and Protection:**

- ○ **Protective Measures:** Isolate the patient to prevent infection and limit further radiation exposure.
- ○ **Decontamination:** Remove contaminated clothing and wash the skin thoroughly to reduce external contamination.

- **Fluid and Electrolyte Management:**

  - ○ **Intravenous Fluids:** Administer IV fluids to maintain hydration and correct electrolyte imbalances.
  - ○ **Electrolyte Replacement:** Monitor and replace electrolytes as needed.

Symptomatic Treatment:

- **Antiemetics:** Administer antiemetics such as ondansetron to control nausea and vomiting.
- **Analgesics:** Use pain relief medications to manage headache and general discomfort.

Hematopoietic Support:

- **Bone Marrow Stimulants:**

  - ○ **G-CSF (Granulocyte Colony-Stimulating Factor):** To stimulate white blood cell production and reduce infection risk.
  - ○ **Erythropoietin:** To stimulate red blood cell production and manage anemia.

- **Blood Transfusions:** Provide platelet and red blood cell transfusions as needed to manage thrombocytopenia and anemia.
- **Antibiotics:** Administer broad-spectrum antibiotics prophylactically or to treat infections due to immunosuppression.

Gastrointestinal Support:

- **Antidiarrheal Agents:** Administer antidiarrheal medications to control severe diarrhea.

- **Nutritional Support:** Provide parenteral nutrition if gastrointestinal absorption is impaired.

Neurological and Cardiovascular Support:

- **Seizure Management:** Administer anticonvulsants to control seizures.
- **Cardiovascular Support:** Monitor and manage blood pressure and cardiac function. Use vasopressors if necessary to maintain blood pressure.

Specific Treatments:

- **Potassium Iodide (KI):** Administer KI to block thyroid uptake of radioactive iodine, reducing the risk of thyroid cancer. Effective if given within hours of exposure.
- **Prussian Blue:** Used to treat internal contamination with cesium-137 or thallium by enhancing excretion.
- **Diethylenetriamine Pentaacetic Acid (DTPA):** Used to chelate and enhance excretion of radioactive plutonium, americium, and curium.

Long-Term Monitoring and Follow-Up:

- **Regular Check-ups:** Monitor blood counts, renal and liver function, and overall health.
- **Psychological Support:** Provide counseling and support to address the psychological impact of radiation exposure.
- **Cancer Surveillance:** Long-term monitoring for the development of radiation-induced cancers, particularly thyroid cancer and leukemia.

Preventive Measures:

- **Public Education:** Educate the public about the risks of radiation exposure and appropriate protective measures.
- **Emergency Preparedness:** Develop and implement emergency response plans for radiation accidents, including stockpiling of protective agents like KI and Prussian Blue.
- **Workplace Safety:** Implement strict safety protocols in industries and facilities where radiation exposure risk is high, and ensure workers have

access to protective equipment and training.

Chapter 8: Clinical Symptoms and Management of Chronic Poisoning

Introduction

Chronic poisoning, unlike acute poisoning, results from prolonged exposure to toxic substances at lower doses. This type of poisoning can be insidious, with symptoms developing gradually over time, often making diagnosis and management more challenging. Chronic poisoning can occur due to occupational exposure, environmental contamination, lifestyle choices, or long-term use of certain medications.

Importance of Understanding Chronic Poisoning

Understanding chronic poisoning is critical for several reasons. Firstly, it often affects multiple organ systems, leading to complex clinical presentations that require comprehensive medical evaluations. Secondly, chronic poisoning can have long-lasting or irreversible health effects, making early detection and intervention crucial for preventing severe outcomes. Lastly, chronic exposure to toxins can impact not just individuals but entire communities, necessitating public health measures and policies to mitigate risks.

Scope of the Chapter

This chapter will provide an in-depth examination of the clinical symptoms and management strategies for various types of chronic poisoning. The focus will be on identifying the common sources of chronic toxins, understanding their pathophysiology, recognizing clinical manifestations, and implementing effective management and preventive strategies.

Key Areas Covered

1. **Common Sources of Chronic Toxic Exposure:**

   - **Heavy Metals:** Lead, mercury, arsenic, and cadmium are prevalent in various industrial processes, contaminated water supplies, and some traditional medicines.
   - **Pesticides:** Persistent organic pollutants such as DDT and organophosphates used in agriculture.
   - **Industrial Chemicals:** Benzene, asbestos, and other chemicals used in manufacturing and construction.
   - **Medications:** Long-term use of drugs like acetaminophen, NSAIDs, and certain psychiatric medications can lead to chronic toxicity.
   - **Environmental Toxins:** Air pollutants, contaminated food, and water.

2. **Clinical Symptoms of Chronic Poisoning:**

   - **General Symptoms:** Fatigue, malaise, weight loss, and chronic pain.
   - **Neurological Symptoms:** Cognitive decline, peripheral neuropathy, tremors, and mood disturbances.
   - **Gastrointestinal Symptoms:** Chronic nausea, vomiting, abdominal pain, and altered bowel habits.
   - **Hematological Symptoms:** Anemia, leukopenia, and thrombocytopenia.
   - **Dermatological Symptoms:** Chronic dermatitis, pigmentation changes, and hair loss.
   - **Respiratory Symptoms:** Chronic cough, dyspnea, and reduced lung function.
   - **Renal and Hepatic Symptoms:** Chronic kidney disease, hepatotoxicity, and associated metabolic disturbances.

3. **Diagnostic Approaches:**

   - **History and Physical Examination:** Comprehensive assessment to identify potential sources of exposure and clinical signs of toxicity.
   - **Laboratory Tests:** Blood and urine tests to detect and quantify toxins and assess organ function.
   - **Imaging Studies:** X-rays, CT scans, and MRIs to identify organ damage and guide further evaluation.

- **Specialized Tests:** Hair, nail, and bone marrow analysis for detecting specific toxins.

4. **Management Strategies:**

- **Elimination of Exposure:** Identifying and removing the source of the toxin to prevent further exposure.
- **Symptomatic Treatment:** Managing symptoms through supportive care, medications, and therapeutic interventions.
- **Specific Antidotes and Chelation Therapy:** Using agents like EDTA, dimercaprol, and succimer for heavy metal poisoning.
- **Nutritional Support:** Providing vitamins, minerals, and dietary modifications to support recovery and mitigate deficiencies caused by chronic toxicity.
- **Monitoring and Follow-Up:** Regular monitoring of clinical status, laboratory parameters, and organ function to assess treatment efficacy and detect complications.

5. **Preventive Measures:**

- **Public Health Policies:** Implementing regulations and guidelines to reduce environmental and occupational exposure to toxins.
- **Education and Awareness:** Raising awareness among healthcare providers and the public about the risks of chronic poisoning and the importance of preventive measures.
- **Safety Protocols:** Developing and enforcing safety standards in industries and workplaces to protect workers from toxic exposures.
- **Community Interventions:** Initiating community-based programs to address and mitigate the effects of environmental contamination.

8.1 Heavy Metals Poisoning

8.1.1 Arsenic

Arsenic is a naturally occurring element found in the earth's crust, and it exists in both organic and inorganic forms. Inorganic arsenic compounds, particularly arsenic trioxide, are highly toxic and can lead to chronic poisoning when individuals are exposed to contaminated water, soil, or industrial processes.

8.1.1.1 Clinical Symptoms

Chronic arsenic poisoning, also known as arsenicosis, presents with a variety of symptoms that develop over time due to prolonged exposure. These symptoms can affect multiple organ systems and vary in severity.

Dermatological Symptoms:

- **Hyperpigmentation:** Darkening of the skin, especially on the palms and soles.
- **Hypopigmentation:** Lightening of the skin in a spotted pattern, often appearing alongside hyperpigmentation.
- **Keratosis:** Thickening of the skin, particularly on the palms and soles, leading to rough, wart-like lesions.
- **Mees' Lines:** White lines that appear across the fingernails and toenails.

Neurological Symptoms:

- **Peripheral Neuropathy:** Tingling, numbness, and pain in the hands and feet due to nerve damage.
- **Cognitive Decline:** Memory loss, difficulty concentrating, and other cognitive impairments.
- **Headaches:** Persistent headaches are common.

Gastrointestinal Symptoms:

- **Abdominal Pain:** Chronic pain and cramping.
- **Nausea and Vomiting:** Frequent gastrointestinal distress.
- **Diarrhea:** Recurrent episodes of watery stools.

Cardiovascular Symptoms:

- **Hypertension:** Elevated blood pressure.
- **Arrhythmias:** Irregular heartbeats.

Hematological Symptoms:

- **Anemia:** Fatigue, pallor, and other symptoms associated with low red blood cell count.

Respiratory Symptoms:

- **Chronic Cough:** Persistent coughing and irritation of the respiratory tract.

Renal and Hepatic Symptoms:

- **Renal Dysfunction:** Chronic kidney disease and associated symptoms.
- **Hepatotoxicity:** Liver damage, often indicated by jaundice and elevated liver enzymes.

Cancer Risk:

- **Increased Risk of Cancers:** Chronic arsenic exposure is associated with higher risks of skin, lung, bladder, and liver cancers.

8.1.1.2 Management Strategies

Effective management of chronic arsenic poisoning involves several steps, including identification and elimination of the source of exposure, supportive care, and specific treatments to remove arsenic from the body and mitigate its effects.

Elimination of Exposure:

- **Identify Source:** Determine the source of arsenic exposure, such as contaminated water, food, or occupational hazards.
- **Remove or Avoid Source:** Implement measures to eliminate or reduce exposure, such as using alternative water sources, improving occupational safety, and regulating industrial emissions.

Supportive Care:

- **Hydration:** Ensure adequate hydration to support renal function and facilitate arsenic excretion.
- **Nutritional Support:** Provide a balanced diet with adequate vitamins and minerals to support overall health and recovery.

Specific Treatments:

- **Chelation Therapy:** Chelation agents bind to arsenic, allowing it to be excreted in the urine. Commonly used chelating agents include:

  - **Dimercaprol (BAL):** Administered intramuscularly, effective for acute and chronic arsenic poisoning.
  - **Dimercaptosuccinic Acid (DMSA):** Administered orally, preferred for its safety profile and ease of use.
  - **Dimercaptopropane Sulfonate (DMPS):** Another oral chelator that can be used in chronic arsenic poisoning.

Symptomatic Treatment:

- **Pain Management:** Use analgesics to manage pain associated with peripheral neuropathy and other symptoms.
- **Antihypertensives:** Administer medications to control high blood pressure.
- **Dermatological Care:** Topical treatments and skin care regimens to manage keratosis and other skin lesions.

Monitoring and Follow-Up:

- **Regular Assessments:** Conduct regular medical check-ups to monitor the patient's clinical status and response to treatment.
- **Laboratory Tests:** Monitor blood arsenic levels, renal and liver function tests, and complete blood counts to assess the extent of poisoning and organ function.
- **Neurological Evaluations:** Perform regular neurological assessments to monitor for changes in peripheral neuropathy and cognitive function.

Preventive Measures:

- **Public Education:** Educate communities about the risks of arsenic exposure and the importance of using safe water sources.
- **Regulation and Safety Standards:** Implement and enforce regulations to limit arsenic levels in drinking water, food, and industrial emissions.

- **Occupational Safety:** Ensure workers in industries using arsenic are provided with appropriate personal protective equipment (PPE) and safety training.

Environmental and Community Interventions:

- **Water Treatment:** Develop and implement water treatment solutions to remove arsenic from contaminated water supplies.
- **Soil Remediation:** Initiate soil remediation projects to reduce arsenic levels in agricultural and residential areas.

8.1 Heavy Metals Poisoning

8.1.2 Lead

Lead is a toxic heavy metal that can cause a wide range of health problems, particularly affecting the nervous system, kidneys, and blood. Chronic lead poisoning occurs due to prolonged exposure to lead from sources such as contaminated water, lead-based paints, industrial processes, and certain traditional medicines.

8.1.2.1 Clinical Symptoms

Chronic lead poisoning can affect multiple organ systems, and its symptoms vary based on the level of exposure, age, and individual susceptibility.

Neurological Symptoms:

- **Cognitive Decline:** Reduced attention span, memory loss, and learning difficulties, especially in children.
- **Peripheral Neuropathy:** Numbness, tingling, and weakness in the extremities, often seen as "wrist drop" or "foot drop."
- **Headaches:** Frequent and persistent headaches.
- **Irritability and Mood Changes:** Increased irritability, mood swings, and in severe cases, depression.

Gastrointestinal Symptoms:

- **Abdominal Pain:** Colicky and intermittent pain, often referred to as "lead colic."
- **Nausea and Vomiting:** Gastrointestinal upset.
- **Constipation:** Common due to the effects of lead on the gastrointestinal tract.

Hematological Symptoms:

- **Anemia:** Fatigue, pallor, and weakness due to impaired hemoglobin synthesis. Often characterized by basophilic stippling of red blood cells.
- **Lead Lines:** Bluish lines on the gums, known as Burton's lines.

Renal Symptoms:

- **Chronic Kidney Disease:** Impaired renal function, often resulting in proteinuria and decreased glomerular filtration rate (GFR).

Musculoskeletal Symptoms:

- **Joint and Muscle Pain:** Arthralgia and myalgia due to lead deposition in bones and tissues.

Reproductive Symptoms:

- **Infertility:** Both males and females may experience reduced fertility.
- **Miscarriages and Stillbirths:** Increased risk in pregnant women.

General Symptoms:

- **Fatigue:** General feeling of tiredness and weakness.
- **Weight Loss:** Unintentional loss of weight.

8.1.2.2 Management Strategies

Management of chronic lead poisoning involves identifying and eliminating the source of exposure, providing supportive care, and administering specific treatments to remove lead from the body.

Elimination of Exposure:

- **Identify Source:** Determine the source of lead exposure, such as contaminated water, paint, soil, or occupational hazards.
- **Remove or Avoid Source:** Implement measures to eliminate or reduce exposure, such as using lead-free paints, treating water, and improving occupational safety practices.

Supportive Care:

- **Nutritional Support:** Provide a diet rich in calcium, iron, and vitamin C to help reduce lead absorption and mitigate anemia.
- **Hydration:** Ensure adequate hydration to support renal function and facilitate lead excretion.

Specific Treatments:

- **Chelation Therapy:** Chelation agents bind to lead, allowing it to be excreted in the urine. Commonly used chelating agents include:

  - **Dimercaptosuccinic Acid (DMSA):** Oral chelator preferred for its safety profile and ease of use.
  - **Calcium Disodium EDTA:** Intravenous chelator used for more severe cases.
  - **Dimercaprol (BAL):** Intramuscular chelator used in conjunction with EDTA for severe poisoning.

Symptomatic Treatment:

- **Pain Management:** Use analgesics to manage abdominal pain, headaches, and musculoskeletal pain.
- **Antihypertensives:** Administer medications to control high blood pressure if renal impairment leads to hypertension.
- **Treatment of Anemia:** Provide iron supplements and, if necessary, blood transfusions to manage severe anemia.

Monitoring and Follow-Up:

- **Regular Assessments:** Conduct regular medical check-ups to monitor the patient's clinical status and response to treatment.

- **Laboratory Tests:** Monitor blood lead levels, renal function tests, liver function tests, and complete blood counts to assess the extent of poisoning and organ function.
- **Neurological Evaluations:** Perform regular neurological assessments to monitor changes in cognitive function and peripheral neuropathy.

Preventive Measures:

- **Public Education:** Educate communities about the risks of lead exposure and the importance of using safe water sources, lead-free paints, and safe occupational practices.
- **Regulation and Safety Standards:** Implement and enforce regulations to limit lead levels in drinking water, paint, soil, and industrial emissions.
- **Occupational Safety:** Ensure workers in industries using lead are provided with appropriate personal protective equipment (PPE) and safety training.

Environmental and Community Interventions:

- **Water Treatment:** Develop and implement water treatment solutions to remove lead from contaminated water supplies.
- **Soil Remediation:** Initiate soil remediation projects to reduce lead levels in agricultural and residential areas.
- **Lead Abatement Programs:** Implement lead abatement programs to remove or encapsulate lead-based paints in homes, schools, and public buildings.

8.1 Heavy Metals Poisoning

8.1.3 Mercury

Mercury is a heavy metal that poses significant health risks when humans are exposed to it. Mercury exists in three forms: elemental (metallic) mercury, inorganic mercury compounds, and organic mercury compounds (such as methylmercury). Each form has different routes of exposure and toxicity profiles.

8.1.3.1 Clinical Symptoms
Elemental Mercury:
Inhalation Exposure:

- **Neurological Symptoms:**

  - **Tremors:** Also known as "mercurial tremor," characterized by fine, involuntary shaking.
  - **Emotional Instability:** Irritability, mood swings, and shyness, often referred to as "erethism."
  - **Memory Loss and Cognitive Decline:** Difficulty concentrating and impaired short-term memory.

- **Respiratory Symptoms:**

  - **Cough and Shortness of Breath:** Due to inhalation of mercury vapors.
  - **Pneumonitis:** Inflammation of lung tissue in severe cases.

Inorganic Mercury:
Ingestion or Dermal Exposure:

- **Gastrointestinal Symptoms:**

  - **Metallic Taste:** Unpleasant taste in the mouth.
  - **Nausea, Vomiting, and Diarrhea:** Gastrointestinal upset and damage.
  - **Abdominal Pain:** Cramping and discomfort.

- **Renal Symptoms:**

  - **Nephrotic Syndrome:** Proteinuria, edema, and elevated blood urea nitrogen (BUN) and creatinine levels.
  - **Acute Kidney Injury:** Reduced renal function.

Organic Mercury (Methylmercury):
Ingestion (primarily from contaminated fish):

- **Neurological Symptoms:**

- ◦ **Paresthesia:** Tingling or numbness in the hands and feet.
- ◦ **Ataxia:** Uncoordinated movements and difficulty with balance.
- ◦ **Dysarthria:** Slurred speech.
- ◦ **Visual and Hearing Impairment:** Constriction of the visual field and difficulty hearing.
- ◦ **Cognitive and Motor Dysfunction:** Severe cases can lead to profound cognitive deficits and motor impairments, including cerebral palsy-like symptoms in children exposed in utero.

General Symptoms Across All Forms:

- **Fatigue:** General feeling of tiredness and weakness.
- **Weight Loss:** Unintentional loss of weight.
- **Dermatological Symptoms:**

- ◦ **Rashes and Dermatitis:** Skin irritation and inflammation, particularly with dermal exposure.

8.1.3.2 Management Strategies

Effective management of mercury poisoning involves identifying and eliminating the source of exposure, providing supportive care, and administering specific treatments to remove mercury from the body.

Elimination of Exposure:

- **Identify Source:** Determine the source of mercury exposure, such as broken thermometers, industrial processes, or consumption of contaminated fish.
- **Remove or Avoid Source:** Implement measures to eliminate or reduce exposure, such as proper disposal of mercury-containing products, improving workplace safety, and avoiding consumption of high-mercury fish.

Supportive Care:

- **Hydration:** Ensure adequate hydration to support renal function and facilitate mercury excretion.
- **Nutritional Support:** Provide a balanced diet to support overall health and recovery.

Specific Treatments:

- **Chelation Therapy:** Chelation agents bind to mercury, allowing it to be excreted in the urine. Commonly used chelating agents include:

  - **Dimercaprol (BAL):** Administered intramuscularly, used for severe cases of mercury poisoning.
  - **Dimercaptosuccinic Acid (DMSA):** Administered orally, preferred for its safety profile and ease of use.
  - **Dimercaptopropane Sulfonate (DMPS):** Another oral chelator that can be used for mercury poisoning.

Symptomatic Treatment:

- **Pain Management:** Use analgesics to manage pain associated with tremors, gastrointestinal symptoms, and other discomforts.
- **Antihypertensives:** Administer medications to control high blood pressure if renal impairment leads to hypertension.
- **Treatment of Neurological Symptoms:** Provide medications and therapies to manage tremors, ataxia, and cognitive symptoms.

Monitoring and Follow-Up:

- **Regular Assessments:** Conduct regular medical check-ups to monitor the patient's clinical status and response to treatment.
- **Laboratory Tests:** Monitor blood and urine mercury levels, renal function tests, liver function tests, and complete blood counts to assess the extent of poisoning and organ function.
- **Neurological Evaluations:** Perform regular neurological assessments to monitor changes in cognitive function, motor skills, and sensory function.

Preventive Measures:

- **Public Education:** Educate communities about the risks of mercury exposure and the importance of using mercury-free alternatives and avoiding high-mercury fish.

- **Regulation and Safety Standards:** Implement and enforce regulations to limit mercury emissions in industrial processes and to control the use of mercury in products.
- **Occupational Safety:** Ensure workers in industries using mercury are provided with appropriate personal protective equipment (PPE) and safety training.

Environmental and Community Interventions:

- **Cleanup of Contaminated Sites:** Implement cleanup projects for areas contaminated with mercury, including industrial sites and water bodies.
- **Fish Consumption Advisories:** Issue guidelines and advisories to inform the public about safe consumption levels of fish, particularly for vulnerable populations such as pregnant women and children.

8.1 Heavy Metals Poisoning

8.1.4 Iron

Iron poisoning, or iron toxicity, is a serious condition that can result from the excessive ingestion of iron supplements or products. It is more common in children due to accidental ingestion of iron-containing supplements, often marketed as vitamins. Chronic iron poisoning can also occur due to repeated blood transfusions or excessive dietary intake.

8.1.4.1 Clinical Symptoms

Acute Iron Poisoning:

Acute iron poisoning is characterized by a progression through several stages, each with distinct clinical symptoms.

Stage 1 (0-6 hours):

- **Gastrointestinal Symptoms:**

  - **Nausea and Vomiting:** Often with blood (hematemesis).
  - **Diarrhea:** Watery stools, sometimes bloody.
  - **Abdominal Pain:** Severe and crampy pain.

Stage 2 (6-24 hours):

- **Latent Phase:** Symptoms may temporarily improve, giving a false sense of recovery.

Stage 3 (12-48 hours):

- **Systemic Toxicity:**

  - **Metabolic Acidosis:** Due to iron's effect on cellular metabolism.
  - **Hypotension and Shock:** Resulting from vasodilation and fluid loss.
  - **Fever:** Due to inflammatory response.
  - **CNS Symptoms:** Lethargy, drowsiness, and potentially coma.

Stage 4 (2-5 days):

- **Hepatic Toxicity:**

  - **Liver Dysfunction:** Elevated liver enzymes (AST, ALT), jaundice, and hepatic failure.
  - **Coagulopathy:** Impaired blood clotting.

Stage 5 (2-6 weeks):

- **Gastrointestinal Obstruction:** Due to healing of the gastrointestinal mucosa, leading to scarring and strictures.

Chronic Iron Poisoning:
Chronic iron overload, often due to repeated blood transfusions or excessive dietary intake, leads to gradual accumulation of iron in various organs, causing damage over time.

- **Hepatic Symptoms:**

  - **Liver Enlargement (Hepatomegaly):** Due to iron deposition.
  - **Cirrhosis:** Chronic liver damage and scarring.
  - **Hepatic Failure:** In severe cases.

- **Cardiovascular Symptoms:**

    - **Cardiomyopathy:** Iron-induced damage to the heart muscle.
    - **Arrhythmias:** Irregular heartbeats.

- **Endocrine Symptoms:**

    - **Diabetes Mellitus:** Due to pancreatic damage.
    - **Hypogonadism:** Reduced function of the gonads.

- **Skin Symptoms:**

    - **Bronzing:** Skin hyperpigmentation due to iron deposition.

8.1.4.2 Management Strategies

Effective management of iron poisoning involves immediate and appropriate interventions to prevent severe complications and improve outcomes.

Acute Iron Poisoning:
Supportive Care:

- **Airway Management:** Ensure airway patency and provide supplemental oxygen.
- **Circulatory Support:** Administer intravenous fluids to maintain blood pressure and hydration. Use vasopressors if necessary to treat shock.

Decontamination:

- **Gastric Lavage:** Consider gastric lavage if the patient presents within 1 hour of ingestion and has a significant amount of iron in the stomach.
- **Activated Charcoal:** Not effective for iron as it does not adsorb iron effectively.

Specific Treatments:

- **Whole Bowel Irrigation:** Use polyethylene glycol (PEG) solution to flush the gastrointestinal tract, especially if radiopaque iron tablets are visible on an abdominal X-ray.

- **Chelation Therapy:** Administer deferoxamine, a chelating agent that binds to free iron, facilitating its excretion.

  - **Deferoxamine:** Initial dose of 15 mg/kg/hour intravenously, adjusted based on the severity of poisoning and serum iron levels.

Symptomatic Treatment:

- **Metabolic Acidosis:** Correct with intravenous sodium bicarbonate.
- **Pain Management:** Use analgesics to manage abdominal pain.

Monitoring and Follow-Up:

- **Vital Signs:** Continuous monitoring of respiratory rate, oxygen saturation, heart rate, and blood pressure.
- **Laboratory Tests:** Monitor serum iron levels, total iron-binding capacity (TIBC), liver function tests, renal function tests, and blood gases.
- **Imaging:** Abdominal X-ray to check for retained iron tablets.

Chronic Iron Poisoning:
Supportive Care:

- **Nutritional Support:** Provide a balanced diet with appropriate caloric and nutrient intake.

Specific Treatments:

- **Chelation Therapy:** Regular administration of deferoxamine or other chelating agents to reduce iron overload.

  - **Deferasirox:** An oral chelator used for chronic iron overload.
  - **Deferiprone:** Another oral chelator that can be used in combination with other treatments.

Monitoring and Follow-Up:

- **Regular Assessments:** Conduct periodic medical evaluations to monitor the patient's clinical status and response to treatment.

- **Laboratory Tests:** Regularly monitor serum ferritin, liver function tests, cardiac function tests, and endocrine function tests.
- **Imaging:** MRI to assess iron deposition in the liver and heart.

Preventive Measures:

- **Public Education:** Educate communities about the risks of iron overdose, particularly the dangers of iron supplements to children.
- **Safe Storage:** Advise safe storage of iron-containing products to prevent accidental ingestion.
- **Screening Programs:** Implement screening for individuals at risk of chronic iron overload, such as those with hereditary hemochromatosis or receiving frequent blood transfusions.

8.1 Heavy Metals Poisoning

8.1.5 Copper

Copper is an essential trace element involved in various biological processes. However, excessive copper intake or impaired copper metabolism can lead to toxicity. Copper poisoning can be acute or chronic and is often associated with industrial exposure, contaminated water supplies, or genetic disorders such as Wilson's disease.

8.1.5.1 Clinical Symptoms

Acute Copper Poisoning:

Acute copper poisoning typically results from ingestion of a large amount of copper salts or contaminated water.

Gastrointestinal Symptoms:

- **Nausea and Vomiting:** Often severe and may include vomiting of green or blue material.
- **Abdominal Pain:** Sharp and crampy pain.
- **Diarrhea:** May be bloody due to gastrointestinal mucosal irritation.

Systemic Symptoms:

- **Metallic Taste:** Unpleasant metallic taste in the mouth.
- **Hypotension and Shock:** Due to fluid loss and direct cardiovascular effects of copper.
- **Hemolysis:** Destruction of red blood cells leading to jaundice and hemoglobinuria.
- **Renal Failure:** Resulting from hemoglobinuria and direct nephrotoxic effects of copper.
- **Hepatic Necrosis:** Severe liver damage, elevated liver enzymes, and jaundice.

Neurological Symptoms:

- **Headache and Dizziness:** Common in acute poisoning.
- **Confusion and Lethargy:** Due to severe systemic effects and organ damage.

Chronic Copper Poisoning:

Chronic copper poisoning, often associated with conditions like Wilson's disease, results from prolonged exposure or impaired copper metabolism.

Hepatic Symptoms:

- **Chronic Hepatitis:** Inflammation of the liver.
- **Cirrhosis:** Scarring and dysfunction of the liver.
- **Portal Hypertension:** Increased blood pressure in the portal vein.

Neurological Symptoms:

- **Movement Disorders:** Tremors, dystonia, and unsteady gait.
- **Cognitive Impairment:** Memory loss, difficulty concentrating, and mood changes.
- **Psychiatric Symptoms:** Depression, anxiety, and behavioral changes.

Ocular Symptoms:

- **Kayser-Fleischer Rings:** Brownish or greenish rings around the cornea due to copper deposition.

Renal Symptoms:

- **Proteinuria:** Excess protein in the urine.
- **Nephrocalcinosis:** Calcium deposits in the kidneys.

8.1.5.2 Management Strategies

Effective management of copper poisoning involves prompt diagnosis, removal of the source of exposure, supportive care, and specific treatments to reduce copper levels in the body.

Elimination of Exposure:

- **Identify Source:** Determine the source of copper exposure, such as contaminated water, industrial exposure, or dietary supplements.
- **Remove or Avoid Source:** Implement measures to eliminate or reduce exposure, such as treating water supplies, improving workplace safety, and discontinuing the use of copper-containing supplements.

Supportive Care:

- **Hydration:** Ensure adequate hydration to support renal function and facilitate copper excretion.
- **Nutritional Support:** Provide a balanced diet to support overall health and recovery.

Specific Treatments:

- **Chelation Therapy:** Chelating agents bind to copper, allowing it to be excreted in the urine. Commonly used chelating agents include:
  - **Penicillamine:** An oral chelator that is effective in binding copper.
  - **Trientine:** Another oral chelator used for copper toxicity, particularly in patients intolerant to penicillamine.
  - **Zinc Acetate:** Used to block the absorption of copper in the gastrointestinal tract.

Symptomatic Treatment:

- **Pain Management:** Use analgesics to manage abdominal pain and other discomforts.
- **Anti-Emetics:** Administer anti-emetics to control severe nausea and vomiting.
- **Blood Transfusions:** May be necessary in cases of severe hemolysis and anemia.

Monitoring and Follow-Up:

- **Regular Assessments:** Conduct regular medical check-ups to monitor the patient's clinical status and response to treatment.
- **Laboratory Tests:** Monitor serum copper levels, liver function tests, renal function tests, complete blood counts, and urine copper levels.
- **Neurological Evaluations:** Perform regular neurological assessments to monitor changes in cognitive function and motor skills.

Preventive Measures:

- **Public Education:** Educate communities about the risks of copper exposure and the importance of using safe water sources and avoiding excessive use of copper-containing supplements.
- **Regulation and Safety Standards:** Implement and enforce regulations to limit copper levels in drinking water and industrial emissions.
- **Occupational Safety:** Ensure workers in industries using copper are provided with appropriate personal protective equipment (PPE) and safety training.

Environmental and Community Interventions:

- **Water Treatment:** Develop and implement water treatment solutions to remove copper from contaminated water supplies.
- **Soil Remediation:** Initiate soil remediation projects to reduce copper levels in agricultural and residential areas.

Chapter 9: Venomous Snake Bites

Introduction

Venomous snake bites represent a significant medical emergency worldwide, particularly in tropical and subtropical regions. The World Health Organization (WHO) identifies snakebite envenoming as a high-priority neglected tropical disease due to its substantial impact on public health. Each year, millions of people are bitten by venomous snakes, leading to hundreds of thousands of envenomings and tens of thousands of deaths. The morbidity associated with snake bites includes severe local tissue damage, systemic effects, and long-term disabilities.

Importance of Understanding Venomous Snake Bites

Understanding venomous snake bites is crucial for several reasons. Firstly, timely and effective medical intervention can be life-saving and can significantly reduce morbidity. Secondly, the diverse range of venomous snakes and their varied venom compositions necessitate specific treatment protocols tailored to the type of snake and the nature of the venom. Finally, awareness and education about snakebite prevention and first aid can greatly reduce the incidence and severity of snakebite envenoming.

Scope of the Chapter

This chapter aims to provide a comprehensive overview of venomous snake bites, focusing on the clinical presentation, diagnosis, and management of envenomings. It will cover the following key areas:

1. **Epidemiology and Impact:**

    ◦ Global distribution of venomous snakes.
    ◦ Prevalence and incidence of snake bites.
    ◦ Public health impact and burden of snakebite envenoming.

2. **Classification of Venomous Snakes:**

    ◦ Taxonomy and identification of major venomous snake families (e.g., Elapidae, Viperidae, and Atractaspididae).
    ◦ Characteristics and behavior of venomous snakes.

3. **Venom Composition and Mechanisms of Action:**

- Biochemical components of snake venoms.
- Pathophysiological effects of venom components on the human body.

4. **Clinical Presentation of Snake Bites:**

- Local Effects: Pain, swelling, necrosis, and compartment syndrome.
- Systemic Effects: Neurotoxicity, hemotoxicity, cytotoxicity, and myotoxicity.
- Specific symptoms associated with different types of snake venoms.

5. **Diagnosis and Assessment:**

- History and physical examination of snakebite victims.
- Laboratory investigations and imaging studies.
- Identification of the offending snake species when possible.

6. **Management and Treatment:**

- First aid measures and initial management at the bite site.
- Hospital management and medical treatment protocols.
- Administration of antivenom: indications, dosing, and potential adverse reactions.
- Supportive care and management of complications.

7. **Prevention and Education:**

- Strategies for preventing snake bites.
- Community education and awareness programs.
- Training healthcare providers in the recognition and management of snake bites.

9.1 Families of Venomous Snakes

9.1.1 Elapidae

The Elapidae family, commonly known as elapids, includes some of the most dangerous and widely recognized venomous snakes in the world. This family encompasses species such as cobras, kraits, mambas, and coral snakes.

Characteristics:

- **Venom:** Elapid venom is predominantly neurotoxic, affecting the nervous system. It contains a mixture of toxins, including neurotoxins, cardiotoxins, and myotoxins.
- **Fangs:** Elapids have short, fixed front fangs that efficiently deliver venom.
- **Habitat:** These snakes are found in a variety of environments, including forests, grasslands, deserts, and coastal regions.
- **Behavior:** Elapids are generally agile and active hunters, feeding on a range of prey such as rodents, birds, and other reptiles.

Notable Species:

- **Cobras (Genus Naja):** Known for their iconic hood and defensive posture. Cobras can deliver a potent neurotoxic venom and, in some species, spit venom as a defense mechanism.
- **Kraits (Genus Bungarus):** Typically nocturnal, kraits have highly toxic venom that causes paralysis and respiratory failure.
- **Mambas (Genus Dendroaspis):** Found in Africa, mambas are fast and highly venomous. The black mamba is particularly notorious for its lethal bite.
- **Coral Snakes (Various Genera):** Recognizable by their brightly colored bands, coral snakes have a potent neurotoxic venom.

9.1.2 Viperidae

The Viperidae family, commonly known as vipers, includes pit vipers, true vipers, and bush vipers. This family is characterized by long, hinged fangs that allow deep penetration of venom.

Characteristics:

- **Venom:** Viperid venom is primarily hemotoxic, causing tissue damage, coagulopathy, and systemic bleeding. It contains a complex mixture of enzymes and proteins that disrupt blood clotting and damage tissues.
- **Fangs:** Vipers have long, retractable fangs that can inject venom deep into the tissues of their prey or aggressors.
- **Habitat:** Vipers are adaptable and can be found in diverse habitats, including forests, deserts, mountains, and swamps.
- **Behavior:** Vipers are typically ambush predators, relying on camouflage and stealth to capture their prey.

Notable Species:

- **Russell's Viper (Daboia russelii):** Found in Asia, this viper is responsible for many snakebite incidents and has a potent hemotoxic venom.
- **Saw-scaled Viper (Echis carinatus):** Known for its distinctive scale-rubbing sound, this small but dangerous viper is found in Africa, the Middle East, and South Asia.
- **Pit Vipers (Subfamily Crotalinae):** This group includes rattlesnakes, copperheads, and water moccasins. They possess heat-sensing pits that help locate warm-blooded prey.
- **Gaboon Viper (Bitis gabonica):** Found in Africa, it has the longest fangs of any snake and a powerful venom that combines hemotoxic and cytotoxic effects.

9.1.3 Hydrophiidae

The Hydrophiidae family, commonly known as sea snakes, comprises snakes that are highly adapted to marine environments. This family includes sea kraits and true sea snakes.

Characteristics:

- **Venom:** Sea snake venom is extremely potent and primarily neurotoxic, causing paralysis and respiratory failure. It also contains myotoxins that damage muscle tissue.
- **Fangs:** Sea snakes have small, fixed fangs designed to deliver venom to their prey, which consists mainly of fish and eels.

- **Habitat:** Sea snakes are found in warm coastal waters, particularly in the Indian and Pacific Oceans. They are excellent swimmers and can remain submerged for extended periods.
- **Behavior:** Sea snakes are generally not aggressive towards humans and bites are rare. However, they can be highly dangerous if provoked.

Notable Species:

- **Belcher's Sea Snake (Hydrophis belcheri):** Often cited as one of the most venomous snakes in the world, though bites to humans are rare.
- **Yellow-bellied Sea Snake (Hydrophis platurus):** Recognizable by its yellow underbelly, it has a widespread distribution across the Indo-Pacific region.
- **Banded Sea Krait (Laticauda colubrina):** Distinguished by its black and white bands, this species is semi-aquatic and often comes ashore to rest and lay eggs.

9.2 Clinical Effects of Venoms

Venomous snakes possess a variety of toxins in their venom, each affecting the human body in different ways. The clinical effects of snake venom can be broadly categorized into neurotoxic, hemotoxic, and myotoxic effects. Understanding these effects is crucial for the effective treatment of snakebite envenomings.

9.2.1 Neurotoxic Effects

Neurotoxic venoms primarily affect the nervous system. Snakes from the Elapidae family, such as cobras, kraits, mambas, and sea snakes, typically have neurotoxic venom. These toxins interfere with nerve signal transmission, leading to paralysis and other neurological symptoms.

Mechanisms of Action:

- **Presynaptic Neurotoxins:** These toxins damage nerve endings, preventing the release of neurotransmitters. Examples include β-bungarotoxin found in kraits.

- **Postsynaptic Neurotoxins:** These toxins bind to acetylcholine receptors at the neuromuscular junction, blocking nerve signal transmission. Examples include α-bungarotoxin found in cobras.

Clinical Symptoms:

- **Muscle Weakness:** Progressive weakness starting from the head and neck muscles, often descending to involve respiratory muscles.
- **Ptosis:** Drooping of the upper eyelids due to paralysis of the eyelid muscles.
- **Diplopia:** Double vision caused by paralysis of the eye muscles.
- **Dysphagia:** Difficulty swallowing due to paralysis of the throat muscles.
- **Respiratory Paralysis:** Severe cases can lead to respiratory failure due to paralysis of the diaphragm and intercostal muscles, requiring mechanical ventilation.

9.2.2 Hemotoxic Effects

Hemotoxic venoms primarily affect the blood and vascular systems. Snakes from the Viperidae family, such as pit vipers and true vipers, typically have hemotoxic venom. These toxins disrupt blood clotting mechanisms and damage blood vessels.

Mechanisms of Action:

- **Procoagulants:** These toxins activate clotting factors, leading to the formation of small clots throughout the bloodstream, which can deplete clotting factors and result in coagulopathy.
- **Anticoagulants:** These toxins inhibit clotting factors, preventing blood clotting and causing excessive bleeding.
- **Vascular Toxins:** These toxins damage the lining of blood vessels, leading to increased permeability and hemorrhage.

Clinical Symptoms:

- **Bleeding:** Prolonged bleeding from the bite site, gums, nose, and other mucosal surfaces.
- **Bruising:** Widespread bruising due to internal bleeding.

- **Hypotension:** Low blood pressure resulting from fluid loss and vascular damage.
- **Hemorrhagic Shock:** Severe blood loss leading to shock, characterized by rapid heart rate, low blood pressure, and organ failure.
- **DIC (Disseminated Intravascular Coagulation):** A serious condition where widespread clotting and bleeding occur simultaneously.

9.2.3 Myotoxic Effects

Myotoxic venoms primarily affect muscle tissue. Some snakes from the Elapidae and Viperidae families, as well as sea snakes from the Hydrophiidae family, have myotoxic venom. These toxins cause muscle damage and necrosis.

Mechanisms of Action:

- **Phospholipases:** These enzymes break down cell membranes, leading to muscle cell destruction.
- **Myotoxins:** These toxins directly damage muscle fibers, causing muscle necrosis and the release of muscle breakdown products into the bloodstream.

Clinical Symptoms:

- **Muscle Pain:** Intense pain and tenderness at the bite site and affected muscles.
- **Swelling:** Significant swelling and inflammation around the bite site.
- **Myoglobinuria:** Dark urine due to the presence of myoglobin, a muscle breakdown product, which can cause kidney damage.
- **Rhabdomyolysis:** Extensive muscle breakdown leading to the release of muscle cell contents into the bloodstream, potentially causing kidney failure.
- **Weakness and Paralysis:** Localized or generalized muscle weakness due to muscle damage.

9.3 General Management and First Aid

Effective management of venomous snake bites involves immediate first aid measures to reduce the severity of envenoming and hospital management to treat the systemic effects of the venom. Prompt and appropriate actions can significantly improve patient outcomes and reduce the risk of complications.

9.3.1 Immediate First Aid Measures

Immediate first aid measures aim to slow the spread of venom and stabilize the patient until they can receive medical care. It is essential to follow evidence-based practices to minimize harm.

Key First Aid Principles:

- **Stay Calm and Reassure the Victim:** Keeping the victim calm can help slow the spread of venom by reducing their heart rate and metabolic rate.
- **Immobilize the Affected Limb:** Use a splint or any rigid object to immobilize the limb to slow the spread of venom. Keep the limb at or slightly below heart level.
- **Remove Constrictive Items:** Remove rings, watches, or tight clothing from the affected limb to prevent complications from swelling.
- **Clean the Wound:** Gently clean the bite site with soap and water to reduce the risk of secondary infection. Do not attempt to suck out the venom or make incisions.

Do Not:

- **Do Not Apply a Tourniquet:** Tourniquets can cause severe damage to the limb and are not recommended.
- **Do Not Apply Ice:** Ice can cause local tissue damage and is ineffective at reducing venom spread.
- **Do Not Give the Victim Alcohol or Caffeine:** These substances can increase the absorption of venom.

Specific First Aid Techniques:

- **Pressure Immobilization Bandage:** This technique is recommended for neurotoxic bites (e.g., from elapids) but should be used with caution. Wrap a bandage firmly around the entire bitten limb, starting from the bite site and moving upwards, without cutting off circulation. Immobilize the limb with a splint.

- **Basic Life Support (BLS):** If the victim shows signs of respiratory distress or cardiac arrest, provide BLS as needed, including rescue breathing and chest compressions.

9.3.2 Hospital Management

Hospital management focuses on stabilizing the patient, administering antivenom, and treating complications arising from the venom.

Initial Assessment:

- **History and Examination:** Obtain a detailed history of the bite incident, including the time and location of the bite, the type of snake (if known), and the progression of symptoms. Conduct a thorough physical examination.
- **Vital Signs Monitoring:** Continuously monitor the patient's vital signs, including heart rate, blood pressure, respiratory rate, and oxygen saturation.
- **Laboratory Investigations:** Perform baseline blood tests, including complete blood count (CBC), coagulation profile, electrolytes, renal function tests, and liver function tests. Obtain a urine sample to check for hematuria and myoglobinuria.

Specific Treatments:

- **Antivenom Administration:** Antivenom is the primary treatment for envenoming and should be administered as soon as possible.

  - **Selection:** Use the appropriate antivenom for the snake species involved. If the species is unknown, use a polyvalent antivenom.
  - **Dosage:** Administer the recommended initial dose of antivenom based on the severity of envenoming and the guidelines provided with the antivenom product. Monitor for any signs of allergic reaction.
  - **Infusion:** Antivenom is typically given intravenously, diluted in saline, and infused slowly.

- **Supportive Care:**

  - **Fluid Resuscitation:** Administer intravenous fluids to maintain blood pressure and hydration.
  - **Pain Management:** Use analgesics to manage pain at the bite site and other affected areas.
  - **Tetanus Prophylaxis:** Administer tetanus prophylaxis if the patient's immunization status is not up to date.

- **Treatment of Specific Effects:**

  - **Neurotoxic Effects:** Monitor respiratory function closely. Provide mechanical ventilation if the patient shows signs of respiratory failure.
  - **Hemotoxic Effects:** Monitor coagulation parameters and administer fresh frozen plasma or clotting factors if there is significant coagulopathy.
  - **Myotoxic Effects:** Monitor renal function and treat rhabdomyolysis with aggressive hydration and possibly alkalinization of urine to prevent kidney damage.

Monitoring and Follow-Up:

- **Observation:** Keep the patient under close observation for at least 24 hours after antivenom administration to monitor for delayed effects and complications.
- **Repeat Antivenom Doses:** Administer additional doses of antivenom if symptoms persist or worsen, based on clinical assessment and laboratory results.
- **Long-Term Care:** Provide follow-up care for wound management, rehabilitation, and treatment of any long-term complications such as chronic pain or neurological deficits.

9.4 Early Manifestations and Complications

Venomous snake bites can cause a range of early manifestations and complications, which can be categorized into local and systemic effects.

Understanding these effects is crucial for timely and effective management of snakebite envenomings.

9.4.1 Local Effects

Local effects refer to the symptoms and signs that appear at and around the site of the snake bite. These effects can vary depending on the type of snake, the amount of venom injected, and the victim's response to the venom.
Common Local Effects:

- **Pain:** Immediate and severe pain at the bite site, which can radiate to surrounding areas.
- **Swelling:** Rapid swelling of the affected limb or area, which can progress significantly within hours.
- **Redness and Warmth:** Inflammation around the bite site, with the skin becoming red and warm to the touch.
- **Bruising:** Hemorrhagic spots and bruises can develop due to local bleeding.
- **Blistering:** Formation of blisters filled with clear or blood-stained fluid.
- **Necrosis:** Tissue death may occur, leading to blackened, necrotic areas around the bite site, particularly with hemotoxic venoms.

Severe Local Complications:

- **Compartment Syndrome:** Severe swelling within an enclosed muscle compartment can restrict blood flow and damage nerves, leading to severe pain, numbness, and weakness. This condition requires urgent medical intervention, often surgical.
- **Secondary Infection:** The bite wound can become infected, leading to cellulitis, abscess formation, and systemic infection if not properly managed.

9.4.2 Systemic Effects

Systemic effects refer to the widespread symptoms and signs that occur throughout the body as the venom spreads. These effects depend on the venom composition and can include neurotoxic, hemotoxic, and myotoxic manifestations.

Neurotoxic Effects:

Neurotoxic venoms primarily affect the nervous system, leading to a range of neurological symptoms.

- **Muscle Weakness:** Generalized weakness that often starts in the muscles closest to the bite and progresses.
- **Ptosis:** Drooping of the upper eyelids due to paralysis of the eyelid muscles.
- **Diplopia:** Double vision caused by paralysis of the eye muscles.
- **Dysphagia:** Difficulty swallowing due to paralysis of the throat muscles.
- **Respiratory Paralysis:** Severe cases can lead to respiratory failure due to paralysis of the diaphragm and intercostal muscles.

Hemotoxic Effects:

Hemotoxic venoms affect the blood and vascular systems, leading to significant bleeding and clotting disorders.

- **Coagulopathy:** Disruption of blood clotting, leading to prolonged bleeding from the bite site and other areas.
- **Hemorrhage:** Internal bleeding in various organs, which can manifest as hematuria (blood in urine), hematemesis (vomiting blood), and melena (black, tarry stools).
- **Hypotension:** Low blood pressure resulting from blood loss and vascular damage, which can progress to shock.
- **DIC (Disseminated Intravascular Coagulation):** A severe condition where widespread clotting and bleeding occur simultaneously, leading to multiple organ failure.

Myotoxic Effects:

Myotoxic venoms primarily affect muscle tissue, leading to muscle damage and systemic effects.

- **Muscle Pain and Swelling:** Intense pain and swelling in the affected muscles.
- **Myoglobinuria:** Presence of myoglobin (a muscle breakdown product) in the urine, causing dark-colored urine and potential kidney damage.

- **Rhabdomyolysis:** Extensive muscle breakdown, leading to the release of muscle cell contents into the bloodstream, potentially causing acute kidney injury.

Severe Systemic Complications:

- **Acute Kidney Injury (AKI):** Due to hemoglobinuria or myoglobinuria, resulting in reduced urine output and elevated creatinine levels.
- **Respiratory Failure:** Due to neurotoxic paralysis of respiratory muscles or severe pulmonary hemorrhage.
- **Cardiac Arrhythmias:** Irregular heartbeats due to electrolyte imbalances and direct cardiac toxicity.
- **Multi-Organ Failure:** Severe envenoming can lead to failure of multiple organ systems, requiring intensive care.

9.5 Snake Bite Injuries

Snake bite injuries can result in a range of immediate and long-term complications, depending on the type of snake, the amount of venom injected, and the promptness and appropriateness of medical treatment. Understanding the types of injuries and their potential long-term complications is essential for providing comprehensive care to snakebite victims.

9.5.1 Types of Injuries

The types of injuries resulting from snake bites can be categorized into local and systemic effects, as well as specific types of physical and physiological damage.

Local Injuries:

- **Puncture Wounds:** The initial injury from a snake bite typically consists of two puncture marks from the snake's fangs. These wounds may be surrounded by bruising and swelling.

- **Tissue Necrosis:** Venom-induced cell death can lead to necrosis, characterized by blackened, dead tissue around the bite site. This is common with viper bites.
- **Blisters and Ulcers:** Formation of fluid-filled blisters that can progress to deep ulcers due to venom cytotoxicity.
- **Compartment Syndrome:** Severe swelling within an enclosed muscle compartment can lead to increased pressure, reduced blood flow, and nerve damage. This condition requires prompt surgical intervention.

Systemic Injuries:

- **Coagulopathy:** Disruption of the blood clotting system, leading to widespread bleeding, including internal hemorrhages.
- **Neurotoxicity:** Paralysis and respiratory failure due to the neurotoxic effects of certain snake venoms, particularly those of elapids.
- **Myotoxicity:** Muscle breakdown and rhabdomyolysis, resulting in the release of muscle breakdown products into the bloodstream, potentially leading to kidney damage.

9.5.2 Long-Term Complications

Long-term complications from snake bites can affect various organ systems and lead to chronic health issues. These complications often depend on the severity of the initial envenoming, the type of venom, and the timeliness of medical intervention.

Chronic Pain and Disability:

- **Neuropathic Pain:** Persistent pain due to nerve damage caused by the venom.
- **Chronic Inflammation:** Ongoing inflammation around the bite site, leading to pain and discomfort.
- **Physical Disability:** Loss of function or mobility in the affected limb due to muscle and nerve damage, scarring, or amputation.

Renal Complications:

- **Chronic Kidney Disease:** Long-term damage to the kidneys due to hemoglobinuria or myoglobinuria from hemolysis or rhabdomyolysis.
- **Renal Failure:** Progression to end-stage renal disease requiring dialysis or kidney transplantation.

Cardiovascular Complications:

- **Hypertension:** Long-term high blood pressure resulting from kidney damage or direct cardiovascular effects of the venom.
- **Cardiac Arrhythmias:** Persistent irregular heartbeats due to venom-induced damage to the heart.

Hematological Complications:

- **Persistent Coagulopathy:** Ongoing issues with blood clotting, leading to easy bruising and prolonged bleeding.
- **Anemia:** Chronic anemia due to ongoing blood loss or hemolysis.

Psychological and Emotional Complications:

- **Post-Traumatic Stress Disorder (PTSD):** Psychological trauma from the snakebite experience, leading to anxiety, nightmares, and hypervigilance.
- **Depression and Anxiety:** Mental health issues arising from the physical and emotional impact of the snake bite and its long-term consequences.

Dermatological Complications:

- **Scarring:** Significant scarring at the bite site and areas of necrosis, which can affect mobility and appearance.
- **Skin Grafts:** Need for skin grafting to repair extensive tissue damage, which can lead to complications such as graft rejection or infection.

Chapter 10: Plant Poisoning

Introduction

Plant poisoning, also known as phytotoxicosis, occurs when individuals come into contact with or ingest toxic substances found in certain plants. While plants are a crucial part of our ecosystem and provide numerous benefits, including food, medicine, and aesthetics, some contain chemicals that can be harmful or even deadly to humans and animals. Plant poisoning can result from accidental ingestion, inhalation of plant particles, or dermal contact with toxic plants.

Importance of Understanding Plant Poisoning

Understanding plant poisoning is essential for several reasons. Firstly, many cases of plant poisoning, especially in children, are preventable with proper education and awareness. Secondly, accurate identification and knowledge of toxic plants and their effects can lead to timely and effective treatment, reducing morbidity and mortality. Finally, healthcare providers need to be equipped with the knowledge to manage plant poisoning cases, given the diversity of toxic plants and the wide range of clinical symptoms they can cause.

Scope of the Chapter

This chapter aims to provide a comprehensive overview of plant poisoning, focusing on the identification of common toxic plants, the clinical manifestations of plant poisoning, and the management strategies for affected individuals. Key areas covered will include:

1. **Common Toxic Plants:**

   - Identification and classification of plants known to cause poisoning.
   - Geographic distribution and common habitats of toxic plants.
   - Seasonal variations in plant toxicity.

2. **Mechanisms of Plant Toxicity:**

   - Overview of toxic compounds found in plants (e.g., alkaloids, glycosides, saponins, terpenes).

- How these compounds affect human physiology.

3. **Clinical Manifestations of Plant Poisoning:**

   - Symptoms and signs associated with ingestion, inhalation, and dermal contact with toxic plants.
   - Organ systems commonly affected by plant toxins.

4. **Diagnosis of Plant Poisoning:**

   - Steps to accurately diagnose plant poisoning, including patient history, physical examination, and laboratory tests.
   - Importance of identifying the specific plant involved.

5. **Management and Treatment:**

   - Immediate first aid measures for plant poisoning.
   - Hospital management, including decontamination, symptomatic treatment, and specific antidotes if available.
   - Long-term care and follow-up for severe cases of poisoning.

6. **Prevention and Education:**

   - Strategies for preventing plant poisoning in various settings, such as homes, schools, and workplaces.
   - Educational initiatives to raise awareness about toxic plants and safe practices.

10.1 Common Poisonous Plants

10.1.1 Identification and Characteristics

Identifying poisonous plants is crucial for preventing plant poisoning. Poisonous plants can be found in various environments, including gardens, parks, forests, and even homes as ornamental plants. Understanding the characteristics of these plants helps in recognizing and avoiding them.

Oleander (Nerium oleander): Oleander is a popular ornamental shrub known for its beautiful flowers, which can be red, pink, white, or yellow. Despite its attractiveness, every part of the oleander plant is highly toxic, including its leaves, flowers, and stems. Oleander contains cardiac glycosides, which can cause severe cardiovascular issues, including arrhythmias and cardiac arrest, if ingested. The plant's leathery, lance-shaped leaves and dense clusters of flowers make it easily identifiable.

Castor Bean (Ricinus communis): The castor bean plant is easily recognizable by its large, palmate leaves and spiky, capsule-like fruits. These fruits contain seeds, known as castor beans, which are highly toxic due to the presence of ricin. Ricin is a potent protein toxin that can inhibit protein synthesis in cells, leading to severe symptoms such as vomiting, diarrhea, abdominal pain, and potentially fatal organ damage. The castor bean plant is often grown for ornamental purposes and for its oil, which is used in various industrial applications.

Deadly Nightshade (Atropa belladonna): Deadly nightshade, also known as belladonna, is a perennial herb that can be identified by its bell-shaped, purple flowers and shiny, black berries. All parts of the plant contain tropane alkaloids, such as atropine and scopolamine, which affect the nervous system. Ingestion can lead to dilated pupils, dry mouth, difficulty swallowing, hallucinations, and even death. The plant's dark green leaves and distinctive berries make it recognizable, but its toxicity necessitates caution.

Hemlock (Conium maculatum): Hemlock is a highly poisonous biennial plant that can be identified by its tall, hollow stems, which are often purple-spotted, and its small, white, umbrella-like clusters of flowers. The plant contains coniine, a potent neurotoxin that disrupts the central nervous system, leading to symptoms such as muscle paralysis, respiratory failure, and death. Hemlock is commonly found in moist, shaded areas such as riverbanks and ditches.

Foxglove (Digitalis purpurea): Foxglove is a biennial or perennial plant known for its tall spikes of tubular, purple, pink, or white flowers. The plant contains cardiac glycosides, similar to those in oleander, which can cause serious heart problems. Symptoms of foxglove poisoning include nausea, vomiting, diarrhea, confusion, and irregular heartbeats. The plant's striking flowers and large, woolly leaves make it easy to identify in gardens and wild areas.

10.1.2 Common Toxic Compounds

Understanding the toxic compounds found in poisonous plants is essential for recognizing the potential dangers and symptoms of poisoning. These compounds vary widely in their chemical structure and effects on the human body.

Cardiac Glycosides: Cardiac glycosides are found in plants such as oleander and foxglove. These compounds affect the heart by increasing the force of cardiac contractions and altering the electrical activity of the heart. Symptoms of cardiac glycoside poisoning include nausea, vomiting, diarrhea, abdominal pain, confusion, and severe arrhythmias. Ingesting even a small amount of plants containing these toxins can be fatal.

Ricin: Ricin, found in the seeds of the castor bean plant, is one of the most potent toxins known. It inhibits protein synthesis within cells, leading to cell death. Symptoms of ricin poisoning include severe abdominal pain, vomiting, diarrhea, dehydration, and multi-organ failure. Ricin is highly toxic, and exposure to even a small amount can be lethal.

Tropane Alkaloids: Tropane alkaloids, such as atropine and scopolamine, are found in deadly nightshade and other plants of the Solanaceae family. These alkaloids affect the nervous system by blocking acetylcholine receptors. Symptoms of tropane alkaloid poisoning include dry mouth, blurred vision, hallucinations, confusion, seizures, and death. These compounds are highly toxic and can cause severe symptoms with minimal exposure.

Coniine: Coniine is a neurotoxin found in hemlock. It affects the peripheral nervous system by disrupting the transmission of nerve impulses. Symptoms of coniine poisoning include muscle paralysis, respiratory distress, tremors, and death. Hemlock poisoning can be fatal even in small doses, making it one of the most dangerous plants.

Oxalates: Oxalates are found in plants such as rhubarb leaves and dieffenbachia. These compounds can cause irritation and swelling of the mouth, throat, and gastrointestinal tract. In severe cases, ingestion of oxalates can lead to kidney damage and hypocalcemia. Symptoms include burning sensations, difficulty swallowing, vomiting, and, in severe cases, convulsions and renal failure.

10.2 Mushrooms Poisoning

Mushroom poisoning, also known as mycetism, occurs when toxic species of mushrooms are ingested. Mushrooms are a diverse group of fungi, and while many are edible and nutritious, others contain potent toxins that can cause severe illness or death. Proper identification and awareness of toxic mushrooms are essential to prevent poisoning.

10.2.1 Toxic Species

Identifying toxic mushroom species is critical for preventing mushroom poisoning. Several species are particularly dangerous due to their potent toxins.

Amanita Phalloides (Death Cap): The death cap is one of the most poisonous mushrooms. It is typically found in deciduous forests and can be mistaken for edible mushrooms. The cap is usually greenish to yellowish, the gills are white, and it has a bulbous base with a white volva. It contains amatoxins, which inhibit RNA polymerase and cause severe liver damage.

Amanita Muscaria (Fly Agaric): This iconic mushroom is easily recognizable by its bright red cap with white spots. It contains ibotenic acid and muscimol, which affect the central nervous system. Ingestion can cause hallucinations, seizures, and delirium.

Galerina Marginata (Deadly Galerina): This small brown mushroom is often found on decaying wood. It contains amatoxins similar to those in the death cap, leading to severe liver and kidney damage.

Gyromitra Esculenta (False Morel): False morels resemble true morels but contain gyromitrin, which is converted to monomethylhydrazine (MMH) in the body. MMH is toxic to the liver and central nervous system, causing seizures and organ failure.

Cortinarius Species: Several Cortinarius species contain orellanine, a toxin that causes delayed kidney failure. Symptoms may not appear until several days after ingestion, making diagnosis and treatment challenging.

Lepiota Species: Some small Lepiota species contain amatoxins and can cause severe liver damage. They are often mistaken for edible mushrooms, leading to accidental poisoning.

10.2.2 Clinical Symptoms

Clinical symptoms of mushroom poisoning vary depending on the species ingested and the toxins involved. Symptoms can range from mild gastrointestinal distress to severe organ failure.

Gastrointestinal Symptoms:

- **Nausea and Vomiting:** Common early symptoms after ingesting toxic mushrooms.
- **Abdominal Pain:** Cramping and severe pain in the abdomen.
- **Diarrhea:** Watery or bloody stools, leading to dehydration.

Hepatic Symptoms:

- **Jaundice:** Yellowing of the skin and eyes due to liver damage.
- **Hepatomegaly:** Enlargement of the liver.
- **Liver Failure:** Severe cases can lead to acute liver failure, characterized by confusion, coagulopathy, and multi-organ failure.

Neurological Symptoms:

- **Hallucinations:** Visual and auditory hallucinations, particularly with Amanita muscaria and Psilocybe species.
- **Seizures:** Convulsions due to neurotoxins affecting the central nervous system.
- **Delirium:** Confusion, agitation, and altered mental status.

Renal Symptoms:

- **Hematuria:** Blood in the urine due to kidney damage.
- **Oliguria:** Reduced urine output.
- **Acute Kidney Injury (AKI):** Severe cases can lead to kidney failure, requiring dialysis.

Delayed Symptoms:

- **Delayed Onset:** Some toxins, like orellanine, have a delayed onset of symptoms, which can appear days to weeks after ingestion.
- **Chronic Organ Damage:** Long-term exposure to certain toxins can lead to chronic liver or kidney damage.

10.2.3 Management Strategies

Effective management of mushroom poisoning requires prompt identification, supportive care, and specific treatments to mitigate the effects of the toxins.

Immediate First Aid:

- **Induce Vomiting:** Only if advised by a poison control center or healthcare provider and if the patient is alert.
- **Activated Charcoal:** Administer activated charcoal to absorb toxins and reduce their absorption in the gastrointestinal tract.
- **Gastric Lavage:** Consider gastric lavage if the patient presents within a few hours of ingestion and is symptomatic.

Supportive Care:

- **Hydration:** Provide intravenous fluids to maintain hydration and correct electrolyte imbalances.
- **Symptomatic Treatment:** Manage symptoms such as nausea, vomiting, and pain with appropriate medications.

Specific Treatments:

- **Antidotes:** Administer specific antidotes if available and appropriate for the type of mushroom ingested.

  - **Silibinin:** Used to treat amatoxin poisoning, it helps protect the liver and improve outcomes.
  - **Pyridoxine (Vitamin B6):** Administered for gyromitrin poisoning to counteract the effects of MMH.

Monitoring and Follow-Up:

- **Vital Signs:** Continuously monitor the patient's vital signs, including heart rate, blood pressure, respiratory rate, and oxygen saturation.
- **Laboratory Tests:** Perform regular blood tests to monitor liver and kidney function, coagulation profile, and electrolyte levels.

- **Imaging:** Conduct imaging studies, such as ultrasound or CT scans, to assess organ damage.

Prevention and Education:

- **Public Awareness:** Educate the public about the risks of mushroom foraging and the importance of accurate identification.
- **Proper Identification:** Encourage the use of reliable field guides and expert consultation when foraging for wild mushrooms.
- **Avoiding Unknown Mushrooms:** Advise against consuming any wild mushrooms unless they are positively identified as safe by an expert.

10.3 Mycotoxins Poisoning

Mycotoxins are toxic secondary metabolites produced by certain species of molds. These compounds can contaminate food and feed, posing serious health risks to humans and animals. Understanding the different types of mycotoxins, their clinical symptoms, and management strategies is crucial for preventing and treating mycotoxin poisoning.

10.3.1 Types of Mycotoxins

Mycotoxins are produced by various fungi, primarily Aspergillus, Penicillium, and Fusarium species. Several types of mycotoxins are of significant concern due to their widespread occurrence and toxicity.

Aflatoxins: Aflatoxins are produced by Aspergillus species, particularly A. flavus and A. parasiticus. They are commonly found in contaminated grains, nuts, and legumes. Aflatoxin B1 is the most toxic and carcinogenic. Aflatoxins can cause acute liver damage, immune suppression, and are potent carcinogens, particularly affecting the liver.

Ochratoxins: Ochratoxins are produced by Aspergillus and Penicillium species. Ochratoxin A is the most prevalent and toxic. It contaminates a wide range of food products, including cereals, coffee, dried fruits, and wine. Ochratoxin A primarily affects the kidneys, leading to nephrotoxicity and potential kidney failure. It is also a potential carcinogen.

Trichothecenes: Trichothecenes are produced by Fusarium species and include a variety of toxins such as deoxynivalenol (DON) and T-2 toxin.

They contaminate cereals and grains. Trichothecenes inhibit protein synthesis, causing gastrointestinal issues, immune suppression, and skin toxicity. T-2 toxin is particularly toxic, leading to severe hemorrhagic lesions.

Fumonisins: Fumonisins are produced by Fusarium species, primarily F. verticillioides and F. proliferatum. They are commonly found in maize and maize-based products. Fumonisins disrupt sphingolipid metabolism, leading to hepatotoxicity, nephrotoxicity, and increased risk of esophageal cancer. They are also associated with neural tube defects.

Zearalenone: Zearalenone is produced by Fusarium species and contaminates cereals, particularly maize. It has estrogenic effects, causing reproductive issues such as infertility, spontaneous abortions, and feminization in animals and humans.

10.3.2 Clinical Symptoms

The clinical symptoms of mycotoxin poisoning vary depending on the type of mycotoxin, the dose, and the duration of exposure. Symptoms can range from acute to chronic and affect multiple organ systems.

Aflatoxins:

- **Acute Poisoning:** Symptoms include fever, vomiting, abdominal pain, and jaundice. Severe cases can lead to acute liver failure and death.
- **Chronic Exposure:** Long-term exposure can result in liver cancer, immunosuppression, stunted growth in children, and chronic liver disease.

Ochratoxins:

- **Acute Poisoning:** Symptoms include abdominal pain, diarrhea, vomiting, and kidney pain.
- **Chronic Exposure:** Long-term exposure can lead to chronic kidney disease, immunosuppression, and increased risk of cancer, particularly in the urinary tract.

Trichothecenes:

- **Acute Poisoning:** Symptoms include nausea, vomiting, diarrhea, abdominal pain, and bleeding. Skin exposure can cause dermatitis.
- **Chronic Exposure:** Long-term exposure can lead to immunosuppression, chronic gastrointestinal issues, and potential cancer risk.

Fumonisins:

- **Acute Poisoning:** Symptoms include abdominal pain, diarrhea, and signs of liver and kidney toxicity.
- **Chronic Exposure:** Long-term exposure can lead to liver and kidney damage, esophageal cancer, and neural tube defects in fetuses.

Zearalenone:

- **Acute Poisoning:** Symptoms are less common but may include abdominal pain and hormonal disruptions.
- **Chronic Exposure:** Long-term exposure can lead to reproductive issues, such as infertility and developmental problems in fetuses.

10.3.3 Management Strategies

Effective management of mycotoxin poisoning involves preventing exposure, symptomatic treatment, and specific interventions to reduce toxin levels in the body.

Prevention:

- **Food Safety:** Implement stringent food safety measures to prevent mold contamination in crops and food products. This includes proper storage, drying, and monitoring of moisture levels.
- **Regulation:** Enforce regulations and standards for acceptable mycotoxin levels in food and feed products.
- **Public Awareness:** Educate the public about the risks of mycotoxins and safe food handling practices.

Symptomatic Treatment:

- **Supportive Care:** Provide hydration, electrolyte balance, and nutritional support for affected individuals.
- **Gastrointestinal Decontamination:** In cases of acute ingestion, consider activated charcoal to reduce toxin absorption.
- **Pain Management:** Use analgesics to manage abdominal pain and other discomforts.

Specific Interventions:

- **Antioxidants:** Administer antioxidants, such as vitamin E and selenium, to mitigate oxidative stress caused by mycotoxins.
- **Chelation Therapy:** For certain mycotoxins, chelation therapy may help reduce toxin levels. However, this is not commonly used and depends on the specific mycotoxin involved.

Monitoring and Follow-Up:

- **Regular Assessments:** Conduct regular medical check-ups to monitor the patient's clinical status and response to treatment.
- **Laboratory Tests:** Perform blood tests to assess liver and kidney function, as well as specific tests for mycotoxin levels if available.
- **Long-Term Care:** Provide long-term monitoring and supportive care for individuals with chronic exposure to mycotoxins to prevent long-term health complications.

10.4 Symptoms and Management

Mycotoxin poisoning can present with various symptoms, affecting different organ systems. The management of these symptoms involves supportive care and specific treatments based on the type and severity of symptoms.

10.4.1 Gastrointestinal Symptoms

Gastrointestinal symptoms are common in mycotoxin poisoning due to the ingestion of contaminated food. These symptoms can range from mild discomfort to severe, life-threatening conditions.

Common Gastrointestinal Symptoms:

- **Nausea and Vomiting:** These are often the first symptoms to appear after ingestion of mycotoxins.
- **Abdominal Pain:** Cramping and severe pain in the abdomen are common.
- **Diarrhea:** Watery or bloody stools can lead to dehydration and electrolyte imbalances.
- **Hematemesis:** Vomiting blood, which indicates severe gastrointestinal bleeding.

Management of Gastrointestinal Symptoms:

- **Hydration:** Provide intravenous fluids to maintain hydration and correct electrolyte imbalances.
- **Antiemetics:** Administer antiemetic medications such as ondansetron to control nausea and vomiting.
- **Analgesics:** Use analgesics like acetaminophen or ibuprofen to manage abdominal pain.
- **Activated Charcoal:** In cases of recent ingestion, activated charcoal can help absorb the mycotoxins and reduce their systemic absorption.
- **Gastrointestinal Decontamination:** Consider gastric lavage if the patient presents within a few hours of ingestion and is symptomatic.

10.4.2 Neurological Symptoms

Neurological symptoms occur due to the neurotoxic effects of certain mycotoxins, affecting the central and peripheral nervous systems. These symptoms can be acute or develop over time with chronic exposure.

Common Neurological Symptoms:

- **Headaches:** Persistent and severe headaches.
- **Dizziness and Vertigo:** Sensations of spinning and imbalance.
- **Seizures:** Convulsions due to severe neurotoxicity.
- **Hallucinations:** Visual and auditory hallucinations, particularly with certain mycotoxins like those from Amanita muscaria.

- **Confusion and Delirium:** Altered mental status, agitation, and disorientation.
- **Peripheral Neuropathy:** Tingling, numbness, and weakness in the extremities.

Management of Neurological Symptoms:

- **Anticonvulsants:** Administer anticonvulsant medications such as diazepam or phenytoin to control seizures.
- **Sedatives:** Use sedatives to manage severe agitation and delirium.
- **Hydration and Electrolyte Balance:** Maintain adequate hydration and correct electrolyte imbalances, which can exacerbate neurological symptoms.
- **Supportive Care:** Provide supportive care, including monitoring of vital signs and neurological status.
- **Chelation Therapy:** For specific mycotoxins, chelation therapy may help reduce toxin levels and mitigate neurological symptoms.

10.4.3 Dermatological Symptoms

Dermatological symptoms can result from direct skin contact with mycotoxins or secondary effects of systemic toxicity. These symptoms may include irritation, allergic reactions, and more severe skin conditions.

Common Dermatological Symptoms:

- **Rashes:** Red, itchy, and inflamed skin.
- **Dermatitis:** Severe skin inflammation, often resulting from direct contact with mycotoxins.
- **Blisters:** Fluid-filled blisters that can be painful and prone to infection.
- **Erythema:** Redness of the skin due to increased blood flow.
- **Ulceration:** Severe cases can lead to skin ulcers and necrosis.

Management of Dermatological Symptoms:

- **Topical Treatments:** Apply topical corticosteroids to reduce inflammation and itching. Antibiotic ointments can prevent secondary infections.

- **Oral Antihistamines:** Use oral antihistamines like diphenhydramine to control allergic reactions and itching.
- **Hydration:** Maintain adequate hydration to support skin healing and overall health.
- **Wound Care:** Properly clean and dress blisters and ulcers to prevent infection and promote healing.
- **Avoidance of Exposure:** Prevent further contact with the source of mycotoxins and use protective clothing to minimize skin exposure.

Chapter 11: Food Poisoning

Introduction

Food poisoning, also known as foodborne illness, is a widespread and significant public health issue affecting millions of people worldwide each year. It is caused by consuming contaminated food or beverages containing harmful microorganisms, toxins, chemicals, or other hazardous substances. The symptoms of food poisoning can range from mild gastrointestinal discomfort to severe, life-threatening conditions. Understanding the causes, symptoms, and management of food poisoning is essential for preventing outbreaks and ensuring food safety.

Importance of Understanding Food Poisoning

Understanding food poisoning is crucial for several reasons. Firstly, it helps in identifying the sources and pathways of contamination, enabling the implementation of effective preventive measures. Secondly, knowledge of the various pathogens and toxins involved in food poisoning can aid in prompt diagnosis and treatment, reducing morbidity and mortality. Lastly, raising awareness about food safety practices among consumers, food handlers, and regulatory authorities can significantly reduce the incidence of foodborne illnesses.

Scope of the Chapter

This chapter aims to provide a comprehensive overview of food poisoning, focusing on the types of pathogens and toxins responsible, the clinical manifestations of foodborne illnesses, and the strategies for prevention and management. Key areas covered will include:

1. **Types of Food Poisoning:**

   - **Bacterial:** Common bacterial pathogens such as Salmonella, Escherichia coli, Listeria, and Campylobacter.
   - **Viral:** Viral agents including norovirus, hepatitis A, and rotavirus.
   - **Parasitic:** Parasitic infections caused by organisms such as Giardia, Cryptosporidium, and Toxoplasma.
   - **Chemical:** Poisoning from chemical contaminants like pesticides, heavy metals, and food additives.
   - **Toxins:** Illnesses caused by natural toxins found in certain plants, seafood, and mushrooms.

2. **Pathways of Contamination:**

   - **Food Production and Processing:** Contamination during harvesting, processing, and packaging.
   - **Food Handling and Preparation:** Cross-contamination and improper food handling practices.
   - **Storage and Transportation:** Inadequate temperature control and sanitation during storage and transportation.

3. **Clinical Manifestations:**

   - **Gastrointestinal Symptoms:** Nausea, vomiting, diarrhea, abdominal pain, and cramping.
   - **Systemic Symptoms:** Fever, headache, muscle aches, and dehydration.
   - **Severe Complications:** Hemolytic uremic syndrome, septicemia, and neurological symptoms.

4. **Diagnosis and Management:**

- ○ **Diagnostic Techniques:** Laboratory tests, stool cultures, and identification of specific pathogens.
- ○ **Supportive Care:** Hydration, electrolyte balance, and symptomatic treatment.
- ○ **Specific Treatments:** Antibiotics, antivirals, and antiparasitic medications when indicated.
- ○ **Hospitalization:** Criteria for hospital admission and management of severe cases.

5. **Prevention and Control:**

- ○ **Food Safety Practices:** Guidelines for safe food handling, cooking, and storage.
- ○ **Regulatory Standards:** Food safety regulations and inspection protocols.
- ○ **Public Health Interventions:** Surveillance, outbreak investigation, and public education campaigns.

11.1 Causes and Types of Food Poisoning

Food poisoning is caused by the ingestion of food or beverages contaminated with harmful microorganisms, toxins, or chemicals. These contaminants can lead to various types of foodborne illnesses, each with distinct causes and clinical manifestations. Understanding the different types of food poisoning is essential for effective prevention, diagnosis, and management.

11.1.1 Bacterial Food Poisoning

Bacterial food poisoning is one of the most common types of foodborne illnesses. It occurs when food or beverages are contaminated with pathogenic bacteria that produce toxins or directly infect the gastrointestinal tract.

Common Bacterial Pathogens:

- **Salmonella:**

- ◦ **Sources:** Contaminated poultry, eggs, meat, dairy products, and produce.
- ◦ **Symptoms:** Nausea, vomiting, abdominal cramps, diarrhea, fever, and headache. Symptoms usually appear 6-48 hours after ingestion and can last 4-7 days.
- ◦ **Complications:** Severe cases can lead to dehydration and septicemia, particularly in young children, the elderly, and immunocompromised individuals.

- **Escherichia coli (E. coli):**

  - ◦ **Sources:** Contaminated beef, unpasteurized milk, fresh produce, and water.
  - ◦ **Symptoms:** Severe abdominal cramps, bloody diarrhea, and vomiting. Symptoms typically appear 3-4 days after exposure and can last up to 10 days.
  - ◦ **Complications:** Some strains, such as E. coli O157

, can cause hemolytic uremic syndrome (HUS), leading to kidney failure and hemolysis.

- **Listeria monocytogenes:**

  - ◦ **Sources:** Contaminated deli meats, unpasteurized dairy products, and ready-to-eat foods.
  - ◦ **Symptoms:** Fever, muscle aches, nausea, and diarrhea. Invasive listeriosis can lead to severe complications like meningitis and septicemia.
  - ◦ **Complications:** High risk for pregnant women, newborns, the elderly, and immunocompromised individuals. Can cause miscarriages, stillbirths, and neonatal infections.

- **Campylobacter:**

  - ◦ **Sources:** Contaminated poultry, unpasteurized milk, and untreated water.
  - ◦ **Symptoms:** Diarrhea (often bloody), fever, nausea, vomiting, and abdominal pain. Symptoms usually appear 2-5 days after ingestion

and can last about a week.

- ◦ **Complications:** Severe dehydration, Guillain-Barré syndrome, and reactive arthritis in some cases.

11.1.2 Viral Food Poisoning

Viral food poisoning is caused by viruses that contaminate food or water. These viruses are highly infectious and can spread rapidly through contaminated food, water, or person-to-person contact.

Common Viral Pathogens:

- **Norovirus:**

  - ◦ **Sources:** Contaminated shellfish, fresh produce, and ready-to-eat foods. Often spread in settings like restaurants, cruise ships, and nursing homes.
  - ◦ **Symptoms:** Nausea, vomiting, watery diarrhea, abdominal pain, and fever. Symptoms typically appear 12-48 hours after exposure and last 1-3 days.
  - ◦ **Complications:** Dehydration, particularly in young children, the elderly, and immunocompromised individuals.

- **Hepatitis A:**

  - ◦ **Sources:** Contaminated shellfish, raw produce, and water. Often spread through poor hygiene and sanitation practices.
  - ◦ **Symptoms:** Fever, fatigue, nausea, vomiting, abdominal pain, dark urine, jaundice, and liver inflammation. Symptoms usually appear 15-50 days after exposure and can last several weeks to months.
  - ◦ **Complications:** Liver failure in severe cases, particularly in individuals with pre-existing liver conditions.

- **Rotavirus:**

  - ◦ **Sources:** Contaminated water and food, particularly in areas with poor sanitation.

- **Symptoms:** Severe diarrhea, vomiting, fever, and abdominal pain. Common in infants and young children, with symptoms appearing 1-3 days after exposure and lasting 3-8 days.
- **Complications:** Severe dehydration, particularly in young children, requiring hospitalization and rehydration therapy.

11.1.3 Chemical Food Poisoning

Chemical food poisoning occurs when food or beverages are contaminated with harmful chemicals. These chemicals can be naturally occurring in certain foods or result from contamination during food production, processing, or storage.

Common Chemical Contaminants:

- **Pesticides:**

  - **Sources:** Residues on fruits, vegetables, and grains from agricultural use.
  - **Symptoms:** Nausea, vomiting, diarrhea, abdominal pain, headache, dizziness, and in severe cases, convulsions and respiratory distress.
  - **Complications:** Long-term exposure can lead to chronic health issues, including neurological damage and cancer.

- **Heavy Metals:**

  - **Sources:** Contaminated water and food, particularly seafood. Common heavy metals include lead, mercury, and cadmium.
  - **Symptoms:** Nausea, vomiting, abdominal pain, diarrhea, and neurological symptoms such as tremors, headaches, and cognitive impairment.
  - **Complications:** Chronic exposure can cause organ damage, developmental issues in children, and increased cancer risk.

- **Food Additives and Preservatives:**

  - **Sources:** Additives used to enhance flavor, color, and shelf-life of food products. Common additives include sulfites, nitrates, and artificial sweeteners.

- ◦ **Symptoms:** Allergic reactions, gastrointestinal symptoms, headaches, and in some cases, respiratory distress.
- ◦ **Complications:** Long-term health effects are still being studied, but some additives have been linked to hyperactivity in children and other health concerns.

11.2 Clinical Symptoms

Food poisoning can present with a wide range of clinical symptoms, primarily affecting the gastrointestinal system but also causing systemic effects. The severity and type of symptoms depend on the pathogen or toxin involved, the amount ingested, and the individual's health status.

11.2.1 Gastrointestinal Symptoms

Gastrointestinal symptoms are the most common and immediate indicators of food poisoning. These symptoms result from the direct effects of pathogens or toxins on the digestive tract.

Common Gastrointestinal Symptoms:

- **Nausea:** A feeling of unease and discomfort in the stomach with an urge to vomit. Nausea often precedes vomiting and can be caused by a variety of pathogens, including bacteria, viruses, and toxins.
- **Vomiting:** The forceful expulsion of stomach contents through the mouth. Vomiting can be a protective mechanism to expel harmful substances but can lead to dehydration if severe or prolonged.
- **Diarrhea:** Frequent, loose, or watery stools. Diarrhea is a common symptom of food poisoning caused by bacteria such as Salmonella, E. coli, and viruses like norovirus. It can lead to significant fluid loss and dehydration.
- **Abdominal Pain and Cramping:** Sharp or cramping pain in the abdomen. This pain is due to inflammation and irritation of the gastrointestinal tract caused by the infection or toxin.
- **Bloody Stools:** The presence of blood in stools indicates severe infection and inflammation, often associated with pathogens like E. coli O157

and Shigella. Bloody diarrhea is a medical emergency requiring prompt evaluation.

- **Fever:** Elevated body temperature as the body responds to the infection. Fever is common with bacterial food poisoning and can help differentiate infectious causes from non-infectious causes of gastrointestinal distress.

11.2.2 Systemic Symptoms

Systemic symptoms arise when the infection or toxin spreads beyond the gastrointestinal tract, affecting other organs and systems. These symptoms indicate a more severe or widespread infection.

Common Systemic Symptoms:

- **Fever and Chills:** Fever, often accompanied by chills, indicates an immune response to systemic infection. It is common in bacterial and viral food poisoning.
- **Headache:** Generalized headache can result from dehydration, fever, or direct effects of toxins on the nervous system.
- **Muscle Aches (Myalgia):** Generalized muscle pain and discomfort. Myalgia can be associated with viral food poisoning, such as norovirus or rotavirus.
- **Fatigue and Weakness:** Generalized tiredness and weakness due to the body's efforts to fight off the infection, dehydration, and loss of nutrients.
- **Dehydration:** Severe vomiting and diarrhea can lead to significant fluid loss, resulting in dehydration. Symptoms include dry mouth, decreased urine output, dark-colored urine, dizziness, and confusion. Severe dehydration can lead to hypovolemic shock and requires immediate medical intervention.
- **Jaundice:** Yellowing of the skin and eyes due to liver involvement, seen in cases of hepatitis A virus infection. Jaundice indicates liver inflammation and requires medical evaluation.
- **Neurological Symptoms:** In severe cases, certain toxins and pathogens can affect the nervous system, leading to symptoms such as dizziness, confusion, seizures, and, in extreme cases, coma. Neurological

symptoms are more commonly associated with chemical food poisoning and severe bacterial infections.

11.3 Management and Prevention

Effective management and prevention of food poisoning involve addressing symptoms, treating the underlying cause, and implementing strategies to prevent future occurrences. This section outlines the approaches to symptomatic treatment and preventive measures.

11.3.1 Symptomatic Treatment

Symptomatic treatment focuses on relieving the symptoms of food poisoning and preventing complications such as dehydration and severe illness.

Hydration:

- **Oral Rehydration Solutions (ORS):** These solutions contain a balanced mix of salts and sugars to replace lost fluids and electrolytes. They are especially important for children and the elderly, who are more susceptible to dehydration.
- **Intravenous Fluids:** In severe cases of dehydration, intravenous (IV) fluids may be necessary to quickly restore hydration and electrolyte balance.

Antiemetics:

- **Medications:** Drugs such as ondansetron or promethazine can help control nausea and vomiting, making it easier for patients to keep down fluids and avoid dehydration.

Antidiarrheals:

- **Medications:** Loperamide can reduce the frequency of diarrhea, but it should be used with caution. It is not recommended for bacterial infections like E. coli O157 or Shigella, where slowing down the gastrointestinal tract may be harmful.

Analgesics:

- **Pain Relievers:** Acetaminophen or ibuprofen can help relieve abdominal pain and fever. Aspirin should be avoided in children due to the risk of Reye's syndrome.

Antibiotics:

- **When Indicated:** Antibiotics may be prescribed for certain bacterial infections, such as severe cases of Campylobacter or Salmonella, or for vulnerable populations such as the elderly, infants, and immunocompromised individuals. However, antibiotics are generally not recommended for E. coli O157

infections due to the risk of hemolytic uremic syndrome (HUS).
Rest and Recovery:

- **Bed Rest:** Encouraging rest to allow the body to recover from the illness.
- **Gradual Reintroduction of Food:** Starting with bland, easy-to-digest foods like rice, bananas, toast, and clear broths, and gradually returning to a normal diet as tolerated.

11.3.2 Preventive Measures

Preventive measures are crucial to reduce the risk of food poisoning and ensure food safety at all stages, from production to consumption.
Food Handling and Preparation:

- **Hand Washing:** Wash hands thoroughly with soap and water before and after handling food, especially raw meat, poultry, seafood, and eggs.
- **Separate Cutting Boards:** Use separate cutting boards and utensils for raw and cooked foods to avoid cross-contamination.
- **Proper Cooking:** Cook foods to the appropriate temperatures to kill harmful pathogens. Use a food thermometer to ensure meats, poultry, and seafood reach safe internal temperatures.

- ◦ **Poultry:** 165°F (74°C)
- ◦ **Ground meats:** 160°F (71°C)
- ◦ **Fish:** 145°F (63°C)

- **Chilling:** Refrigerate perishable foods promptly. Keep the refrigerator temperature at or below 40°F (4°C) and the freezer at or below 0°F (-18°C).
- **Avoiding Raw Foods:** Avoid consuming raw or undercooked meats, poultry, seafood, and eggs. Be cautious with raw milk and products made from it.

Food Storage:

- **Proper Storage:** Store food in clean, airtight containers to prevent contamination. Keep raw and cooked foods separate in the refrigerator.
- **Labeling and Dating:** Label and date leftovers and consume them within a safe period, typically 3-4 days for most perishable foods.
- **FIFO Principle:** Follow the "First In, First Out" principle to use older stock before newer stock to minimize spoilage.

Food Safety Practices:

- **Cleaning:** Keep kitchen surfaces, utensils, and equipment clean. Use hot, soapy water to wash dishes and cooking tools, and sanitize cutting boards and countertops regularly.
- **Avoiding Contaminated Water:** Use safe, potable water for drinking, cooking, and washing food. Be cautious when traveling to areas with questionable water quality.
- **Educating Food Handlers:** Train food handlers in proper food safety practices to minimize the risk of contamination in commercial and institutional settings.

Regulatory Standards and Public Health Interventions:

- **Regulations:** Adhere to local and international food safety standards and regulations to ensure food production, processing, and distribution are safe.

- **Surveillance and Monitoring:** Implement foodborne disease surveillance systems to detect and respond to outbreaks promptly.
- **Public Awareness Campaigns:** Conduct public health campaigns to educate consumers and food handlers about the importance of food safety and hygiene practices.

Chapter 12: Envenomations – Arthropod Bites and Stings

Introduction

Envenomations resulting from arthropod bites and stings are a common and significant health concern worldwide. Arthropods, a diverse group of invertebrates that include insects, arachnids, and crustaceans, can deliver venom through bites or stings, causing a range of reactions from mild discomfort to severe systemic effects. While many arthropod bites and stings are benign and self-limiting, some can lead to serious medical conditions requiring prompt intervention.

Importance of Understanding Arthropod Envenomations

Understanding arthropod envenomations is crucial for several reasons. Firstly, it enables healthcare providers to recognize and manage envenomations effectively, reducing morbidity and mortality. Secondly, knowledge of the diverse range of arthropods and their venoms helps in preventing and controlling envenomations, particularly in endemic areas. Lastly, public awareness and education about the risks and appropriate responses to arthropod bites and stings can significantly reduce the incidence and severity of envenomations.

Scope of the Chapter

This chapter aims to provide a comprehensive overview of arthropod envenomations, focusing on the identification of common venomous arthropods, the clinical manifestations of their bites and stings, and the management strategies for affected individuals. Key areas covered will include:

1. **Common Venomous Arthropods:**

   ◦ Identification and classification of arthropods known to cause envenomations.
   ◦ Geographic distribution and common habitats of venomous arthropods.
   ◦ Seasonal variations in arthropod activity and envenomation risk.

2. **Mechanisms of Venom Action:**

   ◦ Overview of the toxic compounds found in arthropod venoms.
   ◦ How these compounds affect human physiology.

3. **Clinical Manifestations of Envenomations:**

   ◦ Local Effects: Pain, swelling, redness, and necrosis at the bite or sting site.
   ◦ Systemic Effects: Allergic reactions, anaphylaxis, neurotoxicity, and organ damage.
   ◦ Specific symptoms associated with different types of arthropod venoms.

4. **Diagnosis and Assessment:**

   ◦ History and physical examination of envenomation victims.
   ◦ Laboratory investigations and imaging studies.
   ◦ Identification of the offending arthropod when possible.

5. **Management and Treatment:**

   ◦ First aid measures and initial management at the bite or sting site.
   ◦ Hospital management and medical treatment protocols.
   ◦ Administration of antivenoms, when available and indicated.
   ◦ Supportive care and management of complications.

6. **Prevention and Education:**

   ◦ Strategies for preventing arthropod bites and stings.

- Community education and awareness programs.
- Training healthcare providers in the recognition and management of arthropod envenomations.

12.1 Types of Arthropod Envenomations

Arthropod envenomations occur when venomous insects and arachnids bite or sting, injecting venom into their victims. This section will cover the types of arthropod envenomations, focusing on insect bites and stings, as well as arachnid bites and stings.

12.1.1 Insect Bites and Stings

Insects are a diverse group of arthropods that include species capable of delivering venom through bites or stings. These envenomations can cause a range of symptoms, from mild local reactions to severe systemic effects.

Common Venomous Insects:

- **Bees (Family Apidae):**

  - **Description:** Bees, including honeybees and bumblebees, are commonly found worldwide. They have barbed stingers, which detach from their bodies after stinging.
  - **Venom:** Bee venom contains melittin, phospholipase A2, and hyaluronidase, which can cause pain, swelling, and allergic reactions.
  - **Symptoms:** Localized pain, swelling, redness, and itching. In allergic individuals, bee stings can cause anaphylaxis, characterized by difficulty breathing, hives, and shock.

- **Wasps (Family Vespidae):**

  - **Description:** Wasps, including yellow jackets and hornets, are aggressive and can sting multiple times. They have smooth stingers that do not detach.
  - **Venom:** Wasp venom contains a mix of toxins, including peptides and enzymes, which cause pain and inflammation.

- ◦ **Symptoms:** Immediate pain, swelling, redness, and itching at the sting site. Systemic allergic reactions can occur in sensitive individuals.

- **Ants (Family Formicidae):**

  - ◦ **Description:** Fire ants and bullet ants are notorious for their painful stings. Fire ants inject venom through their mandibles and sting multiple times.
  - ◦ **Venom:** Fire ant venom contains alkaloids, such as solenopsin, which cause intense pain and pustules.
  - ◦ **Symptoms:** Burning pain, swelling, and pustule formation. Severe allergic reactions and anaphylaxis can occur.

- **Mosquitoes (Family Culicidae):**

  - ◦ **Description:** Mosquitoes are widespread and feed on blood using their proboscis. They inject saliva containing anticoagulants and anesthetics.
  - ◦ **Venom:** Mosquito saliva contains proteins that trigger immune responses.
  - ◦ **Symptoms:** Itchy red bumps, localized swelling, and in some cases, allergic reactions. Mosquitoes can transmit diseases such as malaria, dengue fever, and Zika virus.

12.1.2 Arachnid Bites and Stings

Arachnids, including spiders and scorpions, are another group of arthropods capable of envenomation. Their bites and stings can cause a range of symptoms, from mild to severe.

Common Venomous Arachnids:

- **Spiders (Order Araneae):**

  - ◦ **Black Widow Spider (Latrodectus spp.):**

    - ▪ **Description:** Black widow spiders are found in temperate regions worldwide. They have a shiny black body with a distinctive red hourglass marking on the abdomen.

- **Venom:** Contains neurotoxins, particularly latrotoxin, which affects the nervous system.
- **Symptoms:** Severe pain, muscle cramps, abdominal pain, sweating, and hypertension. In rare cases, envenomation can be fatal, especially in young children and the elderly.

- **Brown Recluse Spider (Loxosceles spp.):**

  - **Description:** Brown recluse spiders are found in the United States. They have a violin-shaped marking on their back.
  - **Venom:** Contains necrotizing enzymes, particularly sphingomyelinase D, which causes tissue damage.
  - **Symptoms:** Initially painless, followed by severe pain, blistering, and necrosis at the bite site. Systemic symptoms can include fever, chills, and hemolysis.

- **Scorpions (Order Scorpiones):**

  - **Description:** Scorpions are found in various regions, including deserts and tropical areas. They have a segmented tail with a venomous stinger.
  - **Venom:** Contains a mix of neurotoxins and enzymes that affect the nervous system and cardiovascular system.
  - **Symptoms:** Intense localized pain, swelling, and redness. Systemic symptoms can include numbness, muscle twitching, sweating, and in severe cases, respiratory distress, convulsions, and cardiovascular collapse.

12.2 Clinical Symptoms

The clinical symptoms of arthropod envenomations can vary widely depending on the species involved, the amount of venom injected, and the individual's response. Symptoms can be broadly categorized into local and systemic effects.

12.2.1 Local Symptoms

Local symptoms occur at or near the site of the bite or sting. These symptoms are usually the first to appear and can range from mild to severe.
Pain:

- **Immediate Pain:** Many arthropod bites and stings cause immediate sharp or burning pain. For example, bee stings and fire ant bites are known for their intense pain.
- **Delayed Pain:** Some bites, like those from brown recluse spiders, may initially be painless but develop severe pain over time.

Swelling and Redness:

- **Localized Swelling:** Swelling around the bite or sting site is common. It can range from mild to significant, potentially extending beyond the initial area.
- **Redness:** The skin around the bite or sting often becomes red and inflamed due to the body's immune response to the venom.

Itching and Irritation:

- **Pruritus:** Itching is a common symptom, particularly with mosquito bites. It can lead to scratching, which may cause secondary infections.
- **Urticaria:** Raised, itchy welts (hives) may develop at the site, especially in allergic reactions.

Blistering and Ulceration:

- **Blisters:** Some bites and stings, such as those from fire ants or brown recluse spiders, can cause blisters to form, filled with clear or bloody fluid.
- **Ulceration:** Severe envenomations, particularly from brown recluse spiders, can lead to skin necrosis and ulceration, causing open sores that may require medical attention.

Necrosis:

- **Tissue Death:** Venom from certain arachnids, like the brown recluse spider, can cause necrosis, leading to blackened, dead tissue around the bite site. This may require surgical intervention to remove dead tissue and promote healing.

12.2.2 Systemic Symptoms

Systemic symptoms occur when venom spreads through the bloodstream, affecting various organs and systems. These symptoms can be more severe and require urgent medical attention.

Allergic Reactions:

- **Anaphylaxis:** A severe, life-threatening allergic reaction that can occur rapidly after a sting or bite. Symptoms include difficulty breathing, swelling of the face and throat, rapid heartbeat, low blood pressure, and loss of consciousness. Immediate administration of epinephrine is critical.
- **Generalized Urticaria:** Widespread hives and itching beyond the bite or sting site.

Neurological Symptoms:

- **Muscle Cramps and Spasms:** Neurotoxic venoms, such as those from black widow spiders, can cause severe muscle cramps and spasms.
- **Paralysis:** Some venoms can cause temporary paralysis, particularly in severe cases of scorpion stings or certain spider bites.
- **Headache and Dizziness:** General neurological effects can include headaches, dizziness, and confusion.

Cardiovascular Symptoms:

- **Hypertension or Hypotension:** Blood pressure changes, either high or low, can occur depending on the venom and individual response.
- **Tachycardia or Bradycardia:** Increased or decreased heart rate may result from the body's response to venom.

Respiratory Symptoms:

- **Difficulty Breathing:** Swelling of the airways and respiratory distress can occur, particularly in severe allergic reactions or with neurotoxic venom.
- **Pulmonary Edema:** Fluid accumulation in the lungs may occur in severe cases, leading to breathing difficulties and requiring urgent medical intervention.

Gastrointestinal Symptoms:

- **Nausea and Vomiting:** Common symptoms following envenomation, especially in systemic reactions.
- **Abdominal Pain:** Severe abdominal cramps and pain can be associated with certain envenomations, such as black widow spider bites.

Renal and Hematological Symptoms:

- **Hemolysis:** Destruction of red blood cells can occur with certain venoms, leading to hemolytic anemia.
- **Renal Failure:** Severe systemic envenomations, particularly those involving hemolysis, can lead to acute kidney injury and renal failure.

12.3 Management and Treatment

Effective management and treatment of arthropod envenomations involve prompt first aid measures followed by appropriate medical intervention. This approach can significantly reduce the severity of symptoms, prevent complications, and improve patient outcomes.

12.3.1 First Aid Measures

Immediate first aid measures are crucial in minimizing the impact of venom and stabilizing the patient until professional medical help can be obtained.
General First Aid for Bites and Stings:

- **Stay Calm:** Keeping the patient calm can help slow the spread of venom.
- **Move to a Safe Area:** Remove the patient from the vicinity of the arthropod to prevent further bites or stings.

- **Positioning:** If bitten on an extremity, keep the affected limb at or slightly below heart level to reduce venom spread.

Specific First Aid Techniques:

- **For Bee and Wasp Stings:**

  - **Remove the Stinger:** If the stinger is still present, scrape it off with a straight-edged object like a credit card. Avoid using tweezers as they can squeeze more venom into the skin.
  - **Apply Cold Compresses:** Use a cold pack or a cloth soaked in cold water to reduce pain and swelling.
  - **Clean the Area:** Wash the affected area with soap and water to prevent infection.
  - **Antihistamines:** Oral antihistamines like diphenhydramine can help reduce itching and swelling.

- **For Ant Bites and Stings:**

  - **Cold Compresses:** Apply cold packs to reduce swelling and pain.
  - **Topical Treatments:** Use hydrocortisone cream or calamine lotion to alleviate itching.
  - **Elevation:** Elevate the affected limb to reduce swelling.

- **For Spider Bites:**

  - **Clean the Bite:** Wash the bite site with soap and water to prevent infection.
  - **Apply Ice:** Use an ice pack to reduce swelling and numb the area.
  - **Pain Relief:** Over-the-counter pain relievers such as ibuprofen or acetaminophen can help manage pain.

- **For Scorpion Stings:**

  - **Immobilize the Limb:** Keep the affected limb still and at rest.
  - **Apply Cold Compresses:** Use cold packs to reduce pain and swelling.
  - **Seek Medical Attention:** Scorpion stings can be serious, particularly in children and the elderly. Immediate medical evaluation is

recommended.

- **For Tick Bites:**

  - **Remove the Tick:** Use fine-tipped tweezers to grasp the tick as close to the skin as possible and pull upward with steady pressure. Do not twist or jerk the tick.
  - **Clean the Area:** Wash the bite area with soap and water, then apply an antiseptic.
  - **Monitor for Symptoms:** Observe for signs of tick-borne illnesses such as Lyme disease or Rocky Mountain spotted fever.

12.3.2 Medical Treatment

Medical treatment is necessary for severe envenomations or when first aid measures are insufficient to manage symptoms. It involves supportive care, specific treatments, and management of complications.

Supportive Care:

- **Hydration:** Administer intravenous fluids to maintain hydration and electrolyte balance, especially in cases of severe vomiting, diarrhea, or systemic reactions.
- **Pain Management:** Provide analgesics for pain relief. For severe pain, stronger medications such as opioids may be necessary.
- **Monitoring:** Continuous monitoring of vital signs, including heart rate, blood pressure, respiratory rate, and oxygen saturation.

Specific Treatments:

- **Antivenom:** Administer antivenom when indicated, such as for black widow spider bites or scorpion stings. Antivenom can neutralize the venom and prevent severe complications.

  - **Dosage and Administration:** Follow specific guidelines for dosing and administration. Monitor for potential allergic reactions to the antivenom.

- **Antihistamines and Corticosteroids:** Use antihistamines for allergic reactions and corticosteroids for severe inflammation and anaphylaxis.

  - ◦ **Epinephrine:** Administer epinephrine in cases of anaphylaxis to counteract severe allergic reactions and stabilize the patient.

Management of Complications:

- **Infection Control:** Prescribe antibiotics if there is evidence of secondary bacterial infection at the bite or sting site.
- **Tetanus Prophylaxis:** Ensure the patient is up to date with tetanus immunization. Administer a tetanus booster if needed.
- **Surgical Intervention:** In cases of severe necrosis or ulceration, surgical debridement may be necessary to remove dead tissue and promote healing.
- **Neurological and Cardiovascular Support:** Provide appropriate interventions for severe systemic symptoms such as respiratory distress, cardiovascular instability, or neurological impairment.

Chapter 13: Substance Abuse

Introduction

Substance abuse, also known as substance use disorder, is a widespread and complex issue that affects individuals, families, and societies globally. It involves the harmful or hazardous use of psychoactive substances, including alcohol, illicit drugs, and prescription medications. Substance abuse can lead to addiction, physical and mental health problems, and significant social and economic consequences. Understanding the nature of substance abuse, its causes, and its impact is essential for developing effective prevention, treatment, and rehabilitation strategies.

Importance of Understanding Substance Abuse

Understanding substance abuse is crucial for several reasons. Firstly, it helps in identifying the underlying causes and risk factors that contribute to the development of substance use disorders. Secondly, knowledge of the various substances and their effects on the body and mind can aid in early detection and intervention. Lastly, raising awareness about substance abuse and its consequences can promote healthier lifestyles and reduce the stigma associated with addiction, encouraging individuals to seek help.

Scope of the Chapter

This chapter aims to provide a comprehensive overview of substance abuse, focusing on the types of substances commonly abused, the clinical manifestations of substance use disorders, and the strategies for prevention and treatment. Key areas covered will include:

1. **Types of Substances:**

    - **Alcohol:** Patterns of use, effects, and associated health risks.
    - **Illicit Drugs:** Commonly abused drugs such as cannabis, cocaine, heroin, methamphetamine, and ecstasy.
    - **Prescription Medications:** Misuse of prescription drugs, including opioids, benzodiazepines, and stimulants.
    - **Other Substances:** Abuse of substances such as inhalants, anabolic steroids, and synthetic drugs.

2. **Causes and Risk Factors:**

    - **Genetic Factors:** The role of genetics in predisposition to substance abuse.
    - **Environmental Factors:** Influence of family, peers, and socio-economic conditions.
    - **Psychological Factors:** Mental health disorders, trauma, and stress as contributing factors.
    - **Social and Cultural Factors:** Cultural attitudes and societal norms related to substance use.

3. **Clinical Manifestations:**

    - **Physical Symptoms:** Health effects of substance abuse, including organ damage, infections, and overdose.

- **Psychological Symptoms:** Mental health issues such as depression, anxiety, psychosis, and cognitive impairment.
- **Behavioral Symptoms:** Changes in behavior, including neglect of responsibilities, risky behaviors, and criminal activities.

4. **Diagnosis and Assessment:**

- **Screening Tools:** Methods for identifying substance use disorders, including questionnaires and interviews.
- **Clinical Evaluation:** Comprehensive assessment of substance use, medical history, and psychosocial factors.
- **Laboratory Tests:** Drug testing and other laboratory investigations to confirm substance use.

5. **Treatment and Rehabilitation:**

- **Detoxification:** Medical management of withdrawal symptoms and stabilization.
- **Therapeutic Interventions:** Behavioral therapies, counseling, and support groups.
- **Medications:** Pharmacological treatments for addiction, such as methadone, buprenorphine, and naltrexone.
- **Relapse Prevention:** Strategies to maintain sobriety and prevent relapse, including aftercare and ongoing support.

6. **Prevention and Education:**

- **Public Health Initiatives:** Community-based programs and policies to reduce substance abuse.
- **Education and Awareness:** Promoting awareness about the risks of substance use and healthy alternatives.
- **Family and Peer Support:** The role of family and social networks in preventing and addressing substance abuse.

13.1 Signs and Symptoms of Substance Abuse

Recognizing the signs and symptoms of substance abuse is crucial for early intervention and treatment. Substance abuse can manifest through a variety of physical and behavioral signs, which may vary depending on the type of substance used, the duration of use, and the individual's overall health.

13.1.1 Physical Signs

Physical signs of substance abuse are often the most noticeable and can affect various body systems. These signs may develop gradually and can become severe if substance use continues.

General Physical Signs:

- **Changes in Appearance:** Sudden weight loss or gain, neglected personal hygiene, and unusual body odor.
- **Bloodshot or Glazed Eyes:** Red, bloodshot eyes or pupils that are larger or smaller than usual.
- **Frequent Nosebleeds:** Especially common with snorting drugs like cocaine or methamphetamine.
- **Unusual Bruises or Track Marks:** Marks on the arms or other parts of the body from intravenous drug use.

Specific Substance-Related Physical Signs:

- **Alcohol:**

  - **Slurred Speech:** Difficulty speaking clearly and coherently.
  - **Impaired Coordination:** Difficulty walking, clumsiness, and frequent accidents.
  - **Tremors:** Shaking hands, particularly in the morning.

- **Opioids (e.g., heroin, prescription painkillers):**

  - **Drowsiness:** Excessive sleepiness or "nodding off."
  - **Constricted Pupils:** Pinpoint pupils that do not respond to changes in light.
  - **Respiratory Depression:** Slow or shallow breathing.

- **Stimulants (e.g., cocaine, methamphetamine):**

- ○ **Increased Energy:** Hyperactivity, excessive talking, and restlessness.
- ○ **Dilated Pupils:** Enlarged pupils that are sensitive to light.
- ○ **Teeth Grinding:** Jaw clenching and teeth grinding, especially with methamphetamine use.

- **Cannabis:**

- ○ **Red Eyes:** Bloodshot eyes with dilated pupils.
- ○ **Increased Appetite:** Cravings for food, often referred to as "the munchies."
- ○ **Dry Mouth:** Persistent dry mouth and thirst.

- **Hallucinogens (e.g., LSD, psilocybin mushrooms):**

- ○ **Visual Disturbances:** Hallucinations, seeing things that are not there.
- ○ **Changes in Perception:** Altered sense of time, space, and reality.
- ○ **Pupil Dilation:** Large pupils that do not constrict in bright light.

13.1.2 Behavioral Signs

Behavioral signs of substance abuse often involve changes in an individual's actions, habits, and overall lifestyle. These changes can be subtle initially but may become more pronounced as substance use continues.

General Behavioral Signs:

- **Changes in Social Behavior:** Withdrawal from family and friends, secretive behavior, and isolation.
- **Decline in Academic or Work Performance:** Poor attendance, declining grades, or work performance.
- **Financial Problems:** Unexplained need for money, borrowing or stealing money, or financial difficulties.

Specific Behavioral Signs:

- **Alcohol:**

- ○ **Increased Tolerance:** Needing more alcohol to achieve the same effect.
- ○ **Blackouts:** Inability to remember events that occurred while drinking.
- ○ **Drinking Alone:** Consuming alcohol in isolation or at inappropriate times.

- **Opioids:**

  - ○ **Doctor Shopping:** Visiting multiple doctors to obtain prescriptions.
  - ○ **Neglect of Responsibilities:** Ignoring personal, professional, or social responsibilities.
  - ○ **Withdrawal Symptoms:** Experiencing symptoms such as nausea, sweating, and agitation when not using.

- **Stimulants:**

  - ○ **Aggressive Behavior:** Increased irritability, agitation, and potential for violence.
  - ○ **Paranoia:** Suspicion or mistrust of others, feeling persecuted.
  - ○ **Risky Behaviors:** Engaging in dangerous activities or taking unnecessary risks.

- **Cannabis:**

  - ○ **Lack of Motivation:** Decreased interest in activities, lethargy, and apathy.
  - ○ **Memory Problems:** Short-term memory impairment and difficulty concentrating.
  - ○ **Changes in Social Circles:** Associating with new groups of friends who use substances.

- **Hallucinogens:**

  - ○ **Erratic Behavior:** Unpredictable mood swings and bizarre actions.
  - ○ **Flashbacks:** Re-experiencing hallucinations or altered states of perception long after the substance was used.

- ○ **Poor Judgment:** Making illogical decisions and engaging in risky activities.

13.2 Treatment of Dependence

Effective treatment of substance dependence involves a comprehensive approach that addresses both the physiological and psychological aspects of addiction. This section will focus on the treatment of dependence on Central Nervous System (CNS) stimulants, particularly amphetamines, and outline clinical management strategies.

13.2.1 CNS Stimulants: Amphetamine

Amphetamines are a class of potent CNS stimulants that include drugs such as Adderall, Dexedrine, and methamphetamine. These substances are commonly abused for their stimulating effects, which include increased energy, euphoria, and heightened concentration. However, chronic use can lead to dependence and a range of adverse health effects.

13.2.1.1 Clinical Management

The clinical management of amphetamine dependence involves several key steps: detoxification, pharmacological treatment, behavioral therapies, and long-term support to prevent relapse.

Detoxification:

Detoxification is the first step in managing amphetamine dependence. This process involves safely managing withdrawal symptoms as the drug is eliminated from the body.

- **Medical Supervision:** Detoxification should be conducted under medical supervision to monitor and manage withdrawal symptoms, which can include fatigue, depression, increased appetite, and intense cravings.
- **Supportive Care:** Providing a supportive environment, adequate hydration, nutrition, and rest is crucial during detoxification.

Pharmacological Treatment:

Currently, there are no FDA-approved medications specifically for the treatment of amphetamine dependence. However, certain medications can be used off-label to manage withdrawal symptoms and support recovery.

- **Antidepressants:** SSRIs (Selective Serotonin Reuptake Inhibitors) like fluoxetine or sertraline may be prescribed to manage depressive symptoms during withdrawal.
- **Benzodiazepines:** These can be used short-term to manage severe anxiety and agitation during the initial phase of detoxification.
- **Antipsychotics:** In cases of severe agitation or psychosis, antipsychotic medications may be necessary.

Behavioral Therapies:

Behavioral therapies are a cornerstone of treatment for amphetamine dependence. These therapies address the psychological aspects of addiction and help individuals develop coping strategies to maintain sobriety.

- **Cognitive-Behavioral Therapy (CBT):** CBT helps patients recognize and change negative thought patterns and behaviors associated with drug use. It also teaches coping skills to handle stress and triggers.
- **Contingency Management:** This approach uses positive reinforcement to encourage abstinence. Patients receive rewards for meeting treatment goals, such as maintaining sobriety or attending therapy sessions.
- **Motivational Interviewing:** This client-centered approach helps individuals find the motivation to change their behavior and commit to treatment.
- **12-Step Programs:** Participation in 12-step programs like Narcotics Anonymous (NA) can provide peer support and a structured framework for recovery.

Long-Term Support and Relapse Prevention:

Long-term support is essential to prevent relapse and maintain recovery. This involves ongoing therapy, support groups, and strategies to manage triggers and stress.

- **Aftercare Programs:** Structured aftercare programs provide ongoing support and resources to help individuals maintain sobriety after completing initial treatment.
- **Relapse Prevention Planning:** Developing a relapse prevention plan that identifies triggers, coping strategies, and support networks can help

individuals manage cravings and avoid relapse.

- **Family Therapy:** Involving family members in therapy can improve communication, resolve conflicts, and provide a supportive environment for recovery.
- **Lifestyle Changes:** Encouraging healthy lifestyle changes, such as regular exercise, a balanced diet, and stress management techniques, can support overall well-being and reduce the risk of relapse.

13.2.2 Opioids

Opioid dependence is a significant public health concern due to the high potential for addiction, the risk of overdose, and the serious health consequences associated with long-term use. Effective clinical management of opioid dependence involves a comprehensive approach that includes detoxification, pharmacological treatment, behavioral therapies, and ongoing support to prevent relapse.

13.2.2.1 Clinical Management

Detoxification:

Detoxification is the initial step in the treatment of opioid dependence. The goal is to manage withdrawal symptoms and prepare the patient for ongoing treatment.

- **Medical Supervision:** Detoxification should be conducted under medical supervision to monitor and manage withdrawal symptoms, which can include agitation, anxiety, muscle aches, sweating, abdominal cramping, diarrhea, nausea, and vomiting.
- **Supportive Care:** Providing a supportive environment with adequate hydration, nutrition, and comfort measures is essential during detoxification.

Pharmacological Treatment:

Pharmacological treatment is a critical component in the management of opioid dependence. Medications are used to manage withdrawal symptoms, reduce cravings, and prevent relapse.

- **Methadone:** A long-acting opioid agonist that helps reduce withdrawal symptoms and cravings. It is administered daily in a controlled clinical setting.

- **Buprenorphine:** A partial opioid agonist that reduces withdrawal symptoms and cravings. It can be prescribed in various formulations, including buprenorphine-naloxone combinations (e.g., Suboxone) to reduce the potential for misuse.
- **Naltrexone:** An opioid antagonist that blocks the effects of opioids. It is available in oral and extended-release injectable forms. Naltrexone is used after detoxification to prevent relapse.
- **Clonidine:** An alpha-2 adrenergic agonist used off-label to manage certain withdrawal symptoms such as anxiety, agitation, and muscle aches.

Behavioral Therapies:

Behavioral therapies are essential for addressing the psychological aspects of opioid dependence and supporting long-term recovery.

- **Cognitive-Behavioral Therapy (CBT):** CBT helps patients identify and change negative thought patterns and behaviors related to drug use. It also teaches coping skills for managing stress and triggers.
- **Contingency Management:** This approach uses positive reinforcement to encourage abstinence. Patients receive rewards for meeting treatment goals, such as maintaining sobriety or attending therapy sessions.
- **Motivational Interviewing:** This client-centered approach helps individuals find the motivation to change their behavior and commit to treatment.
- **12-Step Programs:** Participation in 12-step programs like Narcotics Anonymous (NA) provides peer support and a structured framework for recovery.

Long-Term Support and Relapse Prevention:

Long-term support is crucial to prevent relapse and sustain recovery. This involves ongoing therapy, support groups, and strategies to manage triggers and stress.

- **Aftercare Programs:** Structured aftercare programs offer ongoing support and resources to help individuals maintain sobriety after completing initial treatment.

- **Relapse Prevention Planning:** Developing a relapse prevention plan that identifies triggers, coping strategies, and support networks can help individuals manage cravings and avoid relapse.
- **Family Therapy:** Involving family members in therapy can improve communication, resolve conflicts, and provide a supportive environment for recovery.
- **Lifestyle Changes:** Encouraging healthy lifestyle changes, such as regular exercise, a balanced diet, and stress management techniques, supports overall well-being and reduces the risk of relapse.

13.2.3 CNS Depressants

CNS depressants, including benzodiazepines, barbiturates, and certain sleep medications, are commonly prescribed for anxiety, insomnia, and other conditions. However, their potential for dependence and abuse requires careful management.

13.2.3.1 Clinical Management

Detoxification:

Detoxification from CNS depressants should be managed carefully due to the risk of severe withdrawal symptoms, including seizures.

- **Gradual Tapering:** Slowly reducing the dose of the CNS depressant under medical supervision is crucial to minimize withdrawal symptoms. A tapering schedule is individualized based on the specific drug, dose, and duration of use.
- **Medical Supervision:** Monitoring for signs of withdrawal, such as anxiety, tremors, sweating, insomnia, and seizures, is essential. In severe cases, hospitalization may be required.

Pharmacological Treatment:

- **Benzodiazepine Tapering:** For benzodiazepine dependence, a gradual taper using a long-acting benzodiazepine, such as diazepam or clonazepam, can help manage withdrawal symptoms.
- **Anticonvulsants:** Medications such as gabapentin or valproate may be used to prevent seizures during detoxification.

- **Beta-Blockers:** These can help manage autonomic symptoms such as tremors and tachycardia.

Behavioral Therapies:

Behavioral therapies are essential to address the psychological aspects of dependence on CNS depressants.

- **Cognitive-Behavioral Therapy (CBT):** CBT helps individuals identify and change maladaptive thought patterns and behaviors related to drug use and develop coping strategies for stress and anxiety.
- **Motivational Interviewing:** This approach helps individuals find the motivation to change their behavior and commit to treatment.
- **Support Groups:** Participation in support groups, such as those offered by Narcotics Anonymous (NA), can provide peer support and a sense of community.

Long-Term Support and Relapse Prevention:

- **Aftercare Programs:** Structured aftercare programs provide ongoing support and resources to help individuals maintain sobriety.
- **Relapse Prevention Planning:** Developing a relapse prevention plan that identifies triggers, coping strategies, and support networks can help manage cravings and avoid relapse.
- **Family Therapy:** Involving family members in therapy can improve communication, resolve conflicts, and provide a supportive environment for recovery.

13.2.4 Hallucinogens: LSD

Lysergic acid diethylamide (LSD) is a potent hallucinogen that can cause profound changes in perception, mood, and cognition. While physical dependence is less common, psychological dependence and adverse psychological reactions can occur.

13.2.4.1 Clinical Management

Management of Acute Reactions:

- **Supportive Care:** In the case of an acute LSD reaction, providing a calm and safe environment is crucial. Reassuring the individual and reducing sensory stimulation can help alleviate anxiety and paranoia.
- **Benzodiazepines:** Medications like diazepam or lorazepam can be used to manage severe anxiety, agitation, or panic attacks during an acute LSD reaction.
- **Antipsychotics:** In cases of severe psychotic reactions, antipsychotic medications such as haloperidol may be necessary.

Long-Term Treatment:

- **Psychotherapy:** Long-term treatment focuses on addressing underlying psychological issues and preventing further substance use.

  - **Cognitive-Behavioral Therapy (CBT):** CBT can help individuals understand the psychological reasons for their LSD use and develop healthier coping mechanisms.
  - **Motivational Interviewing:** This approach can help individuals recognize the negative impact of their substance use and find the motivation to change.

Relapse Prevention:

- **Education:** Educating individuals about the risks and potential long-term effects of LSD use can help prevent relapse.
- **Support Groups:** Participation in support groups, such as those provided by organizations like Narcotics Anonymous (NA), can offer ongoing support and a sense of community.
- **Lifestyle Changes:** Encouraging healthy lifestyle changes, such as regular exercise, a balanced diet, and stress management techniques, can support overall well-being and reduce the risk of relapse.13.2.5 Cannabis Group

Cannabis, commonly known as marijuana, is widely used for both recreational and medicinal purposes. While physical dependence on cannabis is less pronounced than on other substances, psychological dependence and withdrawal symptoms can still occur.

13.2.5.1 Clinical Management

Detoxification:
Detoxification from cannabis is generally less severe than from other substances, but it still requires supportive care to manage withdrawal symptoms.

- **Medical Supervision:** Although cannabis withdrawal is not typically life-threatening, symptoms such as irritability, anxiety, insomnia, and appetite changes should be monitored.
- **Supportive Care:** Providing a supportive environment, hydration, nutrition, and sleep hygiene can help ease withdrawal symptoms.

Pharmacological Treatment:
There are no specific medications approved for treating cannabis dependence, but certain drugs can help manage withdrawal symptoms and co-occurring disorders.

- **Antidepressants:** SSRIs (Selective Serotonin Reuptake Inhibitors) such as fluoxetine or sertraline may be used to manage symptoms of depression and anxiety associated with cannabis withdrawal.
- **Anxiolytics:** Short-term use of medications like buspirone can help manage anxiety during withdrawal.

Behavioral Therapies:
Behavioral therapies are the primary treatment approach for cannabis dependence.

- **Cognitive-Behavioral Therapy (CBT):** CBT helps individuals recognize and change patterns of marijuana use and develop coping strategies for triggers and stress.
- **Motivational Enhancement Therapy (MET):** This therapy helps individuals increase their motivation to change their cannabis use behaviors and engage in treatment.
- **Contingency Management:** This approach uses positive reinforcement to encourage abstinence from cannabis, providing rewards for meeting treatment goals.

Long-Term Support and Relapse Prevention:

- **Aftercare Programs:** Participation in structured aftercare programs provides ongoing support and resources to maintain sobriety.
- **Relapse Prevention Planning:** Developing a relapse prevention plan that includes identifying triggers, coping strategies, and support networks is essential.
- **Support Groups:** Involvement in support groups, such as Marijuana Anonymous (MA), can offer peer support and a sense of community.

13.2.6 Tobacco

Tobacco dependence is a significant public health issue due to its highly addictive nature and the severe health risks associated with long-term use, including respiratory diseases, cardiovascular diseases, and various cancers.

13.2.6.1 Clinical Management

Detoxification:

Detoxification from nicotine, the addictive substance in tobacco, involves managing withdrawal symptoms, which can be intense but are not typically life-threatening.

- **Medical Supervision:** While medical supervision is not always necessary, support from healthcare providers can help manage withdrawal symptoms such as irritability, anxiety, difficulty concentrating, increased appetite, and cravings.
- **Supportive Care:** Encouraging hydration, proper nutrition, and physical activity can help ease withdrawal symptoms.

Pharmacological Treatment:

Several medications are available to help individuals quit smoking and manage withdrawal symptoms.

- **Nicotine Replacement Therapy (NRT):** NRT products, such as patches, gum, lozenges, nasal sprays, and inhalers, provide a controlled dose of nicotine to reduce withdrawal symptoms and cravings.
- **Bupropion (Zyban):** An atypical antidepressant that helps reduce nicotine cravings and withdrawal symptoms. It is usually started one to two weeks before quitting smoking.

- **Varenicline (Chantix):** A medication that reduces cravings and withdrawal symptoms by partially stimulating nicotine receptors in the brain. It is typically started one week before the quit date.

Behavioral Therapies:
Behavioral therapies are essential for addressing the psychological aspects of tobacco dependence.

- **Cognitive-Behavioral Therapy (CBT):** CBT helps individuals identify and change smoking-related thoughts and behaviors and develop coping strategies for triggers and stress.
- **Motivational Interviewing:** This approach helps individuals find the motivation to quit smoking and commit to a quit plan.
- **Contingency Management:** This method uses positive reinforcement to encourage smoking cessation, providing rewards for meeting smoking cessation goals.

Long-Term Support and Relapse Prevention:

- **Aftercare Programs:** Participation in structured aftercare programs provides ongoing support and resources to maintain smoking cessation.
- **Relapse Prevention Planning:** Developing a relapse prevention plan that includes identifying triggers, coping strategies, and support networks is essential.
- **Support Groups:** Involvement in support groups, such as Nicotine Anonymous (NicA), can offer peer support and a sense of community.
- **Smoking Cessation Programs:** Enrolling in smoking cessation programs that offer counseling, education, and support can significantly increase the chances of successfully quitting.

CHAPTER IV

Gut Decontamination

Introduction

Gut decontamination is a critical aspect of managing acute poisoning cases. The primary goal of gut decontamination is to remove or neutralize ingested toxins before they can be absorbed into the systemic circulation. This intervention can significantly reduce the severity of poisoning and improve patient outcomes.

Gut decontamination involves various techniques and agents, each with specific indications, mechanisms of action, and limitations. The choice of method depends on factors such as the type of toxin, the time since ingestion, the patient's clinical condition, and the risks and benefits of the procedure.

4.1 Indications for Gut Decontamination

Gut decontamination is not universally indicated for all poisoning cases. Specific criteria must be met to justify its use, ensuring that the benefits outweigh the potential risks. Understanding the indications and criteria for gut decontamination is essential for making informed clinical decisions.

4.1.1 Criteria for Use

Criteria for the use of gut decontamination involve assessing the type of toxin, the time elapsed since ingestion, and the patient's overall condition. The decision to proceed with gut decontamination should be based on the following considerations:

Type of Toxin:

- **Potentially Life-Threatening Toxins:** Gut decontamination is particularly indicated for ingestions involving toxins that are highly toxic or potentially fatal, such as cyanide, methanol, ethylene glycol, certain pesticides, and large doses of medications like tricyclic antidepressants or calcium channel blockers.

- **Substances with Delayed Absorption:** Toxins that have delayed gastrointestinal absorption, such as sustained-release or enteric-coated medications, may benefit from gut decontamination even if several hours have passed since ingestion.
- **Substances Not Effectively Removed by Other Means:** Some toxins are poorly removed by hemodialysis or other extracorporeal methods, making gut decontamination a preferred option.

Time Since Ingestion:

- **Within One Hour:** Gut decontamination is most effective when performed within one hour of toxin ingestion. This is when the toxin is still primarily located in the stomach and upper gastrointestinal tract.
- **Beyond One Hour:** In certain cases, gut decontamination may be considered beyond one hour if the toxin has a prolonged gastric retention time, the patient has ingested a large amount, or if the toxin is known to form bezoars or slow-release formulations.

Patient's Clinical Condition:

- **Stable Vital Signs:** The patient should have stable vital signs or be stabilized to ensure safe decontamination. Unstable patients may require initial stabilization before gut decontamination can be safely attempted.
- **Protected Airway:** Patients should have a protected airway, either naturally or through intubation, to prevent aspiration, especially during procedures like gastric lavage or when administering activated charcoal.
- **Cooperation and Consciousness:** Conscious and cooperative patients are more likely to tolerate procedures like activated charcoal administration. In unconscious or uncooperative patients, the risk of complications may outweigh the benefits.

Contraindications:

- **Caustic or Corrosive Ingestions:** Gut decontamination is contraindicated in cases of caustic or corrosive substance ingestion, as it can cause additional injury to the gastrointestinal tract and increase the risk of perforation.

- **Hydrocarbon Ingestions:** For hydrocarbons, such as gasoline or kerosene, gut decontamination is generally contraindicated due to the high risk of aspiration and chemical pneumonitis.
- **Risk of Aspiration:** Patients with an unprotected airway or those at high risk of aspiration should not undergo gut decontamination procedures that increase this risk.

Specific Considerations:

- **Activated Charcoal:** Indicated for a wide range of toxins, especially those that bind well to charcoal. Not effective for metals, alcohols, and certain other substances.
- **Gastric Lavage:** Considered for life-threatening ingestions if performed within one hour. Requires careful consideration of risks versus benefits.
- **Whole Bowel Irrigation:** Indicated for substances that do not bind well to activated charcoal or have a delayed release. Suitable for ingestions of sustained-release formulations or body packers.

4.1 Indications for Gut Decontamination

4.1.2 Timing and Effectiveness

The **timing** of gut decontamination is a crucial factor in its effectiveness. The sooner the intervention is performed after toxin ingestion, the more likely it is to prevent significant absorption of the toxin and reduce its systemic effects. Understanding the relationship between timing and effectiveness is essential for making informed clinical decisions about gut decontamination.

Timing Considerations:

- **Within One Hour:**

  - **Peak Effectiveness:** Gut decontamination is most effective when performed within the first hour after ingestion. During this time, the majority of the ingested toxin is likely to be present in the stomach, where it can be effectively removed or adsorbed.

- **Activated Charcoal:** Administering activated charcoal within one hour can adsorb a significant amount of the toxin, preventing its absorption into the bloodstream. It is the preferred method for many toxins due to its broad efficacy and safety profile.
- **Gastric Lavage:** This method is generally recommended only within the first hour for life-threatening ingestions, as the procedure itself carries risks and is less effective once the toxin has moved beyond the stomach.

- **Beyond One Hour:**

  - **Reduced Effectiveness:** The effectiveness of gut decontamination decreases significantly as more time elapses after ingestion. Toxins are progressively absorbed into the bloodstream or move further along the gastrointestinal tract, making removal more difficult.
  - **Special Cases:** Certain situations may still warrant gut decontamination beyond the one-hour mark:

    - **Delayed-Release Formulations:** Ingestions involving sustained-release or enteric-coated medications, which can remain in the gastrointestinal tract longer, may benefit from continued gut decontamination efforts.
    - **Bezoars and Body Packers:** In cases where large quantities of drugs form bezoars (solid masses) or body packers ingest packets of drugs, whole bowel irrigation or repeated doses of activated charcoal can be effective beyond the initial hour.

Effectiveness of Different Methods:

- **Activated Charcoal:**

  - **Mechanism:** Activated charcoal adsorbs toxins onto its surface, reducing their absorption in the gastrointestinal tract. It is effective for a wide range of substances, including many drugs and chemicals.
  - **Administration:** Typically given as a single dose (50-100 grams for adults, 25-50 grams for children), but multiple doses may be administered in specific cases like sustained-release drug ingestion or enterohepatic recirculation of the toxin.

- ○ **Timing:** Most effective when given within one hour of ingestion. Its effectiveness diminishes over time but can still provide some benefit if given later, especially in cases of delayed gastric emptying.

- **Gastric Lavage:**

  - ○ **Mechanism:** Involves the insertion of a large-bore orogastric tube and the repeated instillation and aspiration of small volumes of saline or water to wash out the stomach contents.
  - ○ **Administration:** Performed within one hour of a life-threatening ingestion. Requires careful consideration of risks, such as aspiration and esophageal perforation.
  - ○ **Timing:** Effectiveness is greatest within the first hour, with rapidly diminishing returns thereafter. It is rarely indicated beyond this period due to the risks involved.

- **Whole Bowel Irrigation:**

  - ○ **Mechanism:** Uses a polyethylene glycol-electrolyte solution to flush out the entire gastrointestinal tract, preventing further absorption of the toxin.
  - ○ **Administration:** Indicated for substances not effectively adsorbed by activated charcoal, such as iron, lithium, and certain sustained-release medications.
  - ○ **Timing:** Can be effective beyond the first hour, particularly in cases where the toxin remains in the gastrointestinal tract for an extended period.

Monitoring and Reassessment:

- **Clinical Monitoring:** Continuous monitoring of the patient's vital signs, mental status, and overall condition is essential during and after gut decontamination procedures.
- **Laboratory Tests:** Regular assessment of blood chemistry, toxicology screens, and other relevant laboratory tests helps guide ongoing management and determine the effectiveness of decontamination efforts.

- **Reevaluation:** Reevaluate the need for further decontamination or additional interventions based on the patient's response to initial treatments and evolving clinical status.

4.2 Methods of Gut Decontamination

4.2.1 Induced Emesis

Induced emesis involves the deliberate induction of vomiting to expel ingested toxins from the stomach. Historically, it has been used as a method of gut decontamination, but its use has become more limited due to the availability of more effective and safer alternatives.

4.2.1.1 Indications and Contraindications
Indications:

- **Specific Toxin Ingestions:** Induced emesis may be considered for certain ingestions where other methods are not feasible, and the toxin is not caustic or hydrocarbon-based.
- **Early Presentation:** It is most effective when the patient presents very soon after ingestion, ideally within one hour, when the toxin is still in the stomach.
- **Limited Resources:** In settings where activated charcoal or other decontamination methods are unavailable, induced emesis might be considered as an interim measure.

Contraindications:

- **Caustic Substances:** Ingestions involving caustic substances (e.g., acids, alkalis) can cause further injury to the esophagus and oral mucosa if vomited.
- **Hydrocarbons:** Vomiting hydrocarbons (e.g., gasoline, kerosene) increases the risk of aspiration and chemical pneumonitis.
- **Reduced Consciousness:** Patients with a decreased level of consciousness or those unable to protect their airway are at high risk of aspiration and should not be induced to vomit.

- **Seizure Disorders:** Patients with a history of seizures or currently seizing are at increased risk of aspiration.
- **Age Considerations:** Young children and elderly patients are at higher risk for complications and may not be suitable candidates for induced emesis.

4.2.1.2 Techniques and Complications
Techniques:

- **Syrup of Ipecac:**

  - **Administration:** Ipecac syrup was traditionally used to induce vomiting. The recommended dose was 15-30 mL in adults and 10-15 mL in children, followed by 240 mL of water. Vomiting typically occurs within 15-30 minutes.
  - **Availability:** Its use has declined significantly, and it is no longer recommended in many guidelines due to the potential for adverse effects and the availability of better alternatives.

- **Mechanical Stimulation:**

  - **Technique:** Mechanical stimulation of the pharynx (e.g., using a finger or other object) to induce a gag reflex and vomiting.
  - **Risks:** This method is not recommended due to the risk of trauma to the oropharynx and the potential for aspiration.

Complications:

- **Aspiration:** One of the most serious complications, especially in patients with compromised airway protection or reduced consciousness.
- **Esophageal and Gastric Injury:** Induced vomiting can cause tears, perforations, or other injuries to the esophagus and stomach, particularly with caustic substances.
- **Electrolyte Imbalances:** Repeated vomiting can lead to significant electrolyte disturbances, including hypokalemia and metabolic alkalosis.
- **Persistent Vomiting:** Some patients may experience prolonged vomiting, leading to dehydration and further complications.

- **Ineffectiveness:** Induced emesis may not effectively remove all or even a significant portion of the ingested toxin, especially if delayed beyond the optimal time frame.

4.2 Methods of Gut Decontamination

4.2.2 Gastric Lavage

Gastric lavage is a procedure that involves the insertion of a tube into the stomach, followed by the repeated instillation and aspiration of fluid to remove ingested toxins. While its use has declined with the advent of more effective and safer methods, gastric lavage may still be considered in specific clinical scenarios.

4.2.2.1 Indications and Contraindications
Indications:

- **Life-Threatening Ingestions:** Considered when a potentially life-threatening amount of a toxin has been ingested, especially if the ingestion occurred within one hour.
- **Large Ingestions:** Particularly large ingestions of substances that do not bind well to activated charcoal, such as iron or lithium.
- **Toxins Not Amenable to Other Methods:** Situations where other methods, such as activated charcoal, are not suitable or available.
- **Delayed Gastric Emptying:** Certain cases where delayed gastric emptying is suspected, such as with bezoars or large pill masses.

Contraindications:

- **Caustic or Corrosive Substances:** Ingestions involving acids or alkalis, which can cause further damage to the esophagus and stomach if gastric lavage is performed.
- **Hydrocarbons:** Risk of aspiration and chemical pneumonitis outweighs the potential benefits.
- **Compromised Airway Protection:** Patients with a decreased level of consciousness who do not have a secured airway (e.g., intubation) are at high risk of aspiration.

- **High Risk of Perforation:** Situations where there is a high risk of gastrointestinal perforation, such as in cases of recent surgery or known pathology.

4.2.2.2 Techniques and Complications
Techniques:

1. **Preparation:**

   - **Patient Positioning:** Place the patient in the left lateral decubitus position with the head slightly lower than the body to reduce the risk of aspiration.
   - **Equipment Preparation:** Use a large-bore orogastric tube (36-40 French for adults, 24-28 French for children), syringes or lavage set, and saline or water for lavage.

2. **Procedure:**

   - **Insertion of the Tube:** Insert the orogastric tube gently through the mouth or nose into the stomach, confirming placement by auscultation (listening for air insufflated through the tube) and aspiration of stomach contents.
   - **Initial Aspiration:** Aspirate as much gastric content as possible before beginning lavage.
   - **Lavage Process:** Instill 200-300 mL of warm saline or water into the stomach and then aspirate back the fluid. Repeat this process until the returned fluid is clear. For children, use smaller volumes (10 mL/kg).
   - **Monitoring:** Continuously monitor the patient's vital signs and oxygen saturation throughout the procedure.

Complications:

- **Aspiration:** One of the most serious complications, particularly if the patient's airway is not adequately protected. This can lead to aspiration pneumonia or chemical pneumonitis.
- **Esophageal or Gastric Perforation:** Risk of perforation, especially if excessive force is used during tube insertion or if the patient has underlying gastrointestinal pathology.

- **Electrolyte Imbalances:** Repeated lavage with large volumes of fluid can lead to electrolyte disturbances, particularly if electrolyte-free solutions are used.
- **Hypothermia:** Using large volumes of cold lavage fluid can lead to hypothermia, especially in small children or elderly patients.
- **Mechanical Injury:** Trauma to the oropharynx, esophagus, or stomach can occur, leading to bleeding or other complications.
- **Ineffectiveness:** If performed too late after ingestion, gastric lavage may not effectively remove the toxin, especially if it has already moved beyond the stomach or been absorbed.

4.2 Methods of Gut Decontamination

4.2.3 Activated Charcoal

Activated charcoal is a widely used method of gut decontamination in poisoning cases. It works by adsorbing toxins in the gastrointestinal tract, preventing their absorption into the bloodstream. Due to its effectiveness and relative safety, activated charcoal is often the preferred method for many types of poisoning.

4.2.3.1 Mechanism and Indications

Mechanism of Action:

- **Adsorption:** Activated charcoal has a large surface area due to its porous structure, which allows it to adsorb a wide range of toxins. The toxins adhere to the surface of the charcoal particles, reducing their absorption from the gastrointestinal tract into the bloodstream.
- **Prevention of Enterohepatic Recirculation:** In some cases, activated charcoal can interrupt the enterohepatic recirculation of certain toxins, further enhancing its effectiveness in reducing toxin levels in the body.

Indications:

- **Broad Range of Toxins:** Activated charcoal is effective for many drugs and chemicals, including acetaminophen, aspirin, barbiturates, tricyclic antidepressants, and many others.

- **Early Presentation:** Most effective when administered within one hour of toxin ingestion. It may still be beneficial beyond this period for certain substances with delayed absorption or prolonged gastric retention.
- **Multiple Doses:** In cases of substances that undergo enterohepatic recirculation (e.g., carbamazepine, phenobarbital) or sustained-release formulations, multiple doses of activated charcoal may be indicated.

Substances Not Effectively Adsorbed by Activated Charcoal:

- **Metals:** Iron, lithium, lead.
- **Alcohols:** Ethanol, methanol, ethylene glycol.
- **Corrosives:** Acids and alkalis.
- **Hydrocarbons:** Gasoline, kerosene.

4.2.3.2 Dosage and Administration
Dosage:

- **Single Dose:**

  - **Adults:** 50-100 grams of activated charcoal.
  - **Children:** 25-50 grams of activated charcoal.

- **Multiple Doses:** Used in specific cases where prolonged adsorption is beneficial. Subsequent doses are typically 12.5 grams per hour, 25 grams every 2 hours, or 50 grams every 4 hours, depending on the clinical scenario and toxin involved.

Administration:

1. **Preparation:**

   - **Formulation:** Activated charcoal is usually available as a powder that is mixed with water to form a slurry, or as a pre-prepared suspension. The slurry should be mixed thoroughly to ensure even distribution.
   - **Palatability:** Activated charcoal has an unpleasant taste and gritty texture. It can be mixed with a flavored beverage (e.g., juice) to improve palatability, though this should not significantly dilute the charcoal.

2. **Administration Technique:**

   - **Oral Route:** The charcoal slurry is given orally if the patient is conscious and able to swallow. Encourage the patient to drink the entire dose.
   - **Nasogastric Tube:** In cases where the patient is unconscious or unable to swallow, activated charcoal can be administered via a nasogastric tube. Confirm proper tube placement before administration to avoid complications.

3. **Post-Administration Care:**

   - **Hydration:** Ensure the patient stays adequately hydrated to facilitate gastrointestinal transit and reduce the risk of constipation.
   - **Monitoring:** Monitor for signs of gastrointestinal obstruction or aspiration, particularly in patients with decreased consciousness or compromised airway reflexes.

Complications:

- **Aspiration:** Risk of aspiration, particularly in patients with a decreased level of consciousness or those unable to protect their airway. This risk underscores the importance of securing the airway in at-risk patients.
- **Gastrointestinal Obstruction:** Rarely, activated charcoal can lead to intestinal obstruction, particularly with multiple doses. Ensure adequate hydration and monitor for signs of obstruction.
- **Emesis:** Vomiting is a common side effect and can complicate the administration, especially if large volumes are given quickly.

4.2 Methods of Gut Decontamination

4.2.4 Whole Bowel Irrigation

Whole bowel irrigation (WBI) is a method of gut decontamination that involves the administration of large volumes of an osmotically balanced polyethylene glycol-electrolyte solution to cleanse the entire gastrointestinal tract. This technique is used to prevent the absorption of ingested toxins by flushing them out of the gastrointestinal tract.

4.2.4.1 Indications and Contraindications

Indications:

- **Sustained-Release or Enteric-Coated Drugs:** WBI is particularly useful for ingestions involving sustained-release or enteric-coated medications that are not effectively removed by other methods.
- **Drugs Not Adsorbed by Activated Charcoal:** Substances such as iron, lithium, and certain heavy metals that do not bind well to activated charcoal.
- **Body Packers:** Individuals who have ingested packets of illicit drugs (e.g., cocaine, heroin) to smuggle them. WBI can help evacuate the packets before they rupture and cause severe toxicity.
- **Large Ingestions:** Situations where a significant amount of a toxin has been ingested, and rapid clearance from the gastrointestinal tract is desired.

Contraindications:

- **Bowel Obstruction or Perforation:** WBI is contraindicated in patients with known or suspected bowel obstruction or gastrointestinal perforation due to the risk of worsening the condition.
- **Gastrointestinal Bleeding:** Active gastrointestinal bleeding is a contraindication as WBI can exacerbate bleeding.
- **Unprotected Airway:** Patients with a compromised airway or those who cannot protect their airway are at risk of aspiration.
- **Hemodynamic Instability:** Patients who are hemodynamically unstable may not tolerate the large fluid volumes required for WBI.
- **Caustic Ingestions:** Ingestions involving caustic substances (e.g., acids, alkalis) should not undergo WBI as it can cause further injury to the gastrointestinal tract.

4.2.4.2 Techniques and Complications

Techniques:

1. **Preparation:**

- **Solution:** Use a polyethylene glycol-electrolyte solution (e.g., GoLYTELY, Colyte). This solution is isotonic and osmotically balanced to prevent significant fluid and electrolyte shifts.
- **Equipment:** A large-bore nasogastric tube may be necessary for administration, especially in unconscious or uncooperative patients.

2. Administration:

- **Oral Route:** If the patient is conscious and cooperative, the solution can be ingested orally. Typically, the patient drinks 1.5-2 liters per hour until the effluent (stool) is clear.
- **Nasogastric Tube:** In unconscious or uncooperative patients, the solution is administered via a nasogastric tube. The rate is similar, 1.5-2 liters per hour, until the effluent is clear.
- **Duration:** The procedure usually lasts 4-6 hours but can vary depending on the amount of toxin ingested and the patient's gastrointestinal transit time.

3. Monitoring:

- **Vital Signs:** Continuous monitoring of vital signs to detect any signs of hemodynamic instability.
- **Electrolytes:** Regular monitoring of electrolyte levels, especially in patients with underlying medical conditions that could be exacerbated by large fluid volumes.
- **Output:** Monitor the output and clarity of the effluent to determine when the irrigation can be stopped.

Complications:

- **Nausea and Vomiting:** Common during the procedure and can complicate the administration of the solution.
- **Abdominal Distension:** The large volumes of fluid can cause discomfort and distension, particularly in patients with delayed gastric emptying.
- **Electrolyte Imbalances:** Although the solution is isotonic, there is still a risk of electrolyte disturbances, particularly if the procedure is prolonged or the patient has pre-existing electrolyte abnormalities.

- **Aspiration:** Risk of aspiration, especially in patients with compromised airway reflexes. This underscores the importance of airway protection in at-risk patients.
- **Mechanical Complications:** Insertion and use of a nasogastric tube can cause nasal or esophageal trauma, especially if not performed correctly.

CHAPTER V

Elimination Enhancement

Introduction

Elimination enhancement refers to a range of medical interventions designed to accelerate the removal of toxins from the body. While the body's natural processes, primarily through the liver and kidneys, gradually eliminate most poisons, these processes can be too slow to prevent significant harm in cases of severe poisoning. Enhancing elimination can significantly reduce the duration of toxin exposure, mitigate its effects, and improve patient outcomes.

This chapter explores various techniques used to enhance the elimination of toxins, including urinary alkalinization, hemodialysis, hemoperfusion, and other extracorporeal methods. Each technique has specific indications, mechanisms of action, and potential complications. Understanding when and how to use these methods is critical for effectively managing cases of poisoning, particularly when dealing with substances that are highly toxic or have prolonged half-lives.

Scope of the Chapter

This chapter will cover the following key areas:

1. **Urinary Alkalinization:** Discussing its role in enhancing the renal excretion of certain toxins, particularly weak acids like salicylates and phenobarbital.
2. **Hemodialysis:** Exploring its effectiveness in removing toxins that are water-soluble, have low molecular weight, and are not highly protein-bound. This includes a discussion on indications, procedure, and potential complications.
3. **Hemoperfusion:** Detailing its use for removing toxins that are poorly removed by hemodialysis, such as those with high protein binding or large molecular size, including the setup, indications, and limitations.

4. **Other Extracorporeal Methods:** Briefly covering additional techniques like continuous renal replacement therapy (CRRT) and exchange transfusion, highlighting their specific applications and effectiveness in poisoning cases.

Importance of Elimination Enhancement

The primary goal of elimination enhancement is to reduce the toxin burden on the body more rapidly than would occur naturally. This is particularly important in the following scenarios:

- **Severe Poisoning:** When the ingested toxin is highly toxic and poses an immediate threat to life.
- **Prolonged Half-Life:** When the toxin has a long half-life, leading to sustained exposure and potential cumulative damage.
- **Impaired Natural Elimination:** In patients with compromised renal or hepatic function, where the natural elimination processes are insufficient to handle the toxin load.

5.1 Principles of Elimination Enhancement

5.1.1 Mechanisms of Enhanced Elimination

Enhanced elimination techniques are employed to accelerate the removal of toxins from the body. These mechanisms are particularly valuable when natural elimination processes are insufficient to mitigate the toxic effects rapidly enough. The primary mechanisms include urinary manipulation, extracorporeal removal, and chemical modification.

Urinary Manipulation:

- **Urinary Alkalinization:**

  - **Mechanism:** This process involves the administration of alkaline substances, such as sodium bicarbonate, to increase the pH of urine. Alkaline urine increases the ionization of weak acids, reducing their reabsorption in the renal tubules and enhancing their excretion.

- ○ **Applications:** Effective for toxins such as salicylates and phenobarbital. It enhances the renal clearance of these substances by trapping them in their ionized form within the urinary tract.

Extracorporeal Removal:

- **Hemodialysis:**

  - ○ **Mechanism:** Hemodialysis uses a semipermeable membrane to facilitate the diffusion of toxins from the blood into a dialysate solution, which is then removed from the body. It is effective for substances that are water-soluble, have low molecular weight, and are not highly protein-bound.
  - ○ **Applications:** Commonly used for toxins such as methanol, ethylene glycol, lithium, and certain barbiturates.

- **Hemoperfusion:**

  - ○ **Mechanism:** In hemoperfusion, blood passes through a column containing adsorbent materials (e.g., activated charcoal or resin), which bind and remove toxins from the bloodstream. This technique is particularly useful for toxins that are highly protein-bound or have large molecular weights.
  - ○ **Applications:** Effective for substances like theophylline, carbamazepine, and certain pesticides.

Chemical Modification:

- **Use of Antidotes:**

  - ○ **Mechanism:** Some antidotes can chemically modify toxins, rendering them less harmful or more easily excretable. For example, N-acetylcysteine in acetaminophen poisoning helps replenish glutathione, facilitating detoxification.
  - ○ **Applications:** Specific antidotes are used based on the type of poisoning and the mechanism of the toxin.

5.1.2 Indications and Contraindications

Indications for Enhanced Elimination:

- **Severe Poisoning:**

  - **Life-Threatening Toxins:** When the ingested toxin poses an immediate and severe risk to life, enhanced elimination is critical.
  - **Examples:** Severe cases of methanol or ethylene glycol poisoning, significant salicylate toxicity, and life-threatening lithium overdose.

- **Prolonged Half-Life:**

  - **Toxins with Long Half-Lives:** Substances that remain in the body for extended periods, leading to prolonged toxic effects.
  - **Examples:** Barbiturates, theophylline, and certain sustained-release formulations.

- **Ineffective Natural Elimination:**

  - **Compromised Renal or Hepatic Function:** Patients with impaired kidney or liver function, where the natural elimination processes are inadequate.
  - **Examples:** Patients with pre-existing renal insufficiency who have ingested lithium or other renally excreted toxins.

Contraindications for Enhanced Elimination:

- **Hemodynamic Instability:**

  - **Unstable Patients:** Procedures like hemodialysis and hemoperfusion require stable hemodynamics. Severely unstable patients may not tolerate these procedures without first being stabilized.
  - **Management:** Initial stabilization of blood pressure and cardiovascular status is necessary before proceeding.

- **Coagulopathies:**

- ○ **Risk of Bleeding:** Patients with bleeding disorders or those at high risk of bleeding may not be suitable candidates for extracorporeal procedures.
- ○ **Considerations:** Careful assessment and correction of coagulopathies are essential before initiating procedures like hemodialysis or hemoperfusion.

- **Inadequate Access:**

  - ○ **Vascular Access Issues:** Difficulty in establishing reliable vascular access can preclude the use of certain extracorporeal techniques.
  - ○ **Alternatives:** Consider alternative methods of elimination or prioritize other supportive care measures.

- **Specific Toxin Properties:**

  - ○ **Ineffectiveness of Technique:** Not all toxins are amenable to enhanced elimination techniques. For instance, highly lipid-soluble or protein-bound toxins may not be effectively removed by hemodialysis.
  - ○ **Evaluation:** A thorough evaluation of the toxin's pharmacokinetics and properties is necessary to determine the appropriateness of the chosen method.

5.2 Methods of Elimination Enhancement

5.2.1 Urinary Alkalinization

5.2.1.1 Mechanism and Indications
Mechanism:

Urinary alkalinization involves the administration of substances that increase the pH of urine, typically sodium bicarbonate. This process enhances the renal excretion of certain toxins, particularly weak acids. When the urine becomes more alkaline, weak acids become ionized and less lipid-soluble. This ionized form is less likely to be reabsorbed by the renal tubules and more likely to be excreted in the urine. This mechanism is crucial for toxins like salicylates and phenobarbital, which are weak acids and can cause significant toxicity. By increasing the urinary pH to a target range of 7.5 to 8.0, these substances are trapped in the urine, facilitating their elimination from the body.

Indications:

Urinary alkalinization is primarily indicated for poisoning with weak acids that benefit from increased renal excretion. One of the most common indications is **salicylate poisoning.** Salicylates, found in medications like aspirin, can cause metabolic acidosis, respiratory alkalosis, and various systemic effects. Alkalinizing the urine enhances the elimination of salicylates, reducing their toxic effects. Another indication is **phenobarbital overdose,** a barbiturate that can cause central nervous system depression and respiratory failure. By promoting the excretion of phenobarbital, urinary alkalinization helps to decrease its sedative effects. Additionally, urinary alkalinization can be used for poisoning with other weak acids, although it is less commonly employed for these cases.

5.2.1.2 Techniques and Complications

Techniques:

To achieve urinary alkalinization, **sodium bicarbonate** is typically administered intravenously. The initial dose is usually **1-2 mEq/kg,** administered as an intravenous bolus. Following the bolus, a continuous infusion of sodium bicarbonate may be initiated. The infusion rate is adjusted based on the patient's urine pH and serum bicarbonate levels. The goal is to maintain the urine pH between 7.5 and 8.0. Frequent monitoring of urine pH is essential to ensure that the target range is achieved and maintained. In addition to urine pH, **serum electrolytes** and **blood gases** should be monitored regularly to avoid complications such as metabolic alkalosis and electrolyte imbalances. Potassium supplementation may be necessary because alkalinization can lead to hypokalemia.

Complications:

While urinary alkalinization can be highly effective, it is not without risks. One of the primary complications is **metabolic alkalosis,** which can occur if the bicarbonate dose is too high or if the patient has pre-existing conditions that predispose them to alkalosis. Metabolic alkalosis can cause symptoms such as confusion, muscle twitching, and cardiac arrhythmias. To prevent this, careful monitoring of blood gases and serum bicarbonate levels is necessary. Another potential complication is **hypokalemia,** which occurs because increasing the urinary pH enhances potassium excretion.

Hypokalemia can lead to muscle weakness, cramps, and arrhythmias. Regular monitoring of serum potassium levels and appropriate supplementation are crucial. Additionally, rapid administration of sodium bicarbonate can lead to **volume overload** and **hypernatremia**, especially in patients with renal or cardiac dysfunction. It is important to adjust the rate of infusion and monitor fluid balance closely to avoid these issues.

5.2 Methods of Elimination Enhancement

5.2.2 Hemodialysis

5.2.2.1 Mechanism and Indications

Mechanism:

Hemodialysis is a procedure that utilizes a dialysis machine and a semipermeable membrane to remove toxins from the blood. The patient's blood is pumped through a dialyzer, where it flows on one side of the membrane while a dialysis solution (dialysate) flows on the opposite side. The semipermeable membrane allows small molecules, such as toxins and electrolytes, to diffuse from the blood into the dialysate based on concentration gradients. Large molecules and blood cells are retained, while toxins move into the dialysate, which is then discarded. This process effectively reduces the concentration of water-soluble, low molecular weight, and non-protein-bound toxins in the bloodstream, thus decreasing their toxic effects.

Indications:

Hemodialysis is indicated for the removal of specific toxins that meet certain criteria:

- **Water-Soluble Toxins:** Hemodialysis is effective for substances that are highly soluble in water.
- **Low Molecular Weight Toxins:** Toxins with low molecular weights can easily pass through the semipermeable membrane of the dialyzer.
- **Low Protein Binding:** Toxins that are not extensively bound to plasma proteins are more readily removed by hemodialysis.

Common indications for hemodialysis in poisoning include:

- **Methanol and Ethylene Glycol:** Both are toxic alcohols that can cause metabolic acidosis and severe organ damage. Hemodialysis rapidly removes these substances and their toxic metabolites.
- **Salicylates:** In cases of severe salicylate poisoning, where levels are dangerously high, hemodialysis can effectively reduce serum salicylate concentrations.
- **Lithium:** Hemodialysis is used in severe lithium toxicity, particularly when serum levels are high or in patients with impaired renal function.
- **Phenobarbital:** For barbiturate poisoning, especially when complicated by prolonged coma or significant respiratory depression, hemodialysis can enhance drug elimination.
- **Theophylline:** In cases of severe theophylline poisoning, hemodialysis can be used to rapidly reduce toxic levels, especially when standard therapies fail.

5.2.2.2 Techniques and Complications
Techniques:

1. **Vascular Access:**

   - **Central Venous Catheter:** A temporary large-bore catheter is placed in a central vein (e.g., femoral, jugular, or subclavian) to facilitate high blood flow rates required for hemodialysis.
   - **AV Fistula or Graft:** In patients requiring long-term dialysis, an arteriovenous (AV) fistula or graft is surgically created, but this is not typically used in acute poisoning scenarios.

2. **Dialysis Procedure:**

   - **Dialyzer Setup:** The dialyzer, containing the semipermeable membrane, is connected to the dialysis machine. The dialysate composition is selected based on the patient's needs, often mirroring normal plasma electrolyte concentrations.
   - **Blood Flow Rates:** Blood flow rates are typically maintained between 200-500 mL/min to ensure efficient toxin removal.
   - **Duration:** The duration of the dialysis session can vary but usually lasts 4-6 hours. In severe cases, continuous renal replacement therapy (CRRT) may be considered.

3. **Monitoring:**

   - **Vital Signs:** Continuous monitoring of blood pressure, heart rate, and respiratory rate is crucial to detect any hemodynamic instability.
   - **Electrolytes and Blood Gases:** Regular checks of serum electrolytes, blood gases, and toxin levels help guide the dialysis process and adjustments in treatment.

Complications:

1. **Hypotension:**

   - **Mechanism:** Rapid removal of fluids and toxins can lead to a drop in blood pressure, particularly in patients who are volume-depleted or have cardiovascular instability.
   - **Management:** Hypotension can be managed by adjusting the ultrafiltration rate, administering intravenous fluids, or using vasopressors if necessary.

2. **Electrolyte Imbalances:**

   - **Mechanism:** Rapid shifts in electrolytes can occur during hemodialysis, leading to imbalances such as hypokalemia or hypocalcemia.
   - **Management:** Regular monitoring and appropriate supplementation of electrolytes are essential to prevent complications.

3. **Dialysis Disequilibrium Syndrome:**

   - **Mechanism:** This condition can occur due to rapid removal of urea and other solutes, leading to cerebral edema. Symptoms include headache, nausea, vomiting, and in severe cases, seizures.
   - **Management:** Gradual reduction in solute removal and careful monitoring of neurological status can help mitigate this risk.

4. **Infections:**

- ◦ **Mechanism:** The use of central venous catheters increases the risk of infections, including bacteremia and sepsis.
- ◦ **Management:** Strict aseptic technique during catheter insertion and maintenance, along with prompt treatment of any signs of infection, is crucial.

5. **Bleeding:**

- ◦ **Mechanism:** Heparin is often used during hemodialysis to prevent clotting in the dialysis circuit, which can increase the risk of bleeding.
- ◦ **Management:** Monitoring coagulation parameters and adjusting heparin dosage as needed can help manage this risk.

5.2 Methods of Elimination Enhancement

5.2.3 Hemoperfusion

5.2.3.1 Mechanism and Indications

Mechanism:

Hemoperfusion involves passing the patient's blood through a cartridge filled with adsorbent materials, such as activated charcoal or resin, which can bind and remove toxins directly from the bloodstream. Unlike hemodialysis, which relies on diffusion across a semipermeable membrane, hemoperfusion uses adsorption to clear substances. The blood flows through the adsorbent material, which captures and holds onto the toxin molecules. This method is particularly effective for substances that are highly protein-bound or have large molecular weights, which are typically difficult to remove by hemodialysis.

Indications:

Hemoperfusion is indicated for certain types of poisonings where traditional methods, such as activated charcoal or hemodialysis, are less effective:

- **Highly Protein-Bound Toxins:** Toxins like theophylline, carbamazepine, and phenobarbital, which bind extensively to plasma proteins, making them poor candidates for hemodialysis.

- **Large Molecular Weight Toxins:** Substances with large molecular sizes, which are inefficiently cleared by hemodialysis membranes.
- **Lipid-Soluble Toxins:** Toxins that are highly lipid-soluble, such as certain pesticides and drugs that are difficult to remove by conventional methods.
- **Severe Poisoning:** Cases of life-threatening toxicity where rapid reduction of toxin levels is critical for patient survival.

5.2.3.2 Techniques and Complications
Techniques:

1. **Preparation:**

   - **Vascular Access:** Similar to hemodialysis, a central venous catheter is typically used to achieve the necessary blood flow rates. This catheter is placed in a large central vein, such as the femoral, jugular, or subclavian vein.
   - **Cartridge Selection:** The type of adsorbent material (activated charcoal or resin) is chosen based on the specific toxin to be removed. Each cartridge has specific properties suited to different types of toxins.

2. **Procedure:**

   - **Blood Flow:** Blood is drawn from the patient and pumped through the hemoperfusion cartridge. The flow rate is usually maintained between 200-300 mL/min to ensure efficient adsorption of toxins.
   - **Adsorption:** As blood passes through the cartridge, toxins bind to the adsorbent material, while the cleansed blood is returned to the patient. The duration of the procedure is typically 2-4 hours, depending on the severity of poisoning and the efficiency of toxin removal.
   - **Monitoring:** Continuous monitoring of vital signs, blood flow rates, and the condition of the hemoperfusion cartridge is essential to ensure the procedure's effectiveness and patient safety.

Complications:

1. **Hypotension:**

   - **Mechanism:** Rapid removal of large volumes of blood and the adsorption of certain substances can cause a drop in blood pressure.
   - **Management:** Hypotension can be managed by adjusting blood flow rates, administering intravenous fluids, or using vasopressors if necessary.

2. **Thrombocytopenia:**

   - **Mechanism:** The adsorbent materials in the cartridge can adsorb platelets and clotting factors, leading to a reduction in platelet count and an increased risk of bleeding.
   - **Management:** Regular monitoring of platelet counts and coagulation parameters is necessary. If thrombocytopenia is significant, the procedure may need to be discontinued, or additional supportive measures, such as platelet transfusions, may be required.

3. **Electrolyte Imbalances:**

   - **Mechanism:** Similar to hemodialysis, hemoperfusion can cause shifts in electrolyte levels, particularly calcium, potassium, and magnesium.
   - **Management:** Frequent monitoring of electrolytes and appropriate supplementation are essential to prevent complications.

4. **Cartridge Saturation:**

   - **Mechanism:** Over time, the adsorbent material in the cartridge can become saturated with toxins, reducing its effectiveness.
   - **Management:** The cartridge may need to be replaced during the procedure to maintain optimal toxin adsorption.

5. **Infections:**

   - **Mechanism:** The use of central venous catheters increases the risk of bloodstream infections.
   - **Management:** Strict aseptic techniques during catheter insertion and maintenance are essential, along with prompt treatment of any signs

of infection.

6. **Coagulopathy:**

   ○ **Mechanism:** Adsorption of clotting factors can lead to coagulopathy, increasing the risk of bleeding.
   ○ **Management:** Monitoring coagulation parameters and adjusting treatment as necessary can help manage this risk.

5.2 Methods of Elimination Enhancement

5.2.4 Peritoneal Dialysis

5.2.4.1 Mechanism and Indications

Mechanism:

Peritoneal dialysis (PD) is a technique that uses the patient's peritoneal membrane as a semi-permeable dialysis membrane. A dialysis solution, or dialysate, is infused into the peritoneal cavity, where it remains for a period, allowing toxins and excess solutes from the blood to diffuse across the peritoneal membrane into the dialysate. After an appropriate dwell time, the dialysate, now containing the waste products and toxins, is drained out of the peritoneal cavity and replaced with fresh dialysate. This process can be repeated multiple times to enhance the removal of toxins from the bloodstream.

Indications:

Peritoneal dialysis is indicated in situations where other methods of enhanced elimination are not feasible or are contraindicated:

- **Limited Access to Hemodialysis:** In settings where hemodialysis facilities are not available, peritoneal dialysis can be an alternative for toxin removal.
- **Hemodynamic Instability:** Patients who are hemodynamically unstable and cannot tolerate the rapid fluid shifts associated with hemodialysis may benefit from the gentler nature of peritoneal dialysis.
- **Specific Toxins:** Although less commonly used for toxin removal compared to hemodialysis, peritoneal dialysis can be effective for certain

toxins, particularly those that are water-soluble and have low molecular weights.

- **Pediatric Patients:** Peritoneal dialysis is often preferred in young children due to the relative ease of the procedure and the avoidance of large vascular access.

5.2.4.2 Techniques and Complications
Techniques:

1. **Catheter Insertion:**

   - **Peritoneal Catheter:** A peritoneal dialysis catheter is surgically or percutaneously inserted into the peritoneal cavity. This catheter provides access for infusing and draining the dialysate.
   - **Placement:** The catheter is placed under sterile conditions to reduce the risk of infection and is typically positioned in the lower abdomen.

2. **Dialysate Infusion:**

   - **Dialysate Composition:** The dialysate is an osmotic solution containing glucose or other osmotic agents, electrolytes, and sometimes buffers. The composition is selected based on the patient's needs and the specific toxins involved.
   - **Infusion Process:** The dialysate is infused into the peritoneal cavity through the catheter. The volume of dialysate used can vary, but typical volumes range from 1.5 to 2.5 liters per exchange.

3. **Dwell Time:**

   - **Duration:** The dialysate is allowed to dwell in the peritoneal cavity for a prescribed period, usually between 1 to 4 hours, depending on the specific protocol and the patient's condition.
   - **Diffusion and Osmosis:** During the dwell time, toxins and excess solutes diffuse from the blood vessels in the peritoneal membrane into the dialysate, driven by concentration gradients.

4. **Drain and Exchange:**

- ◦ **Draining:** After the dwell time, the dialysate, now containing the removed toxins and waste products, is drained out of the peritoneal cavity.
- ◦ **Exchange:** Fresh dialysate is then infused to start a new cycle. This process is repeated several times per day, depending on the severity of poisoning and the efficiency of toxin removal.

Complications:

1. **Peritonitis:**

   - ◦ **Mechanism:** Infection of the peritoneal cavity is a significant risk and can occur due to contamination during catheter insertion or dialysate exchanges.
   - ◦ **Symptoms:** Signs of peritonitis include abdominal pain, fever, cloudy dialysate, and elevated white blood cell count in the dialysate.
   - ◦ **Management:** Treatment involves prompt administration of intraperitoneal or systemic antibiotics, and in severe cases, removal and replacement of the catheter.

2. **Catheter-Related Issues:**

   - ◦ **Obstruction:** The peritoneal catheter can become obstructed by fibrin, blood clots, or kinks, preventing effective dialysate flow.
   - ◦ **Management:** Flushing the catheter, repositioning, or in some cases, surgical revision may be necessary to restore proper function.

3. **Fluid Overload:**

   - ◦ **Mechanism:** Inadequate removal of fluid during exchanges can lead to fluid retention and overload, causing symptoms such as edema, hypertension, and respiratory distress.
   - ◦ **Management:** Careful monitoring of fluid balance and adjusting the dialysate volume and dwell times can help prevent and manage fluid overload.

4. **Electrolyte Imbalances:**

- ○ **Mechanism:** Peritoneal dialysis can cause shifts in electrolytes, leading to imbalances such as hypokalemia or hyperglycemia (due to the glucose content in the dialysate).
- ○ **Management:** Regular monitoring of serum electrolyte levels and appropriate adjustments to the dialysate composition or supplementation are necessary to maintain electrolyte balance.

5. **Mechanical Complications:**

- ○ **Leakage:** Leakage of dialysate around the catheter insertion site can occur, leading to suboptimal dialysis and risk of infection.
- ○ **Hernias:** Increased intra-abdominal pressure from the dialysate can contribute to the development of hernias, particularly in patients with pre-existing risk factors.
- ○ **Management:** Addressing leakage may require adjustments in the catheter placement or securement, and hernias may require surgical intervention.

CHAPTER VI

Toxicokinetics

Introduction

Toxicokinetics is the study of how toxins are absorbed, distributed, metabolized, and excreted by the body. Understanding these processes is essential for effectively managing poisoning cases and developing appropriate treatment strategies. The principles of toxicokinetics help predict the behavior of toxins within the body, influencing decisions about decontamination, antidote administration, and supportive care.

Toxicokinetics is closely related to pharmacokinetics, the study of how drugs move through the body, but focuses specifically on substances that cause harmful effects. By analyzing toxicokinetic data, healthcare providers can better understand the time course of toxin exposure and its impact on different organs and systems.

Scope of the Chapter

This chapter will cover the following key areas:

1. **Absorption:** How toxins enter the body through various routes, including oral, inhalation, dermal, and parenteral. Factors affecting the rate and extent of absorption will be discussed.
2. **Distribution:** The process by which toxins are transported throughout the body and distributed to various tissues and organs. This section will explore the concepts of volume of distribution, protein binding, and tissue affinity.
3. **Metabolism:** How the body biotransforms toxins into more or less harmful substances. The roles of the liver and other metabolic pathways, including phase I and phase II reactions, will be examined.
4. **Excretion:** The mechanisms by which toxins and their metabolites are eliminated from the body, primarily through the kidneys, liver, and lungs. Factors influencing renal and hepatic clearance will be discussed.

5. **Kinetic Models:** An overview of the different models used to describe the kinetic behavior of toxins, including zero-order and first-order kinetics, and how these models help predict toxin levels over time.

Importance of Toxicokinetics

Understanding toxicokinetics is crucial for several reasons:

- **Treatment Planning:** By knowing how a toxin is absorbed, distributed, metabolized, and excreted, healthcare providers can develop targeted treatment plans to enhance elimination and mitigate toxic effects.
- **Dose-Response Relationships:** Toxicokinetics helps elucidate the relationship between the dose of a toxin and its observed effects, aiding in the assessment of toxicity and risk.
- **Timing of Interventions:** Knowledge of toxicokinetic principles enables clinicians to time interventions, such as the administration of antidotes or enhanced elimination techniques, to maximize their effectiveness.
- **Predicting Outcomes:** By analyzing toxicokinetic data, it is possible to predict the likely course of poisoning and anticipate potential complications, leading to more proactive and effective management.

6.1 Absorption

6.1.1 Mechanisms of Absorption

Mechanisms of Absorption refer to the processes by which toxins enter the body and move from the site of exposure into the bloodstream. Understanding these mechanisms is crucial for predicting the onset and severity of toxic effects and for determining appropriate decontamination strategies.

Gastrointestinal Absorption:

- **Passive Diffusion:** Most toxins are absorbed through passive diffusion, where molecules move from an area of higher concentration (the gut) to an area of lower concentration (the blood) across the intestinal mucosa.

This process does not require energy and depends on the concentration gradient.

- **Active Transport:** Some toxins, particularly those that resemble essential nutrients, are absorbed via active transport. This process involves carrier proteins and requires energy (ATP) to move substances against their concentration gradient. Examples include certain metals like lead, which mimic calcium.
- **Facilitated Diffusion:** This is similar to passive diffusion but involves specific carrier proteins that help transport molecules across the cell membrane without using energy.
- **Endocytosis:** Larger molecules or particles may be absorbed through endocytosis, where the cell membrane engulfs the toxin and forms a vesicle to transport it into the cell. This mechanism is less common but important for some biological toxins.

Dermal Absorption:

- **Transdermal Penetration:** Toxins can penetrate the skin through the outermost layer, the stratum corneum. Lipid-soluble substances penetrate more easily than water-soluble ones.
- **Intercellular Route:** Toxins can move between the cells of the stratum corneum, following the lipid matrix.
- **Transcellular Route:** This involves toxins moving through the cells of the epidermis.
- **Appendageal Route:** Some toxins enter through hair follicles and sweat glands, bypassing the stratum corneum.

Inhalational Absorption:

- **Alveolar Diffusion:** Gases and vapors are absorbed through the alveoli in the lungs by simple diffusion. The large surface area and rich blood supply of the alveoli facilitate rapid absorption.
- **Aerosol and Particulate Absorption:** Particles can be absorbed through the alveolar membrane or deposited in the respiratory tract and absorbed through the mucosa.

Parenteral Absorption:

- **Intravenous Injection:** Toxins introduced directly into the bloodstream provide immediate absorption and distribution.
- **Intramuscular and Subcutaneous Injection:** Toxins are absorbed from the injection site into the surrounding tissue and then into the bloodstream. This absorption depends on blood flow to the injection site.

6.1.2 Factors Influencing Absorption

Factors Influencing Absorption involve a variety of physiological and chemical characteristics that affect how quickly and efficiently toxins are absorbed into the body.

Physicochemical Properties of the Toxin:

- **Molecular Size and Weight:** Smaller molecules generally diffuse more easily across cell membranes compared to larger molecules.
- **Lipid Solubility:** Lipid-soluble toxins penetrate cell membranes more readily than water-soluble toxins, affecting absorption rates.
- **Ionization State:** The degree of ionization of a toxin affects its absorption. Non-ionized (neutral) molecules cross cell membranes more easily than ionized molecules. The ionization state is influenced by the pH of the environment and the pKa of the substance.

Concentration of the Toxin:

- **Concentration Gradient:** A higher concentration of the toxin at the site of exposure creates a stronger gradient, promoting faster absorption through passive diffusion.

Surface Area of the Absorptive Site:

- **Gastrointestinal Tract:** The extensive surface area of the intestines, with villi and microvilli, enhances absorption.
- **Lungs:** The alveoli provide a large surface area for gas and vapor absorption.
- **Skin:** The surface area available for dermal absorption can be increased with larger exposure areas.

Blood Flow to the Absorptive Site:

- **Enhanced Perfusion:** Increased blood flow to the site of absorption (e.g., intestines, lungs) enhances the removal of absorbed toxins, maintaining the concentration gradient and promoting further absorption.
- **Reduced Perfusion:** Conditions that decrease blood flow can reduce absorption rates.

Presence of Food or Other Substances:

- **Food in the Stomach:** The presence of food can slow gastric emptying, thereby slowing the absorption of some toxins but potentially increasing the absorption of lipid-soluble toxins due to bile secretion.
- **Interactions with Other Substances:** Some substances can bind to toxins, reducing their absorption. For example, activated charcoal binds many toxins in the gastrointestinal tract, preventing their absorption.

Physiological Conditions:

- **Age and Health Status:** Age-related changes, such as decreased gastric acidity and slowed gastrointestinal motility in the elderly, can influence absorption. Health conditions, such as gastrointestinal diseases, can also affect absorption.
- **Genetic Factors:** Genetic variations can influence enzyme activity and transporter proteins involved in toxin absorption and metabolism.

Exposure Route and Duration:

- **Route of Exposure:** Different routes (oral, inhalation, dermal, parenteral) have distinct absorption characteristics. For instance, inhalation provides rapid absorption due to the large surface area and rich blood supply of the alveoli.
- **Duration of Exposure:** Prolonged exposure can lead to increased absorption and accumulation of the toxin in the body.

6.2 Distribution

6.2.1 Mechanisms of Distribution

Mechanisms of Distribution describe how toxins move from the bloodstream to various tissues and organs after absorption. This process is influenced by the toxin's physicochemical properties and the body's physiological characteristics.

Blood Flow and Perfusion:

- **Initial Distribution:** Toxins are initially distributed to highly perfused organs such as the liver, kidneys, brain, and heart. These organs receive a large proportion of the cardiac output, leading to rapid distribution.
- **Subsequent Redistribution:** Over time, toxins redistribute to less perfused tissues like muscle and fat. This process depends on the toxin's solubility and affinity for different tissues.

Plasma Protein Binding:

- **Binding to Plasma Proteins:** Many toxins bind to plasma proteins, such as albumin and globulins. The extent of binding affects the free (unbound) fraction of the toxin available for distribution to tissues.
- **Equilibrium:** A dynamic equilibrium exists between the bound and unbound forms of the toxin. Only the unbound fraction can cross cell membranes and exert toxic effects or be metabolized and excreted.

Capillary Permeability:

- **Continuous Capillaries:** These capillaries, found in the brain and muscles, have tight junctions that restrict the movement of large molecules and hydrophilic substances. The blood-brain barrier (BBB) is an example of a continuous capillary system with selective permeability.
- **Fenestrated Capillaries:** Found in organs like the kidneys and endocrine glands, these capillaries have pores that allow larger molecules and hydrophilic substances to pass through more easily.
- **Discontinuous Capillaries:** Present in the liver and spleen, these capillaries have large gaps, permitting the passage of larger molecules and cells.

Transport Mechanisms:

- **Passive Diffusion:** Toxins move across cell membranes from areas of higher concentration to lower concentration. Lipid-soluble toxins diffuse more readily through the lipid bilayer of cell membranes.
- **Active Transport:** Some toxins are transported into cells via active transport mechanisms, involving specific carrier proteins and energy expenditure.
- **Facilitated Diffusion:** Carrier proteins facilitate the movement of toxins across cell membranes without using energy, driven by concentration gradients.
- **Endocytosis:** Cells engulf toxins through endocytosis, forming vesicles that transport the toxins into the cell. This mechanism is important for large molecules and particulate matter.

6.2.2 Factors Influencing Distribution

Factors Influencing Distribution involve various characteristics of the toxin and the physiological state of the body, affecting how toxins are distributed to different tissues and organs.

Physicochemical Properties of the Toxin:

- **Molecular Size:** Smaller molecules distribute more easily through capillary walls and cell membranes compared to larger molecules.
- **Lipid Solubility:** Lipid-soluble toxins readily cross cell membranes and are distributed to tissues with high lipid content, such as the brain and adipose tissue.
- **Ionization State:** The degree of ionization affects a toxin's ability to cross cell membranes. Non-ionized (neutral) molecules cross membranes more easily than ionized molecules.

Tissue Perfusion:

- **Highly Perfused Tissues:** Organs with high blood flow, such as the liver, kidneys, brain, and heart, receive a significant amount of the toxin quickly after absorption.

- **Less Perfused Tissues:** Tissues with lower blood flow, such as muscle and fat, receive the toxin more slowly. Redistribution to these tissues occurs over time.

Plasma Protein Binding:

- **Extent of Binding:** The proportion of the toxin bound to plasma proteins affects the free fraction available for distribution. Highly protein-bound toxins have a limited free fraction, reducing their immediate distribution to tissues.
- **Reversible Binding:** Binding to plasma proteins is usually reversible, allowing a dynamic equilibrium between bound and unbound toxin. Changes in binding dynamics can influence distribution.

Barriers to Distribution:

- **Blood-Brain Barrier (BBB):** The BBB restricts the passage of many toxins into the brain, protecting the central nervous system. Only lipid-soluble or actively transported toxins can cross the BBB easily.
- **Placental Barrier:** The placental barrier provides partial protection to the fetus from maternal toxins, although many substances can still cross and affect fetal development.

Tissue Affinity:

- **Tissue Binding:** Some toxins have a high affinity for specific tissues, leading to accumulation. For example, lead accumulates in bones, and certain pesticides accumulate in adipose tissue.
- **Receptor Interactions:** Toxins that interact with specific cellular receptors may have targeted distribution based on receptor availability in different tissues.

Pathophysiological Conditions:

- **Disease States:** Conditions such as liver or kidney disease can alter toxin distribution by affecting blood flow, plasma protein levels, and tissue permeability.

- **Age and Development:** Age-related changes, such as decreased plasma protein levels in neonates or altered blood-brain barrier function in the elderly, can influence toxin distribution.
- **Body Composition:** Variations in body fat and muscle mass affect the distribution of lipid-soluble and water-soluble toxins, respectively.

Drug Interactions:

- **Competitive Binding:** Co-administered drugs that bind to the same plasma proteins can displace toxins, increasing the free fraction available for distribution.
- **Metabolic Interactions:** Drugs that induce or inhibit metabolic enzymes can alter the distribution of toxins by affecting their metabolism and subsequent availability for distribution.

6.3 Metabolism

6.3.1 Mechanisms of Metabolism

Mechanisms of Metabolism refer to the biochemical processes by which the body transforms toxins into more water-soluble compounds that can be more easily excreted. These processes primarily occur in the liver but can also take place in other tissues such as the kidneys, lungs, and intestines. Metabolism of toxins generally occurs in two phases: Phase I and Phase II reactions.

Phase I Reactions:

- **Oxidation:** These reactions involve the addition of oxygen or the removal of hydrogen from the toxin, typically catalyzed by the cytochrome P450 enzyme system (CYP450). Common oxidative reactions include hydroxylation, dealkylation, and deamination.

  - **Example:** The oxidation of ethanol to acetaldehyde by alcohol dehydrogenase.

- **Reduction:** These reactions involve the gain of electrons or hydrogen by the toxin. Reduction reactions are less common than oxidation and often occur in anaerobic environments or low oxygen conditions.

  - **Example:** The reduction of nitro compounds to amines.

- **Hydrolysis:** These reactions involve the cleavage of bonds by the addition of water, typically catalyzed by esterases, amidases, and other hydrolases.

  - **Example:** The hydrolysis of aspirin (acetylsalicylic acid) to salicylic acid and acetic acid.

Phase II Reactions:

- **Conjugation:** Phase II reactions involve the addition of endogenous substrates to the toxin or its Phase I metabolites, making them more water-soluble and easier to excrete.

  - **Glucuronidation:** Addition of glucuronic acid, catalyzed by UDP-glucuronosyltransferase (UGT).
  - **Sulfation:** Addition of sulfate groups, catalyzed by sulfotransferases.
  - **Acetylation:** Addition of acetyl groups, catalyzed by N-acetyltransferases.
  - **Glutathione Conjugation:** Addition of glutathione, catalyzed by glutathione S-transferase.

These metabolic reactions transform lipophilic toxins into hydrophilic metabolites, which can be readily excreted by the kidneys or through bile.

6.3.2 Factors Influencing Metabolism

Factors Influencing Metabolism encompass a variety of physiological, genetic, and environmental factors that can affect the rate and efficiency of toxin metabolism.

Genetic Factors:

- **Genetic Polymorphisms:** Variations in genes encoding metabolic enzymes can lead to differences in metabolic activity. For instance, polymorphisms in the CYP450 enzymes can result in individuals being classified as poor, intermediate, extensive, or ultra-rapid metabolizers.

  - **Example:** CYP2D6 polymorphisms can affect the metabolism of drugs like codeine and its conversion to morphine.

Age:

- **Neonates and Infants:** Immature liver enzyme systems in neonates and infants can lead to slower metabolism and prolonged effects of toxins.

  - **Example:** The deficiency of UDP-glucuronosyltransferase in newborns can cause prolonged jaundice due to inefficient bilirubin conjugation.

- **Elderly:** Aging can reduce the metabolic capacity due to decreased liver size, blood flow, and enzyme activity.

  - **Example:** Decreased Phase I enzyme activity in elderly individuals can slow the metabolism of certain medications and toxins.

Sex:

- **Sex Differences:** Hormonal differences between males and females can influence the expression and activity of certain metabolic enzymes.

  - **Example:** Female sex hormones can modulate the activity of CYP3A4, affecting the metabolism of various drugs and toxins.

Diet and Nutrition:

- **Dietary Influences:** Certain foods and nutrients can induce or inhibit metabolic enzymes, affecting toxin metabolism.

  - **Induction:** Cruciferous vegetables and charbroiled meats can induce CYP1A2, increasing the metabolism of some drugs.

- ○ **Inhibition:** Grapefruit juice contains compounds that inhibit CYP3A4, leading to decreased metabolism of certain toxins and drugs.

Disease States:

- **Liver Disease:** Conditions such as hepatitis, cirrhosis, or liver cancer can impair hepatic metabolism, reducing the clearance of toxins.

  - ○ **Example:** Cirrhosis can decrease the activity of CYP450 enzymes, leading to the accumulation of toxins and drugs.

- **Renal Disease:** Impaired renal function can affect the excretion of metabolites, leading to their accumulation and potential toxicity.

  - ○ **Example:** Chronic kidney disease can reduce the elimination of conjugated metabolites, prolonging their effects.

Environmental Factors:

- **Exposure to Chemicals:** Environmental pollutants and chemicals, such as industrial solvents and pesticides, can induce or inhibit metabolic enzymes.

  - ○ **Induction:** Exposure to polycyclic aromatic hydrocarbons (PAHs) can induce CYP1A1 and CYP1B1, affecting toxin metabolism.
  - ○ **Inhibition:** Heavy metals like lead and mercury can inhibit various metabolic enzymes, reducing toxin clearance.

Drug Interactions:

- **Inducers and Inhibitors:** Concurrent use of drugs that induce or inhibit metabolic enzymes can significantly alter the metabolism of toxins.

  - ○ **Induction:** Rifampin, an antibiotic, induces CYP3A4, increasing the metabolism of drugs and toxins.
  - ○ **Inhibition:** Ketoconazole, an antifungal, inhibits CYP3A4, decreasing the metabolism of many substances.

Physiological Conditions:

- **Pregnancy:** Hormonal changes and increased blood volume during pregnancy can affect the metabolism of toxins.

  - **Example:** Increased activity of CYP2D6 and CYP3A4 during pregnancy can enhance the metabolism of certain drugs.

6.4 Excretion

6.4.1 Mechanisms of Excretion

Mechanisms of Excretion involve the processes by which toxins and their metabolites are eliminated from the body. Excretion is a critical component of toxicokinetics, as it determines how long a toxin remains in the body and continues to exert its effects. The primary organs involved in excretion are the kidneys, liver, lungs, and to a lesser extent, the skin and gastrointestinal tract.

Renal Excretion:

- **Glomerular Filtration:** Blood is filtered through the glomeruli in the kidneys, allowing small, water-soluble molecules and unbound toxins to pass into the filtrate, forming urine. The rate of glomerular filtration depends on the blood flow to the kidneys and the integrity of the glomerular filtration barrier.

  - **Example:** Small, hydrophilic toxins like methanol and ethylene glycol are efficiently excreted through glomerular filtration.

- **Tubular Secretion:** Toxins and metabolites that did not enter the filtrate through glomerular filtration can be actively secreted into the renal tubules from the peritubular capillaries. This process involves specific transporter proteins and energy expenditure.

  - **Example:** Organic acids and bases, such as penicillin and morphine, are actively secreted into the renal tubules.

- **Tubular Reabsorption:** Some toxins and metabolites may be reabsorbed from the tubular fluid back into the bloodstream, depending on their lipid solubility and ionization state. Urinary pH can influence reabsorption; for example, alkaline urine enhances the excretion of weak acids by reducing their reabsorption.

  ◦ **Example:** Weak acids like salicylates are reabsorbed less in alkaline urine, promoting their excretion.

Hepatic Excretion:

- **Biliary Excretion:** The liver plays a significant role in excreting toxins via bile. Hepatocytes secrete conjugated metabolites into the bile, which is then transported to the gallbladder and released into the intestines. Toxins can be eliminated in feces or undergo enterohepatic recirculation if reabsorbed from the intestines.

  ◦ **Example:** Conjugated bilirubin and certain drug metabolites are excreted into the bile.

- **Enterohepatic Recirculation:** Some toxins and metabolites excreted in bile can be reabsorbed in the intestines and returned to the liver via the portal circulation. This recycling process can prolong the presence of the toxin in the body.

  ◦ **Example:** Enterohepatic recirculation of estrogen metabolites can extend their biological activity.

Pulmonary Excretion:

- **Exhalation:** Volatile substances and gases can be excreted through the lungs by diffusion across the alveolar-capillary membrane. The rate of pulmonary excretion depends on the concentration gradient between the blood and alveolar air and the blood flow to the lungs.

  ◦ **Example:** Alcohol, anesthetic gases, and volatile solvents like benzene are excreted through exhalation.

Gastrointestinal Excretion:

- **Direct Excretion into the Gut:** Some toxins can be directly excreted into the gastrointestinal tract from the bloodstream. This mechanism is less common but can be significant for certain substances.

  - ○ **Example:** Heavy metals like mercury can be excreted into the intestines and eliminated in feces.

Other Routes of Excretion:

- **Sweat and Saliva:** Minor routes of excretion include sweat and saliva. Toxins excreted in sweat can cause skin irritation, while those in saliva may lead to a metallic taste or other oral symptoms.

  - ○ **Example:** Small amounts of drugs like amphetamines can be excreted in sweat and saliva.

- **Milk:** Lactating mothers can excrete toxins into breast milk, posing a risk to nursing infants. The excretion into milk depends on the toxin's lipid solubility and protein binding.

  - ○ **Example:** Lipid-soluble drugs like diazepam can be excreted into breast milk.

6.4 Excretion

6.4.2 Factors Influencing Excretion

Factors Influencing Excretion include various physiological, biochemical, and external factors that affect how efficiently toxins and their metabolites are eliminated from the body. Understanding these factors is essential for predicting the duration of toxic effects and for designing effective treatment strategies.

Physiological Factors:

- **Renal Function:** The efficiency of renal excretion is directly related to kidney function. Conditions like chronic kidney disease (CKD) or acute kidney injury (AKI) can significantly reduce the elimination of toxins, leading to prolonged toxicity.

  - **Example:** Impaired renal function in patients with CKD can lead to the accumulation of drugs like digoxin, requiring dose adjustments.

- **Hepatic Function:** Liver health is crucial for the metabolism and subsequent excretion of many toxins. Liver diseases such as hepatitis or cirrhosis can impair hepatic metabolism and biliary excretion, leading to increased toxicity.

  - **Example:** Reduced hepatic function in cirrhosis can impair the excretion of bilirubin, leading to jaundice.

- **Age:** Both very young and elderly individuals often have reduced excretory capacity. Neonates have immature renal and hepatic functions, while elderly individuals may experience age-related declines in kidney and liver function.

  - **Example:** Newborns have immature glucuronidation pathways, affecting the excretion of drugs like chloramphenicol, which can lead to "gray baby syndrome."

- **Body Fluid pH:** The pH of body fluids, particularly urine, can influence the excretion of weak acids and bases. Alkaline urine enhances the excretion of weak acids by ionizing them, while acidic urine promotes the excretion of weak bases.

  - **Example:** Alkalinizing the urine with sodium bicarbonate is used to enhance the excretion of salicylates in cases of overdose.

Biochemical Factors:

- **Protein Binding:** Toxins that are highly bound to plasma proteins have a reduced free fraction available for filtration and excretion. Only the unbound fraction is freely filtered by the kidneys.

- ○ **Example:** Warfarin is highly protein-bound, limiting its renal excretion.

- **Molecular Size and Lipid Solubility:** Small, water-soluble molecules are more readily excreted by the kidneys, while larger, lipid-soluble molecules may require metabolism to more water-soluble forms before excretion.

  - ○ **Example:** Lipid-soluble drugs like diazepam undergo hepatic metabolism to form more water-soluble metabolites for renal excretion.

- **Transporter Proteins:** Specific transport proteins in the kidneys and liver facilitate the secretion and reabsorption of various toxins and drugs. Genetic variations or drug interactions can affect the function of these transporters.

  - ○ **Example:** P-glycoprotein is a transporter that pumps drugs out of cells and can influence the excretion of drugs like digoxin.

External Factors:

- **Drug Interactions:** Concurrent use of multiple drugs can affect the excretion of toxins through competition for the same transporters or enzymes, or through changes in urine pH.

  - ○ **Example:** Probenecid inhibits the renal excretion of penicillin, prolonging its plasma levels and therapeutic effects.

- **Hydration Status:** Adequate hydration enhances renal excretion by increasing urine flow and dilution of toxins. Dehydration can reduce renal perfusion and urine output, slowing toxin elimination.

  - ○ **Example:** Adequate hydration is crucial for patients receiving methotrexate to prevent renal toxicity.

- **Diet and Nutrition:** Certain dietary components can influence the excretion of toxins. For example, a high-protein diet can acidify the urine, affecting the excretion of weak bases.

- ◦ **Example:** A diet rich in green vegetables can alkalinize the urine, enhancing the excretion of weak acids.

- **Environmental Factors:** Exposure to environmental toxins, such as heavy metals, can saturate excretory pathways, reducing the body's ability to eliminate other toxins.

- ◦ **Example:** Chronic exposure to lead can impair renal function, reducing the excretion of other nephrotoxic substances.

Pathophysiological Conditions:

- **Infections and Inflammation:** Conditions that affect the kidneys or liver, such as infections or inflammatory diseases, can impair the excretion of toxins.

- ◦ **Example:** Acute pyelonephritis can impair renal function and reduce the excretion of drugs like aminoglycosides.

- **Genetic Disorders:** Genetic disorders affecting metabolic enzymes or transport proteins can significantly alter the excretion of toxins.

- ◦ **Example:** Individuals with Gilbert's syndrome have a deficiency in glucuronosyltransferase, affecting the excretion of bilirubin and certain drugs.

6.5 Factors Affecting Toxicokinetics

6.5.1 Age and Gender

Age:

- **Neonates and Infants:**

- **Absorption:** Gastrointestinal absorption is variable due to immature digestive enzymes and altered gastric pH. Dermal absorption is higher due to thinner skin.
- **Distribution:** Higher body water content and lower fat content influence the distribution of hydrophilic and lipophilic toxins, respectively. Plasma protein binding is reduced due to lower albumin levels.
- **Metabolism:** Liver enzyme activity is immature, leading to slower metabolism of many toxins.
- **Excretion:** Renal function is immature, reducing glomerular filtration, tubular secretion, and reabsorption.

- **Elderly:**

  - **Absorption:** Gastrointestinal motility and blood flow decrease with age, potentially altering absorption rates.
  - **Distribution:** Increased body fat and decreased lean body mass affect the distribution of lipophilic and hydrophilic substances. Plasma protein binding may be reduced due to lower albumin levels.
  - **Metabolism:** Hepatic enzyme activity and liver blood flow decline, slowing the metabolism of many toxins.
  - **Excretion:** Renal function declines, reducing the clearance of toxins.

Gender:

- **Hormonal Differences:** Sex hormones influence the expression and activity of metabolic enzymes and transporters. For example, estrogen and progesterone can modulate CYP450 enzyme activity.
- **Body Composition:** Women generally have higher body fat percentages, affecting the distribution of lipophilic toxins. Men typically have higher lean body mass, influencing the distribution of hydrophilic toxins.
- **Renal Function:** Glomerular filtration rate (GFR) may differ slightly between genders, influencing renal excretion rates.

6.5.2 Genetic Factors

- **Genetic Polymorphisms:** Variations in genes encoding metabolic enzymes, transporters, and receptors can lead to differences in toxin metabolism and excretion among individuals.

  - **CYP450 Enzymes:** Polymorphisms in CYP2D6, CYP2C19, and CYP2C9 can lead to variations in the metabolism of many drugs and toxins, resulting in poor, intermediate, extensive, or ultra-rapid metabolizer phenotypes.
  - **Transport Proteins:** Variations in genes encoding transporters like P-glycoprotein (ABCB1) and organic anion transporters (OATs) can affect the uptake and efflux of toxins in tissues and organs.

- **Metabolic Enzymes:**

  - **UDP-Glucuronosyltransferases (UGTs):** Polymorphisms in UGT1A1 can affect the glucuronidation and excretion of bilirubin and drugs like irinotecan.
  - **N-Acetyltransferases (NATs):** Polymorphisms in NAT2 can lead to slow or fast acetylator phenotypes, affecting the metabolism of drugs like isoniazid.

- **Receptor Variants:** Genetic variations in receptors can alter sensitivity to toxins and influence their toxicokinetic profiles.

6.5.3 Disease States

Liver Disease:

- **Cirrhosis and Hepatitis:** These conditions impair hepatic metabolism and reduce the clearance of many toxins. Liver dysfunction can alter the synthesis of plasma proteins, affecting toxin binding and distribution.
- **Liver Enzyme Activity:** Enzyme activity may be reduced, leading to slower Phase I and Phase II reactions, which impairs the detoxification process.

Kidney Disease:

- **Chronic Kidney Disease (CKD):** Reduced glomerular filtration, tubular secretion, and reabsorption impair renal excretion of toxins. Accumulation of uremic toxins can interfere with the metabolism and excretion of other substances.
- **Acute Kidney Injury (AKI):** Sudden loss of renal function can lead to rapid accumulation of toxins and their metabolites, requiring immediate medical intervention.

Cardiovascular Disease:

- **Heart Failure:** Reduced cardiac output decreases blood flow to the liver and kidneys, impairing the metabolism and excretion of toxins.
- **Peripheral Edema:** Fluid accumulation can alter the distribution of hydrophilic toxins.

Endocrine Disorders:

- **Diabetes:** Diabetic nephropathy can impair renal function, while alterations in glucose metabolism can influence the metabolism of certain toxins.
- **Thyroid Disorders:** Hyperthyroidism and hypothyroidism can affect the metabolism and distribution of toxins due to changes in metabolic rate and protein binding.

Respiratory Disease:

- **Chronic Obstructive Pulmonary Disease (COPD):** Impaired pulmonary function can reduce the excretion of volatile toxins and affect the overall metabolic capacity.

Gastrointestinal Disorders:

- **Malabsorption Syndromes:** Conditions like celiac disease or Crohn's disease can alter the absorption of toxins and nutrients, influencing their toxicokinetic profiles.

CHAPTER VII

Clinical Symptoms and Management of Acute Poisoning Introduction

Acute poisoning is a critical medical emergency that requires prompt recognition and management to prevent severe morbidity and mortality. The clinical presentation of acute poisoning can vary widely depending on the type of toxin, the route of exposure, the dose, and the patient's individual characteristics. Understanding the clinical symptoms and appropriate management strategies is crucial for healthcare providers to effectively address poisoning cases.

Acute poisoning can result from various substances, including pharmaceuticals, household chemicals, industrial agents, environmental toxins, and biological agents. The symptoms can range from mild, nonspecific complaints to severe, life-threatening conditions. Effective management involves a systematic approach to assessment, stabilization, diagnosis, and treatment.

Scope of the Chapter

This chapter will cover the following key areas:

1. **Clinical Symptoms:**

   ° Identification of common and specific clinical signs and symptoms associated with various types of poisoning.
   ° Understanding the pathophysiology behind the symptoms to aid in accurate diagnosis and management.

2. **Initial Assessment and Stabilization:**

   ° A systematic approach to the initial assessment of poisoned patients, focusing on airway, breathing, and circulation (ABCs).
   ° Rapid identification of life-threatening conditions and implementation of immediate stabilization measures.

3. **Diagnosis:**

   - Strategies for obtaining a detailed patient history, including exposure history and previous medical conditions.
   - Utilization of laboratory tests, imaging studies, and toxicology screens to identify the causative agent and assess the severity of poisoning.

4. **Decontamination:**

   - Techniques for removing or neutralizing the toxin from the patient's body, including activated charcoal, gastric lavage, and whole bowel irrigation.
   - Indications, contraindications, and potential complications of each decontamination method.

5. **Supportive Care:**

   - Providing symptomatic and supportive care tailored to the specific needs of the poisoned patient.
   - Monitoring vital signs, fluid and electrolyte balance, and organ function to prevent and manage complications.

6. **Specific Antidotes:**

   - Overview of commonly used antidotes for specific toxins, including their mechanisms of action, indications, and administration protocols.
   - Case studies highlighting the use of antidotes in real-world clinical scenarios.

7. **Elimination Enhancement:**

   - Methods to enhance the elimination of toxins from the body, such as urinary alkalinization, hemodialysis, hemoperfusion, and peritoneal dialysis.
   - Indications, techniques, and potential complications of each method.

8. **Prevention and Education:**

   - Strategies for preventing poisoning incidents through public education, safe storage of hazardous substances, and regulatory measures.
   - Importance of educating patients and caregivers about the risks and management of potential poisoning exposures.

Importance of Understanding Clinical Symptoms and Management

Effective management of acute poisoning requires a thorough understanding of the clinical symptoms and appropriate treatment protocols. Prompt recognition and intervention can significantly improve patient outcomes by preventing the progression of poisoning and minimizing complications. Healthcare providers must be equipped with the knowledge and skills to:

- **Identify Toxic Syndromes:** Recognize patterns of symptoms that suggest specific types of poisoning, enabling timely and accurate diagnosis.
- **Stabilize Patients:** Implement immediate stabilization measures to address life-threatening conditions and maintain vital functions.
- **Administer Appropriate Treatments:** Utilize the correct decontamination methods, supportive care, antidotes, and elimination enhancement techniques based on the specific toxin and patient condition.
- **Educate and Prevent:** Provide education to patients, families, and communities to prevent poisoning incidents and promote safe practices.

7.1 Pesticide Poisoning

7.1.1 Organophosphorous Compounds

Organophosphorous (OP) compounds are a group of pesticides that inhibit acetylcholinesterase, an enzyme responsible for breaking down acetylcholine in the nervous system. The accumulation of acetylcholine leads to overstimulation of cholinergic receptors, resulting in a wide range of clinical symptoms.

7.1.1.1 Clinical Symptoms

The clinical symptoms of organophosphorous poisoning can be divided into three categories: muscarinic, nicotinic, and central nervous system (CNS) effects. The onset of symptoms can be rapid, occurring within minutes to hours after exposure.

Muscarinic Effects:

- **Respiratory Symptoms:**

  - **Bronchorrhea:** Excessive secretion of mucus in the airways.
  - **Bronchospasm:** Constriction of the bronchi, leading to difficulty in breathing.
  - **Dyspnea:** Shortness of breath due to increased secretions and bronchospasm.

- **Gastrointestinal Symptoms:**

  - **Salivation:** Excessive salivation.
  - **Lacrimation:** Increased tearing.
  - **Diarrhea:** Watery stools due to increased gastrointestinal motility.
  - **Vomiting:** Stimulation of the emetic center in the brain.

- **Ophthalmic Symptoms:**

  - **Miosis:** Constriction of the pupils.
  - **Blurred Vision:** Due to the constriction of the pupils and increased tear production.

- **Cardiovascular Symptoms:**

  - **Bradycardia:** Slowed heart rate.
  - **Hypotension:** Low blood pressure due to vasodilation.

Nicotinic Effects:

- **Muscle Weakness:** Due to overstimulation of the nicotinic receptors at the neuromuscular junction.
- **Fasciculations:** Involuntary muscle twitching.
- **Paralysis:** Severe cases can lead to paralysis, including respiratory muscles, necessitating mechanical ventilation.

CNS Effects:

- **Anxiety:** Increased restlessness and nervousness.
- **Confusion:** Mental disorientation.
- **Seizures:** Due to overstimulation of the CNS.
- **Coma:** Severe poisoning can lead to loss of consciousness and coma.

7.1.1.2 Management Strategies

The management of organophosphorous poisoning involves a combination of supportive care, decontamination, and specific antidotal therapy. Prompt recognition and treatment are crucial to improve outcomes.

Supportive Care:

- **Airway Management:** Ensure a clear airway and provide oxygen. Mechanical ventilation may be necessary in cases of respiratory failure.
- **Cardiovascular Support:** Monitor heart rate and blood pressure. Administer intravenous fluids and vasopressors if needed to maintain blood pressure.

Decontamination:

- **Skin Decontamination:** Remove contaminated clothing and wash the skin thoroughly with soap and water to reduce dermal absorption of the toxin.
- **Gastric Lavage:** Consider gastric lavage if the patient presents within one hour of ingestion, especially if a large amount of pesticide has been ingested. Ensure airway protection before performing gastric lavage.
- **Activated Charcoal:** Administer activated charcoal to reduce gastrointestinal absorption if the patient is alert and within one hour of ingestion.

Antidotal Therapy:

- **Atropine:** Atropine is a muscarinic antagonist that counteracts the muscarinic effects of acetylcholine. Administer an initial dose of 2-5 mg IV in adults (0.05 mg/kg in children), repeating every 5-10 minutes until secretions are dry, and bradycardia is resolved. Higher doses may be required in severe cases.
- **Pralidoxime (2-PAM):** Pralidoxime reactivates acetylcholinesterase by removing the organophosphorous compound from the enzyme. Administer an initial dose of 1-2 g IV in adults (20-50 mg/kg in children), followed by a continuous infusion if necessary. Repeat dosing may be required based on the clinical response.
- **Benzodiazepines:** Administer benzodiazepines, such as diazepam, to control seizures and reduce CNS agitation.

Monitoring and Follow-Up:

- **Vital Signs:** Continuously monitor vital signs, including heart rate, blood pressure, respiratory rate, and oxygen saturation.
- **Neurological Status:** Regularly assess the patient's neurological status, including mental status, muscle strength, and reflexes.
- **Laboratory Tests:** Perform serial blood tests to monitor acetylcholinesterase activity, electrolyte levels, and organ function.

Preventive Measures:

- **Education:** Educate patients and communities about the safe use and storage of pesticides to prevent accidental poisoning.
- **Personal Protective Equipment (PPE):** Encourage the use of PPE, such as gloves and masks, when handling pesticides.
- **Regulation:** Advocate for the regulation and control of organophosphorous pesticides to reduce the risk of poisoning.

7.1 Pesticide Poisoning

7.1.2 Carbamates

Carbamates are a class of pesticides similar to organophosphates in their mechanism of action but with some key differences in their clinical presentation and management. Like organophosphates, carbamates inhibit acetylcholinesterase, leading to an accumulation of acetylcholine and subsequent overstimulation of cholinergic receptors. However, carbamate poisoning tends to be less severe and of shorter duration compared to organophosphate poisoning because carbamates bind reversibly to acetylcholinesterase.

7.1.2.1 Clinical Symptoms

The clinical symptoms of carbamate poisoning are similar to those of organophosphate poisoning and can be categorized into muscarinic, nicotinic, and central nervous system (CNS) effects. Symptoms usually manifest within minutes to hours of exposure.

Muscarinic Effects:

- **Respiratory Symptoms:**

  - **Bronchorrhea:** Increased mucus production in the airways.
  - **Bronchospasm:** Constriction of the bronchial muscles, causing difficulty in breathing.
  - **Dyspnea:** Shortness of breath due to increased secretions and bronchospasm.

- **Gastrointestinal Symptoms:**

  - **Salivation:** Excessive production of saliva.
  - **Lacrimation:** Increased tear production.
  - **Diarrhea:** Frequent, watery bowel movements.
  - **Vomiting:** Expulsion of stomach contents through the mouth.

- **Ophthalmic Symptoms:**

  - **Miosis:** Constriction of the pupils, leading to blurred vision.
  - **Blurred Vision:** Due to pupil constriction and increased tear production.

- **Cardiovascular Symptoms:**

  - ◦ **Bradycardia:** Slow heart rate.
  - ◦ **Hypotension:** Low blood pressure due to vasodilation.

Nicotinic Effects:

- **Muscle Weakness:** Generalized muscle weakness due to overstimulation of nicotinic receptors at the neuromuscular junction.
- **Fasciculations:** Involuntary muscle twitching.
- **Paralysis:** Severe cases may lead to paralysis, including respiratory muscles, necessitating mechanical ventilation.

CNS Effects:

- **Anxiety:** Increased nervousness and restlessness.
- **Confusion:** Disorientation and difficulty in thinking clearly.
- **Seizures:** Convulsions due to excessive stimulation of the central nervous system.
- **Coma:** Loss of consciousness in severe poisoning cases.

7.1.2.2 Management Strategies

The management of carbamate poisoning involves supportive care, decontamination, and specific antidotal therapy. Given that carbamate poisoning tends to be less severe and shorter in duration than organophosphate poisoning, the management strategies are tailored accordingly.

Supportive Care:

- **Airway Management:** Ensure a clear airway and provide supplemental oxygen. Mechanical ventilation may be required in cases of severe respiratory compromise.
- **Cardiovascular Support:** Monitor heart rate and blood pressure. Administer intravenous fluids and vasopressors if necessary to maintain adequate blood pressure.

Decontamination:

- **Skin Decontamination:** Remove contaminated clothing and wash the skin thoroughly with soap and water to reduce further absorption of the toxin.
- **Gastric Lavage:** Consider gastric lavage if the patient presents within one hour of ingestion, especially if a large amount of carbamate has been ingested. Ensure airway protection before performing gastric lavage.
- **Activated Charcoal:** Administer activated charcoal to reduce gastrointestinal absorption if the patient is alert and presents within one hour of ingestion.

Antidotal Therapy:

- **Atropine:** Atropine is a muscarinic antagonist that counteracts the muscarinic effects of acetylcholine. Administer an initial dose of 1-2 mg IV in adults (0.05 mg/kg in children), repeating every 5-10 minutes until secretions are dry and bradycardia is resolved. Higher doses may be required in severe cases.
- **Pralidoxime (2-PAM):** Unlike in organophosphate poisoning, pralidoxime is generally not indicated in carbamate poisoning because carbamates bind reversibly to acetylcholinesterase, and the enzyme reactivates spontaneously. However, in cases of severe poisoning where differentiation from organophosphate poisoning is unclear, pralidoxime may be administered.

Monitoring and Follow-Up:

- **Vital Signs:** Continuously monitor vital signs, including heart rate, blood pressure, respiratory rate, and oxygen saturation.
- **Neurological Status:** Regularly assess the patient's neurological status, including mental status, muscle strength, and reflexes.
- **Laboratory Tests:** Perform serial blood tests to monitor acetylcholinesterase activity, electrolyte levels, and organ function.

Preventive Measures:

- **Education:** Educate patients and communities about the safe use and storage of carbamate pesticides to prevent accidental poisoning.

- **Personal Protective Equipment (PPE):** Encourage the use of PPE, such as gloves and masks, when handling carbamate pesticides.
- **Regulation:** Advocate for the regulation and control of carbamate pesticides to reduce the risk of poisoning.

7.1 Pesticide Poisoning

7.1.3 Organochlorines

Organochlorines are a class of pesticides known for their environmental persistence and bioaccumulation in the food chain. These compounds include well-known pesticides such as DDT, chlordane, and lindane. They exert their toxic effects primarily by interfering with the normal function of the nervous system, particularly by prolonging the opening of sodium channels in nerve cells, leading to prolonged depolarization and subsequent neurotoxicity.

7.1.3.1 Clinical Symptoms

The clinical symptoms of organochlorine poisoning can vary depending on the level and duration of exposure. Symptoms may appear acutely or after chronic exposure due to the cumulative nature of these compounds.

Acute Exposure Symptoms:

- **Neurological Symptoms:**

  - **Seizures:** Prolonged depolarization of neurons can lead to seizures, which may be difficult to control.
  - **Tremors:** Muscle twitching and tremors due to overstimulation of nerves.
  - **Hyperexcitability:** Increased sensitivity to stimuli, resulting in exaggerated reflexes and restlessness.
  - **Dizziness and Headache:** General symptoms of central nervous system irritation.

- **Gastrointestinal Symptoms:**

- ○ **Nausea and Vomiting:** Common symptoms due to the irritative effects of organochlorines on the gastrointestinal tract.
- ○ **Abdominal Pain:** Discomfort and pain due to toxin exposure.

- **Dermatological Symptoms:**

- ○ **Rashes:** Skin irritation and rashes can occur upon dermal exposure.

Chronic Exposure Symptoms:

- **Neurological Symptoms:**

- ○ **Peripheral Neuropathy:** Long-term exposure can lead to sensory and motor deficits.
- ○ **Cognitive Impairment:** Memory loss, confusion, and other cognitive deficits due to chronic neurotoxicity.

- **Endocrine Disruption:**

- ○ **Hormonal Imbalances:** Organochlorines can interfere with endocrine function, leading to reproductive and metabolic disorders.

- **Carcinogenic Effects:**

- ○ **Increased Cancer Risk:** Chronic exposure to certain organochlorines is associated with an increased risk of cancers, particularly liver and breast cancer.

7.1.3.2 Management Strategies

Management of organochlorine poisoning involves supportive care, decontamination, and specific interventions to manage symptoms. Due to their persistence and bioaccumulation, long-term monitoring may also be necessary.

Supportive Care:

- **Neurological Support:**

- **Seizure Management:** Administer benzodiazepines such as diazepam or lorazepam to control seizures. Refractory seizures may require additional anticonvulsants like phenobarbital.
- **Monitoring:** Continuous monitoring of neurological status is essential to detect and manage ongoing neurotoxic effects.

- **Gastrointestinal Support:**

  - **Antiemetics:** Administer antiemetics such as ondansetron to control nausea and vomiting.
  - **Fluid and Electrolyte Balance:** Ensure adequate hydration and correct any electrolyte imbalances caused by vomiting or diarrhea.

Decontamination:

- **Skin Decontamination:**

  - **Immediate Washing:** Remove contaminated clothing and wash the skin thoroughly with soap and water to reduce further absorption.
  - **Activated Charcoal:** Administer activated charcoal if ingestion occurred within an hour and the patient is alert, to limit gastrointestinal absorption.

Specific Interventions:

- **Seizure Control:**

  - **Benzodiazepines:** Administer benzodiazepines for initial seizure control.
  - **Additional Anticonvulsants:** Use phenobarbital or phenytoin if seizures are refractory to benzodiazepines.

- **Monitoring and Follow-Up:**

  - **Vital Signs:** Continuous monitoring of vital signs, including heart rate, blood pressure, and respiratory rate, to manage acute symptoms.
  - **Neurological Assessments:** Regular neurological assessments to detect changes in mental status, seizure activity, and other neurotoxic

effects.

- ◦ **Laboratory Tests:** Perform blood tests to monitor organ function and detect any metabolic abnormalities.

Preventive Measures:

- **Public Education:** Educate the public about the dangers of organochlorine exposure and the importance of proper handling and disposal.

  - ◦ **Regulation:** Advocate for stricter regulations and monitoring of organochlorine use to minimize environmental contamination and human exposure.
  - ◦ **Personal Protective Equipment (PPE):** Encourage the use of PPE, such as gloves and masks, when handling organochlorines to reduce the risk of exposure.

Long-Term Monitoring:

- **Neurological Monitoring:** Regular follow-up to monitor for long-term neurological effects, such as peripheral neuropathy and cognitive impairment.
- **Cancer Screening:** Periodic screening for cancers associated with chronic organochlorine exposure, particularly liver and breast cancer.

7.1 Pesticide Poisoning

7.1.4 Pyrethroids

Pyrethroids are a class of synthetic insecticides modeled after natural pyrethrins derived from chrysanthemum flowers. They are widely used due to their high insecticidal potency and relatively low toxicity to humans. However, in cases of significant exposure, pyrethroids can cause acute toxicity, particularly affecting the nervous system.

7.1.4.1 Clinical Symptoms

The clinical symptoms of pyrethroid poisoning primarily involve the nervous system but can also include other systemic effects. Symptoms vary depending on the type of pyrethroid (Type I or Type II) and the level of exposure.

Type I Pyrethroids (e.g., permethrin, tetramethrin):

- **Neurological Symptoms:**

  - **Tremors:** Fine, involuntary muscle twitching and shaking.
  - **Hyperexcitability:** Increased sensitivity to stimuli, leading to exaggerated reflexes.
  - **Ataxia:** Lack of muscle coordination, resulting in unsteady movements.

- **Systemic Symptoms:**

  - **Nausea and Vomiting:** Common gastrointestinal symptoms due to systemic absorption.
  - **Respiratory Distress:** Mild respiratory symptoms such as coughing and throat irritation.

Type II Pyrethroids (e.g., cypermethrin, deltamethrin):

- **Neurological Symptoms:**

  - **Seizures:** Convulsions due to overstimulation of the nervous system.
  - **Paresthesia:** Tingling or burning sensation on the skin, particularly at the site of contact.
  - **Choreoathetosis:** Involuntary, writhing movements of the limbs and trunk.

- **Systemic Symptoms:**

  - **Salivation:** Increased production of saliva.
  - **Lacrimation:** Excessive tearing.
  - **Bradycardia:** Slow heart rate.

General Symptoms:

- **Dermal Symptoms:**

  - **Skin Irritation:** Redness, itching, and burning sensation at the site of exposure.
  - **Allergic Reactions:** In rare cases, contact dermatitis or urticaria.

- **Respiratory Symptoms:**

  - **Respiratory Irritation:** Coughing, wheezing, and shortness of breath due to inhalation of pyrethroid particles.

7.1.4.2 Management Strategies

Management of pyrethroid poisoning involves supportive care, decontamination, and symptom-specific treatments. Prompt recognition and appropriate management are crucial to minimize toxicity and improve outcomes.

Supportive Care:

- **Neurological Support:**

  - **Seizure Management:** Administer benzodiazepines such as diazepam or lorazepam to control seizures. Severe cases may require additional anticonvulsants like phenobarbital.
  - **Monitoring:** Continuous monitoring of neurological status is essential to detect and manage ongoing neurotoxic effects.

- **Respiratory Support:**

  - **Oxygen Therapy:** Provide supplemental oxygen to patients experiencing respiratory distress.
  - **Ventilatory Support:** Mechanical ventilation may be necessary in cases of severe respiratory compromise.

Decontamination:

- **Skin Decontamination:**

- ◦ **Immediate Washing:** Remove contaminated clothing and wash the skin thoroughly with soap and water to reduce further absorption.
- ◦ **Activated Charcoal:** Administer activated charcoal if ingestion occurred within an hour and the patient is alert, to limit gastrointestinal absorption.

Symptom-Specific Treatments:

- **Tremors and Hyperexcitability:**

  - ◦ **Benzodiazepines:** Administer benzodiazepines to reduce tremors and hyperexcitability.
  - ◦ **Antihistamines:** Use antihistamines to alleviate skin irritation and paresthesia.

- **Gastrointestinal Symptoms:**

  - ◦ **Antiemetics:** Administer antiemetics such as ondansetron to control nausea and vomiting.
  - ◦ **Hydration:** Ensure adequate hydration to prevent dehydration from vomiting.

- **Respiratory Symptoms:**

  - ◦ **Bronchodilators:** Use bronchodilators to relieve bronchospasm and improve airflow.
  - ◦ **Corticosteroids:** Administer corticosteroids in severe cases of respiratory irritation and inflammation.

Monitoring and Follow-Up:

- **Vital Signs:** Continuous monitoring of vital signs, including heart rate, blood pressure, respiratory rate, and oxygen saturation.
- **Neurological Assessments:** Regular neurological assessments to detect changes in mental status, seizure activity, and other neurotoxic effects.
- **Laboratory Tests:** Perform blood tests to monitor organ function and detect any metabolic abnormalities.

Preventive Measures:

- **Public Education:** Educate the public about the safe use and storage of pyrethroid pesticides to prevent accidental poisoning.
- **Personal Protective Equipment (PPE):** Encourage the use of PPE, such as gloves and masks, when handling pyrethroids to reduce the risk of exposure.
- **Regulation:** Advocate for stricter regulations and monitoring of pyrethroid use to minimize environmental contamination and human exposure.

7.2 Opiates Overdose

7.2.1 Clinical Symptoms

Opiates are a class of drugs that include natural, synthetic, and semi-synthetic compounds derived from the opium poppy or designed to mimic its effects. Common opiates include morphine, heroin, codeine, oxycodone, and fentanyl. Overdose of opiates can lead to a range of symptoms, primarily due to their depressant effects on the central nervous system (CNS) and respiratory system.

Central Nervous System Symptoms:

- **Depressed Mental Status:** Opiate overdose typically results in marked sedation, drowsiness, and lethargy. Patients may become unresponsive or difficult to arouse.
- **Coma:** In severe cases, opiate overdose can lead to profound unconsciousness or coma.
- **Miosis:** Pinpoint pupils are a classic sign of opiate overdose, though this may not be present in cases involving mixed drug overdoses.

Respiratory Symptoms:

- **Respiratory Depression:** A hallmark of opiate overdose is slowed or absent breathing. This can lead to hypoxia, hypercapnia, and potentially fatal respiratory arrest.

- **Cyanosis:** Blue discoloration of the skin and mucous membranes due to inadequate oxygenation of the blood.

Cardiovascular Symptoms:

- **Hypotension:** Low blood pressure may occur due to the vasodilatory effects of opiates.
- **Bradycardia:** Slowed heart rate is common, although in severe cases, the heart rate may become erratic or lead to cardiac arrest.

Gastrointestinal Symptoms:

- **Nausea and Vomiting:** Common symptoms due to the activation of the chemoreceptor trigger zone.
- **Decreased Bowel Sounds:** Opiates can reduce gastrointestinal motility, leading to constipation or ileus.

7.2.2 Management Strategies

The management of opiate overdose focuses on supportive care, the administration of specific antidotes, and addressing any complications that arise. Timely intervention is critical to prevent severe outcomes and fatalities.

Supportive Care:

- **Airway Management:** Ensure the patient's airway is open. Use the jaw-thrust maneuver if necessary, and consider placing an oropharyngeal or nasopharyngeal airway to maintain patency.
- **Breathing Support:** Administer supplemental oxygen to all patients with suspected opiate overdose. For patients with significant respiratory depression, provide assisted ventilation using a bag-valve mask. Endotracheal intubation and mechanical ventilation may be required in severe cases.
- **Circulatory Support:** Monitor blood pressure and heart rate. Administer intravenous fluids to treat hypotension. Vasopressors may be necessary if hypotension persists despite fluid resuscitation.

Antidotal Therapy:

- **Naloxone:** Naloxone is a competitive opioid receptor antagonist that rapidly reverses the effects of opiates. It can be administered intravenously, intramuscularly, subcutaneously, or intranasally.

  - **Initial Dose:** Administer 0.4 to 2 mg of naloxone IV, IM, or SC. If there is no response, repeat every 2 to 3 minutes, up to a total dose of 10 mg. For intranasal administration, 2 to 4 mg can be given, and repeated as necessary.
  - **Observation:** After naloxone administration, monitor the patient closely for recurrent respiratory depression, as the duration of action of naloxone is shorter than that of many opiates. Additional doses may be required.
  - **Infusion:** In cases of long-acting opiate overdose, a continuous infusion of naloxone may be necessary to maintain adequate ventilation.

Monitoring and Follow-Up:

- **Vital Signs:** Continuous monitoring of respiratory rate, oxygen saturation, heart rate, and blood pressure.
- **Neurological Status:** Regular assessments of the patient's level of consciousness and neurological status.
- **Laboratory Tests:** Perform blood tests, including arterial blood gases (ABGs), to assess oxygenation, ventilation, and acid-base status. Check electrolytes, glucose, and renal function to detect any metabolic abnormalities.

Preventive Measures:

- **Education and Awareness:** Educate patients, families, and communities about the risks of opiate use and overdose. Promote the availability of naloxone kits for individuals at risk of overdose.
- **Safe Prescribing Practices:** Encourage healthcare providers to follow guidelines for the safe prescribing of opiates and to consider alternative pain management strategies.

- **Substance Abuse Treatment:** Refer patients with opiate dependence to addiction treatment programs and provide resources for long-term support.

Long-Term Management:

- **Observation:** Patients who have received naloxone should be observed for at least 2 to 4 hours after the last dose to ensure that respiratory depression does not recur.
- **Psychosocial Support:** Offer counseling and support services to address underlying issues related to opiate use and addiction.
- **Harm Reduction:** Promote harm reduction strategies, such as needle exchange programs and supervised injection sites, to reduce the risk of overdose and other complications.

7.3 Antidepressants Overdose

7.3.1 Clinical Symptoms

Antidepressants are a diverse group of medications used to treat depression and other psychiatric disorders. Overdoses can be life-threatening and present with a wide range of symptoms depending on the class of antidepressant involved. The main classes include tricyclic antidepressants (TCAs), selective serotonin reuptake inhibitors (SSRIs), serotonin-norepinephrine reuptake inhibitors (SNRIs), and monoamine oxidase inhibitors (MAOIs).

Tricyclic Antidepressants (TCAs):

- **Neurological Symptoms:**

  - **Sedation:** Patients may present with drowsiness, confusion, and coma in severe cases.
  - **Seizures:** TCAs lower the seizure threshold, leading to convulsions.

- **Cardiovascular Symptoms:**

- **Tachycardia:** Increased heart rate.
- **Hypotension:** Low blood pressure due to vasodilation and reduced cardiac output.
- **Arrhythmias:** Life-threatening arrhythmias, including ventricular tachycardia and fibrillation.
- **QRS Prolongation:** Widening of the QRS complex on ECG, indicative of sodium channel blockade.

- **Anticholinergic Effects:**

  - **Dry Mouth, Blurred Vision, Urinary Retention, Constipation:** Due to muscarinic receptor antagonism.

Selective Serotonin Reuptake Inhibitors (SSRIs):

- **Neurological Symptoms:**

  - **Agitation, Confusion:** Mild to moderate overdose can cause increased anxiety and confusion.
  - **Seizures:** Rare but can occur in severe overdoses.
  - **Serotonin Syndrome:** Characterized by agitation, hyperreflexia, tremor, clonus, and hyperthermia. It can be life-threatening.

- **Gastrointestinal Symptoms:**

  - **Nausea, Vomiting, Diarrhea:** Common due to increased serotonin in the gastrointestinal tract.

Serotonin-Norepinephrine Reuptake Inhibitors (SNRIs):

- **Neurological Symptoms:**

  - **Agitation, Confusion, Seizures:** Similar to SSRIs, with additional risk of increased blood pressure.

- **Cardiovascular Symptoms:**

- ◦ **Hypertension:** Increased blood pressure due to norepinephrine reuptake inhibition.
- ◦ **Tachycardia:** Increased heart rate.

Monoamine Oxidase Inhibitors (MAOIs):

- **Neurological Symptoms:**

  - ◦ **Agitation, Confusion, Seizures:** Due to excessive neurotransmitter accumulation.

- **Cardiovascular Symptoms:**

  - ◦ **Hypertension:** Severe, potentially leading to hypertensive crisis.
  - ◦ **Tachycardia:** Increased heart rate.

- **Serotonin Syndrome:** Especially when combined with other serotonergic agents.

7.3.2 Management Strategies

The management of antidepressant overdose involves supportive care, specific antidotal therapies where applicable, and careful monitoring to manage complications. Early recognition and treatment are crucial.

Supportive Care:

- **Airway Management:** Ensure a clear airway and provide supplemental oxygen as needed. Intubation and mechanical ventilation may be required in cases of severe respiratory depression or coma.
- **Circulatory Support:** Monitor blood pressure and heart rate. Administer intravenous fluids to maintain adequate blood pressure. Vasopressors may be necessary if hypotension persists despite fluid resuscitation.

Decontamination:

- **Activated Charcoal:** Administer activated charcoal if the patient presents within one hour of ingestion and is alert, to limit gastrointestinal absorption of the drug.

- **Gastric Lavage:** Consider gastric lavage if the patient presents within one hour of a large overdose and airway protection is assured.

Specific Treatments:

- **Tricyclic Antidepressants (TCAs):**

  - **Sodium Bicarbonate:** Administer sodium bicarbonate IV to treat QRS prolongation and arrhythmias. Typical dose is 1-2 mEq/kg, repeated as necessary based on ECG findings.
  - **Benzodiazepines:** Use benzodiazepines to control seizures and agitation.
  - **Lipid Emulsion Therapy:** Consider lipid emulsion therapy for severe, refractory cases, especially with significant cardiovascular instability.

- **Selective Serotonin Reuptake Inhibitors (SSRIs) and Serotonin-Norepinephrine Reuptake Inhibitors (SNRIs):**

  - **Benzodiazepines:** Administer benzodiazepines for seizures and severe agitation.
  - **Cyproheptadine:** An antihistamine with serotonin antagonistic properties, used to treat serotonin syndrome. The initial dose is 12 mg, followed by 2 mg every 2 hours as needed.
  - **Cooling Measures:** Use cooling blankets and antipyretics to manage hyperthermia associated with serotonin syndrome.

- **Monoamine Oxidase Inhibitors (MAOIs):**

  - **Phentolamine or Nitroprusside:** Administer phentolamine or nitroprusside IV to manage hypertensive crisis. Start with 1-5 mg of phentolamine IV or 0.3 mcg/kg/min of nitroprusside, titrated to effect.
  - **Benzodiazepines:** Use benzodiazepines for seizure control.

Monitoring and Follow-Up:

- **Vital Signs:** Continuous monitoring of respiratory rate, oxygen saturation, heart rate, and blood pressure.
- **ECG Monitoring:** Regular ECG monitoring to detect and manage arrhythmias, particularly in TCA overdose.
- **Neurological Status:** Frequent assessments of the patient's level of consciousness and neurological status.
- **Laboratory Tests:** Perform blood tests, including electrolytes, renal function, and toxicology screens, to assess the extent of the overdose and organ function.

Preventive Measures:

- **Patient Education:** Educate patients and caregivers about the risks of overdose and the importance of adhering to prescribed dosages.
- **Safe Prescribing Practices:** Encourage healthcare providers to follow guidelines for the safe prescribing of antidepressants and to consider alternative treatments for patients at risk of overdose.
- **Mental Health Support:** Provide resources and referrals for mental health support and counseling to address underlying issues related to depression and suicidal ideation.

7.4 Barbiturates and Benzodiazepines Overdose

7.4.1 Clinical Symptoms

Barbiturates and **benzodiazepines** are both central nervous system (CNS) depressants but differ in their mechanisms of action and toxicity profiles. Overdoses of these substances can lead to significant morbidity and mortality, particularly when taken in combination with other depressants such as alcohol.

Barbiturates:

- **Neurological Symptoms:**

  - **Sedation:** Profound drowsiness, lethargy, and, in severe cases, coma.

- ◦ **Respiratory Depression:** Slowed or absent breathing due to CNS depression.
- ◦ **Ataxia:** Lack of coordination and unsteady movements.
- ◦ **Nystagmus:** Rapid involuntary eye movements.

- **Cardiovascular Symptoms:**

- ◦ **Hypotension:** Low blood pressure due to vasodilation and decreased cardiac output.
- ◦ **Bradycardia:** Slowed heart rate.

- **Gastrointestinal Symptoms:**

- ◦ **Nausea and Vomiting:** Common due to CNS effects on the vomiting center.

Benzodiazepines:

- **Neurological Symptoms:**

- ◦ **Sedation:** Drowsiness, confusion, and difficulty in arousal.
- ◦ **Ataxia:** Unsteady gait and impaired coordination.
- ◦ **Dysarthria:** Slurred speech.
- ◦ **Respiratory Depression:** Less common compared to barbiturates but can occur, especially with high doses or in combination with other CNS depressants.

- **Cardiovascular Symptoms:**

- ◦ **Hypotension:** Less common but possible, especially in cases of severe overdose.

- **Paradoxical Reactions:**

- ◦ **Agitation:** In rare cases, particularly in children and the elderly, paradoxical agitation and hyperactivity may occur.

7.4.2 Management Strategies

The management of barbiturate and benzodiazepine overdose involves supportive care, the use of specific antidotes, and addressing any complications that arise. Prompt recognition and appropriate intervention are crucial for improving patient outcomes.

Supportive Care:

- **Airway Management:** Ensure the patient's airway is open. Use the jaw-thrust maneuver if necessary, and consider placing an oropharyngeal or nasopharyngeal airway to maintain patency.
- **Breathing Support:** Administer supplemental oxygen to all patients with suspected overdose. For patients with significant respiratory depression, provide assisted ventilation using a bag-valve mask. Endotracheal intubation and mechanical ventilation may be required in severe cases.
- **Circulatory Support:** Monitor blood pressure and heart rate. Administer intravenous fluids to maintain adequate blood pressure. Vasopressors may be necessary if hypotension persists despite fluid resuscitation.

Decontamination:

- **Activated Charcoal:** Administer activated charcoal if the patient presents within one hour of ingestion and is alert, to limit gastrointestinal absorption of the drug. This is more effective for barbiturates than benzodiazepines.
- **Gastric Lavage:** Consider gastric lavage if the patient presents within one hour of a large overdose and airway protection is assured.

Specific Treatments:

- **Barbiturates:**

  - **Alkaline Diuresis:** For long-acting barbiturates like phenobarbital, consider using sodium bicarbonate to alkalinize the urine and enhance renal excretion. This involves administering 1-2 mEq/kg of sodium bicarbonate IV, followed by a continuous infusion to maintain urine pH above 7.5.

- ○ **Hemodialysis:** In severe cases of barbiturate overdose, particularly with long-acting agents, hemodialysis or hemoperfusion may be necessary to enhance drug clearance.

- **Benzodiazepines:**

  - ○ **Flumazenil:** Flumazenil is a competitive benzodiazepine receptor antagonist that can reverse the effects of benzodiazepines. However, it should be used with caution due to the risk of precipitating seizures, particularly in patients with a history of seizures, benzodiazepine dependence, or co-ingestion of proconvulsant substances.

    - **Initial Dose:** Administer 0.2 mg IV over 15 seconds. If there is no response, give an additional 0.3 mg IV over 30 seconds. Further doses of 0.5 mg can be administered at 1-minute intervals, up to a total dose of 3 mg.

Monitoring and Follow-Up:

- **Vital Signs:** Continuous monitoring of respiratory rate, oxygen saturation, heart rate, and blood pressure.
- **Neurological Status:** Frequent assessments of the patient's level of consciousness and neurological status.
- **Laboratory Tests:** Perform blood tests, including electrolytes, renal function, and toxicology screens, to assess the extent of the overdose and organ function.

Preventive Measures:

- **Patient Education:** Educate patients and caregivers about the risks of overdose and the importance of adhering to prescribed dosages.
- **Safe Prescribing Practices:** Encourage healthcare providers to follow guidelines for the safe prescribing of barbiturates and benzodiazepines and to consider alternative treatments for patients at risk of overdose.
- **Mental Health Support:** Provide resources and referrals for mental health support and counseling to address underlying issues related to substance use and dependency.

Long-Term Management:

- **Observation:** Patients who have received treatment for barbiturate or benzodiazepine overdose should be observed for several hours to ensure that symptoms do not recur.
- **Substance Abuse Treatment:** Refer patients with a history of substance abuse to addiction treatment programs and provide resources for long-term support.

7.5 Alcohol Poisoning

7.5.1 Ethanol

Ethanol is the type of alcohol found in alcoholic beverages. Ethanol poisoning, also known as alcohol intoxication, occurs when a person consumes a large amount of ethanol in a short period, leading to toxic effects on the central nervous system and other organs.

7.5.1.1 Clinical Symptoms

The clinical symptoms of ethanol poisoning vary depending on the blood alcohol concentration (BAC) and the individual's tolerance to alcohol. Symptoms can range from mild to severe.

Mild to Moderate Intoxication:

- **Euphoria:** Feeling of well-being and reduced inhibition.
- **Impaired Judgment:** Poor decision-making and risk-taking behavior.
- **Coordination Problems:** Unsteady gait, difficulty with fine motor skills.
- **Slurred Speech:** Difficulty articulating words clearly.
- **Nausea and Vomiting:** Gastrointestinal irritation and potential for aspiration.

Severe Intoxication:

- **Confusion:** Disorientation and impaired cognitive function.
- **Stupor:** Significant reduction in mental and physical activity, difficult to arouse.

- **Hypothermia:** Low body temperature due to vasodilation and impaired thermoregulation.
- **Hypoglycemia:** Low blood sugar levels, especially in individuals with poor nutritional status.
- **Respiratory Depression:** Slowed or irregular breathing, potentially leading to respiratory arrest.
- **Coma:** Unconsciousness, unresponsive to stimuli.
- **Death:** In severe cases, respiratory arrest, aspiration, or cardiac arrhythmias can lead to death.

7.5.1.2 Management Strategies

Management of ethanol poisoning focuses on supportive care, monitoring, and preventing complications.

Supportive Care:

- **Airway Management:** Ensure the airway is open and protected, especially if the patient is vomiting or has a reduced level of consciousness. Consider endotracheal intubation if there is a risk of aspiration.
- **Breathing Support:** Provide supplemental oxygen if needed. Assist ventilation if there is significant respiratory depression.
- **Circulatory Support:** Monitor blood pressure and heart rate. Administer intravenous fluids to maintain hydration and blood pressure. Correct electrolyte imbalances as needed.

Decontamination:

- **Activated Charcoal:** Not typically indicated for ethanol poisoning as it is not effective in adsorbing alcohol.

Symptomatic Treatment:

- **Hypoglycemia:** Administer intravenous glucose to treat or prevent hypoglycemia, particularly in children and individuals with poor nutritional status.
- **Thiamine:** Administer thiamine (100 mg IV or IM) to prevent Wernicke's encephalopathy, especially in chronic alcohol users.

- **Hypothermia:** Rewarm patients with hypothermia using external warming devices and warm IV fluids.

Monitoring and Follow-Up:

- **Vital Signs:** Continuous monitoring of respiratory rate, oxygen saturation, heart rate, and blood pressure.
- **Neurological Status:** Regular assessments of the patient's level of consciousness and neurological status.
- **Laboratory Tests:** Perform blood tests, including blood alcohol level, glucose, electrolytes, and liver function tests.

Preventive Measures:

- **Patient Education:** Educate patients about the dangers of excessive alcohol consumption and provide resources for alcohol use disorder treatment.
- **Safe Practices:** Encourage safe drinking practices and the use of designated drivers or alternative transportation.

7.5.2 Methanol

Methanol is a toxic alcohol found in industrial products, antifreeze, and some household products. Methanol poisoning occurs when methanol is ingested, inhaled, or absorbed through the skin. Methanol is metabolized to formaldehyde and formic acid, which are highly toxic.

7.5.2.1 Clinical Symptoms

The clinical symptoms of methanol poisoning can be delayed, typically appearing 12-24 hours after exposure, and are primarily due to the toxic metabolites.

Initial Symptoms:

- **Central Nervous System Symptoms:**

  - **Headache:** Common early symptom.
  - **Dizziness and Confusion:** Impaired cognitive function.
  - **Nausea and Vomiting:** Gastrointestinal distress.

- **Visual Symptoms:**

  - **Blurred Vision:** Difficulty focusing.
  - **Photophobia:** Sensitivity to light.
  - **"Snowfield" Vision:** Described as seeing a "snowstorm" effect in the visual field, which can progress to blindness.

Severe Symptoms:

- **Metabolic Acidosis:**

  - **Hyperventilation:** Rapid breathing to compensate for acidosis.
  - **Abdominal Pain:** Due to severe metabolic acidosis.
  - **Coma:** Depressed level of consciousness, potentially leading to coma.

- **Ocular Damage:**

  - **Optic Neuropathy:** Permanent damage to the optic nerve, leading to blindness.

- **Multi-Organ Failure:**

  - **Cardiovascular Collapse:** Severe hypotension and shock.
  - **Renal Failure:** Due to severe metabolic acidosis and toxicity.

7.5.2.2 Management Strategies

Management of methanol poisoning involves supportive care, specific antidotal therapy, and enhanced elimination techniques.

Supportive Care:

- **Airway Management:** Ensure the airway is open and protected. Consider intubation if the patient has a depressed level of consciousness.
- **Breathing Support:** Provide supplemental oxygen and assist ventilation if needed. Monitor for respiratory failure due to metabolic acidosis.
- **Circulatory Support:** Monitor blood pressure and heart rate. Administer intravenous fluids and vasopressors if necessary to maintain blood pressure.

Decontamination:

- **Activated Charcoal:** Not effective for methanol poisoning and not recommended.

Specific Treatments:

- **Antidotes:**

  - **Ethanol:** Competitive inhibition of alcohol dehydrogenase. Administer ethanol IV or orally to maintain a blood ethanol concentration of 100-150 mg/dL.
  - **Fomepizole:** Preferred antidote, inhibits alcohol dehydrogenase. Initial dose is 15 mg/kg IV, followed by 10 mg/kg every 12 hours.

- **Folic Acid:** Enhances the metabolism of formic acid to non-toxic metabolites. Administer folic acid (50 mg IV every 4-6 hours).
- **Correction of Metabolic Acidosis:**

  - **Sodium Bicarbonate:** Administer sodium bicarbonate IV to correct severe metabolic acidosis and maintain blood pH above 7.3.

Enhanced Elimination:

- **Hemodialysis:** Highly effective in removing methanol and its toxic metabolites. Indicated in cases of severe poisoning, significant metabolic acidosis, visual disturbances, or renal failure.

Monitoring and Follow-Up:

- **Vital Signs:** Continuous monitoring of respiratory rate, oxygen saturation, heart rate, and blood pressure.
- **Neurological Status:** Regular assessments of the patient's level of consciousness and neurological status.
- **Laboratory Tests:** Perform serial blood tests to monitor methanol levels, electrolytes, blood pH, and renal function.

Preventive Measures:

- **Public Education:** Educate the public about the dangers of methanol-containing products and the importance of safe storage and handling.
- **Regulation:** Advocate for stricter regulations on the availability and labeling of methanol-containing products to prevent accidental ingestion.

7.6 Paracetamol and Salicylates Overdose

7.6.1 Clinical Symptoms

Paracetamol (Acetaminophen)

Paracetamol overdose is one of the most common causes of poisoning worldwide. It can lead to severe liver damage and potentially fatal hepatic failure if not promptly treated. Symptoms of paracetamol overdose typically present in stages.

Stage 1 (0-24 hours):

- **Nausea and Vomiting:** Initial symptoms may include gastrointestinal upset.
- **Diaphoresis:** Excessive sweating.
- **Malaise:** General feeling of discomfort or unease.

Stage 2 (24-72 hours):

- **Right Upper Quadrant Pain:** Due to liver enlargement and damage.
- **Elevated Liver Enzymes:** AST and ALT levels begin to rise, indicating liver injury.
- **Jaundice:** Yellowing of the skin and eyes may start to appear.
- **Coagulopathy:** Impaired blood clotting due to liver dysfunction.

Stage 3 (72-96 hours):

- **Peak Hepatic Damage:** Liver enzymes peak, and hepatic failure may ensue.
- **Encephalopathy:** Confusion, altered mental status due to liver failure.
- **Hypoglycemia:** Low blood sugar levels.

- **Lactic Acidosis:** Metabolic acidosis due to liver failure.
- **Renal Failure:** Kidney injury may occur in severe cases.

Stage 4 (4 days to 2 weeks):

- **Recovery or Death:** Patients may either recover with supportive care and treatment or progress to multi-organ failure and death.

Salicylates (Aspirin)

Salicylate poisoning can result from acute overdose or chronic ingestion. Symptoms result from direct toxicity and metabolic disturbances.

Early Symptoms (0-12 hours):

- **Tinnitus:** Ringing in the ears.
- **Nausea and Vomiting:** Gastrointestinal upset is common.
- **Hyperventilation:** Due to stimulation of the respiratory center in the brain.
- **Respiratory Alkalosis:** Early acid-base disturbance from hyperventilation.

Progressive Symptoms (12-24 hours):

- **Metabolic Acidosis:** Accumulation of salicylic acid and lactic acid.
- **Dehydration:** Due to vomiting, hyperventilation, and fever.
- **Hyperthermia:** Elevated body temperature.
- **Confusion and Agitation:** Central nervous system effects from salicylate toxicity.

Severe Symptoms (24+ hours):

- **Seizures:** Due to severe metabolic disturbances.
- **Pulmonary Edema:** Fluid accumulation in the lungs.
- **Hypoglycemia:** Low blood sugar levels.
- **Renal Failure:** Due to direct toxicity and dehydration.
- **Coma:** Severe cases can lead to coma and death.

7.6.2 Management Strategies

Paracetamol (Acetaminophen)
Supportive Care:

- **Airway Management:** Ensure airway patency and provide supplemental oxygen if needed.
- **Circulatory Support:** Administer intravenous fluids to maintain hydration and blood pressure.

Decontamination:

- **Activated Charcoal:** Administer activated charcoal if the patient presents within 1-2 hours of ingestion to limit gastrointestinal absorption of the drug.

Specific Treatments:

- **N-acetylcysteine (NAC):** NAC replenishes glutathione stores and enhances the detoxification of NAPQI, the toxic metabolite of paracetamol.

  - **Oral NAC:** Loading dose of 140 mg/kg followed by 70 mg/kg every 4 hours for 17 doses.
  - **Intravenous NAC:** Loading dose of 150 mg/kg over 1 hour, followed by 50 mg/kg over 4 hours, then 100 mg/kg over 16 hours.

Monitoring and Follow-Up:

- **Vital Signs:** Continuous monitoring of respiratory rate, oxygen saturation, heart rate, and blood pressure.
- **Liver Function Tests:** Regular assessment of AST, ALT, bilirubin, and coagulation parameters.
- **Renal Function Tests:** Monitor creatinine and urine output to detect renal involvement.

Preventive Measures:

- **Patient Education:** Educate patients about the risks of paracetamol overdose and the importance of adhering to recommended dosages.
- **Safe Storage:** Advise safe storage of paracetamol-containing products to prevent accidental ingestion, especially in children.

Salicylates (Aspirin)
Supportive Care:

- **Airway Management:** Ensure airway patency and provide supplemental oxygen if needed.
- **Circulatory Support:** Administer intravenous fluids to correct dehydration and maintain blood pressure.

Decontamination:

- **Activated Charcoal:** Administer activated charcoal if the patient presents within 1-2 hours of ingestion to limit gastrointestinal absorption of the drug.
- **Gastric Lavage:** Consider gastric lavage if the patient presents within 1 hour of a large overdose and airway protection is assured.

Specific Treatments:

- **Alkalinization:** Sodium bicarbonate IV to alkalinize the urine and promote renal excretion of salicylates.

  - **Initial Dose:** 1-2 mEq/kg IV bolus followed by continuous infusion to maintain urine pH above 7.5.

- **Hemodialysis:** Indicated in severe cases with renal failure, severe metabolic acidosis, or refractory symptoms. Hemodialysis effectively removes salicylates from the blood.

Monitoring and Follow-Up:

- **Vital Signs:** Continuous monitoring of respiratory rate, oxygen saturation, heart rate, and blood pressure.

- **Electrolytes and Acid-Base Status:** Regular assessment of electrolytes, blood gases, and bicarbonate levels.
- **Renal Function Tests:** Monitor creatinine and urine output to detect renal involvement.

Preventive Measures:

- **Patient Education:** Educate patients about the risks of salicylate overdose and the importance of adhering to recommended dosages.
- **Safe Storage:** Advise safe storage of salicylate-containing products to prevent accidental ingestion, especially in children.

7.7 Non-Steroidal Anti-Inflammatory Drugs (NSAIDs) Overdose

7.7.1 Clinical Symptoms

Non-Steroidal Anti-Inflammatory Drugs (NSAIDs) are commonly used medications for pain, inflammation, and fever. Overdose can lead to a variety of clinical symptoms, ranging from mild gastrointestinal discomfort to severe multi-organ toxicity.

Mild to Moderate Overdose:

- **Gastrointestinal Symptoms:**

  - **Nausea and Vomiting:** Common early symptoms due to direct irritation of the gastric mucosa.
  - **Abdominal Pain:** Often related to gastrointestinal irritation and potential for gastritis or peptic ulceration.
  - **Diarrhea:** Occasional symptom related to gastrointestinal upset.

- **Central Nervous System Symptoms:**

  - **Headache:** Common symptom, often mild.
  - **Dizziness:** Feeling of lightheadedness or unsteadiness.

- **Tinnitus:** Ringing in the ears, especially with salicylate-based NSAIDs.

Severe Overdose:

- **Renal Symptoms:**

  - **Acute Kidney Injury (AKI):** NSAIDs can cause reduced renal blood flow and direct renal toxicity, leading to AKI. Symptoms include decreased urine output, fluid retention, and elevated creatinine levels.
  - **Electrolyte Imbalances:** Hyperkalemia and hyponatremia can occur due to impaired renal function.

- **Cardiovascular Symptoms:**

  - **Hypertension:** Elevated blood pressure due to fluid retention and renal effects.
  - **Arrhythmias:** Rare but possible in severe overdose, particularly with medications like ibuprofen and naproxen.

- **Central Nervous System Symptoms:**

  - **Seizures:** Rare but possible, particularly with severe overdose or in individuals with underlying risk factors.
  - **Coma:** In very severe cases, CNS depression can lead to coma.

- **Gastrointestinal Symptoms:**

  - **Gastrointestinal Bleeding:** Significant risk in severe overdose, particularly with chronic use or pre-existing gastrointestinal conditions.
  - **Perforation:** Rare but serious complication due to severe gastrointestinal ulceration.

- **Metabolic Symptoms:**

- **Metabolic Acidosis:** Can occur in severe overdose, particularly with NSAIDs like ibuprofen.

7.7.2 Management Strategies

Management of NSAID overdose focuses on supportive care, decontamination, monitoring, and addressing any complications that arise.
Supportive Care:

- **Airway Management:** Ensure airway patency and provide supplemental oxygen if needed.
- **Circulatory Support:** Administer intravenous fluids to maintain hydration and blood pressure, particularly if there is evidence of renal impairment or significant gastrointestinal loss.

Decontamination:

- **Activated Charcoal:** Administer activated charcoal if the patient presents within 1-2 hours of ingestion and is alert, to limit gastrointestinal absorption of the drug.

Symptomatic Treatment:

- **Gastrointestinal Protection:**

  - **Proton Pump Inhibitors (PPIs):** Administer PPIs (e.g., omeprazole) to reduce gastric acid secretion and protect the gastric mucosa.
  - **H2 Receptor Antagonists:** As an alternative to PPIs, H2 receptor antagonists (e.g., ranitidine) can also be used to reduce gastric acid secretion.

- **Renal Support:**

  - **Hydration:** Ensure adequate hydration to support renal function and promote excretion of the drug.
  - **Monitoring:** Regularly monitor renal function through serum creatinine and urine output. Adjust treatment based on renal

function.

- **Electrolyte Management:**

  - **Hyperkalemia:** Treat hyperkalemia with measures such as sodium polystyrene sulfonate, insulin with glucose, or calcium gluconate, depending on severity.
  - **Hyponatremia:** Correct hyponatremia with appropriate intravenous fluids, avoiding rapid correction.

Monitoring and Follow-Up:

- **Vital Signs:** Continuous monitoring of respiratory rate, oxygen saturation, heart rate, and blood pressure.
- **Laboratory Tests:** Perform serial blood tests to monitor renal function, electrolytes, blood gases, and any evidence of metabolic acidosis.
- **Neurological Status:** Frequent assessments of the patient's level of consciousness and neurological status.

Preventive Measures:

- **Patient Education:** Educate patients about the risks of NSAID overdose and the importance of adhering to recommended dosages.
- **Safe Storage:** Advise safe storage of NSAID-containing products to prevent accidental ingestion, especially in children.
- **Regular Monitoring:** For patients on long-term NSAID therapy, ensure regular monitoring of renal function, gastrointestinal health, and cardiovascular status.

7.8 Hydrocarbons Poisoning

7.8.1 Petroleum Products

Petroleum products such as gasoline, kerosene, and motor oil are common hydrocarbons that can cause poisoning. Exposure can occur through ingestion, inhalation, or dermal contact, leading to a range of clinical symptoms.

7.8.1.1 Clinical Symptoms

Ingestion:

- **Gastrointestinal Symptoms:**

  - **Nausea and Vomiting:** Common initial symptoms.
  - **Abdominal Pain:** Due to irritation of the gastrointestinal tract.
  - **Diarrhea:** Occasionally seen following ingestion.

- **Central Nervous System Symptoms:**

  - **Headache and Dizziness:** Early neurological symptoms.
  - **Confusion and Drowsiness:** Progression to more severe CNS depression.
  - **Seizures and Coma:** Severe cases can lead to seizures and coma.

- **Respiratory Symptoms:**

  - **Coughing and Choking:** Due to aspiration risk.
  - **Respiratory Distress:** Difficulty breathing, wheezing, and cyanosis.
  - **Chemical Pneumonitis:** Inflammation of the lungs due to aspiration, leading to coughing, fever, and chest pain.

Inhalation:

- **Respiratory Symptoms:**

  - **Coughing and Wheezing:** Due to airway irritation.
  - **Shortness of Breath:** Difficulty breathing.
  - **Pulmonary Edema:** Severe cases can lead to fluid accumulation in the lungs.

- **Central Nervous System Symptoms:**

  - **Headache and Dizziness:** Common symptoms due to CNS effects.
  - **Confusion and Ataxia:** Impaired coordination and mental status.
  - **Unconsciousness:** In severe cases.

Dermal Contact:

- **Skin Irritation:** Redness, itching, and burning sensation.
- **Dermatitis:** Prolonged exposure can lead to skin inflammation and blistering.

7.8.1.2 Management Strategies
Supportive Care:

- **Airway Management:** Ensure airway patency and provide supplemental oxygen. Consider intubation if the patient has significant respiratory distress or risk of aspiration.
- **Breathing Support:** Administer supplemental oxygen and provide ventilatory support if needed. Monitor for signs of chemical pneumonitis.
- **Circulatory Support:** Administer intravenous fluids to maintain hydration and blood pressure.

Decontamination:

- **Ingestion:**

  - **Activated Charcoal:** Generally not recommended due to the risk of aspiration.
  - **Gastric Lavage:** Contraindicated due to the high risk of aspiration and chemical pneumonitis.
  - **Do Not Induce Vomiting:** Avoid inducing vomiting to prevent aspiration.

- **Inhalation:**

  - **Remove from Exposure:** Move the patient to fresh air immediately.
  - **Oxygen Therapy:** Provide high-flow oxygen to improve oxygenation.

- **Dermal Contact:**

  - **Skin Decontamination:** Remove contaminated clothing and wash the skin thoroughly with soap and water.

Symptomatic Treatment:

- **Respiratory Support:**

  - **Bronchodilators:** Administer bronchodilators such as albuterol to relieve bronchospasm.
  - **Corticosteroids:** Consider corticosteroids for severe inflammation and chemical pneumonitis.

- **Neurological Support:**

  - **Benzodiazepines:** Administer benzodiazepines for seizure control if necessary.

Monitoring and Follow-Up:

- **Vital Signs:** Continuous monitoring of respiratory rate, oxygen saturation, heart rate, and blood pressure.
- **Chest X-Ray:** Perform a chest x-ray to assess for chemical pneumonitis or pulmonary edema.
- **Laboratory Tests:** Monitor blood gases, electrolytes, and renal function.

Preventive Measures:

- **Public Education:** Educate the public about the dangers of hydrocarbon exposure and the importance of proper storage and handling.
- **Workplace Safety:** Implement safety protocols and provide personal protective equipment (PPE) in workplaces handling hydrocarbons.

7.8.2 Polyethylene Glycol (PEG)

Polyethylene glycol (PEG) is commonly used as a laxative and in various industrial applications. While generally considered safe, excessive ingestion can lead to toxicity.

7.8.2.1 Clinical Symptoms
Gastrointestinal Symptoms:

- **Nausea and Vomiting:** Common initial symptoms.
- **Abdominal Pain:** Cramping and discomfort.
- **Diarrhea:** Due to the osmotic effect of PEG in the gastrointestinal tract.
- **Dehydration:** Resulting from excessive diarrhea and fluid loss.

Central Nervous System Symptoms:

- **Dizziness and Headache:** Mild CNS effects.
- **Confusion:** In severe cases, particularly with significant fluid and electrolyte imbalances.

7.8.2.2 Management Strategies
Supportive Care:

- **Hydration:** Administer oral or intravenous fluids to maintain hydration and correct electrolyte imbalances.
- **Electrolyte Management:** Monitor and correct electrolyte imbalances, particularly sodium and potassium levels.

Decontamination:

- **Activated Charcoal:** Not typically indicated for PEG ingestion due to its poor adsorption of PEG.
- **Gastric Lavage:** Generally not recommended as PEG is rapidly absorbed and lavage is unlikely to be effective.

Symptomatic Treatment:

- **Anti-Nausea Medications:** Administer antiemetics such as ondansetron to control nausea and vomiting.
- **Anti-Diarrheal Medications:** Use cautiously to manage severe diarrhea, ensuring that underlying causes are addressed.

Monitoring and Follow-Up:

- **Vital Signs:** Continuous monitoring of heart rate, blood pressure, and respiratory rate.

- **Laboratory Tests:** Regular assessment of electrolyte levels, renal function, and hydration status.

Preventive Measures:

- **Patient Education:** Educate patients on the proper use of PEG-containing products and the risks of excessive ingestion.
- **Safe Storage:** Advise safe storage of PEG products to prevent accidental ingestion, especially in children.

7.9 Caustics Poisoning

Caustics, or corrosive substances, include inorganic acids and alkalis. These substances can cause severe tissue damage upon contact, leading to significant morbidity. Management of caustics poisoning requires prompt and effective intervention to prevent or minimize tissue injury.

7.9.1 Inorganic Acids

Inorganic acids, such as hydrochloric acid, sulfuric acid, and nitric acid, are commonly used in industrial processes and household cleaning products. Exposure can result from ingestion, inhalation, or dermal contact.

7.9.1.1 Clinical Symptoms
Ingestion:

- **Gastrointestinal Symptoms:**

  - **Severe Pain:** Intense pain in the mouth, throat, chest, and abdomen.
  - **Drooling:** Excessive salivation due to irritation.
  - **Dysphagia:** Difficulty swallowing.
  - **Hematemesis:** Vomiting blood due to gastrointestinal bleeding.
  - **Perforation:** Risk of esophageal or gastric perforation leading to severe pain, peritonitis, and shock.

Inhalation:

- **Respiratory Symptoms:**

- **Coughing:** Due to irritation of the respiratory tract.
- **Dyspnea:** Shortness of breath.
- **Wheezing and Stridor:** Due to airway inflammation and potential obstruction.
- **Pulmonary Edema:** Fluid accumulation in the lungs in severe cases.

Dermal Contact:

- **Skin Symptoms:**

  - **Burns:** Redness, blistering, and severe pain at the site of contact.
  - **Ulceration:** Deep tissue damage can lead to ulcer formation.

7.9.1.2 Management Strategies
Supportive Care:

- **Airway Management:** Ensure airway patency, provide supplemental oxygen, and consider intubation if there is significant respiratory distress.
- **Circulatory Support:** Administer intravenous fluids to maintain hydration and blood pressure, especially if there is significant blood loss or shock.

Decontamination:

- **Ingestion:**

  - **Do Not Induce Vomiting:** Avoid inducing vomiting to prevent further esophageal damage.
  - **Dilution:** Administer small amounts of water or milk to dilute the acid if the patient is conscious and can swallow safely.

- **Inhalation:**

  - **Remove from Exposure:** Move the patient to fresh air immediately.
  - **Oxygen Therapy:** Provide high-flow oxygen to improve oxygenation.

- **Dermal Contact:**

- ◦ **Skin Decontamination:** Remove contaminated clothing and wash the skin thoroughly with copious amounts of water. Continue flushing for at least 15-20 minutes.

Symptomatic Treatment:

- **Pain Management:** Administer analgesics to control pain.
- **Gastrointestinal Protection:** Consider proton pump inhibitors (PPIs) or H2 receptor antagonists to reduce gastric acid secretion and protect the gastric mucosa.

Monitoring and Follow-Up:

- **Vital Signs:** Continuous monitoring of respiratory rate, oxygen saturation, heart rate, and blood pressure.
- **Endoscopy:** Perform early endoscopy (within 24 hours) to assess the extent of gastrointestinal injury and guide further management.
- **Laboratory Tests:** Monitor blood gases, electrolytes, renal function, and complete blood count.

Preventive Measures:

- **Public Education:** Educate the public about the dangers of inorganic acid exposure and the importance of proper storage and handling.
- **Workplace Safety:** Implement safety protocols and provide personal protective equipment (PPE) in workplaces handling inorganic acids.

7.9.2 Alkali

Alkalis, such as sodium hydroxide, potassium hydroxide, and ammonia, are commonly found in industrial cleaners, drain openers, and fertilizers. Alkali exposure can cause deep tissue damage due to liquefactive necrosis.

7.9.2.1 Clinical Symptoms
Ingestion:

- **Gastrointestinal Symptoms:**

- ○ **Severe Pain:** Intense pain in the mouth, throat, chest, and abdomen.
- ○ **Drooling:** Excessive salivation due to irritation.
- ○ **Dysphagia:** Difficulty swallowing.
- ○ **Hematemesis:** Vomiting blood due to gastrointestinal bleeding.
- ○ **Perforation:** Risk of esophageal or gastric perforation leading to severe pain, peritonitis, and shock.

Inhalation:

- **Respiratory Symptoms:**

  - ○ **Coughing:** Due to irritation of the respiratory tract.
  - ○ **Dyspnea:** Shortness of breath.
  - ○ **Wheezing and Stridor:** Due to airway inflammation and potential obstruction.
  - ○ **Pulmonary Edema:** Fluid accumulation in the lungs in severe cases.

Dermal Contact:

- **Skin Symptoms:**

  - ○ **Burns:** Redness, blistering, and severe pain at the site of contact.
  - ○ **Ulceration:** Deep tissue damage can lead to ulcer formation.

7.9.2.2 Management Strategies
Supportive Care:

- **Airway Management:** Ensure airway patency, provide supplemental oxygen, and consider intubation if there is significant respiratory distress.
- **Circulatory Support:** Administer intravenous fluids to maintain hydration and blood pressure, especially if there is significant blood loss or shock.

Decontamination:

- **Ingestion:**

- **Do Not Induce Vomiting:** Avoid inducing vomiting to prevent further esophageal damage.
- **Dilution:** Administer small amounts of water or milk to dilute the alkali if the patient is conscious and can swallow safely.

- **Inhalation:**

  - **Remove from Exposure:** Move the patient to fresh air immediately.
  - **Oxygen Therapy:** Provide high-flow oxygen to improve oxygenation.

- **Dermal Contact:**

  - **Skin Decontamination:** Remove contaminated clothing and wash the skin thoroughly with copious amounts of water. Continue flushing for at least 15-20 minutes.

Symptomatic Treatment:

- **Pain Management:** Administer analgesics to control pain.
- **Gastrointestinal Protection:** Consider proton pump inhibitors (PPIs) or H2 receptor antagonists to reduce gastric acid secretion and protect the gastric mucosa.

Monitoring and Follow-Up:

- **Vital Signs:** Continuous monitoring of respiratory rate, oxygen saturation, heart rate, and blood pressure.
- **Endoscopy:** Perform early endoscopy (within 24 hours) to assess the extent of gastrointestinal injury and guide further management.
- **Laboratory Tests:** Monitor blood gases, electrolytes, renal function, and complete blood count.

Preventive Measures:

- **Public Education:** Educate the public about the dangers of alkali exposure and the importance of proper storage and handling.
- **Workplace Safety:** Implement safety protocols and provide personal protective equipment (PPE) in workplaces handling alkalis.

7.10 Radiation Poisoning

7.10.1 Clinical Symptoms

Radiation poisoning, also known as acute radiation syndrome (ARS), occurs after exposure to a high dose of ionizing radiation over a short period. The severity and onset of symptoms depend on the radiation dose and exposure duration. Clinical symptoms can be grouped into three phases: prodromal, latent, and manifest illness.

Prodromal Phase (Minutes to Days Post-Exposure):

- **Gastrointestinal Symptoms:**

  - **Nausea and Vomiting:** Often the earliest symptoms, occurring within hours of exposure.
  - **Diarrhea:** Can lead to dehydration and electrolyte imbalances.
  - **Anorexia:** Loss of appetite.

- **Neurological Symptoms:**

  - **Headache:** Common due to CNS involvement.
  - **Dizziness:** Feeling of lightheadedness or unsteadiness.
  - **Fatigue and Weakness:** General malaise and loss of energy.

Latent Phase (Hours to Weeks Post-Exposure):

- **Temporary Improvement:** Symptoms may diminish, leading to a deceptive period of well-being.
- **Duration:** Length of the latent phase depends on the radiation dose; higher doses result in shorter latent periods.

Manifest Illness Phase (Weeks to Months Post-Exposure):
Hematopoietic Syndrome (1-10 Gy):

- **Bone Marrow Suppression:**

- ◦ **Leukopenia:** Reduced white blood cell count, increasing infection risk.
- ◦ **Thrombocytopenia:** Reduced platelet count, leading to bleeding and bruising.
- ◦ **Anemia:** Reduced red blood cell count, causing fatigue and pallor.

Gastrointestinal Syndrome (10-50 Gy):

- **Severe Diarrhea and Vomiting:** Leading to dehydration and electrolyte imbalances.
- **Intestinal Damage:** Potential for severe mucosal damage, malabsorption, and bleeding.
- **Sepsis:** High risk due to mucosal barrier breakdown and immunosuppression.

Cardiovascular/Central Nervous System Syndrome (Above 50 Gy):

- **Neurological Symptoms:**

  - ◦ **Confusion and Disorientation:** Altered mental status due to CNS damage.
  - ◦ **Seizures:** Due to severe brain damage.
  - ◦ **Coma:** Loss of consciousness in severe cases.

- **Cardiovascular Collapse:**

  - ◦ **Hypotension:** Low blood pressure leading to shock.
  - ◦ **Multi-Organ Failure:** Due to extensive tissue damage.

7.10.2 Management Strategies

Management of radiation poisoning focuses on supportive care, symptom management, and specific treatments to mitigate the effects of radiation exposure.

Supportive Care:

- **Isolation and Protection:**

- ◦ **Protective Measures:** Isolate the patient to prevent infection and limit further radiation exposure.
- ◦ **Decontamination:** Remove contaminated clothing and wash the skin thoroughly to reduce external contamination.

- **Fluid and Electrolyte Management:**

  - ◦ **Intravenous Fluids:** Administer IV fluids to maintain hydration and correct electrolyte imbalances.
  - ◦ **Electrolyte Replacement:** Monitor and replace electrolytes as needed.

Symptomatic Treatment:

- **Antiemetics:** Administer antiemetics such as ondansetron to control nausea and vomiting.
- **Analgesics:** Use pain relief medications to manage headache and general discomfort.

Hematopoietic Support:

- **Bone Marrow Stimulants:**

  - ◦ **G-CSF (Granulocyte Colony-Stimulating Factor):** To stimulate white blood cell production and reduce infection risk.
  - ◦ **Erythropoietin:** To stimulate red blood cell production and manage anemia.

- **Blood Transfusions:** Provide platelet and red blood cell transfusions as needed to manage thrombocytopenia and anemia.
- **Antibiotics:** Administer broad-spectrum antibiotics prophylactically or to treat infections due to immunosuppression.

Gastrointestinal Support:

- **Antidiarrheal Agents:** Administer antidiarrheal medications to control severe diarrhea.

- **Nutritional Support:** Provide parenteral nutrition if gastrointestinal absorption is impaired.

Neurological and Cardiovascular Support:

- **Seizure Management:** Administer anticonvulsants to control seizures.
- **Cardiovascular Support:** Monitor and manage blood pressure and cardiac function. Use vasopressors if necessary to maintain blood pressure.

Specific Treatments:

- **Potassium Iodide (KI):** Administer KI to block thyroid uptake of radioactive iodine, reducing the risk of thyroid cancer. Effective if given within hours of exposure.
- **Prussian Blue:** Used to treat internal contamination with cesium-137 or thallium by enhancing excretion.
- **Diethylenetriamine Pentaacetic Acid (DTPA):** Used to chelate and enhance excretion of radioactive plutonium, americium, and curium.

Long-Term Monitoring and Follow-Up:

- **Regular Check-ups:** Monitor blood counts, renal and liver function, and overall health.
- **Psychological Support:** Provide counseling and support to address the psychological impact of radiation exposure.
- **Cancer Surveillance:** Long-term monitoring for the development of radiation-induced cancers, particularly thyroid cancer and leukemia.

Preventive Measures:

- **Public Education:** Educate the public about the risks of radiation exposure and appropriate protective measures.
- **Emergency Preparedness:** Develop and implement emergency response plans for radiation accidents, including stockpiling of protective agents like KI and Prussian Blue.
- **Workplace Safety:** Implement strict safety protocols in industries and facilities where radiation exposure risk is high, and ensure workers have

access to protective equipment and training.

Clinical Symptoms and Management of Chronic Poisoning Introduction

Chronic poisoning, unlike acute poisoning, results from prolonged exposure to toxic substances at lower doses. This type of poisoning can be insidious, with symptoms developing gradually over time, often making diagnosis and management more challenging. Chronic poisoning can occur due to occupational exposure, environmental contamination, lifestyle choices, or long-term use of certain medications.

Importance of Understanding Chronic Poisoning

Understanding chronic poisoning is critical for several reasons. Firstly, it often affects multiple organ systems, leading to complex clinical presentations that require comprehensive medical evaluations. Secondly, chronic poisoning can have long-lasting or irreversible health effects, making early detection and intervention crucial for preventing severe outcomes. Lastly, chronic exposure to toxins can impact not just individuals but entire communities, necessitating public health measures and policies to mitigate risks.

Scope of the Chapter

This chapter will provide an in-depth examination of the clinical symptoms and management strategies for various types of chronic poisoning. The focus will be on identifying the common sources of chronic toxins, understanding their pathophysiology, recognizing clinical manifestations, and implementing effective management and preventive strategies.

Key Areas Covered

1. **Common Sources of Chronic Toxic Exposure:**

- ◦ **Heavy Metals:** Lead, mercury, arsenic, and cadmium are prevalent in various industrial processes, contaminated water supplies, and some traditional medicines.
- ◦ **Pesticides:** Persistent organic pollutants such as DDT and organophosphates used in agriculture.
- ◦ **Industrial Chemicals:** Benzene, asbestos, and other chemicals used in manufacturing and construction.
- ◦ **Medications:** Long-term use of drugs like acetaminophen, NSAIDs, and certain psychiatric medications can lead to chronic toxicity.
- ◦ **Environmental Toxins:** Air pollutants, contaminated food, and water.

2. **Clinical Symptoms of Chronic Poisoning:**

- ◦ **General Symptoms:** Fatigue, malaise, weight loss, and chronic pain.
- ◦ **Neurological Symptoms:** Cognitive decline, peripheral neuropathy, tremors, and mood disturbances.
- ◦ **Gastrointestinal Symptoms:** Chronic nausea, vomiting, abdominal pain, and altered bowel habits.
- ◦ **Hematological Symptoms:** Anemia, leukopenia, and thrombocytopenia.
- ◦ **Dermatological Symptoms:** Chronic dermatitis, pigmentation changes, and hair loss.
- ◦ **Respiratory Symptoms:** Chronic cough, dyspnea, and reduced lung function.
- ◦ **Renal and Hepatic Symptoms:** Chronic kidney disease, hepatotoxicity, and associated metabolic disturbances.

3. **Diagnostic Approaches:**

- ◦ **History and Physical Examination:** Comprehensive assessment to identify potential sources of exposure and clinical signs of toxicity.
- ◦ **Laboratory Tests:** Blood and urine tests to detect and quantify toxins and assess organ function.
- ◦ **Imaging Studies:** X-rays, CT scans, and MRIs to identify organ damage and guide further evaluation.
- ◦ **Specialized Tests:** Hair, nail, and bone marrow analysis for detecting specific toxins.

4. **Management Strategies:**

- **Elimination of Exposure:** Identifying and removing the source of the toxin to prevent further exposure.
- **Symptomatic Treatment:** Managing symptoms through supportive care, medications, and therapeutic interventions.
- **Specific Antidotes and Chelation Therapy:** Using agents like EDTA, dimercaprol, and succimer for heavy metal poisoning.
- **Nutritional Support:** Providing vitamins, minerals, and dietary modifications to support recovery and mitigate deficiencies caused by chronic toxicity.
- **Monitoring and Follow-Up:** Regular monitoring of clinical status, laboratory parameters, and organ function to assess treatment efficacy and detect complications.

5. **Preventive Measures:**

- **Public Health Policies:** Implementing regulations and guidelines to reduce environmental and occupational exposure to toxins.
- **Education and Awareness:** Raising awareness among healthcare providers and the public about the risks of chronic poisoning and the importance of preventive measures.
- **Safety Protocols:** Developing and enforcing safety standards in industries and workplaces to protect workers from toxic exposures.
- **Community Interventions:** Initiating community-based programs to address and mitigate the effects of environmental contamination.

8.1 Heavy Metals Poisoning

8.1.1 Arsenic

Arsenic is a naturally occurring element found in the earth's crust, and it exists in both organic and inorganic forms. Inorganic arsenic compounds, particularly arsenic trioxide, are highly toxic and can lead to chronic poisoning when individuals are exposed to contaminated water, soil, or industrial processes.

8.1.1.1 Clinical Symptoms

Chronic arsenic poisoning, also known as arsenicosis, presents with a variety of symptoms that develop over time due to prolonged exposure. These symptoms can affect multiple organ systems and vary in severity.

Dermatological Symptoms:

- **Hyperpigmentation:** Darkening of the skin, especially on the palms and soles.
- **Hypopigmentation:** Lightening of the skin in a spotted pattern, often appearing alongside hyperpigmentation.
- **Keratosis:** Thickening of the skin, particularly on the palms and soles, leading to rough, wart-like lesions.
- **Mees' Lines:** White lines that appear across the fingernails and toenails.

Neurological Symptoms:

- **Peripheral Neuropathy:** Tingling, numbness, and pain in the hands and feet due to nerve damage.
- **Cognitive Decline:** Memory loss, difficulty concentrating, and other cognitive impairments.
- **Headaches:** Persistent headaches are common.

Gastrointestinal Symptoms:

- **Abdominal Pain:** Chronic pain and cramping.
- **Nausea and Vomiting:** Frequent gastrointestinal distress.
- **Diarrhea:** Recurrent episodes of watery stools.

Cardiovascular Symptoms:

- **Hypertension:** Elevated blood pressure.
- **Arrhythmias:** Irregular heartbeats.

Hematological Symptoms:

- **Anemia:** Fatigue, pallor, and other symptoms associated with low red blood cell count.

Respiratory Symptoms:

- **Chronic Cough:** Persistent coughing and irritation of the respiratory tract.

Renal and Hepatic Symptoms:

- **Renal Dysfunction:** Chronic kidney disease and associated symptoms.
- **Hepatotoxicity:** Liver damage, often indicated by jaundice and elevated liver enzymes.

Cancer Risk:

- **Increased Risk of Cancers:** Chronic arsenic exposure is associated with higher risks of skin, lung, bladder, and liver cancers.

8.1.1.2 Management Strategies

Effective management of chronic arsenic poisoning involves several steps, including identification and elimination of the source of exposure, supportive care, and specific treatments to remove arsenic from the body and mitigate its effects.

Elimination of Exposure:

- **Identify Source:** Determine the source of arsenic exposure, such as contaminated water, food, or occupational hazards.
- **Remove or Avoid Source:** Implement measures to eliminate or reduce exposure, such as using alternative water sources, improving occupational safety, and regulating industrial emissions.

Supportive Care:

- **Hydration:** Ensure adequate hydration to support renal function and facilitate arsenic excretion.
- **Nutritional Support:** Provide a balanced diet with adequate vitamins and minerals to support overall health and recovery.

Specific Treatments:

- **Chelation Therapy:** Chelation agents bind to arsenic, allowing it to be excreted in the urine. Commonly used chelating agents include:

  - **Dimercaprol (BAL):** Administered intramuscularly, effective for acute and chronic arsenic poisoning.
  - **Dimercaptosuccinic Acid (DMSA):** Administered orally, preferred for its safety profile and ease of use.
  - **Dimercaptopropane Sulfonate (DMPS):** Another oral chelator that can be used in chronic arsenic poisoning.

Symptomatic Treatment:

- **Pain Management:** Use analgesics to manage pain associated with peripheral neuropathy and other symptoms.
- **Antihypertensives:** Administer medications to control high blood pressure.
- **Dermatological Care:** Topical treatments and skin care regimens to manage keratosis and other skin lesions.

Monitoring and Follow-Up:

- **Regular Assessments:** Conduct regular medical check-ups to monitor the patient's clinical status and response to treatment.
- **Laboratory Tests:** Monitor blood arsenic levels, renal and liver function tests, and complete blood counts to assess the extent of poisoning and organ function.
- **Neurological Evaluations:** Perform regular neurological assessments to monitor for changes in peripheral neuropathy and cognitive function.

Preventive Measures:

- **Public Education:** Educate communities about the risks of arsenic exposure and the importance of using safe water sources.
- **Regulation and Safety Standards:** Implement and enforce regulations to limit arsenic levels in drinking water, food, and industrial emissions.
- **Occupational Safety:** Ensure workers in industries using arsenic are provided with appropriate personal protective equipment (PPE) and safety training.

Environmental and Community Interventions:

- **Water Treatment:** Develop and implement water treatment solutions to remove arsenic from contaminated water supplies.
- **Soil Remediation:** Initiate soil remediation projects to reduce arsenic levels in agricultural and residential areas.

8.1 Heavy Metals Poisoning

8.1.2 Lead

Lead is a toxic heavy metal that can cause a wide range of health problems, particularly affecting the nervous system, kidneys, and blood. Chronic lead poisoning occurs due to prolonged exposure to lead from sources such as contaminated water, lead-based paints, industrial processes, and certain traditional medicines.

8.1.2.1 Clinical Symptoms

Chronic lead poisoning can affect multiple organ systems, and its symptoms vary based on the level of exposure, age, and individual susceptibility.

Neurological Symptoms:

- **Cognitive Decline:** Reduced attention span, memory loss, and learning difficulties, especially in children.
- **Peripheral Neuropathy:** Numbness, tingling, and weakness in the extremities, often seen as "wrist drop" or "foot drop."
- **Headaches:** Frequent and persistent headaches.
- **Irritability and Mood Changes:** Increased irritability, mood swings, and in severe cases, depression.

Gastrointestinal Symptoms:

- **Abdominal Pain:** Colicky and intermittent pain, often referred to as "lead colic."
- **Nausea and Vomiting:** Gastrointestinal upset.

- **Constipation:** Common due to the effects of lead on the gastrointestinal tract.

Hematological Symptoms:

- **Anemia:** Fatigue, pallor, and weakness due to impaired hemoglobin synthesis. Often characterized by basophilic stippling of red blood cells.
- **Lead Lines:** Bluish lines on the gums, known as Burton's lines.

Renal Symptoms:

- **Chronic Kidney Disease:** Impaired renal function, often resulting in proteinuria and decreased glomerular filtration rate (GFR).

Musculoskeletal Symptoms:

- **Joint and Muscle Pain:** Arthralgia and myalgia due to lead deposition in bones and tissues.

Reproductive Symptoms:

- **Infertility:** Both males and females may experience reduced fertility.
- **Miscarriages and Stillbirths:** Increased risk in pregnant women.

General Symptoms:

- **Fatigue:** General feeling of tiredness and weakness.
- **Weight Loss:** Unintentional loss of weight.

8.1.2.2 Management Strategies

Management of chronic lead poisoning involves identifying and eliminating the source of exposure, providing supportive care, and administering specific treatments to remove lead from the body.

Elimination of Exposure:

- **Identify Source:** Determine the source of lead exposure, such as contaminated water, paint, soil, or occupational hazards.

- **Remove or Avoid Source:** Implement measures to eliminate or reduce exposure, such as using lead-free paints, treating water, and improving occupational safety practices.

Supportive Care:

- **Nutritional Support:** Provide a diet rich in calcium, iron, and vitamin C to help reduce lead absorption and mitigate anemia.
- **Hydration:** Ensure adequate hydration to support renal function and facilitate lead excretion.

Specific Treatments:

- **Chelation Therapy:** Chelation agents bind to lead, allowing it to be excreted in the urine. Commonly used chelating agents include:

  - **Dimercaptosuccinic Acid (DMSA):** Oral chelator preferred for its safety profile and ease of use.
  - **Calcium Disodium EDTA:** Intravenous chelator used for more severe cases.
  - **Dimercaprol (BAL):** Intramuscular chelator used in conjunction with EDTA for severe poisoning.

Symptomatic Treatment:

- **Pain Management:** Use analgesics to manage abdominal pain, headaches, and musculoskeletal pain.
- **Antihypertensives:** Administer medications to control high blood pressure if renal impairment leads to hypertension.
- **Treatment of Anemia:** Provide iron supplements and, if necessary, blood transfusions to manage severe anemia.

Monitoring and Follow-Up:

- **Regular Assessments:** Conduct regular medical check-ups to monitor the patient's clinical status and response to treatment.
- **Laboratory Tests:** Monitor blood lead levels, renal function tests, liver function tests, and complete blood counts to assess the extent of

poisoning and organ function.

- **Neurological Evaluations:** Perform regular neurological assessments to monitor changes in cognitive function and peripheral neuropathy.

Preventive Measures:

- **Public Education:** Educate communities about the risks of lead exposure and the importance of using safe water sources, lead-free paints, and safe occupational practices.
- **Regulation and Safety Standards:** Implement and enforce regulations to limit lead levels in drinking water, paint, soil, and industrial emissions.
- **Occupational Safety:** Ensure workers in industries using lead are provided with appropriate personal protective equipment (PPE) and safety training.

Environmental and Community Interventions:

- **Water Treatment:** Develop and implement water treatment solutions to remove lead from contaminated water supplies.
- **Soil Remediation:** Initiate soil remediation projects to reduce lead levels in agricultural and residential areas.
- **Lead Abatement Programs:** Implement lead abatement programs to remove or encapsulate lead-based paints in homes, schools, and public buildings.

8.1 Heavy Metals Poisoning

8.1.3 Mercury

Mercury is a heavy metal that poses significant health risks when humans are exposed to it. Mercury exists in three forms: elemental (metallic) mercury, inorganic mercury compounds, and organic mercury compounds (such as methylmercury). Each form has different routes of exposure and toxicity profiles.

8.1.3.1 Clinical Symptoms
Elemental Mercury:

Inhalation Exposure:

- **Neurological Symptoms:**

  - **Tremors:** Also known as "mercurial tremor," characterized by fine, involuntary shaking.
  - **Emotional Instability:** Irritability, mood swings, and shyness, often referred to as "erethism."
  - **Memory Loss and Cognitive Decline:** Difficulty concentrating and impaired short-term memory.

- **Respiratory Symptoms:**

  - **Cough and Shortness of Breath:** Due to inhalation of mercury vapors.
  - **Pneumonitis:** Inflammation of lung tissue in severe cases.

Inorganic Mercury:
Ingestion or Dermal Exposure:

- **Gastrointestinal Symptoms:**

  - **Metallic Taste:** Unpleasant taste in the mouth.
  - **Nausea, Vomiting, and Diarrhea:** Gastrointestinal upset and damage.
  - **Abdominal Pain:** Cramping and discomfort.

- **Renal Symptoms:**

  - **Nephrotic Syndrome:** Proteinuria, edema, and elevated blood urea nitrogen (BUN) and creatinine levels.
  - **Acute Kidney Injury:** Reduced renal function.

Organic Mercury (Methylmercury):
Ingestion (primarily from contaminated fish):

- **Neurological Symptoms:**

  - **Paresthesia:** Tingling or numbness in the hands and feet.

- ○ **Ataxia:** Uncoordinated movements and difficulty with balance.
- ○ **Dysarthria:** Slurred speech.
- ○ **Visual and Hearing Impairment:** Constriction of the visual field and difficulty hearing.
- ○ **Cognitive and Motor Dysfunction:** Severe cases can lead to profound cognitive deficits and motor impairments, including cerebral palsy-like symptoms in children exposed in utero.

General Symptoms Across All Forms:

- **Fatigue:** General feeling of tiredness and weakness.
- **Weight Loss:** Unintentional loss of weight.
- **Dermatological Symptoms:**

  - ○ **Rashes and Dermatitis:** Skin irritation and inflammation, particularly with dermal exposure.

8.1.3.2 Management Strategies

Effective management of mercury poisoning involves identifying and eliminating the source of exposure, providing supportive care, and administering specific treatments to remove mercury from the body.

Elimination of Exposure:

- **Identify Source:** Determine the source of mercury exposure, such as broken thermometers, industrial processes, or consumption of contaminated fish.
- **Remove or Avoid Source:** Implement measures to eliminate or reduce exposure, such as proper disposal of mercury-containing products, improving workplace safety, and avoiding consumption of high-mercury fish.

Supportive Care:

- **Hydration:** Ensure adequate hydration to support renal function and facilitate mercury excretion.
- **Nutritional Support:** Provide a balanced diet to support overall health and recovery.

Specific Treatments:

- **Chelation Therapy:** Chelation agents bind to mercury, allowing it to be excreted in the urine. Commonly used chelating agents include:

  - **Dimercaprol (BAL):** Administered intramuscularly, used for severe cases of mercury poisoning.
  - **Dimercaptosuccinic Acid (DMSA):** Administered orally, preferred for its safety profile and ease of use.
  - **Dimercaptopropane Sulfonate (DMPS):** Another oral chelator that can be used for mercury poisoning.

Symptomatic Treatment:

- **Pain Management:** Use analgesics to manage pain associated with tremors, gastrointestinal symptoms, and other discomforts.
- **Antihypertensives:** Administer medications to control high blood pressure if renal impairment leads to hypertension.
- **Treatment of Neurological Symptoms:** Provide medications and therapies to manage tremors, ataxia, and cognitive symptoms.

Monitoring and Follow-Up:

- **Regular Assessments:** Conduct regular medical check-ups to monitor the patient's clinical status and response to treatment.
- **Laboratory Tests:** Monitor blood and urine mercury levels, renal function tests, liver function tests, and complete blood counts to assess the extent of poisoning and organ function.
- **Neurological Evaluations:** Perform regular neurological assessments to monitor changes in cognitive function, motor skills, and sensory function.

Preventive Measures:

- **Public Education:** Educate communities about the risks of mercury exposure and the importance of using mercury-free alternatives and avoiding high-mercury fish.

- **Regulation and Safety Standards:** Implement and enforce regulations to limit mercury emissions in industrial processes and to control the use of mercury in products.
- **Occupational Safety:** Ensure workers in industries using mercury are provided with appropriate personal protective equipment (PPE) and safety training.

Environmental and Community Interventions:

- **Cleanup of Contaminated Sites:** Implement cleanup projects for areas contaminated with mercury, including industrial sites and water bodies.
- **Fish Consumption Advisories:** Issue guidelines and advisories to inform the public about safe consumption levels of fish, particularly for vulnerable populations such as pregnant women and children.

8.1 Heavy Metals Poisoning

8.1.4 Iron

Iron poisoning, or iron toxicity, is a serious condition that can result from the excessive ingestion of iron supplements or products. It is more common in children due to accidental ingestion of iron-containing supplements, often marketed as vitamins. Chronic iron poisoning can also occur due to repeated blood transfusions or excessive dietary intake.

8.1.4.1 Clinical Symptoms

Acute Iron Poisoning:

Acute iron poisoning is characterized by a progression through several stages, each with distinct clinical symptoms.

Stage 1 (0-6 hours):

- **Gastrointestinal Symptoms:**

  - **Nausea and Vomiting:** Often with blood (hematemesis).
  - **Diarrhea:** Watery stools, sometimes bloody.
  - **Abdominal Pain:** Severe and crampy pain.

Stage 2 (6-24 hours):

- **Latent Phase:** Symptoms may temporarily improve, giving a false sense of recovery.

Stage 3 (12-48 hours):

- **Systemic Toxicity:**

  - **Metabolic Acidosis:** Due to iron's effect on cellular metabolism.
  - **Hypotension and Shock:** Resulting from vasodilation and fluid loss.
  - **Fever:** Due to inflammatory response.
  - **CNS Symptoms:** Lethargy, drowsiness, and potentially coma.

Stage 4 (2-5 days):

- **Hepatic Toxicity:**

  - **Liver Dysfunction:** Elevated liver enzymes (AST, ALT), jaundice, and hepatic failure.
  - **Coagulopathy:** Impaired blood clotting.

Stage 5 (2-6 weeks):

- **Gastrointestinal Obstruction:** Due to healing of the gastrointestinal mucosa, leading to scarring and strictures.

Chronic Iron Poisoning:
Chronic iron overload, often due to repeated blood transfusions or excessive dietary intake, leads to gradual accumulation of iron in various organs, causing damage over time.

- **Hepatic Symptoms:**

  - **Liver Enlargement (Hepatomegaly):** Due to iron deposition.
  - **Cirrhosis:** Chronic liver damage and scarring.
  - **Hepatic Failure:** In severe cases.

- **Cardiovascular Symptoms:**

  - **Cardiomyopathy:** Iron-induced damage to the heart muscle.
  - **Arrhythmias:** Irregular heartbeats.

- **Endocrine Symptoms:**

  - **Diabetes Mellitus:** Due to pancreatic damage.
  - **Hypogonadism:** Reduced function of the gonads.

- **Skin Symptoms:**

  - **Bronzing:** Skin hyperpigmentation due to iron deposition.

8.1.4.2 Management Strategies

Effective management of iron poisoning involves immediate and appropriate interventions to prevent severe complications and improve outcomes.

Acute Iron Poisoning:
Supportive Care:

- **Airway Management:** Ensure airway patency and provide supplemental oxygen.
- **Circulatory Support:** Administer intravenous fluids to maintain blood pressure and hydration. Use vasopressors if necessary to treat shock.

Decontamination:

- **Gastric Lavage:** Consider gastric lavage if the patient presents within 1 hour of ingestion and has a significant amount of iron in the stomach.
- **Activated Charcoal:** Not effective for iron as it does not adsorb iron effectively.

Specific Treatments:

- **Whole Bowel Irrigation:** Use polyethylene glycol (PEG) solution to flush the gastrointestinal tract, especially if radiopaque iron tablets are visible on an abdominal X-ray.

- **Chelation Therapy:** Administer deferoxamine, a chelating agent that binds to free iron, facilitating its excretion.

  - **Deferoxamine:** Initial dose of 15 mg/kg/hour intravenously, adjusted based on the severity of poisoning and serum iron levels.

Symptomatic Treatment:

- **Metabolic Acidosis:** Correct with intravenous sodium bicarbonate.
- **Pain Management:** Use analgesics to manage abdominal pain.

Monitoring and Follow-Up:

- **Vital Signs:** Continuous monitoring of respiratory rate, oxygen saturation, heart rate, and blood pressure.
- **Laboratory Tests:** Monitor serum iron levels, total iron-binding capacity (TIBC), liver function tests, renal function tests, and blood gases.
- **Imaging:** Abdominal X-ray to check for retained iron tablets.

Chronic Iron Poisoning:
Supportive Care:

- **Nutritional Support:** Provide a balanced diet with appropriate caloric and nutrient intake.

Specific Treatments:

- **Chelation Therapy:** Regular administration of deferoxamine or other chelating agents to reduce iron overload.

  - **Deferasirox:** An oral chelator used for chronic iron overload.
  - **Deferiprone:** Another oral chelator that can be used in combination with other treatments.

Monitoring and Follow-Up:

- **Regular Assessments:** Conduct periodic medical evaluations to monitor the patient's clinical status and response to treatment.

- **Laboratory Tests:** Regularly monitor serum ferritin, liver function tests, cardiac function tests, and endocrine function tests.
- **Imaging:** MRI to assess iron deposition in the liver and heart.

Preventive Measures:

- **Public Education:** Educate communities about the risks of iron overdose, particularly the dangers of iron supplements to children.
- **Safe Storage:** Advise safe storage of iron-containing products to prevent accidental ingestion.
- **Screening Programs:** Implement screening for individuals at risk of chronic iron overload, such as those with hereditary hemochromatosis or receiving frequent blood transfusions.

8.1 Heavy Metals Poisoning

8.1.5 Copper

Copper is an essential trace element involved in various biological processes. However, excessive copper intake or impaired copper metabolism can lead to toxicity. Copper poisoning can be acute or chronic and is often associated with industrial exposure, contaminated water supplies, or genetic disorders such as Wilson's disease.

8.1.5.1 Clinical Symptoms

Acute Copper Poisoning:

Acute copper poisoning typically results from ingestion of a large amount of copper salts or contaminated water.

Gastrointestinal Symptoms:

- **Nausea and Vomiting:** Often severe and may include vomiting of green or blue material.
- **Abdominal Pain:** Sharp and crampy pain.
- **Diarrhea:** May be bloody due to gastrointestinal mucosal irritation.

Systemic Symptoms:

- **Metallic Taste:** Unpleasant metallic taste in the mouth.
- **Hypotension and Shock:** Due to fluid loss and direct cardiovascular effects of copper.
- **Hemolysis:** Destruction of red blood cells leading to jaundice and hemoglobinuria.
- **Renal Failure:** Resulting from hemoglobinuria and direct nephrotoxic effects of copper.
- **Hepatic Necrosis:** Severe liver damage, elevated liver enzymes, and jaundice.

Neurological Symptoms:

- **Headache and Dizziness:** Common in acute poisoning.
- **Confusion and Lethargy:** Due to severe systemic effects and organ damage.

Chronic Copper Poisoning:

Chronic copper poisoning, often associated with conditions like Wilson's disease, results from prolonged exposure or impaired copper metabolism.

Hepatic Symptoms:

- **Chronic Hepatitis:** Inflammation of the liver.
- **Cirrhosis:** Scarring and dysfunction of the liver.
- **Portal Hypertension:** Increased blood pressure in the portal vein.

Neurological Symptoms:

- **Movement Disorders:** Tremors, dystonia, and unsteady gait.
- **Cognitive Impairment:** Memory loss, difficulty concentrating, and mood changes.
- **Psychiatric Symptoms:** Depression, anxiety, and behavioral changes.

Ocular Symptoms:

- **Kayser-Fleischer Rings:** Brownish or greenish rings around the cornea due to copper deposition.

Renal Symptoms:

- **Proteinuria:** Excess protein in the urine.
- **Nephrocalcinosis:** Calcium deposits in the kidneys.

8.1.5.2 Management Strategies

Effective management of copper poisoning involves prompt diagnosis, removal of the source of exposure, supportive care, and specific treatments to reduce copper levels in the body.

Elimination of Exposure:

- **Identify Source:** Determine the source of copper exposure, such as contaminated water, industrial exposure, or dietary supplements.
- **Remove or Avoid Source:** Implement measures to eliminate or reduce exposure, such as treating water supplies, improving workplace safety, and discontinuing the use of copper-containing supplements.

Supportive Care:

- **Hydration:** Ensure adequate hydration to support renal function and facilitate copper excretion.
- **Nutritional Support:** Provide a balanced diet to support overall health and recovery.

Specific Treatments:

- **Chelation Therapy:** Chelating agents bind to copper, allowing it to be excreted in the urine. Commonly used chelating agents include:
  - **Penicillamine:** An oral chelator that is effective in binding copper.
  - **Trientine:** Another oral chelator used for copper toxicity, particularly in patients intolerant to penicillamine.
  - **Zinc Acetate:** Used to block the absorption of copper in the gastrointestinal tract.

Symptomatic Treatment:

- **Pain Management:** Use analgesics to manage abdominal pain and other discomforts.
- **Anti-Emetics:** Administer anti-emetics to control severe nausea and vomiting.
- **Blood Transfusions:** May be necessary in cases of severe hemolysis and anemia.

Monitoring and Follow-Up:

- **Regular Assessments:** Conduct regular medical check-ups to monitor the patient's clinical status and response to treatment.
- **Laboratory Tests:** Monitor serum copper levels, liver function tests, renal function tests, complete blood counts, and urine copper levels.
- **Neurological Evaluations:** Perform regular neurological assessments to monitor changes in cognitive function and motor skills.

Preventive Measures:

- **Public Education:** Educate communities about the risks of copper exposure and the importance of using safe water sources and avoiding excessive use of copper-containing supplements.
- **Regulation and Safety Standards:** Implement and enforce regulations to limit copper levels in drinking water and industrial emissions.
- **Occupational Safety:** Ensure workers in industries using copper are provided with appropriate personal protective equipment (PPE) and safety training.

Environmental and Community Interventions:

- **Water Treatment:** Develop and implement water treatment solutions to remove copper from contaminated water supplies.
- **Soil Remediation:** Initiate soil remediation projects to reduce copper levels in agricultural and residential areas.

CHAPTER IX

Venomous Snake Bites

Introduction

Venomous snake bites represent a significant medical emergency worldwide, particularly in tropical and subtropical regions. The World Health Organization (WHO) identifies snakebite envenoming as a high-priority neglected tropical disease due to its substantial impact on public health. Each year, millions of people are bitten by venomous snakes, leading to hundreds of thousands of envenomings and tens of thousands of deaths. The morbidity associated with snake bites includes severe local tissue damage, systemic effects, and long-term disabilities.

Importance of Understanding Venomous Snake Bites

Understanding venomous snake bites is crucial for several reasons. Firstly, timely and effective medical intervention can be life-saving and can significantly reduce morbidity. Secondly, the diverse range of venomous snakes and their varied venom compositions necessitate specific treatment protocols tailored to the type of snake and the nature of the venom. Finally, awareness and education about snakebite prevention and first aid can greatly reduce the incidence and severity of snakebite envenoming.

Scope of the Chapter

This chapter aims to provide a comprehensive overview of venomous snake bites, focusing on the clinical presentation, diagnosis, and management of envenomings. It will cover the following key areas:

1. **Epidemiology and Impact:**

   - Global distribution of venomous snakes.
   - Prevalence and incidence of snake bites.
   - Public health impact and burden of snakebite envenoming.

392

2. **Classification of Venomous Snakes:**

   - Taxonomy and identification of major venomous snake families (e.g., Elapidae, Viperidae, and Atractaspididae).
   - Characteristics and behavior of venomous snakes.

3. **Venom Composition and Mechanisms of Action:**

   - Biochemical components of snake venoms.
   - Pathophysiological effects of venom components on the human body.

4. **Clinical Presentation of Snake Bites:**

   - Local Effects: Pain, swelling, necrosis, and compartment syndrome.
   - Systemic Effects: Neurotoxicity, hemotoxicity, cytotoxicity, and myotoxicity.
   - Specific symptoms associated with different types of snake venoms.

5. **Diagnosis and Assessment:**

   - History and physical examination of snakebite victims.
   - Laboratory investigations and imaging studies.
   - Identification of the offending snake species when possible.

6. **Management and Treatment:**

   - First aid measures and initial management at the bite site.
   - Hospital management and medical treatment protocols.
   - Administration of antivenom: indications, dosing, and potential adverse reactions.
   - Supportive care and management of complications.

7. **Prevention and Education:**

   - Strategies for preventing snake bites.
   - Community education and awareness programs.
   - Training healthcare providers in the recognition and management of snake bites.

9.1 Families of Venomous Snakes

9.1.1 Elapidae

The Elapidae family, commonly known as elapids, includes some of the most dangerous and widely recognized venomous snakes in the world. This family encompasses species such as cobras, kraits, mambas, and coral snakes.

Characteristics:

- **Venom:** Elapid venom is predominantly neurotoxic, affecting the nervous system. It contains a mixture of toxins, including neurotoxins, cardiotoxins, and myotoxins.
- **Fangs:** Elapids have short, fixed front fangs that efficiently deliver venom.
- **Habitat:** These snakes are found in a variety of environments, including forests, grasslands, deserts, and coastal regions.
- **Behavior:** Elapids are generally agile and active hunters, feeding on a range of prey such as rodents, birds, and other reptiles.

Notable Species:

- **Cobras (Genus Naja):** Known for their iconic hood and defensive posture. Cobras can deliver a potent neurotoxic venom and, in some species, spit venom as a defense mechanism.
- **Kraits (Genus Bungarus):** Typically nocturnal, kraits have highly toxic venom that causes paralysis and respiratory failure.
- **Mambas (Genus Dendroaspis):** Found in Africa, mambas are fast and highly venomous. The black mamba is particularly notorious for its lethal bite.
- **Coral Snakes (Various Genera):** Recognizable by their brightly colored bands, coral snakes have a potent neurotoxic venom.

9.1.2 Viperidae

The Viperidae family, commonly known as vipers, includes pit vipers, true vipers, and bush vipers. This family is characterized by long, hinged fangs that allow deep penetration of venom.

Characteristics:

- **Venom:** Viperid venom is primarily hemotoxic, causing tissue damage, coagulopathy, and systemic bleeding. It contains a complex mixture of enzymes and proteins that disrupt blood clotting and damage tissues.
- **Fangs:** Vipers have long, retractable fangs that can inject venom deep into the tissues of their prey or aggressors.
- **Habitat:** Vipers are adaptable and can be found in diverse habitats, including forests, deserts, mountains, and swamps.
- **Behavior:** Vipers are typically ambush predators, relying on camouflage and stealth to capture their prey.

Notable Species:

- **Russell's Viper (Daboia russelii):** Found in Asia, this viper is responsible for many snakebite incidents and has a potent hemotoxic venom.
- **Saw-scaled Viper (Echis carinatus):** Known for its distinctive scale-rubbing sound, this small but dangerous viper is found in Africa, the Middle East, and South Asia.
- **Pit Vipers (Subfamily Crotalinae):** This group includes rattlesnakes, copperheads, and water moccasins. They possess heat-sensing pits that help locate warm-blooded prey.
- **Gaboon Viper (Bitis gabonica):** Found in Africa, it has the longest fangs of any snake and a powerful venom that combines hemotoxic and cytotoxic effects.

9.1.3 Hydrophiidae

The Hydrophiidae family, commonly known as sea snakes, comprises snakes that are highly adapted to marine environments. This family includes sea kraits and true sea snakes.

Characteristics:

- **Venom:** Sea snake venom is extremely potent and primarily neurotoxic, causing paralysis and respiratory failure. It also contains myotoxins that damage muscle tissue.
- **Fangs:** Sea snakes have small, fixed fangs designed to deliver venom to their prey, which consists mainly of fish and eels.
- **Habitat:** Sea snakes are found in warm coastal waters, particularly in the Indian and Pacific Oceans. They are excellent swimmers and can remain submerged for extended periods.
- **Behavior:** Sea snakes are generally not aggressive towards humans and bites are rare. However, they can be highly dangerous if provoked.

Notable Species:

- **Belcher's Sea Snake (Hydrophis belcheri):** Often cited as one of the most venomous snakes in the world, though bites to humans are rare.
- **Yellow-bellied Sea Snake (Hydrophis platurus):** Recognizable by its yellow underbelly, it has a widespread distribution across the Indo-Pacific region.
- **Banded Sea Krait (Laticauda colubrina):** Distinguished by its black and white bands, this species is semi-aquatic and often comes ashore to rest and lay eggs.

9.2 Clinical Effects of Venoms

Venomous snakes possess a variety of toxins in their venom, each affecting the human body in different ways. The clinical effects of snake venom can be broadly categorized into neurotoxic, hemotoxic, and myotoxic effects. Understanding these effects is crucial for the effective treatment of snakebite envenomings.

9.2.1 Neurotoxic Effects

Neurotoxic venoms primarily affect the nervous system. Snakes from the Elapidae family, such as cobras, kraits, mambas, and sea snakes, typically have neurotoxic venom. These toxins interfere with nerve signal transmission, leading to paralysis and other neurological symptoms.
Mechanisms of Action:

- **Presynaptic Neurotoxins:** These toxins damage nerve endings, preventing the release of neurotransmitters. Examples include β-bungarotoxin found in kraits.
- **Postsynaptic Neurotoxins:** These toxins bind to acetylcholine receptors at the neuromuscular junction, blocking nerve signal transmission. Examples include α-bungarotoxin found in cobras.

Clinical Symptoms:

- **Muscle Weakness:** Progressive weakness starting from the head and neck muscles, often descending to involve respiratory muscles.
- **Ptosis:** Drooping of the upper eyelids due to paralysis of the eyelid muscles.
- **Diplopia:** Double vision caused by paralysis of the eye muscles.
- **Dysphagia:** Difficulty swallowing due to paralysis of the throat muscles.
- **Respiratory Paralysis:** Severe cases can lead to respiratory failure due to paralysis of the diaphragm and intercostal muscles, requiring mechanical ventilation.

9.2.2 Hemotoxic Effects

Hemotoxic venoms primarily affect the blood and vascular systems. Snakes from the Viperidae family, such as pit vipers and true vipers, typically have hemotoxic venom. These toxins disrupt blood clotting mechanisms and damage blood vessels.

Mechanisms of Action:

- **Procoagulants:** These toxins activate clotting factors, leading to the formation of small clots throughout the bloodstream, which can deplete clotting factors and result in coagulopathy.
- **Anticoagulants:** These toxins inhibit clotting factors, preventing blood clotting and causing excessive bleeding.
- **Vascular Toxins:** These toxins damage the lining of blood vessels, leading to increased permeability and hemorrhage.

Clinical Symptoms:

- **Bleeding:** Prolonged bleeding from the bite site, gums, nose, and other mucosal surfaces.
- **Bruising:** Widespread bruising due to internal bleeding.
- **Hypotension:** Low blood pressure resulting from fluid loss and vascular damage.
- **Hemorrhagic Shock:** Severe blood loss leading to shock, characterized by rapid heart rate, low blood pressure, and organ failure.
- **DIC (Disseminated Intravascular Coagulation):** A serious condition where widespread clotting and bleeding occur simultaneously.

9.2.3 Myotoxic Effects

Myotoxic venoms primarily affect muscle tissue. Some snakes from the Elapidae and Viperidae families, as well as sea snakes from the Hydrophiidae family, have myotoxic venom. These toxins cause muscle damage and necrosis.

Mechanisms of Action:

- **Phospholipases:** These enzymes break down cell membranes, leading to muscle cell destruction.
- **Myotoxins:** These toxins directly damage muscle fibers, causing muscle necrosis and the release of muscle breakdown products into the bloodstream.

Clinical Symptoms:

- **Muscle Pain:** Intense pain and tenderness at the bite site and affected muscles.
- **Swelling:** Significant swelling and inflammation around the bite site.
- **Myoglobinuria:** Dark urine due to the presence of myoglobin, a muscle breakdown product, which can cause kidney damage.
- **Rhabdomyolysis:** Extensive muscle breakdown leading to the release of muscle cell contents into the bloodstream, potentially causing kidney failure.
- **Weakness and Paralysis:** Localized or generalized muscle weakness due to muscle damage.

9.3 General Management and First Aid

Effective management of venomous snake bites involves immediate first aid measures to reduce the severity of envenoming and hospital management to treat the systemic effects of the venom. Prompt and appropriate actions can significantly improve patient outcomes and reduce the risk of complications.

9.3.1 Immediate First Aid Measures

Immediate first aid measures aim to slow the spread of venom and stabilize the patient until they can receive medical care. It is essential to follow evidence-based practices to minimize harm.

Key First Aid Principles:

- **Stay Calm and Reassure the Victim:** Keeping the victim calm can help slow the spread of venom by reducing their heart rate and metabolic rate.
- **Immobilize the Affected Limb:** Use a splint or any rigid object to immobilize the limb to slow the spread of venom. Keep the limb at or slightly below heart level.
- **Remove Constrictive Items:** Remove rings, watches, or tight clothing from the affected limb to prevent complications from swelling.
- **Clean the Wound:** Gently clean the bite site with soap and water to reduce the risk of secondary infection. Do not attempt to suck out the venom or make incisions.

Do Not:

- **Do Not Apply a Tourniquet:** Tourniquets can cause severe damage to the limb and are not recommended.
- **Do Not Apply Ice:** Ice can cause local tissue damage and is ineffective at reducing venom spread.
- **Do Not Give the Victim Alcohol or Caffeine:** These substances can increase the absorption of venom.

Specific First Aid Techniques:

- **Pressure Immobilization Bandage:** This technique is recommended for neurotoxic bites (e.g., from elapids) but should be used with caution. Wrap a bandage firmly around the entire bitten limb, starting from the bite site and moving upwards, without cutting off circulation. Immobilize the limb with a splint.
- **Basic Life Support (BLS):** If the victim shows signs of respiratory distress or cardiac arrest, provide BLS as needed, including rescue breathing and chest compressions.

9.3.2 Hospital Management

Hospital management focuses on stabilizing the patient, administering antivenom, and treating complications arising from the venom.

Initial Assessment:

- **History and Examination:** Obtain a detailed history of the bite incident, including the time and location of the bite, the type of snake (if known), and the progression of symptoms. Conduct a thorough physical examination.
- **Vital Signs Monitoring:** Continuously monitor the patient's vital signs, including heart rate, blood pressure, respiratory rate, and oxygen saturation.
- **Laboratory Investigations:** Perform baseline blood tests, including complete blood count (CBC), coagulation profile, electrolytes, renal function tests, and liver function tests. Obtain a urine sample to check for hematuria and myoglobinuria.

Specific Treatments:

- **Antivenom Administration:** Antivenom is the primary treatment for envenoming and should be administered as soon as possible.

  - **Selection:** Use the appropriate antivenom for the snake species involved. If the species is unknown, use a polyvalent antivenom.
  - **Dosage:** Administer the recommended initial dose of antivenom based on the severity of envenoming and the guidelines provided with the antivenom product. Monitor for any signs of allergic

reaction.

- **Infusion:** Antivenom is typically given intravenously, diluted in saline, and infused slowly.

- **Supportive Care:**

  - **Fluid Resuscitation:** Administer intravenous fluids to maintain blood pressure and hydration.
  - **Pain Management:** Use analgesics to manage pain at the bite site and other affected areas.
  - **Tetanus Prophylaxis:** Administer tetanus prophylaxis if the patient's immunization status is not up to date.

- **Treatment of Specific Effects:**

  - **Neurotoxic Effects:** Monitor respiratory function closely. Provide mechanical ventilation if the patient shows signs of respiratory failure.
  - **Hemotoxic Effects:** Monitor coagulation parameters and administer fresh frozen plasma or clotting factors if there is significant coagulopathy.
  - **Myotoxic Effects:** Monitor renal function and treat rhabdomyolysis with aggressive hydration and possibly alkalinization of urine to prevent kidney damage.

Monitoring and Follow-Up:

- **Observation:** Keep the patient under close observation for at least 24 hours after antivenom administration to monitor for delayed effects and complications.
- **Repeat Antivenom Doses:** Administer additional doses of antivenom if symptoms persist or worsen, based on clinical assessment and laboratory results.
- **Long-Term Care:** Provide follow-up care for wound management, rehabilitation, and treatment of any long-term complications such as chronic pain or neurological deficits.

9.4 Early Manifestations and Complications

Venomous snake bites can cause a range of early manifestations and complications, which can be categorized into local and systemic effects. Understanding these effects is crucial for timely and effective management of snakebite envenomings.

9.4.1 Local Effects

Local effects refer to the symptoms and signs that appear at and around the site of the snake bite. These effects can vary depending on the type of snake, the amount of venom injected, and the victim's response to the venom.

Common Local Effects:

- **Pain:** Immediate and severe pain at the bite site, which can radiate to surrounding areas.
- **Swelling:** Rapid swelling of the affected limb or area, which can progress significantly within hours.
- **Redness and Warmth:** Inflammation around the bite site, with the skin becoming red and warm to the touch.
- **Bruising:** Hemorrhagic spots and bruises can develop due to local bleeding.
- **Blistering:** Formation of blisters filled with clear or blood-stained fluid.
- **Necrosis:** Tissue death may occur, leading to blackened, necrotic areas around the bite site, particularly with hemotoxic venoms.

Severe Local Complications:

- **Compartment Syndrome:** Severe swelling within an enclosed muscle compartment can restrict blood flow and damage nerves, leading to severe pain, numbness, and weakness. This condition requires urgent medical intervention, often surgical.
- **Secondary Infection:** The bite wound can become infected, leading to cellulitis, abscess formation, and systemic infection if not properly managed.

9.4.2 Systemic Effects

Systemic effects refer to the widespread symptoms and signs that occur throughout the body as the venom spreads. These effects depend on the venom composition and can include neurotoxic, hemotoxic, and myotoxic manifestations.

Neurotoxic Effects:
Neurotoxic venoms primarily affect the nervous system, leading to a range of neurological symptoms.

- **Muscle Weakness:** Generalized weakness that often starts in the muscles closest to the bite and progresses.
- **Ptosis:** Drooping of the upper eyelids due to paralysis of the eyelid muscles.
- **Diplopia:** Double vision caused by paralysis of the eye muscles.
- **Dysphagia:** Difficulty swallowing due to paralysis of the throat muscles.
- **Respiratory Paralysis:** Severe cases can lead to respiratory failure due to paralysis of the diaphragm and intercostal muscles.

Hemotoxic Effects:
Hemotoxic venoms affect the blood and vascular systems, leading to significant bleeding and clotting disorders.

- **Coagulopathy:** Disruption of blood clotting, leading to prolonged bleeding from the bite site and other areas.
- **Hemorrhage:** Internal bleeding in various organs, which can manifest as hematuria (blood in urine), hematemesis (vomiting blood), and melena (black, tarry stools).
- **Hypotension:** Low blood pressure resulting from blood loss and vascular damage, which can progress to shock.
- **DIC (Disseminated Intravascular Coagulation):** A severe condition where widespread clotting and bleeding occur simultaneously, leading to multiple organ failure.

Myotoxic Effects:
Myotoxic venoms primarily affect muscle tissue, leading to muscle damage and systemic effects.

- **Muscle Pain and Swelling:** Intense pain and swelling in the affected muscles.
- **Myoglobinuria:** Presence of myoglobin (a muscle breakdown product) in the urine, causing dark-colored urine and potential kidney damage.
- **Rhabdomyolysis:** Extensive muscle breakdown, leading to the release of muscle cell contents into the bloodstream, potentially causing acute kidney injury.

Severe Systemic Complications:

- **Acute Kidney Injury (AKI):** Due to hemoglobinuria or myoglobinuria, resulting in reduced urine output and elevated creatinine levels.
- **Respiratory Failure:** Due to neurotoxic paralysis of respiratory muscles or severe pulmonary hemorrhage.
- **Cardiac Arrhythmias:** Irregular heartbeats due to electrolyte imbalances and direct cardiac toxicity.
- **Multi-Organ Failure:** Severe envenoming can lead to failure of multiple organ systems, requiring intensive care.

9.5 Snake Bite Injuries

Snake bite injuries can result in a range of immediate and long-term complications, depending on the type of snake, the amount of venom injected, and the promptness and appropriateness of medical treatment. Understanding the types of injuries and their potential long-term complications is essential for providing comprehensive care to snakebite victims.

9.5.1 Types of Injuries

The types of injuries resulting from snake bites can be categorized into local and systemic effects, as well as specific types of physical and physiological damage.

Local Injuries:

- **Puncture Wounds:** The initial injury from a snake bite typically consists of two puncture marks from the snake's fangs. These wounds may be surrounded by bruising and swelling.
- **Tissue Necrosis:** Venom-induced cell death can lead to necrosis, characterized by blackened, dead tissue around the bite site. This is common with viper bites.
- **Blisters and Ulcers:** Formation of fluid-filled blisters that can progress to deep ulcers due to venom cytotoxicity.
- **Compartment Syndrome:** Severe swelling within an enclosed muscle compartment can lead to increased pressure, reduced blood flow, and nerve damage. This condition requires prompt surgical intervention.

Systemic Injuries:

- **Coagulopathy:** Disruption of the blood clotting system, leading to widespread bleeding, including internal hemorrhages.
- **Neurotoxicity:** Paralysis and respiratory failure due to the neurotoxic effects of certain snake venoms, particularly those of elapids.
- **Myotoxicity:** Muscle breakdown and rhabdomyolysis, resulting in the release of muscle breakdown products into the bloodstream, potentially leading to kidney damage.

9.5.2 Long-Term Complications

Long-term complications from snake bites can affect various organ systems and lead to chronic health issues. These complications often depend on the severity of the initial envenoming, the type of venom, and the timeliness of medical intervention.

Chronic Pain and Disability:

- **Neuropathic Pain:** Persistent pain due to nerve damage caused by the venom.
- **Chronic Inflammation:** Ongoing inflammation around the bite site, leading to pain and discomfort.
- **Physical Disability:** Loss of function or mobility in the affected limb due to muscle and nerve damage, scarring, or amputation.

Renal Complications:

- **Chronic Kidney Disease:** Long-term damage to the kidneys due to hemoglobinuria or myoglobinuria from hemolysis or rhabdomyolysis.
- **Renal Failure:** Progression to end-stage renal disease requiring dialysis or kidney transplantation.

Cardiovascular Complications:

- **Hypertension:** Long-term high blood pressure resulting from kidney damage or direct cardiovascular effects of the venom.
- **Cardiac Arrhythmias:** Persistent irregular heartbeats due to venom-induced damage to the heart.

Hematological Complications:

- **Persistent Coagulopathy:** Ongoing issues with blood clotting, leading to easy bruising and prolonged bleeding.
- **Anemia:** Chronic anemia due to ongoing blood loss or hemolysis.

Psychological and Emotional Complications:

- **Post-Traumatic Stress Disorder (PTSD):** Psychological trauma from the snakebite experience, leading to anxiety, nightmares, and hypervigilance.
- **Depression and Anxiety:** Mental health issues arising from the physical and emotional impact of the snake bite and its long-term consequences.

Dermatological Complications:

- **Scarring:** Significant scarring at the bite site and areas of necrosis, which can affect mobility and appearance.
- **Skin Grafts:** Need for skin grafting to repair extensive tissue damage, which can lead to complications such as graft rejection or infection.

CHAPTER X

Plant Poisoning

Introduction

Plant poisoning, also known as phytotoxicosis, occurs when individuals come into contact with or ingest toxic substances found in certain plants. While plants are a crucial part of our ecosystem and provide numerous benefits, including food, medicine, and aesthetics, some contain chemicals that can be harmful or even deadly to humans and animals. Plant poisoning can result from accidental ingestion, inhalation of plant particles, or dermal contact with toxic plants.

Importance of Understanding Plant Poisoning

Understanding plant poisoning is essential for several reasons. Firstly, many cases of plant poisoning, especially in children, are preventable with proper education and awareness. Secondly, accurate identification and knowledge of toxic plants and their effects can lead to timely and effective treatment, reducing morbidity and mortality. Finally, healthcare providers need to be equipped with the knowledge to manage plant poisoning cases, given the diversity of toxic plants and the wide range of clinical symptoms they can cause.

Scope of the Chapter

This chapter aims to provide a comprehensive overview of plant poisoning, focusing on the identification of common toxic plants, the clinical manifestations of plant poisoning, and the management strategies for affected individuals. Key areas covered will include:

1. **Common Toxic Plants:**

   - Identification and classification of plants known to cause poisoning.
   - Geographic distribution and common habitats of toxic plants.

- Seasonal variations in plant toxicity.

2. **Mechanisms of Plant Toxicity:**

   - Overview of toxic compounds found in plants (e.g., alkaloids, glycosides, saponins, terpenes).
   - How these compounds affect human physiology.

3. **Clinical Manifestations of Plant Poisoning:**

   - Symptoms and signs associated with ingestion, inhalation, and dermal contact with toxic plants.
   - Organ systems commonly affected by plant toxins.

4. **Diagnosis of Plant Poisoning:**

   - Steps to accurately diagnose plant poisoning, including patient history, physical examination, and laboratory tests.
   - Importance of identifying the specific plant involved.

5. **Management and Treatment:**

   - Immediate first aid measures for plant poisoning.
   - Hospital management, including decontamination, symptomatic treatment, and specific antidotes if available.
   - Long-term care and follow-up for severe cases of poisoning.

6. **Prevention and Education:**

   - Strategies for preventing plant poisoning in various settings, such as homes, schools, and workplaces.
   - Educational initiatives to raise awareness about toxic plants and safe practices.

10.1 Common Poisonous Plants

10.1.1 Identification and Characteristics

Identifying poisonous plants is crucial for preventing plant poisoning. Poisonous plants can be found in various environments, including gardens, parks, forests, and even homes as ornamental plants. Understanding the characteristics of these plants helps in recognizing and avoiding them.

Oleander (Nerium oleander): Oleander is a popular ornamental shrub known for its beautiful flowers, which can be red, pink, white, or yellow. Despite its attractiveness, every part of the oleander plant is highly toxic, including its leaves, flowers, and stems. Oleander contains cardiac glycosides, which can cause severe cardiovascular issues, including arrhythmias and cardiac arrest, if ingested. The plant's leathery, lance-shaped leaves and dense clusters of flowers make it easily identifiable.

Castor Bean (Ricinus communis): The castor bean plant is easily recognizable by its large, palmate leaves and spiky, capsule-like fruits. These fruits contain seeds, known as castor beans, which are highly toxic due to the presence of ricin. Ricin is a potent protein toxin that can inhibit protein synthesis in cells, leading to severe symptoms such as vomiting, diarrhea, abdominal pain, and potentially fatal organ damage. The castor bean plant is often grown for ornamental purposes and for its oil, which is used in various industrial applications.

Deadly Nightshade (Atropa belladonna): Deadly nightshade, also known as belladonna, is a perennial herb that can be identified by its bell-shaped, purple flowers and shiny, black berries. All parts of the plant contain tropane alkaloids, such as atropine and scopolamine, which affect the nervous system. Ingestion can lead to dilated pupils, dry mouth, difficulty swallowing, hallucinations, and even death. The plant's dark green leaves and distinctive berries make it recognizable, but its toxicity necessitates caution.

Hemlock (Conium maculatum): Hemlock is a highly poisonous biennial plant that can be identified by its tall, hollow stems, which are often purple-spotted, and its small, white, umbrella-like clusters of flowers. The plant contains coniine, a potent neurotoxin that disrupts the central nervous system, leading to symptoms such as muscle paralysis, respiratory failure, and death. Hemlock is commonly found in moist, shaded areas such as riverbanks and ditches.

Foxglove (Digitalis purpurea): Foxglove is a biennial or perennial plant known for its tall spikes of tubular, purple, pink, or white flowers. The plant contains cardiac glycosides, similar to those in oleander, which can cause serious heart problems. Symptoms of foxglove poisoning include nausea, vomiting, diarrhea, confusion, and irregular heartbeats. The plant's striking flowers and large, woolly leaves make it easy to identify in gardens and wild areas.

10.1.2 Common Toxic Compounds

Understanding the toxic compounds found in poisonous plants is essential for recognizing the potential dangers and symptoms of poisoning. These compounds vary widely in their chemical structure and effects on the human body.

Cardiac Glycosides: Cardiac glycosides are found in plants such as oleander and foxglove. These compounds affect the heart by increasing the force of cardiac contractions and altering the electrical activity of the heart. Symptoms of cardiac glycoside poisoning include nausea, vomiting, diarrhea, abdominal pain, confusion, and severe arrhythmias. Ingesting even a small amount of plants containing these toxins can be fatal.

Ricin: Ricin, found in the seeds of the castor bean plant, is one of the most potent toxins known. It inhibits protein synthesis within cells, leading to cell death. Symptoms of ricin poisoning include severe abdominal pain, vomiting, diarrhea, dehydration, and multi-organ failure. Ricin is highly toxic, and exposure to even a small amount can be lethal.

Tropane Alkaloids: Tropane alkaloids, such as atropine and scopolamine, are found in deadly nightshade and other plants of the Solanaceae family. These alkaloids affect the nervous system by blocking acetylcholine receptors. Symptoms of tropane alkaloid poisoning include dry mouth, blurred vision, hallucinations, confusion, seizures, and death. These compounds are highly toxic and can cause severe symptoms with minimal exposure.

Coniine: Coniine is a neurotoxin found in hemlock. It affects the peripheral nervous system by disrupting the transmission of nerve impulses. Symptoms of coniine poisoning include muscle paralysis, respiratory distress, tremors, and death. Hemlock poisoning can be fatal even in small doses, making it one of the most dangerous plants.

Oxalates: Oxalates are found in plants such as rhubarb leaves and dieffenbachia. These compounds can cause irritation and swelling of the mouth, throat, and gastrointestinal tract. In severe cases, ingestion of oxalates can lead to kidney damage and hypocalcemia. Symptoms include burning sensations, difficulty swallowing, vomiting, and, in severe cases, convulsions and renal failure.

10.2 Mushrooms Poisoning

Mushroom poisoning, also known as mycetism, occurs when toxic species of mushrooms are ingested. Mushrooms are a diverse group of fungi, and while many are edible and nutritious, others contain potent toxins that can cause severe illness or death. Proper identification and awareness of toxic mushrooms are essential to prevent poisoning.

10.2.1 Toxic Species

Identifying toxic mushroom species is critical for preventing mushroom poisoning. Several species are particularly dangerous due to their potent toxins.

Amanita Phalloides (Death Cap): The death cap is one of the most poisonous mushrooms. It is typically found in deciduous forests and can be mistaken for edible mushrooms. The cap is usually greenish to yellowish, the gills are white, and it has a bulbous base with a white volva. It contains amatoxins, which inhibit RNA polymerase and cause severe liver damage.

Amanita Muscaria (Fly Agaric): This iconic mushroom is easily recognizable by its bright red cap with white spots. It contains ibotenic acid and muscimol, which affect the central nervous system. Ingestion can cause hallucinations, seizures, and delirium.

Galerina Marginata (Deadly Galerina): This small brown mushroom is often found on decaying wood. It contains amatoxins similar to those in the death cap, leading to severe liver and kidney damage.

Gyromitra Esculenta (False Morel): False morels resemble true morels but contain gyromitrin, which is converted to monomethylhydrazine (MMH) in the body. MMH is toxic to the liver and central nervous system, causing seizures and organ failure.

Cortinarius Species: Several Cortinarius species contain orellanine, a toxin that causes delayed kidney failure. Symptoms may not appear until several days after ingestion, making diagnosis and treatment challenging.

Lepiota Species: Some small Lepiota species contain amatoxins and can cause severe liver damage. They are often mistaken for edible mushrooms, leading to accidental poisoning.

10.2.2 Clinical Symptoms

Clinical symptoms of mushroom poisoning vary depending on the species ingested and the toxins involved. Symptoms can range from mild gastrointestinal distress to severe organ failure.

Gastrointestinal Symptoms:

- **Nausea and Vomiting:** Common early symptoms after ingesting toxic mushrooms.
- **Abdominal Pain:** Cramping and severe pain in the abdomen.
- **Diarrhea:** Watery or bloody stools, leading to dehydration.

Hepatic Symptoms:

- **Jaundice:** Yellowing of the skin and eyes due to liver damage.
- **Hepatomegaly:** Enlargement of the liver.
- **Liver Failure:** Severe cases can lead to acute liver failure, characterized by confusion, coagulopathy, and multi-organ failure.

Neurological Symptoms:

- **Hallucinations:** Visual and auditory hallucinations, particularly with Amanita muscaria and Psilocybe species.
- **Seizures:** Convulsions due to neurotoxins affecting the central nervous system.
- **Delirium:** Confusion, agitation, and altered mental status.

Renal Symptoms:

- **Hematuria:** Blood in the urine due to kidney damage.
- **Oliguria:** Reduced urine output.
- **Acute Kidney Injury (AKI):** Severe cases can lead to kidney failure, requiring dialysis.

Delayed Symptoms:

- **Delayed Onset:** Some toxins, like orellanine, have a delayed onset of symptoms, which can appear days to weeks after ingestion.
- **Chronic Organ Damage:** Long-term exposure to certain toxins can lead to chronic liver or kidney damage.

10.2.3 Management Strategies

Effective management of mushroom poisoning requires prompt identification, supportive care, and specific treatments to mitigate the effects of the toxins.

Immediate First Aid:

- **Induce Vomiting:** Only if advised by a poison control center or healthcare provider and if the patient is alert.
- **Activated Charcoal:** Administer activated charcoal to absorb toxins and reduce their absorption in the gastrointestinal tract.
- **Gastric Lavage:** Consider gastric lavage if the patient presents within a few hours of ingestion and is symptomatic.

Supportive Care:

- **Hydration:** Provide intravenous fluids to maintain hydration and correct electrolyte imbalances.
- **Symptomatic Treatment:** Manage symptoms such as nausea, vomiting, and pain with appropriate medications.

Specific Treatments:

- **Antidotes:** Administer specific antidotes if available and appropriate for the type of mushroom ingested.

  - **Silibinin:** Used to treat amatoxin poisoning, it helps protect the liver and improve outcomes.
  - **Pyridoxine (Vitamin B6):** Administered for gyromitrin poisoning to counteract the effects of MMH.

Monitoring and Follow-Up:

- **Vital Signs:** Continuously monitor the patient's vital signs, including heart rate, blood pressure, respiratory rate, and oxygen saturation.
- **Laboratory Tests:** Perform regular blood tests to monitor liver and kidney function, coagulation profile, and electrolyte levels.
- **Imaging:** Conduct imaging studies, such as ultrasound or CT scans, to assess organ damage.

Prevention and Education:

- **Public Awareness:** Educate the public about the risks of mushroom foraging and the importance of accurate identification.
- **Proper Identification:** Encourage the use of reliable field guides and expert consultation when foraging for wild mushrooms.
- **Avoiding Unknown Mushrooms:** Advise against consuming any wild mushrooms unless they are positively identified as safe by an expert.

10.3 Mycotoxins Poisoning

Mycotoxins are toxic secondary metabolites produced by certain species of molds. These compounds can contaminate food and feed, posing serious health risks to humans and animals. Understanding the different types of mycotoxins, their clinical symptoms, and management strategies is crucial for preventing and treating mycotoxin poisoning.

10.3.1 Types of Mycotoxins

Mycotoxins are produced by various fungi, primarily Aspergillus, Penicillium, and Fusarium species. Several types of mycotoxins are of significant concern due to their widespread occurrence and toxicity.

Aflatoxins: Aflatoxins are produced by Aspergillus species, particularly A. flavus and A. parasiticus. They are commonly found in contaminated grains, nuts, and legumes. Aflatoxin B1 is the most toxic and carcinogenic. Aflatoxins can cause acute liver damage, immune suppression, and are potent carcinogens, particularly affecting the liver.

Ochratoxins: Ochratoxins are produced by Aspergillus and Penicillium species. Ochratoxin A is the most prevalent and toxic. It contaminates a wide range of food products, including cereals, coffee, dried fruits, and wine. Ochratoxin A primarily affects the kidneys, leading to nephrotoxicity and potential kidney failure. It is also a potential carcinogen.

Trichothecenes: Trichothecenes are produced by Fusarium species and include a variety of toxins such as deoxynivalenol (DON) and T-2 toxin. They contaminate cereals and grains. Trichothecenes inhibit protein synthesis, causing gastrointestinal issues, immune suppression, and skin toxicity. T-2 toxin is particularly toxic, leading to severe hemorrhagic lesions.

Fumonisins: Fumonisins are produced by Fusarium species, primarily F. verticillioides and F. proliferatum. They are commonly found in maize and maize-based products. Fumonisins disrupt sphingolipid metabolism, leading to hepatotoxicity, nephrotoxicity, and increased risk of esophageal cancer. They are also associated with neural tube defects.

Zearalenone: Zearalenone is produced by Fusarium species and contaminates cereals, particularly maize. It has estrogenic effects, causing reproductive issues such as infertility, spontaneous abortions, and feminization in animals and humans.

10.3.2 Clinical Symptoms

The clinical symptoms of mycotoxin poisoning vary depending on the type of mycotoxin, the dose, and the duration of exposure. Symptoms can range from acute to chronic and affect multiple organ systems.

Aflatoxins:

- **Acute Poisoning:** Symptoms include fever, vomiting, abdominal pain, and jaundice. Severe cases can lead to acute liver failure and death.
- **Chronic Exposure:** Long-term exposure can result in liver cancer, immunosuppression, stunted growth in children, and chronic liver disease.

Ochratoxins:

- **Acute Poisoning:** Symptoms include abdominal pain, diarrhea, vomiting, and kidney pain.
- **Chronic Exposure:** Long-term exposure can lead to chronic kidney disease, immunosuppression, and increased risk of cancer, particularly in the urinary tract.

Trichothecenes:

- **Acute Poisoning:** Symptoms include nausea, vomiting, diarrhea, abdominal pain, and bleeding. Skin exposure can cause dermatitis.
- **Chronic Exposure:** Long-term exposure can lead to immunosuppression, chronic gastrointestinal issues, and potential cancer risk.

Fumonisins:

- **Acute Poisoning:** Symptoms include abdominal pain, diarrhea, and signs of liver and kidney toxicity.
- **Chronic Exposure:** Long-term exposure can lead to liver and kidney damage, esophageal cancer, and neural tube defects in fetuses.

Zearalenone:

- **Acute Poisoning:** Symptoms are less common but may include abdominal pain and hormonal disruptions.
- **Chronic Exposure:** Long-term exposure can lead to reproductive issues, such as infertility and developmental problems in fetuses.

10.3.3 Management Strategies

Effective management of mycotoxin poisoning involves preventing exposure, symptomatic treatment, and specific interventions to reduce toxin levels in the body.

Prevention:

- **Food Safety:** Implement stringent food safety measures to prevent mold contamination in crops and food products. This includes proper storage, drying, and monitoring of moisture levels.
- **Regulation:** Enforce regulations and standards for acceptable mycotoxin levels in food and feed products.
- **Public Awareness:** Educate the public about the risks of mycotoxins and safe food handling practices.

Symptomatic Treatment:

- **Supportive Care:** Provide hydration, electrolyte balance, and nutritional support for affected individuals.
- **Gastrointestinal Decontamination:** In cases of acute ingestion, consider activated charcoal to reduce toxin absorption.
- **Pain Management:** Use analgesics to manage abdominal pain and other discomforts.

Specific Interventions:

- **Antioxidants:** Administer antioxidants, such as vitamin E and selenium, to mitigate oxidative stress caused by mycotoxins.
- **Chelation Therapy:** For certain mycotoxins, chelation therapy may help reduce toxin levels. However, this is not commonly used and depends on the specific mycotoxin involved.

Monitoring and Follow-Up:

- **Regular Assessments:** Conduct regular medical check-ups to monitor the patient's clinical status and response to treatment.
- **Laboratory Tests:** Perform blood tests to assess liver and kidney function, as well as specific tests for mycotoxin levels if available.
- **Long-Term Care:** Provide long-term monitoring and supportive care for individuals with chronic exposure to mycotoxins to prevent long-term health complications.

10.4 Symptoms and Management

Mycotoxin poisoning can present with various symptoms, affecting different organ systems. The management of these symptoms involves supportive care and specific treatments based on the type and severity of symptoms.

10.4.1 Gastrointestinal Symptoms

Gastrointestinal symptoms are common in mycotoxin poisoning due to the ingestion of contaminated food. These symptoms can range from mild discomfort to severe, life-threatening conditions.

Common Gastrointestinal Symptoms:

- **Nausea and Vomiting:** These are often the first symptoms to appear after ingestion of mycotoxins.
- **Abdominal Pain:** Cramping and severe pain in the abdomen are common.
- **Diarrhea:** Watery or bloody stools can lead to dehydration and electrolyte imbalances.
- **Hematemesis:** Vomiting blood, which indicates severe gastrointestinal bleeding.

Management of Gastrointestinal Symptoms:

- **Hydration:** Provide intravenous fluids to maintain hydration and correct electrolyte imbalances.
- **Antiemetics:** Administer antiemetic medications such as ondansetron to control nausea and vomiting.
- **Analgesics:** Use analgesics like acetaminophen or ibuprofen to manage abdominal pain.
- **Activated Charcoal:** In cases of recent ingestion, activated charcoal can help absorb the mycotoxins and reduce their systemic absorption.
- **Gastrointestinal Decontamination:** Consider gastric lavage if the patient presents within a few hours of ingestion and is symptomatic.

10.4.2 Neurological Symptoms

Neurological symptoms occur due to the neurotoxic effects of certain mycotoxins, affecting the central and peripheral nervous systems. These symptoms can be acute or develop over time with chronic exposure.

Common Neurological Symptoms:

- **Headaches:** Persistent and severe headaches.
- **Dizziness and Vertigo:** Sensations of spinning and imbalance.
- **Seizures:** Convulsions due to severe neurotoxicity.

- **Hallucinations:** Visual and auditory hallucinations, particularly with certain mycotoxins like those from Amanita muscaria.
- **Confusion and Delirium:** Altered mental status, agitation, and disorientation.
- **Peripheral Neuropathy:** Tingling, numbness, and weakness in the extremities.

Management of Neurological Symptoms:

- **Anticonvulsants:** Administer anticonvulsant medications such as diazepam or phenytoin to control seizures.
- **Sedatives:** Use sedatives to manage severe agitation and delirium.
- **Hydration and Electrolyte Balance:** Maintain adequate hydration and correct electrolyte imbalances, which can exacerbate neurological symptoms.
- **Supportive Care:** Provide supportive care, including monitoring of vital signs and neurological status.
- **Chelation Therapy:** For specific mycotoxins, chelation therapy may help reduce toxin levels and mitigate neurological symptoms.

10.4.3 Dermatological Symptoms

Dermatological symptoms can result from direct skin contact with mycotoxins or secondary effects of systemic toxicity. These symptoms may include irritation, allergic reactions, and more severe skin conditions.

Common Dermatological Symptoms:

- **Rashes:** Red, itchy, and inflamed skin.
- **Dermatitis:** Severe skin inflammation, often resulting from direct contact with mycotoxins.
- **Blisters:** Fluid-filled blisters that can be painful and prone to infection.
- **Erythema:** Redness of the skin due to increased blood flow.
- **Ulceration:** Severe cases can lead to skin ulcers and necrosis.

Management of Dermatological Symptoms:

- **Topical Treatments:** Apply topical corticosteroids to reduce inflammation and itching. Antibiotic ointments can prevent secondary infections.
- **Oral Antihistamines:** Use oral antihistamines like diphenhydramine to control allergic reactions and itching.
- **Hydration:** Maintain adequate hydration to support skin healing and overall health.
- **Wound Care:** Properly clean and dress blisters and ulcers to prevent infection and promote healing.
- **Avoidance of Exposure:** Prevent further contact with the source of mycotoxins and use protective clothing to minimize skin exposure.

CHAPTER XI

Food Poisoning

Introduction

Food poisoning, also known as foodborne illness, is a widespread and significant public health issue affecting millions of people worldwide each year. It is caused by consuming contaminated food or beverages containing harmful microorganisms, toxins, chemicals, or other hazardous substances. The symptoms of food poisoning can range from mild gastrointestinal discomfort to severe, life-threatening conditions. Understanding the causes, symptoms, and management of food poisoning is essential for preventing outbreaks and ensuring food safety.

Importance of Understanding Food Poisoning

Understanding food poisoning is crucial for several reasons. Firstly, it helps in identifying the sources and pathways of contamination, enabling the implementation of effective preventive measures. Secondly, knowledge of the various pathogens and toxins involved in food poisoning can aid in prompt diagnosis and treatment, reducing morbidity and mortality. Lastly, raising awareness about food safety practices among consumers, food handlers, and regulatory authorities can significantly reduce the incidence of foodborne illnesses.

Scope of the Chapter

This chapter aims to provide a comprehensive overview of food poisoning, focusing on the types of pathogens and toxins responsible, the clinical manifestations of foodborne illnesses, and the strategies for prevention and management. Key areas covered will include:

1. **Types of Food Poisoning:**

- **Bacterial:** Common bacterial pathogens such as Salmonella, Escherichia coli, Listeria, and Campylobacter.
- **Viral:** Viral agents including norovirus, hepatitis A, and rotavirus.
- **Parasitic:** Parasitic infections caused by organisms such as Giardia, Cryptosporidium, and Toxoplasma.
- **Chemical:** Poisoning from chemical contaminants like pesticides, heavy metals, and food additives.
- **Toxins:** Illnesses caused by natural toxins found in certain plants, seafood, and mushrooms.

2. **Pathways of Contamination:**

- **Food Production and Processing:** Contamination during harvesting, processing, and packaging.
- **Food Handling and Preparation:** Cross-contamination and improper food handling practices.
- **Storage and Transportation:** Inadequate temperature control and sanitation during storage and transportation.

3. **Clinical Manifestations:**

- **Gastrointestinal Symptoms:** Nausea, vomiting, diarrhea, abdominal pain, and cramping.
- **Systemic Symptoms:** Fever, headache, muscle aches, and dehydration.
- **Severe Complications:** Hemolytic uremic syndrome, septicemia, and neurological symptoms.

4. **Diagnosis and Management:**

- **Diagnostic Techniques:** Laboratory tests, stool cultures, and identification of specific pathogens.
- **Supportive Care:** Hydration, electrolyte balance, and symptomatic treatment.
- **Specific Treatments:** Antibiotics, antivirals, and antiparasitic medications when indicated.
- **Hospitalization:** Criteria for hospital admission and management of severe cases.

5. **Prevention and Control:**

- **Food Safety Practices:** Guidelines for safe food handling, cooking, and storage.
- **Regulatory Standards:** Food safety regulations and inspection protocols.
- **Public Health Interventions:** Surveillance, outbreak investigation, and public education campaigns.

11.1 Causes and Types of Food Poisoning

Food poisoning is caused by the ingestion of food or beverages contaminated with harmful microorganisms, toxins, or chemicals. These contaminants can lead to various types of foodborne illnesses, each with distinct causes and clinical manifestations. Understanding the different types of food poisoning is essential for effective prevention, diagnosis, and management.

11.1.1 Bacterial Food Poisoning

Bacterial food poisoning is one of the most common types of foodborne illnesses. It occurs when food or beverages are contaminated with pathogenic bacteria that produce toxins or directly infect the gastrointestinal tract.

Common Bacterial Pathogens:

- **Salmonella:**

- **Sources:** Contaminated poultry, eggs, meat, dairy products, and produce.
- **Symptoms:** Nausea, vomiting, abdominal cramps, diarrhea, fever, and headache. Symptoms usually appear 6-48 hours after ingestion and can last 4-7 days.
- **Complications:** Severe cases can lead to dehydration and septicemia, particularly in young children, the elderly, and immunocompromised individuals.

- **Escherichia coli (E. coli):**

  - **Sources:** Contaminated beef, unpasteurized milk, fresh produce, and water.
  - **Symptoms:** Severe abdominal cramps, bloody diarrhea, and vomiting. Symptoms typically appear 3-4 days after exposure and can last up to 10 days.
  - **Complications:** Some strains, such as E. coli O157

, can cause hemolytic uremic syndrome (HUS), leading to kidney failure and hemolysis.

- **Listeria monocytogenes:**

  - **Sources:** Contaminated deli meats, unpasteurized dairy products, and ready-to-eat foods.
  - **Symptoms:** Fever, muscle aches, nausea, and diarrhea. Invasive listeriosis can lead to severe complications like meningitis and septicemia.
  - **Complications:** High risk for pregnant women, newborns, the elderly, and immunocompromised individuals. Can cause miscarriages, stillbirths, and neonatal infections.

- **Campylobacter:**

  - **Sources:** Contaminated poultry, unpasteurized milk, and untreated water.
  - **Symptoms:** Diarrhea (often bloody), fever, nausea, vomiting, and abdominal pain. Symptoms usually appear 2-5 days after ingestion and can last about a week.
  - **Complications:** Severe dehydration, Guillain-Barré syndrome, and reactive arthritis in some cases.

11.1.2 Viral Food Poisoning

Viral food poisoning is caused by viruses that contaminate food or water. These viruses are highly infectious and can spread rapidly through contaminated food, water, or person-to-person contact.

Common Viral Pathogens:

- **Norovirus:**

  - **Sources:** Contaminated shellfish, fresh produce, and ready-to-eat foods. Often spread in settings like restaurants, cruise ships, and nursing homes.
  - **Symptoms:** Nausea, vomiting, watery diarrhea, abdominal pain, and fever. Symptoms typically appear 12-48 hours after exposure and last 1-3 days.
  - **Complications:** Dehydration, particularly in young children, the elderly, and immunocompromised individuals.

- **Hepatitis A:**

  - **Sources:** Contaminated shellfish, raw produce, and water. Often spread through poor hygiene and sanitation practices.
  - **Symptoms:** Fever, fatigue, nausea, vomiting, abdominal pain, dark urine, jaundice, and liver inflammation. Symptoms usually appear 15-50 days after exposure and can last several weeks to months.
  - **Complications:** Liver failure in severe cases, particularly in individuals with pre-existing liver conditions.

- **Rotavirus:**

  - **Sources:** Contaminated water and food, particularly in areas with poor sanitation.
  - **Symptoms:** Severe diarrhea, vomiting, fever, and abdominal pain. Common in infants and young children, with symptoms appearing 1-3 days after exposure and lasting 3-8 days.
  - **Complications:** Severe dehydration, particularly in young children, requiring hospitalization and rehydration therapy.

11.1.3 Chemical Food Poisoning

Chemical food poisoning occurs when food or beverages are contaminated with harmful chemicals. These chemicals can be naturally occurring in certain foods or result from contamination during food production, processing, or storage.

Common Chemical Contaminants:

- **Pesticides:**

  - **Sources:** Residues on fruits, vegetables, and grains from agricultural use.
  - **Symptoms:** Nausea, vomiting, diarrhea, abdominal pain, headache, dizziness, and in severe cases, convulsions and respiratory distress.
  - **Complications:** Long-term exposure can lead to chronic health issues, including neurological damage and cancer.

- **Heavy Metals:**

  - **Sources:** Contaminated water and food, particularly seafood. Common heavy metals include lead, mercury, and cadmium.
  - **Symptoms:** Nausea, vomiting, abdominal pain, diarrhea, and neurological symptoms such as tremors, headaches, and cognitive impairment.
  - **Complications:** Chronic exposure can cause organ damage, developmental issues in children, and increased cancer risk.

- **Food Additives and Preservatives:**

  - **Sources:** Additives used to enhance flavor, color, and shelf-life of food products. Common additives include sulfites, nitrates, and artificial sweeteners.
  - **Symptoms:** Allergic reactions, gastrointestinal symptoms, headaches, and in some cases, respiratory distress.
  - **Complications:** Long-term health effects are still being studied, but some additives have been linked to hyperactivity in children and other health concerns.

11.2 Clinical Symptoms

Food poisoning can present with a wide range of clinical symptoms, primarily affecting the gastrointestinal system but also causing systemic effects. The severity and type of symptoms depend on the pathogen or toxin involved, the amount ingested, and the individual's health status.

11.2.1 Gastrointestinal Symptoms

Gastrointestinal symptoms are the most common and immediate indicators of food poisoning. These symptoms result from the direct effects of pathogens or toxins on the digestive tract.
Common Gastrointestinal Symptoms:

- **Nausea:** A feeling of unease and discomfort in the stomach with an urge to vomit. Nausea often precedes vomiting and can be caused by a variety of pathogens, including bacteria, viruses, and toxins.
- **Vomiting:** The forceful expulsion of stomach contents through the mouth. Vomiting can be a protective mechanism to expel harmful substances but can lead to dehydration if severe or prolonged.
- **Diarrhea:** Frequent, loose, or watery stools. Diarrhea is a common symptom of food poisoning caused by bacteria such as Salmonella, E. coli, and viruses like norovirus. It can lead to significant fluid loss and dehydration.
- **Abdominal Pain and Cramping:** Sharp or cramping pain in the abdomen. This pain is due to inflammation and irritation of the gastrointestinal tract caused by the infection or toxin.
- **Bloody Stools:** The presence of blood in stools indicates severe infection and inflammation, often associated with pathogens like E. coli O157

and Shigella. Bloody diarrhea is a medical emergency requiring prompt evaluation.

- **Fever:** Elevated body temperature as the body responds to the infection. Fever is common with bacterial food poisoning and can help differentiate infectious causes from non-infectious causes of gastrointestinal distress.

11.2.2 Systemic Symptoms

Systemic symptoms arise when the infection or toxin spreads beyond the gastrointestinal tract, affecting other organs and systems. These symptoms indicate a more severe or widespread infection.

Common Systemic Symptoms:

- **Fever and Chills:** Fever, often accompanied by chills, indicates an immune response to systemic infection. It is common in bacterial and viral food poisoning.
- **Headache:** Generalized headache can result from dehydration, fever, or direct effects of toxins on the nervous system.
- **Muscle Aches (Myalgia):** Generalized muscle pain and discomfort. Myalgia can be associated with viral food poisoning, such as norovirus or rotavirus.
- **Fatigue and Weakness:** Generalized tiredness and weakness due to the body's efforts to fight off the infection, dehydration, and loss of nutrients.
- **Dehydration:** Severe vomiting and diarrhea can lead to significant fluid loss, resulting in dehydration. Symptoms include dry mouth, decreased urine output, dark-colored urine, dizziness, and confusion. Severe dehydration can lead to hypovolemic shock and requires immediate medical intervention.
- **Jaundice:** Yellowing of the skin and eyes due to liver involvement, seen in cases of hepatitis A virus infection. Jaundice indicates liver inflammation and requires medical evaluation.
- **Neurological Symptoms:** In severe cases, certain toxins and pathogens can affect the nervous system, leading to symptoms such as dizziness, confusion, seizures, and, in extreme cases, coma. Neurological symptoms are more commonly associated with chemical food poisoning and severe bacterial infections.

11.3 Management and Prevention

Effective management and prevention of food poisoning involve addressing symptoms, treating the underlying cause, and implementing strategies to prevent future occurrences. This section outlines the approaches to symptomatic treatment and preventive measures.

11.3.1 Symptomatic Treatment

Symptomatic treatment focuses on relieving the symptoms of food poisoning and preventing complications such as dehydration and severe illness.

Hydration:

- **Oral Rehydration Solutions (ORS):** These solutions contain a balanced mix of salts and sugars to replace lost fluids and electrolytes. They are especially important for children and the elderly, who are more susceptible to dehydration.
- **Intravenous Fluids:** In severe cases of dehydration, intravenous (IV) fluids may be necessary to quickly restore hydration and electrolyte balance.

Antiemetics:

- **Medications:** Drugs such as ondansetron or promethazine can help control nausea and vomiting, making it easier for patients to keep down fluids and avoid dehydration.

Antidiarrheals:

- **Medications:** Loperamide can reduce the frequency of diarrhea, but it should be used with caution. It is not recommended for bacterial infections like E. coli O157

or Shigella, where slowing down the gastrointestinal tract may be harmful.

Analgesics:

- **Pain Relievers:** Acetaminophen or ibuprofen can help relieve abdominal pain and fever. Aspirin should be avoided in children due to the risk of Reye's syndrome.

Antibiotics:

- **When Indicated:** Antibiotics may be prescribed for certain bacterial infections, such as severe cases of Campylobacter or Salmonella, or for vulnerable populations such as the elderly, infants, and immunocompromised individuals. However, antibiotics are generally not recommended for E. coli O157

infections due to the risk of hemolytic uremic syndrome (HUS).
Rest and Recovery:

- **Bed Rest:** Encouraging rest to allow the body to recover from the illness.
- **Gradual Reintroduction of Food:** Starting with bland, easy-to-digest foods like rice, bananas, toast, and clear broths, and gradually returning to a normal diet as tolerated.

11.3.2 Preventive Measures

Preventive measures are crucial to reduce the risk of food poisoning and ensure food safety at all stages, from production to consumption.
Food Handling and Preparation:

- **Hand Washing:** Wash hands thoroughly with soap and water before and after handling food, especially raw meat, poultry, seafood, and eggs.
- **Separate Cutting Boards:** Use separate cutting boards and utensils for raw and cooked foods to avoid cross-contamination.
- **Proper Cooking:** Cook foods to the appropriate temperatures to kill harmful pathogens. Use a food thermometer to ensure meats, poultry, and seafood reach safe internal temperatures.

  - **Poultry:** 165°F (74°C)
  - **Ground meats:** 160°F (71°C)
  - **Fish:** 145°F (63°C)

- **Chilling:** Refrigerate perishable foods promptly. Keep the refrigerator temperature at or below 40°F (4°C) and the freezer at or below 0°F (-18°C).

- **Avoiding Raw Foods:** Avoid consuming raw or undercooked meats, poultry, seafood, and eggs. Be cautious with raw milk and products made from it.

Food Storage:

- **Proper Storage:** Store food in clean, airtight containers to prevent contamination. Keep raw and cooked foods separate in the refrigerator.
- **Labeling and Dating:** Label and date leftovers and consume them within a safe period, typically 3-4 days for most perishable foods.
- **FIFO Principle:** Follow the "First In, First Out" principle to use older stock before newer stock to minimize spoilage.

Food Safety Practices:

- **Cleaning:** Keep kitchen surfaces, utensils, and equipment clean. Use hot, soapy water to wash dishes and cooking tools, and sanitize cutting boards and countertops regularly.
- **Avoiding Contaminated Water:** Use safe, potable water for drinking, cooking, and washing food. Be cautious when traveling to areas with questionable water quality.
- **Educating Food Handlers:** Train food handlers in proper food safety practices to minimize the risk of contamination in commercial and institutional settings.

Regulatory Standards and Public Health Interventions:

- **Regulations:** Adhere to local and international food safety standards and regulations to ensure food production, processing, and distribution are safe.
- **Surveillance and Monitoring:** Implement foodborne disease surveillance systems to detect and respond to outbreaks promptly.
- **Public Awareness Campaigns:** Conduct public health campaigns to educate consumers and food handlers about the importance of food safety and hygiene practices.

CHAPTER XII

Envenomations – Arthropod Bites and Stings

Introduction

Envenomations resulting from arthropod bites and stings are a common and significant health concern worldwide. Arthropods, a diverse group of invertebrates that include insects, arachnids, and crustaceans, can deliver venom through bites or stings, causing a range of reactions from mild discomfort to severe systemic effects. While many arthropod bites and stings are benign and self-limiting, some can lead to serious medical conditions requiring prompt intervention.

Importance of Understanding Arthropod Envenomations

Understanding arthropod envenomations is crucial for several reasons. Firstly, it enables healthcare providers to recognize and manage envenomations effectively, reducing morbidity and mortality. Secondly, knowledge of the diverse range of arthropods and their venoms helps in preventing and controlling envenomations, particularly in endemic areas. Lastly, public awareness and education about the risks and appropriate responses to arthropod bites and stings can significantly reduce the incidence and severity of envenomations.

Scope of the Chapter

This chapter aims to provide a comprehensive overview of arthropod envenomations, focusing on the identification of common venomous arthropods, the clinical manifestations of their bites and stings, and the management strategies for affected individuals. Key areas covered will include:

1. **Common Venomous Arthropods:**

- Identification and classification of arthropods known to cause envenomations.
- Geographic distribution and common habitats of venomous arthropods.
- Seasonal variations in arthropod activity and envenomation risk.

2. **Mechanisms of Venom Action:**

- Overview of the toxic compounds found in arthropod venoms.
- How these compounds affect human physiology.

3. **Clinical Manifestations of Envenomations:**

- Local Effects: Pain, swelling, redness, and necrosis at the bite or sting site.
- Systemic Effects: Allergic reactions, anaphylaxis, neurotoxicity, and organ damage.
- Specific symptoms associated with different types of arthropod venoms.

4. **Diagnosis and Assessment:**

- History and physical examination of envenomation victims.
- Laboratory investigations and imaging studies.
- Identification of the offending arthropod when possible.

5. **Management and Treatment:**

- First aid measures and initial management at the bite or sting site.
- Hospital management and medical treatment protocols.
- Administration of antivenoms, when available and indicated.
- Supportive care and management of complications.

6. **Prevention and Education:**

- Strategies for preventing arthropod bites and stings.
- Community education and awareness programs.

- Training healthcare providers in the recognition and management of arthropod envenomations.

12.1 Types of Arthropod Envenomations

Arthropod envenomations occur when venomous insects and arachnids bite or sting, injecting venom into their victims. This section will cover the types of arthropod envenomations, focusing on insect bites and stings, as well as arachnid bites and stings.

12.1.1 Insect Bites and Stings

Insects are a diverse group of arthropods that include species capable of delivering venom through bites or stings. These envenomations can cause a range of symptoms, from mild local reactions to severe systemic effects.

Common Venomous Insects:

- **Bees (Family Apidae):**

  - **Description:** Bees, including honeybees and bumblebees, are commonly found worldwide. They have barbed stingers, which detach from their bodies after stinging.
  - **Venom:** Bee venom contains melittin, phospholipase A2, and hyaluronidase, which can cause pain, swelling, and allergic reactions.
  - **Symptoms:** Localized pain, swelling, redness, and itching. In allergic individuals, bee stings can cause anaphylaxis, characterized by difficulty breathing, hives, and shock.

- **Wasps (Family Vespidae):**

  - **Description:** Wasps, including yellow jackets and hornets, are aggressive and can sting multiple times. They have smooth stingers that do not detach.
  - **Venom:** Wasp venom contains a mix of toxins, including peptides and enzymes, which cause pain and inflammation.
  - **Symptoms:** Immediate pain, swelling, redness, and itching at the sting site. Systemic allergic reactions can occur in sensitive individuals.

- **Ants (Family Formicidae):**

  - **Description:** Fire ants and bullet ants are notorious for their painful stings. Fire ants inject venom through their mandibles and sting multiple times.
  - **Venom:** Fire ant venom contains alkaloids, such as solenopsin, which cause intense pain and pustules.
  - **Symptoms:** Burning pain, swelling, and pustule formation. Severe allergic reactions and anaphylaxis can occur.

- **Mosquitoes (Family Culicidae):**

  - **Description:** Mosquitoes are widespread and feed on blood using their proboscis. They inject saliva containing anticoagulants and anesthetics.
  - **Venom:** Mosquito saliva contains proteins that trigger immune responses.
  - **Symptoms:** Itchy red bumps, localized swelling, and in some cases, allergic reactions. Mosquitoes can transmit diseases such as malaria, dengue fever, and Zika virus.

12.1.2 Arachnid Bites and Stings

Arachnids, including spiders and scorpions, are another group of arthropods capable of envenomation. Their bites and stings can cause a range of symptoms, from mild to severe.

Common Venomous Arachnids:

- **Spiders (Order Araneae):**

  - **Black Widow Spider (Latrodectus spp.):**

    - **Description:** Black widow spiders are found in temperate regions worldwide. They have a shiny black body with a distinctive red hourglass marking on the abdomen.
    - **Venom:** Contains neurotoxins, particularly latrotoxin, which affects the nervous system.

- **Symptoms:** Severe pain, muscle cramps, abdominal pain, sweating, and hypertension. In rare cases, envenomation can be fatal, especially in young children and the elderly.

  ○ **Brown Recluse Spider (Loxosceles spp.):**

    - **Description:** Brown recluse spiders are found in the United States. They have a violin-shaped marking on their back.
    - **Venom:** Contains necrotizing enzymes, particularly sphingomyelinase D, which causes tissue damage.
    - **Symptoms:** Initially painless, followed by severe pain, blistering, and necrosis at the bite site. Systemic symptoms can include fever, chills, and hemolysis.

- **Scorpions (Order Scorpiones):**

  ○ **Description:** Scorpions are found in various regions, including deserts and tropical areas. They have a segmented tail with a venomous stinger.
  ○ **Venom:** Contains a mix of neurotoxins and enzymes that affect the nervous system and cardiovascular system.
  ○ **Symptoms:** Intense localized pain, swelling, and redness. Systemic symptoms can include numbness, muscle twitching, sweating, and in severe cases, respiratory distress, convulsions, and cardiovascular collapse.

12.2 Clinical Symptoms

The clinical symptoms of arthropod envenomations can vary widely depending on the species involved, the amount of venom injected, and the individual's response. Symptoms can be broadly categorized into local and systemic effects.

12.2.1 Local Symptoms

Local symptoms occur at or near the site of the bite or sting. These symptoms are usually the first to appear and can range from mild to severe.

Pain:

- **Immediate Pain:** Many arthropod bites and stings cause immediate sharp or burning pain. For example, bee stings and fire ant bites are known for their intense pain.
- **Delayed Pain:** Some bites, like those from brown recluse spiders, may initially be painless but develop severe pain over time.

Swelling and Redness:

- **Localized Swelling:** Swelling around the bite or sting site is common. It can range from mild to significant, potentially extending beyond the initial area.
- **Redness:** The skin around the bite or sting often becomes red and inflamed due to the body's immune response to the venom.

Itching and Irritation:

- **Pruritus:** Itching is a common symptom, particularly with mosquito bites. It can lead to scratching, which may cause secondary infections.
- **Urticaria:** Raised, itchy welts (hives) may develop at the site, especially in allergic reactions.

Blistering and Ulceration:

- **Blisters:** Some bites and stings, such as those from fire ants or brown recluse spiders, can cause blisters to form, filled with clear or bloody fluid.
- **Ulceration:** Severe envenomations, particularly from brown recluse spiders, can lead to skin necrosis and ulceration, causing open sores that may require medical attention.

Necrosis:

- **Tissue Death:** Venom from certain arachnids, like the brown recluse spider, can cause necrosis, leading to blackened, dead tissue around the bite site. This may require surgical intervention to remove dead tissue and promote healing.

12.2.2 Systemic Symptoms

Systemic symptoms occur when venom spreads through the bloodstream, affecting various organs and systems. These symptoms can be more severe and require urgent medical attention.

Allergic Reactions:

- **Anaphylaxis:** A severe, life-threatening allergic reaction that can occur rapidly after a sting or bite. Symptoms include difficulty breathing, swelling of the face and throat, rapid heartbeat, low blood pressure, and loss of consciousness. Immediate administration of epinephrine is critical.
- **Generalized Urticaria:** Widespread hives and itching beyond the bite or sting site.

Neurological Symptoms:

- **Muscle Cramps and Spasms:** Neurotoxic venoms, such as those from black widow spiders, can cause severe muscle cramps and spasms.
- **Paralysis:** Some venoms can cause temporary paralysis, particularly in severe cases of scorpion stings or certain spider bites.
- **Headache and Dizziness:** General neurological effects can include headaches, dizziness, and confusion.

Cardiovascular Symptoms:

- **Hypertension or Hypotension:** Blood pressure changes, either high or low, can occur depending on the venom and individual response.
- **Tachycardia or Bradycardia:** Increased or decreased heart rate may result from the body's response to venom.

Respiratory Symptoms:

- **Difficulty Breathing:** Swelling of the airways and respiratory distress can occur, particularly in severe allergic reactions or with neurotoxic venom.

- **Pulmonary Edema:** Fluid accumulation in the lungs may occur in severe cases, leading to breathing difficulties and requiring urgent medical intervention.

Gastrointestinal Symptoms:

- **Nausea and Vomiting:** Common symptoms following envenomation, especially in systemic reactions.
- **Abdominal Pain:** Severe abdominal cramps and pain can be associated with certain envenomations, such as black widow spider bites.

Renal and Hematological Symptoms:

- **Hemolysis:** Destruction of red blood cells can occur with certain venoms, leading to hemolytic anemia.
- **Renal Failure:** Severe systemic envenomations, particularly those involving hemolysis, can lead to acute kidney injury and renal failure.

12.3 Management and Treatment

Effective management and treatment of arthropod envenomations involve prompt first aid measures followed by appropriate medical intervention. This approach can significantly reduce the severity of symptoms, prevent complications, and improve patient outcomes.

12.3.1 First Aid Measures

Immediate first aid measures are crucial in minimizing the impact of venom and stabilizing the patient until professional medical help can be obtained.
General First Aid for Bites and Stings:

- **Stay Calm:** Keeping the patient calm can help slow the spread of venom.
- **Move to a Safe Area:** Remove the patient from the vicinity of the arthropod to prevent further bites or stings.
- **Positioning:** If bitten on an extremity, keep the affected limb at or slightly below heart level to reduce venom spread.

Specific First Aid Techniques:

- **For Bee and Wasp Stings:**

  - **Remove the Stinger:** If the stinger is still present, scrape it off with a straight-edged object like a credit card. Avoid using tweezers as they can squeeze more venom into the skin.
  - **Apply Cold Compresses:** Use a cold pack or a cloth soaked in cold water to reduce pain and swelling.
  - **Clean the Area:** Wash the affected area with soap and water to prevent infection.
  - **Antihistamines:** Oral antihistamines like diphenhydramine can help reduce itching and swelling.

- **For Ant Bites and Stings:**

  - **Cold Compresses:** Apply cold packs to reduce swelling and pain.
  - **Topical Treatments:** Use hydrocortisone cream or calamine lotion to alleviate itching.
  - **Elevation:** Elevate the affected limb to reduce swelling.

- **For Spider Bites:**

  - **Clean the Bite:** Wash the bite site with soap and water to prevent infection.
  - **Apply Ice:** Use an ice pack to reduce swelling and numb the area.
  - **Pain Relief:** Over-the-counter pain relievers such as ibuprofen or acetaminophen can help manage pain.

- **For Scorpion Stings:**

  - **Immobilize the Limb:** Keep the affected limb still and at rest.
  - **Apply Cold Compresses:** Use cold packs to reduce pain and swelling.
  - **Seek Medical Attention:** Scorpion stings can be serious, particularly in children and the elderly. Immediate medical evaluation is recommended.

- **For Tick Bites:**

- **Remove the Tick:** Use fine-tipped tweezers to grasp the tick as close to the skin as possible and pull upward with steady pressure. Do not twist or jerk the tick.
- **Clean the Area:** Wash the bite area with soap and water, then apply an antiseptic.
- **Monitor for Symptoms:** Observe for signs of tick-borne illnesses such as Lyme disease or Rocky Mountain spotted fever.

12.3.2 Medical Treatment

Medical treatment is necessary for severe envenomations or when first aid measures are insufficient to manage symptoms. It involves supportive care, specific treatments, and management of complications.

Supportive Care:

- **Hydration:** Administer intravenous fluids to maintain hydration and electrolyte balance, especially in cases of severe vomiting, diarrhea, or systemic reactions.
- **Pain Management:** Provide analgesics for pain relief. For severe pain, stronger medications such as opioids may be necessary.
- **Monitoring:** Continuous monitoring of vital signs, including heart rate, blood pressure, respiratory rate, and oxygen saturation.

Specific Treatments:

- **Antivenom:** Administer antivenom when indicated, such as for black widow spider bites or scorpion stings. Antivenom can neutralize the venom and prevent severe complications.

  - **Dosage and Administration:** Follow specific guidelines for dosing and administration. Monitor for potential allergic reactions to the antivenom.

- **Antihistamines and Corticosteroids:** Use antihistamines for allergic reactions and corticosteroids for severe inflammation and anaphylaxis.

- **Epinephrine:** Administer epinephrine in cases of anaphylaxis to counteract severe allergic reactions and stabilize the patient.

Management of Complications:

- **Infection Control:** Prescribe antibiotics if there is evidence of secondary bacterial infection at the bite or sting site.
- **Tetanus Prophylaxis:** Ensure the patient is up to date with tetanus immunization. Administer a tetanus booster if needed.
- **Surgical Intervention:** In cases of severe necrosis or ulceration, surgical debridement may be necessary to remove dead tissue and promote healing.
- **Neurological and Cardiovascular Support:** Provide appropriate interventions for severe systemic symptoms such as respiratory distress, cardiovascular instability, or neurological impairment.

CHAPTER XIII

Substance Abuse

Introduction

Substance abuse, also known as substance use disorder, is a widespread and complex issue that affects individuals, families, and societies globally. It involves the harmful or hazardous use of psychoactive substances, including alcohol, illicit drugs, and prescription medications. Substance abuse can lead to addiction, physical and mental health problems, and significant social and economic consequences. Understanding the nature of substance abuse, its causes, and its impact is essential for developing effective prevention, treatment, and rehabilitation strategies.

Importance of Understanding Substance Abuse

Understanding substance abuse is crucial for several reasons. Firstly, it helps in identifying the underlying causes and risk factors that contribute to the development of substance use disorders. Secondly, knowledge of the various substances and their effects on the body and mind can aid in early detection and intervention. Lastly, raising awareness about substance abuse and its consequences can promote healthier lifestyles and reduce the stigma associated with addiction, encouraging individuals to seek help.

Scope of the Chapter

This chapter aims to provide a comprehensive overview of substance abuse, focusing on the types of substances commonly abused, the clinical manifestations of substance use disorders, and the strategies for prevention and treatment. Key areas covered will include:

1. **Types of Substances:**

   - **Alcohol:** Patterns of use, effects, and associated health risks.

- ◦ **Illicit Drugs:** Commonly abused drugs such as cannabis, cocaine, heroin, methamphetamine, and ecstasy.
- ◦ **Prescription Medications:** Misuse of prescription drugs, including opioids, benzodiazepines, and stimulants.
- ◦ **Other Substances:** Abuse of substances such as inhalants, anabolic steroids, and synthetic drugs.

2. **Causes and Risk Factors:**

- ◦ **Genetic Factors:** The role of genetics in predisposition to substance abuse.
- ◦ **Environmental Factors:** Influence of family, peers, and socio-economic conditions.
- ◦ **Psychological Factors:** Mental health disorders, trauma, and stress as contributing factors.
- ◦ **Social and Cultural Factors:** Cultural attitudes and societal norms related to substance use.

3. **Clinical Manifestations:**

- ◦ **Physical Symptoms:** Health effects of substance abuse, including organ damage, infections, and overdose.
- ◦ **Psychological Symptoms:** Mental health issues such as depression, anxiety, psychosis, and cognitive impairment.
- ◦ **Behavioral Symptoms:** Changes in behavior, including neglect of responsibilities, risky behaviors, and criminal activities.

4. **Diagnosis and Assessment:**

- ◦ **Screening Tools:** Methods for identifying substance use disorders, including questionnaires and interviews.
- ◦ **Clinical Evaluation:** Comprehensive assessment of substance use, medical history, and psychosocial factors.
- ◦ **Laboratory Tests:** Drug testing and other laboratory investigations to confirm substance use.

5. **Treatment and Rehabilitation:**

- ◦ **Detoxification:** Medical management of withdrawal symptoms and stabilization.
- ◦ **Therapeutic Interventions:** Behavioral therapies, counseling, and support groups.
- ◦ **Medications:** Pharmacological treatments for addiction, such as methadone, buprenorphine, and naltrexone.
- ◦ **Relapse Prevention:** Strategies to maintain sobriety and prevent relapse, including aftercare and ongoing support.

6. **Prevention and Education:**

- ◦ **Public Health Initiatives:** Community-based programs and policies to reduce substance abuse.
- ◦ **Education and Awareness:** Promoting awareness about the risks of substance use and healthy alternatives.
- ◦ **Family and Peer Support:** The role of family and social networks in preventing and addressing substance abuse.

13.1 Signs and Symptoms of Substance Abuse

Recognizing the signs and symptoms of substance abuse is crucial for early intervention and treatment. Substance abuse can manifest through a variety of physical and behavioral signs, which may vary depending on the type of substance used, the duration of use, and the individual's overall health.

13.1.1 Physical Signs

Physical signs of substance abuse are often the most noticeable and can affect various body systems. These signs may develop gradually and can become severe if substance use continues.

General Physical Signs:

- **Changes in Appearance:** Sudden weight loss or gain, neglected personal hygiene, and unusual body odor.
- **Bloodshot or Glazed Eyes:** Red, bloodshot eyes or pupils that are larger or smaller than usual.

- **Frequent Nosebleeds:** Especially common with snorting drugs like cocaine or methamphetamine.
- **Unusual Bruises or Track Marks:** Marks on the arms or other parts of the body from intravenous drug use.

Specific Substance-Related Physical Signs:

- **Alcohol:**

  - **Slurred Speech:** Difficulty speaking clearly and coherently.
  - **Impaired Coordination:** Difficulty walking, clumsiness, and frequent accidents.
  - **Tremors:** Shaking hands, particularly in the morning.

- **Opioids (e.g., heroin, prescription painkillers):**

  - **Drowsiness:** Excessive sleepiness or "nodding off."
  - **Constricted Pupils:** Pinpoint pupils that do not respond to changes in light.
  - **Respiratory Depression:** Slow or shallow breathing.

- **Stimulants (e.g., cocaine, methamphetamine):**

  - **Increased Energy:** Hyperactivity, excessive talking, and restlessness.
  - **Dilated Pupils:** Enlarged pupils that are sensitive to light.
  - **Teeth Grinding:** Jaw clenching and teeth grinding, especially with methamphetamine use.

- **Cannabis:**

  - **Red Eyes:** Bloodshot eyes with dilated pupils.
  - **Increased Appetite:** Cravings for food, often referred to as "the munchies."
  - **Dry Mouth:** Persistent dry mouth and thirst.

- **Hallucinogens (e.g., LSD, psilocybin mushrooms):**

  - **Visual Disturbances:** Hallucinations, seeing things that are not there.

- ○ **Changes in Perception:** Altered sense of time, space, and reality.
- ○ **Pupil Dilation:** Large pupils that do not constrict in bright light.

13.1.2 Behavioral Signs

Behavioral signs of substance abuse often involve changes in an individual's actions, habits, and overall lifestyle. These changes can be subtle initially but may become more pronounced as substance use continues.
General Behavioral Signs:

- **Changes in Social Behavior:** Withdrawal from family and friends, secretive behavior, and isolation.
- **Decline in Academic or Work Performance:** Poor attendance, declining grades, or work performance.
- **Financial Problems:** Unexplained need for money, borrowing or stealing money, or financial difficulties.

Specific Behavioral Signs:

- **Alcohol:**

  - ○ **Increased Tolerance:** Needing more alcohol to achieve the same effect.
  - ○ **Blackouts:** Inability to remember events that occurred while drinking.
  - ○ **Drinking Alone:** Consuming alcohol in isolation or at inappropriate times.

- **Opioids:**

  - ○ **Doctor Shopping:** Visiting multiple doctors to obtain prescriptions.
  - ○ **Neglect of Responsibilities:** Ignoring personal, professional, or social responsibilities.
  - ○ **Withdrawal Symptoms:** Experiencing symptoms such as nausea, sweating, and agitation when not using.

- **Stimulants:**

- **Aggressive Behavior:** Increased irritability, agitation, and potential for violence.
- **Paranoia:** Suspicion or mistrust of others, feeling persecuted.
- **Risky Behaviors:** Engaging in dangerous activities or taking unnecessary risks.

- **Cannabis:**

  - **Lack of Motivation:** Decreased interest in activities, lethargy, and apathy.
  - **Memory Problems:** Short-term memory impairment and difficulty concentrating.
  - **Changes in Social Circles:** Associating with new groups of friends who use substances.

- **Hallucinogens:**

  - **Erratic Behavior:** Unpredictable mood swings and bizarre actions.
  - **Flashbacks:** Re-experiencing hallucinations or altered states of perception long after the substance was used.
  - **Poor Judgment:** Making illogical decisions and engaging in risky activities.

13.2 Treatment of Dependence

Effective treatment of substance dependence involves a comprehensive approach that addresses both the physiological and psychological aspects of addiction. This section will focus on the treatment of dependence on Central Nervous System (CNS) stimulants, particularly amphetamines, and outline clinical management strategies.

13.2.1 CNS Stimulants: Amphetamine

Amphetamines are a class of potent CNS stimulants that include drugs such as Adderall, Dexedrine, and methamphetamine. These substances are commonly abused for their stimulating effects, which include increased energy, euphoria, and heightened concentration. However, chronic use can lead to dependence and a range of adverse health effects.

13.2.1.1 Clinical Management

The clinical management of amphetamine dependence involves several key steps: detoxification, pharmacological treatment, behavioral therapies, and long-term support to prevent relapse.

Detoxification:

Detoxification is the first step in managing amphetamine dependence. This process involves safely managing withdrawal symptoms as the drug is eliminated from the body.

- **Medical Supervision:** Detoxification should be conducted under medical supervision to monitor and manage withdrawal symptoms, which can include fatigue, depression, increased appetite, and intense cravings.
- **Supportive Care:** Providing a supportive environment, adequate hydration, nutrition, and rest is crucial during detoxification.

Pharmacological Treatment:

Currently, there are no FDA-approved medications specifically for the treatment of amphetamine dependence. However, certain medications can be used off-label to manage withdrawal symptoms and support recovery.

- **Antidepressants:** SSRIs (Selective Serotonin Reuptake Inhibitors) like fluoxetine or sertraline may be prescribed to manage depressive symptoms during withdrawal.
- **Benzodiazepines:** These can be used short-term to manage severe anxiety and agitation during the initial phase of detoxification.
- **Antipsychotics:** In cases of severe agitation or psychosis, antipsychotic medications may be necessary.

Behavioral Therapies:

Behavioral therapies are a cornerstone of treatment for amphetamine dependence. These therapies address the psychological aspects of addiction and help individuals develop coping strategies to maintain sobriety.

- **Cognitive-Behavioral Therapy (CBT):** CBT helps patients recognize and change negative thought patterns and behaviors associated with drug use. It also teaches coping skills to handle stress and triggers.

- **Contingency Management:** This approach uses positive reinforcement to encourage abstinence. Patients receive rewards for meeting treatment goals, such as maintaining sobriety or attending therapy sessions.
- **Motivational Interviewing:** This client-centered approach helps individuals find the motivation to change their behavior and commit to treatment.
- **12-Step Programs:** Participation in 12-step programs like Narcotics Anonymous (NA) can provide peer support and a structured framework for recovery.

Long-Term Support and Relapse Prevention:

Long-term support is essential to prevent relapse and maintain recovery. This involves ongoing therapy, support groups, and strategies to manage triggers and stress.

- **Aftercare Programs:** Structured aftercare programs provide ongoing support and resources to help individuals maintain sobriety after completing initial treatment.
- **Relapse Prevention Planning:** Developing a relapse prevention plan that identifies triggers, coping strategies, and support networks can help individuals manage cravings and avoid relapse.
- **Family Therapy:** Involving family members in therapy can improve communication, resolve conflicts, and provide a supportive environment for recovery.
- **Lifestyle Changes:** Encouraging healthy lifestyle changes, such as regular exercise, a balanced diet, and stress management techniques, can support overall well-being and reduce the risk of relapse.

13.2.2 Opioids

Opioid dependence is a significant public health concern due to the high potential for addiction, the risk of overdose, and the serious health consequences associated with long-term use. Effective clinical management of opioid dependence involves a comprehensive approach that includes detoxification, pharmacological treatment, behavioral therapies, and ongoing support to prevent relapse.

13.2.2.1 Clinical Management

Detoxification:

Detoxification is the initial step in the treatment of opioid dependence. The goal is to manage withdrawal symptoms and prepare the patient for ongoing treatment.

- **Medical Supervision:** Detoxification should be conducted under medical supervision to monitor and manage withdrawal symptoms, which can include agitation, anxiety, muscle aches, sweating, abdominal cramping, diarrhea, nausea, and vomiting.
- **Supportive Care:** Providing a supportive environment with adequate hydration, nutrition, and comfort measures is essential during detoxification.

Pharmacological Treatment:

Pharmacological treatment is a critical component in the management of opioid dependence. Medications are used to manage withdrawal symptoms, reduce cravings, and prevent relapse.

- **Methadone:** A long-acting opioid agonist that helps reduce withdrawal symptoms and cravings. It is administered daily in a controlled clinical setting.
- **Buprenorphine:** A partial opioid agonist that reduces withdrawal symptoms and cravings. It can be prescribed in various formulations, including buprenorphine-naloxone combinations (e.g., Suboxone) to reduce the potential for misuse.
- **Naltrexone:** An opioid antagonist that blocks the effects of opioids. It is available in oral and extended-release injectable forms. Naltrexone is used after detoxification to prevent relapse.
- **Clonidine:** An alpha-2 adrenergic agonist used off-label to manage certain withdrawal symptoms such as anxiety, agitation, and muscle aches.

Behavioral Therapies:

Behavioral therapies are essential for addressing the psychological aspects of opioid dependence and supporting long-term recovery.

- **Cognitive-Behavioral Therapy (CBT):** CBT helps patients identify and change negative thought patterns and behaviors related to drug use. It also teaches coping skills for managing stress and triggers.

- **Contingency Management:** This approach uses positive reinforcement to encourage abstinence. Patients receive rewards for meeting treatment goals, such as maintaining sobriety or attending therapy sessions.
- **Motivational Interviewing:** This client-centered approach helps individuals find the motivation to change their behavior and commit to treatment.
- **12-Step Programs:** Participation in 12-step programs like Narcotics Anonymous (NA) provides peer support and a structured framework for recovery.

Long-Term Support and Relapse Prevention:

Long-term support is crucial to prevent relapse and sustain recovery. This involves ongoing therapy, support groups, and strategies to manage triggers and stress.

- **Aftercare Programs:** Structured aftercare programs offer ongoing support and resources to help individuals maintain sobriety after completing initial treatment.
- **Relapse Prevention Planning:** Developing a relapse prevention plan that identifies triggers, coping strategies, and support networks can help individuals manage cravings and avoid relapse.
- **Family Therapy:** Involving family members in therapy can improve communication, resolve conflicts, and provide a supportive environment for recovery.
- **Lifestyle Changes:** Encouraging healthy lifestyle changes, such as regular exercise, a balanced diet, and stress management techniques, supports overall well-being and reduces the risk of relapse.

13.2.3 CNS Depressants

CNS depressants, including benzodiazepines, barbiturates, and certain sleep medications, are commonly prescribed for anxiety, insomnia, and other conditions. However, their potential for dependence and abuse requires careful management.

13.2.3.1 Clinical Management
Detoxification:

Detoxification from CNS depressants should be managed carefully due to the risk of severe withdrawal symptoms, including seizures.

- **Gradual Tapering:** Slowly reducing the dose of the CNS depressant under medical supervision is crucial to minimize withdrawal symptoms. A tapering schedule is individualized based on the specific drug, dose, and duration of use.
- **Medical Supervision:** Monitoring for signs of withdrawal, such as anxiety, tremors, sweating, insomnia, and seizures, is essential. In severe cases, hospitalization may be required.

Pharmacological Treatment:

- **Benzodiazepine Tapering:** For benzodiazepine dependence, a gradual taper using a long-acting benzodiazepine, such as diazepam or clonazepam, can help manage withdrawal symptoms.
- **Anticonvulsants:** Medications such as gabapentin or valproate may be used to prevent seizures during detoxification.
- **Beta-Blockers:** These can help manage autonomic symptoms such as tremors and tachycardia.

Behavioral Therapies:
Behavioral therapies are essential to address the psychological aspects of dependence on CNS depressants.

- **Cognitive-Behavioral Therapy (CBT):** CBT helps individuals identify and change maladaptive thought patterns and behaviors related to drug use and develop coping strategies for stress and anxiety.
- **Motivational Interviewing:** This approach helps individuals find the motivation to change their behavior and commit to treatment.
- **Support Groups:** Participation in support groups, such as those offered by Narcotics Anonymous (NA), can provide peer support and a sense of community.

Long-Term Support and Relapse Prevention:

- **Aftercare Programs:** Structured aftercare programs provide ongoing support and resources to help individuals maintain sobriety.

- **Relapse Prevention Planning:** Developing a relapse prevention plan that identifies triggers, coping strategies, and support networks can help manage cravings and avoid relapse.
- **Family Therapy:** Involving family members in therapy can improve communication, resolve conflicts, and provide a supportive environment for recovery.

13.2.4 Hallucinogens: LSD

Lysergic acid diethylamide (LSD) is a potent hallucinogen that can cause profound changes in perception, mood, and cognition. While physical dependence is less common, psychological dependence and adverse psychological reactions can occur.

13.2.4.1 Clinical Management

Management of Acute Reactions:

- **Supportive Care:** In the case of an acute LSD reaction, providing a calm and safe environment is crucial. Reassuring the individual and reducing sensory stimulation can help alleviate anxiety and paranoia.
- **Benzodiazepines:** Medications like diazepam or lorazepam can be used to manage severe anxiety, agitation, or panic attacks during an acute LSD reaction.
- **Antipsychotics:** In cases of severe psychotic reactions, antipsychotic medications such as haloperidol may be necessary.

Long-Term Treatment:

- **Psychotherapy:** Long-term treatment focuses on addressing underlying psychological issues and preventing further substance use.

  - **Cognitive-Behavioral Therapy (CBT):** CBT can help individuals understand the psychological reasons for their LSD use and develop healthier coping mechanisms.
  - **Motivational Interviewing:** This approach can help individuals recognize the negative impact of their substance use and find the motivation to change.

Relapse Prevention:

- **Education:** Educating individuals about the risks and potential long-term effects of LSD use can help prevent relapse.
- **Support Groups:** Participation in support groups, such as those provided by organizations like Narcotics Anonymous (NA), can offer ongoing support and a sense of community.
- **Lifestyle Changes:** Encouraging healthy lifestyle changes, such as regular exercise, a balanced diet, and stress management techniques, can support overall well-being and reduce the risk of relapse.13.2.5 Cannabis Group

Cannabis, commonly known as marijuana, is widely used for both recreational and medicinal purposes. While physical dependence on cannabis is less pronounced than on other substances, psychological dependence and withdrawal symptoms can still occur.

13.2.5.1 Clinical Management

Detoxification:

Detoxification from cannabis is generally less severe than from other substances, but it still requires supportive care to manage withdrawal symptoms.

- **Medical Supervision:** Although cannabis withdrawal is not typically life-threatening, symptoms such as irritability, anxiety, insomnia, and appetite changes should be monitored.
- **Supportive Care:** Providing a supportive environment, hydration, nutrition, and sleep hygiene can help ease withdrawal symptoms.

Pharmacological Treatment:

There are no specific medications approved for treating cannabis dependence, but certain drugs can help manage withdrawal symptoms and co-occurring disorders.

- **Antidepressants:** SSRIs (Selective Serotonin Reuptake Inhibitors) such as fluoxetine or sertraline may be used to manage symptoms of depression and anxiety associated with cannabis withdrawal.
- **Anxiolytics:** Short-term use of medications like buspirone can help manage anxiety during withdrawal.

Behavioral Therapies:

Behavioral therapies are the primary treatment approach for cannabis dependence.

- **Cognitive-Behavioral Therapy (CBT):** CBT helps individuals recognize and change patterns of marijuana use and develop coping strategies for triggers and stress.
- **Motivational Enhancement Therapy (MET):** This therapy helps individuals increase their motivation to change their cannabis use behaviors and engage in treatment.
- **Contingency Management:** This approach uses positive reinforcement to encourage abstinence from cannabis, providing rewards for meeting treatment goals.

Long-Term Support and Relapse Prevention:

- **Aftercare Programs:** Participation in structured aftercare programs provides ongoing support and resources to maintain sobriety.
- **Relapse Prevention Planning:** Developing a relapse prevention plan that includes identifying triggers, coping strategies, and support networks is essential.
- **Support Groups:** Involvement in support groups, such as Marijuana Anonymous (MA), can offer peer support and a sense of community.

13.2.6 Tobacco

Tobacco dependence is a significant public health issue due to its highly addictive nature and the severe health risks associated with long-term use, including respiratory diseases, cardiovascular diseases, and various cancers.

13.2.6.1 Clinical Management

Detoxification:

Detoxification from nicotine, the addictive substance in tobacco, involves managing withdrawal symptoms, which can be intense but are not typically life-threatening.

- **Medical Supervision:** While medical supervision is not always necessary, support from healthcare providers can help manage withdrawal symptoms such as irritability, anxiety, difficulty concentrating, increased appetite, and cravings.

- **Supportive Care:** Encouraging hydration, proper nutrition, and physical activity can help ease withdrawal symptoms.

Pharmacological Treatment:

Several medications are available to help individuals quit smoking and manage withdrawal symptoms.

- **Nicotine Replacement Therapy (NRT):** NRT products, such as patches, gum, lozenges, nasal sprays, and inhalers, provide a controlled dose of nicotine to reduce withdrawal symptoms and cravings.
- **Bupropion (Zyban):** An atypical antidepressant that helps reduce nicotine cravings and withdrawal symptoms. It is usually started one to two weeks before quitting smoking.
- **Varenicline (Chantix):** A medication that reduces cravings and withdrawal symptoms by partially stimulating nicotine receptors in the brain. It is typically started one week before the quit date.

Behavioral Therapies:

Behavioral therapies are essential for addressing the psychological aspects of tobacco dependence.

- **Cognitive-Behavioral Therapy (CBT):** CBT helps individuals identify and change smoking-related thoughts and behaviors and develop coping strategies for triggers and stress.
- **Motivational Interviewing:** This approach helps individuals find the motivation to quit smoking and commit to a quit plan.
- **Contingency Management:** This method uses positive reinforcement to encourage smoking cessation, providing rewards for meeting smoking cessation goals.

Long-Term Support and Relapse Prevention:

- **Aftercare Programs:** Participation in structured aftercare programs provides ongoing support and resources to maintain smoking cessation.
- **Relapse Prevention Planning:** Developing a relapse prevention plan that includes identifying triggers, coping strategies, and support networks is

essential.

- **Support Groups:** Involvement in support groups, such as Nicotine Anonymous (NicA), can offer peer support and a sense of community.
- **Smoking Cessation Programs:** Enrolling in smoking cessation programs that offer counseling, education, and support can significantly increase the chances of successfully quitting.

CHAPTER XIV

AUTHORS PROFILE

459

Dr. Santhi Sree Vemulapalli

Dr. Santhi Sree Vemulapalli, a distinguished Professor at Vijaya College of Pharmacy, Hayath Nagar, brings over 16 years of rich experience in pharmaceutical education and leadership. She earned her Ph.D. in Pharmaceutics from Acharya Nagarjuna University, Guntur. Dr. Santhi Sree has an impressive portfolio of numerous articles published in reputed journals and presentations at national and international platforms, focusing on advancements in drug delivery systems and nanotechnology. Her dedication to excellence in teaching has been recognized with several awards. As a member of APTI and a mentor to graduate students, she plays a crucial role in shaping the future professionals in pharmaceutical sciences.

Dr. Anvesh Raj Moturi

Dr. Anvesh Raj Moturi, an Associate Professor at Vijaya College of Pharmacy, Hayath Nagar, has over a decade of extensive experience in pharmaceutical education and leadership. He holds a Ph.D. in Pharmacology from Annamalai University, Chidambaram, Tamil Nadu, Chennai. Dr. Anvesh has published numerous articles in prestigious journals and presented his research at various national and international platforms, focusing on advancements in pharmacy practice. His contributions to teaching have earned him several awards. He is an active member of SPER and LaASA and mentors graduate students, significantly impacting the future of pharmaceutical sciences.

Dr. J. Dinesh Babu

Dr. J. Dinesh Babu, an Associate Professor at Vijaya College of Pharmacy, Hayath Nagar, has over 10 years of dedicated experience in pharmaceutical education and leadership. He earned his Ph.D. in Pharmacology from VELS University, Pallavaram, Tamil Nadu, Chennai. With over 25 articles published in esteemed national and international journals, his research focuses on various phytochemical constituents and their studies in animal subjects. Dr. Dinesh Babu has received several awards recognizing his excellence in teaching. He is a member of SPER and APTI and has guided many UG and PG students, helping shape their careers in pharmaceutical sciences.

Industrial Pharmacy-1 : From theory to Practice By Dr. Santhi Sree Vemulapalli,Dr. Anvesh Raj Moturi &Dr. J. Dinesh Babu